INTERNATIONAL ORGANIZATION AND INDUSTRIAL CHANGE

May 94

To Peter

With all best wishes

Cj

Europe and the International Order

Series Editor: Joel Krieger

Published

Forthcoming

INTERNATIONAL ORGANIZATION AND INDUSTRIAL CHANGE

Global Governance since 1850

Craig N. Murphy

Polity Press

First published in 1994 by Polity Press
in association with Blackwell Publishers.

Editorial office:
Polity Press
65 Bridge Street
Cambridge CB2 1UR, UK

Marketing and production:
Blackwell Publishers
108 Cowley Road
Oxford OX4 1JF, UK

ISBN 0 7456 1223 7
ISBN 0 7456 1224 5 (pbk)

British Library Cataloguing-in-Publication Data
A CIP catalogue record for this book is available from the British Library.

Typeset in 10 1/2 on 12 pt Caslon
by Pure Tech Corporation, Pondicherry, India
Printed in Great Britain by T. J. Press, Padstow, Cornwall

This book is printed on acid-free paper.

CONTENTS

FIGURES

TABLES

ACKNOWLEDGMENTS

This book has been a long time in the making and thus I have incurred many debts that I gratefully acknowledge:

To Wellesley College, the Alfred P. Sloan Foundation through its program for the New Liberal Arts, Harvard University's Center for International Affairs and Department of Government, and the Academic Council on the United Nations System for financial support of my research.

To the New York Public Library, the libraries of Harvard University's Business School and Law School, and the libraries of Wellesley College for the materials that made the research possible.

To my predecessors on the Wellesley faculty, Katharine Lee Bates (of "America the Beautiful" fame), who, like W. T. Stead, was deeply affected by the Columbian Exhibition of 1893 and became fascinated with the idea of applying the "American" system of economic integration to other parts of the world, and Emily Greene Balch, Wellesley's only Nobel laureate (Peace, 1946), for building the College's uniquely rich collection on the history of international cooperation, including bound volumes of pamphlets and reports on the orgins and demise of the gold standard whose jackets suggest that they were last used by a scholar at a neighboring school when he was writing one of the studies that fueled a generation of debate over "hegemonic stability" and its putative decline.

To the Wellesley students, Heather Huddleston, Viana Martinez, Heather Stone, and Michelle Viotti, who made it so much easier to analyze all the materials I found.

To all the scholars who have helped with their comments on my work in progress, including Manuel Adler, John Agnew, Chadwick F.

Alger, Richard K. Ashley, Michael N. Barnett, John Boli, Christopher K. Chase-Dunn, Daniel S. Cheever, Nazli Choucri, Claudio Cioffi-Revilla, Roger A. Coate, Robert W. Cox, Barbara B. Crane, Beverley Crawford, Jack Donnelly, Margaret Doxey, Lawrence S. Finklestein, John E. Fobes, Stephen Gill, Vicki L. Golich, Robert W. Gregg, Ernst B. Haas, Peter M. Haas, Stephan Haggard, Jeffrey A. Hart, Shirley Hazzard, Mark Imber, Harold K. Jacobson, Stephen D. Krasner, Stefanie Lenway, Gene M. Lyons, James M. McCormick, Patrick J. McGowan, Robert I. McLaren, Robert H. Manley, Dale Rogers Marshall, James Mayall, Joel S. Migdal, Linda B. Miller, Bruce Norton, W. Ofuatey-Kodjoe, Robert Paarlberg, M. J. Peterson, Donald Puchala, John Renniger, Alfredo C. Robles, Stephen J. Rosow, John G. Ruggie, Andrew M. Scott, Timothy M. Shaw, Mihaly Simai, Steve Smith, David Spiro, Susan Strange, Paul Streeten, J. Ann Tickner, Bharat Wariawalla, and Peter Willetts, and expecially to Hayward R. Alker, Jr, Robert O. Keohane, Roger Tooze, and Mark W. Zacher, each of whom read a number of chapters in draft with the knowledge that while I would learn from many of their comments, I would also misinterpret some, and probably ignore even more.

To the many people who have recently worked with or within world organizations in Africa, Asia, Europe, and North America who have taken the time to answer my questions and explain what they have done: Fatima Almana, Raymond Almeida, Enrico Augelli, Robert Baker, Andy Ball, Thomas Ball, Peri Barros, Maria de Luz Boal, Louis Brunet, Thomas E. Burke, Enzo Caputo, Gabriella Carbonelli, Osmane Cisse, Lawrence F. Cotton, Baidy Dia, Jürgen Dedering, Timor Dmitrichev, Chuck England, Paula Fortes, Arlette Freitas, Victor Gbeho, Beto de Golf, Susan Goodwillie, Mary Alice Guilford, Joe Hartman, Peer Hijmans, Ryokichi Hirono, James Jonah, Tapio Kanninen, Florence Ladd, Erasmo Lara, Ingrid Lehman, John Lewis, David Lindauer, Olivia Mendes, Tamako Nakanishi, Douglas Nelson, Romero Osveda, Shirley Pinkham, Estavao Rodrigues, Brian Rowe, Robert W. Russell, Piero Sergei, Barbara Thompson, Barbara Upton, Mark Wall, Reavis Ward, Lou Wetherite, Richard H. Wilkinson, Earl Yates, Renée Yates, and those who wished not to be named.

To Joel Krieger and David Roll for their encouragement and to Ann Bone for her careful work and creative suggestions throughout the book's production.

Finally, and most significantly, to my wife, JoAnne Yates, the better historian, whose example has taught me to rein in my social scientist's tendency to treat a generalization as if it were an explanation.

ABBREVIATIONS

AFL-CIO   American Federation of Labor and Congress of
          Industrial Organizations
BCSD   Business Council on Sustainable Development
BIS   Bank for International Settlements
ECLA   Economic Commission for Latin America
FAO   Food and Agriculture Organization of the UN
GAB   General Agreement to Borrow
GATT   General Agreement on Tariffs and Trade
IAEA   International Atomic Energy Agency
IATA   International Air Transport Association
ICAN   Intergovernmental Committee on Aerial Navigation
ICAO   International Civil Aviation Organization
ICR   Intergovernmental Committee on Refugees
IDA   International Development Association
IGO   intergovernmental organization
IIA   International Institute of Agriculture
IIIC   International Institute of Intellectual Cooperation
ILO   International Labor Office, International Labor
          Organization
IMCO   International Maritime Consultative Organization
IMF   International Monetary Fund
IMI   International Management Institute
Intelsat International Telecommunications Satellite Organization
Interpol International Police Organization
IRO   International Refugee Organization
ISO   International Organization for Standardization
ITO   International Trade Organization

ITU	International Telegraph Union, International Telecommunication Union
LDC	less developed country
MFN	most favored nation
NAFTA	North American Free Trade Area
NIC	newly industrializing country
NIEO	New International Economic Order
OECD	Organization for Economic Cooperation and Development
OPEC	Organization of Petroleum Exporting Countries
RTU	Radiotelegraph Union
SDR	Special Drawing Right
SUNFED	Special UN Fund for Economic Development
UIA	Union of International Associations
UN	United Nations
UNCTAD	UN Conference on Trade and Development
UNDP	UN Development Program
UNDRO	UN Disaster Relief Organization
UNEP	UN Environmental Program
UNESCO	UN Educational, Scientific, and Cultural Organization
UNHCR	Office of the UN High Commissioner for Refugees
UNICEF	UN Children's Fund
UNIDO	UN Industrial Development Organization
UNITAR	UN Institute for Training and Research
UNRRA	UN Relief and Rehabilitation Administration
UNRWA	UN Relief and Works Agency
UPU	Universal Postal Union
WHO	World Health Organization
WIPO	World Intellectual Property Organization

INTRODUCTION

Today's system of self-regarding territorial governments recognizing no higher authority can be traced back as far as Italy's early modern trading states, where some of today's oldest private fortunes also began. Dante's *Monarchia*, of around 1310, began the tradition of criticizing this modern – originally, strictly *European* – state system and advocating its replacement with a universal government (Hinsley 1963; Parkinson 1977: 143–54). The tradition continues. We still hear calls for a more universal government, now a *world* government, that would resolve the contradictions within the now globalized European state system and even humanize its fraternal twin, modern capitalism (Lens 1983; Chase-Dunn 1990).

While I, too, am critical of both the state system and the modern world economy, this book is not another call for world government. Nor is it a challenge to shape the nature of a world government that will "inevitably" develop in the near future, like the one issued by Saul Mendlovitz for the World Order Models Project in the early 1970s.[1] Unlike Mendlovitz, I do not believe we are living at the beginning of the first century of world government, although, in some ways, we may be living at its end. I expect that the world government we will have at the end of this century will differ little from the world government that existed when the century began. It will be no more, or less, significant.

One of the best ways to explore *global governance*, what world government we actually have had, is to consider the history of *world organizations*, those intergovernmental and quasi-governmental global agencies that have (nominally) been open to any independent state (even though all states may not have joined). Such institutions have existed since the 1860s, the result of diplomatic efforts that began more than a decade before. Some world organizations have contributed to substantive regulation of world society. Others have pointed to the existence of governance exercised elsewhere, for example, through the widespread adoption of similar national regulations, the enforcement of formal international agreements by a few powerful states, and the global imposition of rules by private, transnational associations. Others, the smallest number, have just been reflections of utopian dreams.

Table 1 suggests the scope of what world government we have today. It lists the one or two world organizations with the largest staffs and budgets in each of the policy areas that global agencies try to affect. While there is some global-level governance of all of these issues, the greatest impact of the world organizations themselves has been on industrial change. They have helped create international markets in industrial goods by linking *communication and transportation infrastructure*, protecting *intellectual property*, and reducing legal and economic barriers to *trade*. As a result, world organizations have played a role in the periodic replacement of lead industries, a critical dynamic of the world economy since the Industrial Revolution: By the mid-1800s the early industrial economy of cotton mills yielded to that of railroads and steel and then to an economy dominated by the mass production of consumer products by the electrical, chemical, and food-processing industries of the turn-of-the-century "Second Industrial Revolution". The automobile and jet age of the twentieth century followed, and today many argue that we are entering another industrial era led by the information industries – computers and telecommunications – and the financial and leisure service sectors they have fostered.

The scale of capitalism has changed with each new set of lead industries. Firms grew. Their markets grew. And the industrial world expanded. World organizations facilitated these changes in scale. By helping secure ever larger market areas for industrial goods, the global agencies helped make it profitable for firms to invest in new technologies. At the same time the world organizations, and the other systems of governance to which they point, have helped mitigate conflicts that go along with the expansion of the industrial system: they privileged some workers in the industrialized nations, insured investment in previously less developed countries (LDCs), and strengthened the states of the less industrialized world. The agencies have also helped perfect the state system itself by extending it to all parts of the globe and mitigating some of the terror

TABLE 1 Major world organizations in 1993 (with abbreviation, location, and main area of responsibility)

Organization	Abbreviation	Location	Area of responsibility
Food and Agriculture Organization	FAO	Rome	Agriculture
General Agreement on Tariffs and Trade	GATT	Geneva	Trade
International Atomic Energy Agency	IAEA	Vienna	Managing interstate conflict
International Civil Aviation Organization	ICAO	Montreal	Transportation infrastructure
International Criminal Police Organization	Interpol	Lyons	Public order and administration
International Labor Organization	ILO	Geneva	Labor
International Monetary Fund	IMF	Washington	Public finance
International Organization for Standardization	ISO	Geneva	Industrial standards
International Telecommunication Union	ITU	Geneva	Communication infrastructure
International Telecommunications Satellite Organization	Intelsat	Washington	Communication infrastructure
United Nations	UN	New York	Managing interstate conflict
UN Development Program	UNDP	New York	Development
Office of the UN Disaster Relief Coordinator	UNDRO	Geneva	Relief and welfare
UN Educational, Scientific, and Cultural Organization	UNESCO	Paris	Education and research
UN Environmental Program	UNEP	Nairobi	Environmental issues
Office of the UN High Commissioner for Refugees	UNHCR	Geneva	Refugees
UN Human Rights Commission	–	Geneva	Human rights
World Bank	–	Washington	Development
World Health Organization	WHO	Geneva	Health
World Intellectual Property Organization	WIPO	Geneva	Intellectual property

inherent in an anarchical system of states armed with the weapons of the industrial age. In strengthening the nation-state and the state system, the global intergovernmental organizations (IGOs) of the UN era also helped encapsulate the major challengers to industrial capitalism, the Soviet and Chinese communist systems, for more than a generation. Today some of the same agencies have been charged with helping reincorporate the postcommunist states into the capitalist world order.

While world organizations may have acted as part of the "super-structure" of the capitalist world economy, they have by no means simply been institutions "functional" to capitalism that somehow were "inevitable" results of the workings of capitalism itself. Their history is part of the dialectic between capitalism and the alternative ways of organizing economic and political life.

In helping encapsulate antagonistic social systems, the world organizations also helped them thrive, at least for a time. In helping to create privileged labor markets in the industrial capitalist world, global IGOs also helped secure the power of part of the industrial working class. And (in the long run, perhaps the most significantly) in seeking the legitimacy needed to carry out their other activities, the global agencies have strengthened social movements that hope to replace today's national governments with universal institutions securing human rights, meeting basic human needs, and preserving the global environment.

Nonetheless, even while the global IGOs may sometimes contribute to forces undermining capitalist industrialism, a prima facie case can be made that they have become necessary for its success. Consider just the period since the early 1970s when both the network of world organizations and the global economy have been in trouble. First, conflict between industrialized capitalist nations and their poorer partners began to split the UN. Then price-fixing by Third World oil producers sent an already weak world economy into a tailspin. Liberal internationalist observers of the simultaneous crises began to argue that the crisis in the world economy would end only if the crisis in international institutions was overcome. Sociologist Daniel Bell contended that the nation-state had become "an ineffective instrument for dealing with the scale of major economic problems" (1977: 134). New, more global arrangements were needed. Business and government leaders in the Club of Rome (Tinbergen 1976) argued for a global kind of Keynesian liberalism under which world organizations would be given the task of boosting production and assuring ever higher standards of living. And the Independent

Commission on International Development Issues under the leader of Germany's Social Democrats, Willy Brandt, proposed reforms of international institutions based on the same global Keynesian design (Brandt Commission 1980, 1983).

Yet the case that effective world organizations are needed before the world economy will revive is far from proven by the experience of the last twenty years. After all, by 1985 the major industrial economies had recovered from the deep recession of the early 1980s, while it took the Gulf War and the dissolution of the Soviet Union to revive the UN system, or at least to have a reinvigorated Security Council intervening in conflicts left over from the Cold War and in the new ones created by the collapse of Europe's communist states (while the International Monetary Fund (IMF) and World Bank tried to ease their transition back into the capitalist world). In the late 1980s even many Keynesian liberals were ready to concede that a reinvigorated world economy had been a matter of the "right" domestic economic policies, and that a reinvigorated system of international organizations was actually a consequence of this economic change, not its cause, a position championed by neoliberal fundamentalists of the Reagan and Thatcher governments.

Yet, despite the signs of a reinvigorated world economy in the late 1980s, most of us continued to experience the hardships of what the Keynesian Paul Krugman (1990a) has called an "age of diminished expectations" which began in the 1970s. The real wages of many industrial workers are no higher in the early 1990s than they were in the early 1960s, while people in the former communist states and most LDCs face even more dismal prospects. Throughout the world the high expectations of a generation raised in the boom years of the 1950s and 1960s have not been met.

Similarly, despite the optimistic image of today's UN forging consensus in hot spots around the world, or even that of the IMF calmly and professionally overseeing the recovery and transformation of dozens of former communist states, a much deeper incoherence remains. The chronically underfunded central organs of the UN can barely make ends meet, while even the better endowed IMF and World Bank do not have the money to complete all the new tasks they have been given. The argument that more fundamental changes in international institutions will be needed before the return of anything like the postwar boom years remains relevant.

This book explores that argument by looking at the history of today's world organizations and their predecessors. I examine the ideas underlying these institutions, the intellectual and political

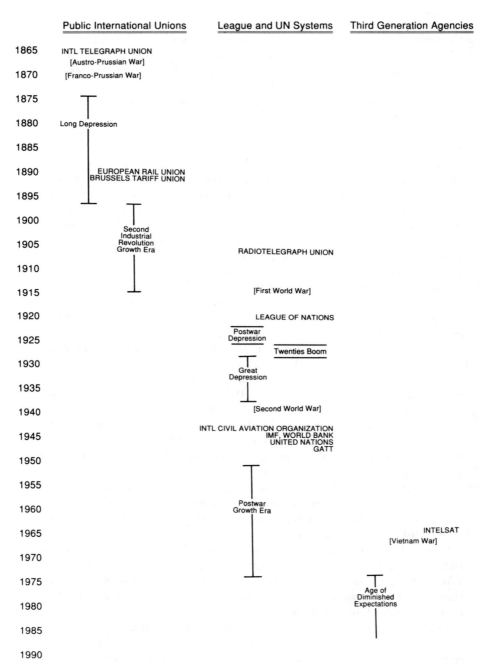

FIGURE 1 Three generations of world organizations

leaders who established them, the tasks the agencies were given, how and to what extent they or other systems of governance carried out those jobs, and what effect these actions have had, especially on the world economy. The venerable liberal internationalist case that such institutions can create widespread and long-lasting prosperity plays a major role in the story because the argument has influenced every generation of world organizations, which is, in part, a consequence of its continuing plausibility.

Yet we can see the best evidence for the liberal argument only if we divide the history of world organizations a little differently than most liberal analysts do. Instead of treating the nineteenth-century "Public International Unions," the League of Nations system, and the postwar UN system as the three successive generations of world organizations, we need to link their history to that of industry by saying that each new generation begins when an agency regulating a revolutionary new communication technology appears. In 1865 the agency was the International Telegraph Union (ITU), the first major Public International Union. In 1906 it was the Radiotelegraph Union (RTU), designed to regulate the airwaves. In 1964 it was Intelsat, the International Telecommunications Satellite Organization, a new kind of world organization, a global public utility, outside the UN system, providing part of the world communications infrastructure instead of just regulating services provided by others (figure 1).

Further experiments in international organization quickly followed each of these three beginnings. The Universal Postal Union and a half-dozen other organizations all appeared before 1890. Agencies serving some of the other new industries of the early twentieth century – the chemical, electrical, and automobile industries – succeeded the RTU, as did the peace organizations created at the 1907 Hague Conference and its successor of 1919, the League of Nations. Similarly, despite recent fears about the future of the UN system, new global agencies have been created in every year since 1965, most of them still inside the UN system, but most, like Intelsat, designed to promote the new industries of the late twentieth century.

Today's crises of international institutions and of the world economy also have their earlier analogues. Each generation of world organizations began in a period of crisis, and its key economic organizations appeared only at the end of the crisis, after years of war involving the great powers and after years of economic malaise. In the late nineteenth century the crisis began with the Austro-Prussian and Franco-Prussian wars and continued through the Long

Depression. The Public International Unions that helped liberalize the world economy after the Long Depression were established only in its last five years. The League of Nations operated in an era of crisis which began with the First World War, ended with the Second World War, and had the Great Depression in between. The economic agencies of the UN era were created as the crisis ended, the IMF and the World Bank at the 1944 Bretton Woods Conference and the General Agreement on Tariffs and Trade (GATT) within three years of the end of the war.

In both generations international transportation agreements immediately preceded the key economic pacts: the European Rail Union (the Central Office for International Rail Transport) in 1890 and the International Civil Aviation Organization (ICAO), the first of the UN specialized agencies, in 1943. Both agencies eventually worked with the earlier communication agency to provide the infrastructure for a larger market in which industrial goods could be traded. The ITU and the Rail Union allowed a Europe-wide market for industrial goods to emerge, while the radio and aviation agencies created a potentially global market.

The actual turn-of-the-century trading area that was partly regulated by the Public International Unions extended the continental market to the overseas dependencies of the European empires. In contrast, the actual trading area partly governed by the IGOs after the Second World War remained smaller than the world linked by radio and the airplane. It covered the Organization for Economic Cooperation and Development (OECD), the club of wealthy market countries (linking western Europe, Canada, the US, Japan, Australia, and New Zealand), and all their economic dependencies in Africa, Asia, the Caribbean, and the Pacific, but excluded China and the Soviet bloc.

Within these geographic limits appeared successive *world orders*, concrete historical political and economic systems, the turn-of-the-century *Interimperial Order*[2] and the postwar *"Free World" Order*.[3] These "interrelated trading area(s)" provide what W. W. Rostow's earliest work on economic development called "the optimum unit for the study of economic history . . . the frame within which many of the most important national, regional, or even international problems must be placed if they are to be fully understood" (1948: 12–23).

The limits of these trading areas were the result of economic agreements that followed the Rail Union and the ICAO. The Brussels-based International Union for the Publication of Customs Tariffs of 1890 signaled the beginning of a wave of European trade liberalization in the 1890s. The GATT marked the beginning of a similar wave throughout the postwar Free World.

Liberal internationalists, both Reagan-era fundamentalists and global Keynesians, argue that the wider markets created in Europe in the 1890s and throughout the capitalist world after the world wars were the keys to the subsequent eras of unprecedented economic growth: Europe's Second Industrial Revolution and the Free World's boom years. If we accept the liberal argument about the earlier eras, we should expect that a new wave of trade liberalization could assure another era of unprecedented prosperity within an even larger trading area that might include China and the postcommunist states.

The argument certainly has some validity. This book demonstrates that global IGOs have played a role in the growth and development of industrial society for over a century. In periods of peace and prosperity they have acted as part of what some social theorists call the "social structures of accumulation" (Gordon 1980, 1988) or "modes of regulation" (Boyer 1990; Lipietz 1987, 1992) that have allowed capitalist industrialism to work as well as it sometimes has. They have also helped industrial societies move out of those times when the system has not worked well – times of economic and geopolitical crisis – by contributing to the rise of the new leading industries of the next era of political order and economic growth.

This book also suggests that contemporary neoliberal fundamentalists underestimate the roles that "world government" must play in the genesis and maintenance of eras of peace and prosperity. Liberalizing trade was never enough. World organizations also encouraged investment in new industries, protected people who could be harmed by further extensions of the industrial system, increased the capabilities of states both within and outside the Interimperial Order and the Free World Order, and encouraged all states to be more open and responsive to their own societies. And now that the environmental consequences of industrialism are finally catching up with us, the agenda for a new generation of global IGOs will be even larger.

At the same time, the longer history of industry and international organization indicates that the task of creating the necessary global institutions may be easier than many of today's liberal commentators believe. They look back to the United States's role in creating the Free World and argue that significant reform of the present system will have to await the rise of another predominant power. Yet the Public International Unions of the Interimperial Order were created without the leadership of the dominant power of the day, Great Britain. Less powerful governments, well-placed citizens, and older global agencies have provided the necessary intellectual and political leadership to create world organizations that have helped fulfill the liberal internationalist vision in the past. They can do so again.

Nevertheless, even if they do, the same institutions may contribute to the forces that eventually end the new era of prosperity and peace. Both the Public International Unions and the UN system did. These institutions contributed to industrial growth but failed to cope with social conflict fostered by that growth. While supporters of the UN system are right when they argue that the men and women who designed it learned from the past and anticipated conflicts the designers of the Public International Unions had ignored, it is also true that their immediate predecessors, the designers of the League, first *forgot* much of what the designers of the Public International Unions once knew. Like today's neoliberal fundamentalists, many of the League's designers overlooked the active role that governments have had to play in building the infrastructure of a liberal industrial economy, as well as in managing the social conflicts that it inevitably creates.

It is easier to remember those lessons if we look at the history of industry and international organization through a lens that is wider than the one provided by the liberals themselves. The social theory developed by the early twentieth-century Italian political strategist, Antonio Gramsci, offers such a lens. Gramsci created a Marxist synthesis of the liberal idealism of the celebrated historian and activist Benedetto Croce with the longer Italian tradition of political realism that goes back to Machiavelli. This synthesis can help us understand the many roles that world organizations have performed – those highlighted by the liberal tradition and those that some liberals discount. At the same time, Gramsci's theory lets us understand the greatest failures of what world government we have had: the eventual disintegration of the two eras of prosperity and peace into periods of war and economic stagnation. Gramsci's framework allows us to integrate the powerful realist and Marxist explanations of these crises, explanations that many liberals discount or ignore.

Gramsci's concept of a unified social order as a *historical bloc* linked by both coercive institutions of *the state proper* and consensual institutions of *civil society* can help us remember that the world organizations, as cooperative institutions of *international* civil society, have only been effective when they have worked alongside a coherent system of coercive power at the international level, a stable military order. And Gramsci's analysis of civil society reminds us to look beyond the regulatory roles played by juridically constituted public institutions to uncover the roles played by less formal domestic, international, and transnational institutions. We need to look for "what world government we've had" outside the multilateral institutions created by sovereign states.

Consider just one key example: the system of mass production and mass consumption that Gramsci dubbed *Fordism* certainly played a central role in the cooperative regulation of the Free World Order. But Fordism began as a matter of industrial relations *within* firms and was later supported by the Keynesian welfare state. The postwar world organizations point to the significance of Fordism and the Keynesian welfare state through the promotion by the International Labor Organization (ILO) of collective bargaining and the IMF's system for encouraging cooperation in public finance, but we would surely misunderstand a critical part of the postwar world order, and of its eventual crisis, if we looked only at the activities of these formal intergovernmental agencies themselves.

Gramsci's ideas also help us understand how a new world order emerges from a crisis. His analysis of the role of *intellectual* and *political leadership* in establishing social orders can help us clear up questions about the mechanics of reform that recent liberal analysts have left in a muddle. When we distinguish between these two types of leadership we can see a wider range of options for effective reform of global IGOs than those recognized by most contemporary liberal internationalists, whether neoliberal fundamentalists or global Keynesians.

Gramsci's method of understanding the role of a particular set of institutions within a larger social order was first to establish the economic and political context in which the social order arose, and then to analyze why the institution was established: the designs of the intellectual leaders who envisioned it and the political process that realized the ideas, including the concrete relationships between intellectual leaders and political leaders, and between both and the larger social forces that they represented. He would then look at the institution's consequences, its contribution (if any) to cementing a new historical bloc, as well as its impact on social forces that might eventually challenge that social order.

Chapter 1 provides an overview of the problem of international organization and industrial change though a critical analysis of liberal internationalism, and then expands on Gramsci's method. Chapters 2, 3, and 4 follow this method to examine the establishment, operation, and consequences of the Public International Unions, Chapters 5, 6, and 7 provide a similar analysis of the League and UN systems. Finally, chapter 8 considers the emerging third generation of world organizations and the prospects for ending the current crises in the world organizations and in the global economy.

1

THE PROMISE OF LIBERAL INTERNATIONALISM

The designers of the Public International Unions, the League of Nations, and the UN all believed that liberal international institutions could create an increasingly prosperous and peaceful world, a conviction that is older than the oldest of the world organizations. This chapter examines the justifications for that conviction provided by liberal internationalism in light of an equally venerable, but more pessimistic tradition that also links industry and international affairs. I show how Gramsci's social theory allows us to combine insights from both traditions in a more complete account that steps beyond the liberals' simplified concept of human motivation and recognizes sites of regulation of the world economy at levels other than those of the nation-state and the state system.

The Liberal Vision and Conflicts It Can Obscure

Both liberal internationalism and world organizations are things of the industrial age. Although liberalism appeared a century before the first modern factories, liberal internationalists honor men of the generation that built those factories, Adam Smith and Immanuel Kant, as the founders of their tradition.

Three characteristics of the industrial age have convinced the followers of Smith and Kant that some form of global governance eventually would be needed if peace and prosperity are to be realized. First, and most significantly, is the propensity of capitalist industry to outgrow any government. The most efficient factories produce more than can be sold in a single country. They fuel desire for that abundance in countries without factories, and combine with the need of competing industrialists to find wider and wider markets. In Marx and Engels's famous words of 1848, the factory system, left to itself, "batters down all Chinese walls . . . [and] creates a world after its own image" (1932: 13).

Second is the link between capitalist industrialism and a republican polity. Industrialism emerged in a society divided among lords, peasants, yeoman farmers, free wage-earners, and the bourgeoisie. Many liberals have always argued that it would remain dynamic only in a society where power is shared among the classes, because, as Adam Smith put it in 1776, the interests of those who gain their income from land and those who gain their income from wages are "strictly connected with the interest of the society," while the bourgeois merchant and manufacturer have immediate interests opposed to those of society as a whole: "profit does not, like rent and wages, rise with the prosperity, and fall with the declension of the society. On the contrary, it is naturally low in rich, and high in poor countries, and it is always the highest in the countries that are going the fastest to ruin" (1981: 265–6). A state controlled only by capitalists would destroy the commonwealth by impoverishing the wage earner and despoiling the land. Competition among capitalists would disappear and they would lose their incentive to invest in new products and new techniques.

Yet – third – on the other hand, even at the beginning of the industrial system, the division of its European birthplace among so many sovereign aristocrats could have thwarted its advance if capitalists had faced excessive demands for investment from statesmen who were preparing for war and pursuing mercantilist policies because they were more interested in extending the limits of their sovereign's rule than in assuring the prosperity of the people and their lands. Therefore champions of the industrial system have always promoted development of those consensual institutions that have transcended the narrow interests of the separate sovereigns since the beginning of the European state system. Industrialism promoted the cooperative institutions of what we might call *international civil society* – both public institutions, including the rules of diplomacy and the growing corpus of international law – and private transnational institutions that have facilitated commerce across Europe's many artificial political boundaries – international banks, insurance schemes that shared the risk of international commerce by sea or land between all parties that might benefit, and business partnerships linking families and firms from many nations, as well as the international fraternity of Europe's aristocracy.

Like their critics, liberals have always had more than mere prosperity in mind when they championed the industrial system. Marx may have seen industry's promise as the generalization of the pride and self-respect that comes from employing our full potential in productive and unalienated work, but Adam Smith's earlier formulation differs only slightly. He saw the promise of the liberal economy in which industry first grew as the universal extension of the esteem and honor we grant to prosperous individuals and societies (Campbell and Skinner 1981: 9–10). For Smith, the ultimate goal of statecraft was to secure and enhance the dignity of a nation and its people. Wealth was just a means to that end. Likewise, for Smith, the factory system – or, to be more precise, anything that contributed to increased productivity (even freer international trade) – was simply a further means to this end and not an end in itself.

In *The Wealth of Nations* Smith celebrates the increasing division of labor – within factories, within societies, and across societies – as the *sine qua non* of the new economic system. Smith clearly understood the prehistory of the industrial system; as Nathan Rosenberg argues, the division of labor across Europe that began in Dante's day was a precondition for the first significant applications of science to the processes of production that finally appeared in Smith's generation (1976: 131). The first results were the innovations that Smith observed in his pin factory: systems for increasing the division of labor among workers by breaking tasks down and using standard materials. The ultimate result would be the startling increase in general productivity that we still call *the* Industrial Revolution. *The Wealth of Nations* argues that the introduction of further industrial innovations would continue to depend on the progressive expansion of the realm of unrestricted trade. As the title of Smith's key third chapter put it, "the Division of Labour [even within the factory] is limited by the Extent of the Market." Economic growth, the generalization of prosperity, would follow.

In *Perpetual Peace* published in 1795 Kant completed the link between industry and international organization by arguing the complement, that the desire to secure these benefits of expanding international commerce would guarantee of the ultimate victory of "world citizenship" over the tradition of warring states. With Kant the institutionalization of a peaceful and prosperous world order became defined as a project of what we might call *progressive* members of the bourgeoisie (those not motivated solely by concerns of immediate profit) and as a natural extension of both bourgeois republicanism and of the norms of the hospitality regularly extended by merchants to foreign colleagues. The emergence of formal intergovernmental institutions would simply be an extension of an emerging cosmopolitan civil society, which was itself the real, ultimate guarantor of peace.

Of course, neither Kant nor Smith were willing to rely on the cosmopolitan bourgeoisie to achieve this happy result by itself. Even if, as Kant said, "the spirit of commerce . . . is incompatible with war" (1957: 32), liberals had to guard against placing governments and international agreements solely in the hands of the merchant and industrial classes; the latter would simply use a monopoly on state power to create and protect real monopolies, the way the East India Company did in England's richest colony, as Smith had pointed out (1981: 630–4). Luckily the republicanism embraced by the bourgeoisie could prevent businessmen from gaining too great an influence over government. Kant and Smith both understood republican constitutions as those incorporating a division of power. In practice, in their day republicanism could only mean counterbalancing the power of the bourgeoisie with that of the older ruling class, the aristocracy, and that of the nascent state class of professionals working in government, the groups to whom Kant and Smith addressed their appeals.

Kant argued for one further check. In his "Secret Article for Perpetual Peace" he required that "The opinions of philosophers on the conditions of the possibility of public peace shall be consulted by those states armed for war" (1957: 33). He thus attempted to balance the powers of all the ruling classes with a new power to be given to what he argued was the most independent and universalistic of the intellectual disciplines represented in the modern university.

In the generation that followed, the new intellectual disciplines that grew out of Kant's and Smith's own field of moral philosophy kept this new liberal internationalist vision alive. Fred Parkinson (1977) gives equal credit for the resulting "functionalist" tradition to Jeremy Bentham and Auguste Comte. Functionalists support the establishment of governmental and intergovernmental institutions to carry out specific, limited activities, the "functions" needed to assure that the promise of a liberal world order will be fulfilled. A prominent twentieth-century functionalist, David Mitrany, summarized their views this way: "Do not ask what is ideal government, but ask what are its functions" (1933: 103). Smith showed the way by delineating three essential roles for government to play, creating and maintaining *national security*, *civil justice*, and necessary *public works* (1981: 687–8). Turning to international affairs, Bentham (1748–

1832), the political economist, argued for limited, purpose-oriented international agreements fostering international commerce and, with it, industrial innovation, prosperity, and peace. Comte (1798–1857), the father of sociology, argued that as long as scientific observation and systematic administration were applied not only to production, but also to the affairs of state, domestic and international conflict could be minimized and prosperity assured.

In Comte's later years these arguments became the key justifications offered for the Public International Unions. They later influenced the designers of the League and the UN – not just Woodrow Wilson, with his vision of an international institution for peace, but also the much wider circle that included John Maynard Keynes. These were the people who preserved the functions of the Public International Unions and later convinced the victors in the Second World War, the original "United Nations," to retain and expand the League's economic and social activities in their postwar "United Nations Organization."

These liberal internationalist ideas have also given rise to an unusually productive scholarly tradition that analyzes those international institutions that have actually been created. Early studies included Paul S. Reinsch's *The Public International Unions* (1911), the empirical parts of John A. Hobson's *Towards International Government* (1915), and Leonard Woolf's *International Government* (1916), as well as a fundamentally new genre of studies on managing conflict at all levels, from the local to the global, pioneered by Mary Parker Follett (1918). Both Follett and Woolf influenced David Mitrany, who in turn inspired the postwar "neofunctionalists" such as Ernst Haas (1958, 1964), who developed a more sophisticated model of politics to explain the real obstacles in what many of their predecessors had seen as a rather easy path to peace and prosperity. Finally, the neofunctionalists have inspired the contemporary generation of more critical analysts of international institutions led by Robert Keohane, who still identify with the larger liberal tradition that affirms "at least the possibility of human progress," even though they dismiss the traditional expectations of what Keohane calls "*republican* and *commercial*" liberal internationalism as something of a myth (Keohane 1989: 10–11).

Yet what myth there is in the liberal internationalist vision differs from some contemporary myths with which it is often contrasted, those propagated by the nineteenth-century nationalist historians who invented elaborate pasts for people who had only recently come to think of themselves as *a* people. Liberal internationalists require no similar distortion of the past, although they may have a distorted overemphasis on some of the possibilities of the present; this may be similar to the distortion found in the closely related myth called by Anthony D. Smith "the myth of the Modern Nation" (1988: 7), something he contrasts with those much simpler mythic national histories. This myth is that the nation is merely a "modern, and therefore temporary, phenomenon, an attribute, more or less basic, of a particular industrial, capitalist or modern phase of history. In the future, when technological and economic conditions have matured, nations and the private roles and attachments they engender, will wither away."

Perhaps this hope could become a reality if every nation could and would emulate the few that social scientists usually cite as exemplars of modernity: the industrialized countries of northwestern Europe and North America. But then the same equally could be said of John Lennon and Yoko Ono's less scholarly conclusion that "War is over, if you want it."

These arguments – the myth of the modern nation and the myth of peace through popular action – each emphasize one possibility of the present, a possibility that would come about if people accepted the argument on faith and then acted as if it were true. They, like the liberal vision of universal peace and prosperity achieved through industry and international organization, are *social myths*, visions that only can become realities if specific people come to believe in them and in their power. Georges Sorel's classic social myth in *Reflections on Violence* of 1906 was that of the General Strike, the moment when the oppressed transform society simply by stopping their work that sustains it; Gramsci wrote that in such myths, "political ideology and political science are fused in the dramatic form" (Forgacs 1988: 238).

Conflicts arising from industry

Gramsci understood that the line between "ideology" and "science," the line between what we wish were true for all time and what is now true at this one moment, is never fixed and clear. "Ideological" commitments only become a problem when we allow our hopes to veil our understanding of the things that thwart their realization. The major blind-spot of this sort in the liberal internationalist vision often obscures conflicts generated by the development and geographical extension of the industrial system itself, conflicts that prevent key social actors from believing the liberal myth and, therefore, from acting in ways that would make it a reality. Other traditions focus on these conflicts and, as a result, offer a more pessimistic image of the link between industry and international affairs. In the words of novelist and essayist Thomas Pynchon:

> By 1945, the factory system – which more than any piece of machinery, was the real and major result of the Industrial Revolution – had been extended to include the Manhattan Project, the German long-range bomber program and the death camps, such as Auschwitz. It has taken no major gift of prophecy to see how these three curves of development might plausibly converge, and before too long. (1984: 41)

Many academic commentators on international affairs have shared this view. Oswald Spengler's *Decline of the West* of 1923 inspired many in the generation of realists who came to dominate the field after the world wars (Farrenkopf 1991: 269). Pitrim Sorokin, who is sometimes claimed by peace researchers as a founder of their field (Eckhardt 1987: 187), also felt Pynchon's pessimism before the nuclear age began (Sorokin 1937). And the earliest systematic analyses of patterns of war between great powers (such as Q. Wright 1942) started with the assumption that the application of science to the techniques of violence made each of the state system's great periodic struggles for predominance potentially more destructive than the last.

Grounds for pessimism have remained as the systematic analysis of great-power war has matured. When Nazli Choucri and Robert North (1975) studied the great-power wars that bracketed the Interimperial Order they concluded that some basic dynamics of industrial society were "master variables" that move the great industrial powers to use their constantly growing capacities to destroy. Both technological change (which appears to be self-reinforcing) and population growth (which in the industrial age has been encouraged by advances in medicine) accelerate demands for resources and for further economic growth, creating *lateral pressure*, "the tendency of a social unit to expand its geographic compass, to push outward the boundaries that partition reality between the 'external' environment and the unit itself, and to draw an ever greater expanse of reality within itself" (Ashley 1980: 14). When Richard Ashley extended this analysis to the postwar Chinese–Soviet–US triangle, the same patterns appeared. To Ashley they pointed toward a more fundamental conclusion about the industrial age: "Technical-rational action has brought progress – progress toward destruction of all it has built" (1980: 214); if we remain subservient to technical rationality in our pursuit of economic growth, we can only end where Pynchon's three curves of development plausibly converge.

Of course, even those who have seen great promise in the industrial system have also warned against making a fetish of technical rationality. Adam Smith worried about the numbing effects that the division of labor could have on the minds and spirit of working men and women (Hirschman 1977: 105–8). At the first appearance of the modern machine, an even more revolutionary and alienating power, acute observers immediately recognized its potential. Charles Babbage, the early Victorian mathematician who designed most of the elements of the modern computer a century before its production would become technically feasible, commented that "The most singular advantages we derive from machinery is in the check which it affords against the inattention, the idleness, or the knavery of human agents" (quoted in J. A. Hobson 1912: 74). Not only were factory workers perfectly subject to discipline automatically meted out by the factory's machines, machines even eliminated the need to consult with workers before changing processes of production. Thus they allowed for a much more complete application of science to production than Smith had observed in his pin factory. As a result, as Engels and Marx recognized, technological innovation became a much more powerful social force than it had ever been before (Rosenberg 1976: 131–5). Hobson argued that these two effects combined to create a "new economy of force and knowledge" (1912: 74), promising expansion of production limited only by human ability to understand and control the physical world, but requiring most men and women to give up hope of ever acting with complete autonomy and responsibility.

With workers Conceivably, of course, every application of science to production could be made contingent on the agreement of those who work with the machines, conserving the revolutionary potential of the "economy of knowledge" while discarding the "economy of force" along with the alienation and disempowerment it entails. This has been the vision of the many socialists from Robert Owen to Herbert Marcuse who recognized that a human need to act with authority cannot be met by what industrial capitalism is best able to provide: prosperity for some. It is the vision that Richard Ashley's studies of lateral pressure led him to embrace.

Liberal internationalists from Smith, to Hobson, and even to Keynes have held out little hope that such a radically democratic society could emerge without destroying capitalist industrialism's capacity for creating wealth. Their best hope has been that the eventual world of plenty created by the industrial system would allow all to experience some of the dignity and humanizing pleasures now enjoyed only by those who most benefit from the machine's economy of force and knowledge. In 1920 Keynes introduced his *Economic Consequences of the Peace* by reminding readers of the "Eldorado" Europeans enjoyed before the Great War (1971: 10); it was an epoch of continent-wide prosperity (for the privileged few) maintained by what Keynes referred to as "the delicate organization" of international institutions that he feared the Treaty of Versailles would doom. In lamenting the world that was lost, Keynes repeated the usual liberal rationalization for the profound global inequality on which the interimperial social order was based: "If only the cake were not cut but allowed to grow . . . perhaps a day might come when . . . overwork, overcrowding, and underfeeding would have come to an end, and men, secure of the comforts and necessities of the body, could proceed to the nobler exercises of their faculties" (ibid.: 21).

David Mitrany and other mid-century functionalists argued that the race to that day when scarcity would end need never be impeded by conflicts between capitalists and workers, if only because a growing economy should always be able to produce enough to compensate the disempowered with ever greater economic rewards. Even so, Mitrany found no way to address Keynes's deeper worry that capitalists would demand so much to keep the economy growing that the disempowered would be left with such small slices of the cake that they might still rebel (cf. Mayall 1975).

More recently, when members of the new generation of global Keynesians discussed reforming international institutions in one of the early reports commissioned by the Club of Rome, they repeated Marcuse's argument that collective decisions about technological change should be taken democratically by all who would be affected (Tinbergen 1976: 82), but they did not explain how that could happen without undermining the system's ability to produce wealth. They did not confront the deeper issue that capitalist industrialism has always rested on inequalities in power: for the system to work, a few must have the ability to change the processes of production, while most must simply submit to the logic of the machine. This contradiction between the demands of industrial system and the demand for democratic control (something that liberals have also long championed) creates the first of the fundamental conflicts that liberal internationalists tend to ignore.

With older social orders A second can appear whenever the industrial system (or even a new stage of industrialism) confronts an older social order, because even if Adam Smith is right and we all pursue honor and esteem above all other values, we do not all pursue these values in the same way. Traditional social relations, threatened by the introduction of industrial capitalism, often remain sources of honor and esteem within societies recently brought into the industrial world. Despite the compensation that may be offered by economic growth, people may fight when technology threatens to transform their lives.

With the less industrialized world Similar conflicts can appear with the geographical extension of the industrial system. Representatives of a preindustrial order will fight for their positions within newly industrializing societies, while other social movements demand the introduction of the industrial system and become frustrated by the slow pace of capitalist investment in industry. Fortunately or unfortunately, as Nigel Harris (1986) argues, capitalist industrialism, even with all its proven dynamism, has been able to expand only so far and so fast. Vast regions of the world have always been left out. The resentment both of those who come from countries which have recently entered a regional, imperial, or global manufacturing system, and of those who cannot do so even if they want to, creates the third kind of conflict that many liberal internationalists overlook.

Among the powers Analogous conflicts can arise within a group of states that have already industrialized. Uneven development occurs within the core of the world industrial economy as well as between its core and its periphery. Elites and masses in one industrialized society can easily come to resent another industrialized country which has developed some new industries or technologies first.

Similarly, the ever increasing prosperity promised by liberal internationalists cannot stop the leaders of expanding industrial states – each internally united by its own sense of national identity – from seeing the peaceful international integration necessary to achieve that vision as a threat to the power of the traditional interests to which national identity and the state have both been linked. Alternative visions of imperial conquest – to assure that the sun never sets on the British Empire or to give Germans *Lebensraum* – may suggest a future in which both the demands of national identity and the needs of an ever-expanding economic system can be served. In fact, a coincidence of desires to preserve an older social order with conflicts arising from uneven development among the industrial powers may provide the best explanation for the apparent connection between lateral pressure and great-power war.

Liberal learning: the critical tradition in liberal internationalism and an evolutionary explanation

When some liberal internationalists recognize one or more of these conflicts they see them only as temporary problems that will be overcome by the more rapid fulfillment of their vision: conflicts over democratic control of the industrial system and conflicts with the less industrial world will be put aside as long as prosperity is assured. Conflicts with the old order and conflicts among unevenly developing industrial powers will be overcome as the "modern nation" withers away, something that is bound to happen as those few necessary functions of government are handed over to global IGOs (cf. Mitrany 1943: 2)

A few liberal internationalists in every generation have gone further and recognized the other half of the same dialectic: opportunities for reasserting a more local sovereignty also grow with international integration, and such reassertions of local control can sometimes solve the conflicts that the industrial system promotes. Reassertions of local sovereignty often play a central role in the early stages of struggles for democracy, as we have seen in eastern Europe since the late 1980s. Similarly, if foreign investors are reluctant to help a society develop new industries, a policy of partial delinking from the larger world economy can sometimes play a progressive role both in the first stages of industrialization and in later struggles to develop new technologies, something the leaders of newly industrializing countries have long understood (cf. Tickner 1987, 1990). Even that iconoclastic sympathizer with the movement to integrate the world economy, Thorstein Veblen – a man who believed as strongly as any liberal internationalist in the myth of the modern nation – argued in 1915 that a temporary delinking from the world economy played an essential role in the industrialization of nineteenth-century Germany (Veblen 1966). Only England, the first country to industrialize and the first "modern" nation, had the opportunity to enter the Industrial Revolution under laissez faire.

A century after the Industrial Revolution, even Britain had an industrial policy. In the late nineteenth century both the British and German governments fostered national industries and both tried to assure that private capitalists would become increasingly dependent on the state; by 1900 a seeming "retrograde" ideology of official nationalism, rooted in justifications for the old order, became as typical of the industrial order in Britain as it was in Germany. Yet, while late-Victorian capitalists may have become, as the great proselytizer of free trade, Richard Cobden, put it, "toadies of a clod-pole aristocracy" (Jones 1987: 194), their investments also continued to provide Britain with the wealth and prestige that Adam Smith considered the ultimate justification of laissez faire; their Tory nationalism even served the laboring poor in being used as a justification for the first laws that alleviated some of their "overwork, overcrowding, and underfeeding," something that the Cobdenite liberal internationalists had only promised.

Later, as James Mayall shows (1990: 88–110), when postwar Keynesian liberals finally were able to keep that promise, they could do so only by allowing a new form of economic nationalism to develop throughout the industrialized core of the Free World. The postwar Keynesians continued an important critical tradition in liberal internationalism that has been willing to embrace some otherwise "retrograde" policies to cope with conflicts that they have recognized as inherent in the industrial system. Keynes not only supported the strong states needed to give large slices of the economic cake to the disempowered, he advocated policies to minimize the uneven development of the powers, and he was one of the initiators of the search for ways both to encourage rapid industrial development in the less industrialized world and to compensate people in those parts of the world where such development would remain unlikely. Today a new generation of global Keynesians, including the men and women who wrote the reports of the Brandt Commission and the Club of Rome, continue this practice.

If we follow the history of the critical tradition, we can see a process in which some liberals have learned about more and more of the conflicts that the larger liberal internationalist vision can obscure. Not only have more of the conflicts been noticed by each generation of critical liberal internationalists, each generation has proposed more effective means for coping with those conflicts. The changing content of these critical theories suggests a broad, evolutionary explanation[1] of both liberal internationalism and the world organizations that have been based on it. It is a theory consistent with Ernst Haas's (1989) explanation of knowledge-driven changes within international institutions, and with Keohane's (1984) explanation of international institutions in terms of their consequences for powerful states.[2] It is an explanation informed by the critical tradition itself, and one that accepts the key assumption of the much broader liberal tradition – that much of human action arises from the rational pursuit of self-interest.

Like all evolutionary explanations, it identifies two social processes: one that generates institutional innovations, and another that selects some to survive. The critical tradition in liberal internationalism itself has provided the innovations. Long before Keynes, the nineteenth-century liberals constantly found new "necessary" functions for international institutions to perform. As Mayall argues, J. S. Mill constantly "expanded his chapter on the 'Limits of laissez-faire' when he realized that only the state could finance a system of universal education and provide public goods" (Mayall 1990: 98–9). Even though governments never have adopted Kant's "Secret Article," the voices of some liberal philosophers have eventually been heard by the powers. Keohane (1984) identifies the key attribute of the process that has selected only some of these experimental institutional innovations to survive: they do so if a sufficiently powerful coalition of national governments learn that they benefit from the state-to-state cooperation that the institutions encourage.

Keohane's work on international institutions concentrates only on the last twenty years. The longer history of world organizations demonstrates that it is not just national governments that must benefit, but also (and perhaps even primarily) a sufficiently powerful coalition of social forces within and across national societies. The changing audiences that successful critical liberal internationalists have addressed tell us something about the content of those coalitions. From Kant's day and throughout the nineteenth century the audience was almost always Europe's aristocracy and also the cosmopolitan bourgeoisie whose interests were to be served by the proposed international institutions. After the turn of the century Hobson and Woolf addressed enlightened businessmen and the traditional state class, and also the newly powerful social democratic parties and the newer class of state functionaries responsible for bringing the masses into the new industrial state. Mary Parker Follett focused on another new class: professional managers operating within the giant industrial firms that first appeared between 1880 and 1920. From the 1920s until the 1980s reformers focused on the business, government, and labor elites of one industrial nation in particular, the United States.

Coalitions of powerful states and social forces "select" international institutions to survive by remaining parties to agreements and by continuing to finance IGOs. The institutions that do not survive are those that key state members leave, stop financing, simply ignore, or fail to renew. Not surprisingly, this kind of "natural selection" is most likely to occur during the fiscal and political crises that come with worldwide depressions and great-power wars. In that way, even events like these that we might consider as the strongest evidence of the limitations of the liberal internationalist vision can also be understood as playing a role in the process that explains the significant degree to which changes in international civil society have followed the path predicted by liberals since Kant.

Of course, this description of the selection mechanism and the evidence we have of a mechanism of innovation do not make a complete evolutionary explanation. We do not know whether the process of selection will continue to assure evolution along the liberal path, or what exactly the process of innovation really is. Theories that focus on changes in leading states and their ruling classes can tell us more about the first question. Similarly, we would need to consult theories about the maintenance and influence of intellectual communities in order to say whether the source of recurring innovation – the intellectual community of liberal internationalists themselves – will be available to suggest experiments in international cooperation in future times of crisis, and whether and why there would be states willing to conduct those experiments.

Gramsci and World Order

Antonio Gramsci's synthesis of liberal, Marxist, and realist social theories provides ways to fill the gaps in this evolutionary explanation and to go beyond it. It helps us to understand the "mythic" element in liberal internationalist thought, the reasons that effective liberal internationalists have always appealed to the kinds of "higher" interests that liberal theory treats as unreliable, and the role of coercive and noncoercive structures at all levels – from the factory floor to the boardrooms of the world organizations – in successive world orders. When we consider these many levels, we can better understand how "retrograde" developments like the reassertion of economic nationalism by the postwar welfare states have contributed to realizing the liberal vision, and why they are likely to be part of any new world order.

Historical blocs

Gramsci's idea of a *historical bloc* – a complex of economic, political, and cultural institutions which permits the normal social development characteristic of a particular period and a particular economic system – helps us combine the most instructive elements of the liberal tradition with theories that account for the wider sources of conflict in the world economy. Gramsci used this concept to overcome some of the misunderstandings that resulted from the traditional Marxist architectural metaphor for society – with its contingent political and cultural "superstructures" resting on a determining foundation or "base." Gramsci recognized the reciprocal determination of base and super-structure. He argued that ideas, culture, politics, and laws are more than simple functions of economic interests and the powers granted to people by their roles in production; these superstructures have an independent existence and force. Moreover, Gramsci believed that no economic system can fully develop – not even the contradictions within its inner logic can fully develop – outside of a conducive political and cultural environment. A historical bloc is "the dialectical unity of base and superstructure, theory and practice, of intellectuals and masses" (Forgacs 1988: 424) that makes such development possible.

A historical bloc is the kind of social formation or social order in which normal processes of social, economic, political, and intellectual development can go on. A historical bloc is not a social order in crisis. It is not a society experiencing a "time of troubles" (Lih 1990). It is not a social formation at the cusp between two dominant modes of production or poised between two industrial epochs. It is certainly not a society at war with itself.

It is easiest to understand Gramsci's concept by recognizing that it, like the older superstructure–base distinction, was developed through metaphor, using analogies to articulate something that had not been recognized in quite the same way before. Thus at various places in Gramsci's work he suggests a whole series of ways in which specific aspects of social life are "like" a *blocco*.

In one sense a historical bloc is simply an alliance – a "bloc" of those whose interests are served and whose aspirations are fulfilled by this economic and social system. In this sense, the cosmopolitan bourgeoisie has always been part of the historical blocs that have partially fulfilled the liberal internationalist vision, but the allies of this class have changed. In 1920 Keynes considered much of the European working class as outside the prewar continental social order whose passing he so regretted. While after the war, with some help from the Keynesians, industrial labor entered the historical bloc *qua* alliance in most parts of the industrial world.

A historical bloc is more than just an alliance. *Blocco* in Italian can also be translated as "block" in English and Gramsci seems to play with the meanings of that word as well. In one sense, a historical bloc is a social order that must be looked at in different ways in order to be understood completely. Its different faces must be examined the way we might examine a block of marble, a child's building block, or a Rubik's cube. Only when we have looked at all of the faces of a historical bloc – its biological-material face, its economic face, its political face, and its cultural and ideological face – can we begin to understand the ways they are internally connected one to another, and therefore begin to understand what makes the characteristic form of its overall social development possible. If we look at periods when the champions of industrial capitalism say it has worked best (such as the quarter-century before the First World War and the quarter-century after the Second), we need to specify the economic relations that were characteristic of the period (what was produced and consumed, where, how, and by whom?) as well as the dominant political institutions and the governing ideas of the time, and look for the interconnections among them.

The same point can be made by considering Gramsci's concept as an architectural metaphor *per se*, one just like the base–superstructure metaphor that it was designed to supersede. A historical bloc is like a complex urban multi-use "block," perhaps one of those massive sets of shops and flats of seven or eight stories centered around a large courtyard and built of brick or stone near the center of so many European cities in the boom years before the First World War, the years when Gramsci first came to industrial Turin from the Sardinian countryside. The depth of the block's foundation, the base, like the mode of production, establishes "limits of the possible" – to use Fernand Braudel's (1981) phrase – for what is above. (No more than seven or eight floors of unreinforced walls can be built on unreinforced foundations of concrete and stone.) Moreover, to remain useful the whole "structure of the superstructure," the building above ground, has to be coherent. Coercive structures (walls, floors, ceilings) have to work with enabling structures (rooms, halls, stairways) in the same way that the institutions of political society must work with those of civil society.

Gramsci's purpose in developing this concept was to emphasize that only within such a coherent ensemble of coercive and enabling institutions – linked to a particular base of technologies and relations of production – can the normal development of society occur. Such a bloc becomes the framework for history, like the Parisian apartment block that George Perec uses to frame *Life: A User's Manual* (1987), a novel formed by a dozen intersecting stories that only could happen in the industrial age. When a historical bloc is stable, life goes on "as it should," following its own inner logic, like the normal day-to-day lives of people sharing the same block of flats. When a society is in crisis, when a historical bloc is crumbling or partially deserted, like a house in a city under siege, normal life cannot go on until the bloc is rebuilt, reclaimed, or other structures found.

Crises, social forces organizing within civil society, and the emergence of new social orders

Gramsci used Marx's political economy and insights from the Italian tradition of realism to identify the sources of social conflict that could undo a historical bloc. Gramsci recognized that fundamental crises, what he called *organic crises* – where the social alliance, economic and political relations, and the ideological glue of a historical bloc are all torn asunder (Gramsci 1971: 210–18) – could originate in regional, sectoral, and ideological conflicts as much as in class conflicts; they could arise from incongruencies that had developed within the so-called "superstructure" as much as from contradictions that had grown between the superstructure and the base. Gramsci's investigations of the complexity of historical blocs as a whole made him leery of any simple, univariate explanations for the periodic crises of capitalist economies. He doubted that one could learn enough simply by tracking traditional Marxist indicators like the "organic composition of capital" or the "falling rate of profit" (ibid.: 469). Nor did he treat any of the fashionable, non-Marxist economic explanations of capitalist crises that came to fore in his day as decisive. Underconsumption, saturation of markets for certain goods, and the "need" for investment in new productive technologies all played a role in Gramsci's accounts, but he treated none as the whole explanation.

Nevertheless, like Marx, Gramsci emphasized that all social crises were part of a historical dialectic; they arose from the *normal* development of a social order. The disempowerment of the workers within the factory was a normal consequence of capitalism when it worked as it should, but at the same time the growing social significance of the working class as a whole was equally a consequence of capitalism's normal development. The two trends together set up the possibility of a social conflict that could transform the social order. Similarly, lateral pressure, different rates of economic development, and the increasing allegiance of both capitalists and workers to the nation-state – in fact, all of the major sources of the organic crisis of the Interimperial Order – could be seen as *normal* consequences of international social orders that were in place when the liberal internationalist vision was being fulfilled.

Much of Gramsci's work focused on the politics that ended such crises. He argued that to understand the genesis of new historical blocs we need to study three aspects of the conjunctures when a new order is being born (Forgacs 1988: 200–9; Chatterjee 1986: 43–9):

The first task, and perhaps the easiest, is to analyze the material limits of the possible. Gramsci, as a follower of Smith via Marx, accepted something of Smith's fundamental claim about techniques of production being limited by the extent of the market. This, after all, was simply an argument that limits of the possible can change. As this book demonstrates, it is a claim that the history of industry and international organization has validated. In 1920 Keynes confronted wider limits of the possible than predecessors had when they first imagined the prewar European social order whose passing he so lamented. Industry could produce much more, with much less effort, in Keynes's day than it could in the 1850s. And, of course, one reason for that was the impetus given to technological innovation by the European market that Keynes hoped to reconstruct.

The second task Gramsci gives us is to examine the relationship of the coercive forces associated with different social movements that are vying to create a new order. Having military predominance may help a social movement establish a coherent social order, but a preponderance of arms is neither a necessary nor a sufficient condition for doing so. The existence of a balanced military system in which no industrial state is encouraged to attack another is the necessary precondition. Thus, while the Interimperial Order may have originated after Germany's defeat of France in 1870, Germany never had military supremacy over Europe's empires; a balance of military force, supplemented by institutions designed to resolve conflicts among the powers, provided the necessary military structure for the late nineteenth-century European order. Similarly, the defeat of the fascists by the wartime United Nations alliance may have been necessary for the establishment of the Free World Order after 1945, but American military predominance in the West was not the essential element of the postwar order that the nuclear balance of terror was.

Finally, and most significantly, Gramsci would have us look at the relation of political forces, "the degree of homogeneity, self-awareness, and organization obtained by various social groups" (Forgacs 1988: 204), all of them functions of both intellectual and political leadership. These political forces tend to operate within what

Gramsci called *civil society*. In normal times, Gramsci argued, this realm of non coercive institutions of social order works alongside the coercive institutions of what he called the *state proper* or *political society*, the institutions exercising central coercive authority (Forgacs 1988: 235), to give a coherent "structure to the superstructure" becoming a polity or, in Gramsci's terms, *a state in the wider, organic sense*. In times of crisis the institutions of civil society remain as the primary site of the cohesion of new political forces that may create a new order.

Gramsci developed this version of the concept of civil society in a critique of the way Hegel (1952: 122–55) and other nineteenth-century theorists used the word to designate the social realm of egoistic interests, the realm in which we act on desires arising from our different positions in the market economy. Hegel considered the vast expansion of this realm to be the fundamental change wrought by capitalism (cf. Polanyi 1957: 111–29). Gramsci argued that it was analytically more fruitful to think of civil society as encompassing the entire realm of voluntary action that predated modern market economies and grew along with them. For Gramsci, civil society became the political space and collective institutions in which and through which individuals form political identities. Gramsci's civil society is the social realm in which abstract economic interests (those the observer can infer as inherent to individuals or groups occupying particular positions within the systems of production and reproduction) take on their actual, concrete, and particular forms as specific aspirations linked to specific world-views. It is the realm of voluntary associations, of the norms and practices which make them possible, and of the collective identities they form, the realm where "I" becomes "we." As such, it is the level of the superstructure typified by active consent and cooperation, not by coercion and force. It is the natural realm in which ideology and intellectual leaders (the makers of ideology) have their greatest impact (Augelli and Murphy 1988: 129–34).

Gramsci noted that industrial societies have tended to support an increasingly articulated civil society. As a result, much of the political struggle that accompanies the periodic crises of capitalist industrialism takes place within the realm of voluntary association and it takes place about the boundaries of that realm. It is the politics of parties, trade unions, and business associations, as well as the politics of churches, private philanthropies, and pluralist interest groups.

In the late 1970s, shortly after the recent world order crisis began, an acute observer of the UN system, Robert W. Cox, began to use some of Gramsci's concepts to reach conclusions about contemporary international institutions that were similar to the ones Gramsci had reached earlier about the noncoercive institutions within industrial states (Cox 1977; Cox and Jacobson 1977). Cox argued that while the stable configuration of UN agencies had helped crystallize the supremacy of the dominant world-views and of the dominant social forces that have governed the western world since 1945, at the same time (and of necessity) the global agencies also provided political space in which opposing social forces could articulate their own world-views and develop counterhegemonic alliances, the political space in which much of the international politics challenging the Free World Order was being conducted (Cox 1980a: 374).

Gramsci himself recognized similar developments which had played a role in the previous world order crises. In the notebooks he compiled from 1929 through 1935, while imprisoned as a leader of the parliamentary opposition to fascism, he included memoranda on contemporary "international institutions" (Gramsci 1992: 291): transportation organizations such as the International Road Conference which reflected the new craze for superhighways (p. 325) and the Maritime Conference where labor played a growing role (p. 358), attempts to establish international responsibility for social welfare (p. 284), the growing role of US businessmen and the US government in international cooperation through the International Chamber of Commerce (p. 291), and the changing array of American proposals for institutions to help resolve the continuing conflicts between Germany and the European victors of the First World War (p. 343). Gramsci wrote, "In the period since 1870 . . . the international organizational relations of the state [have] become more complex and massive," pointing out that this had happened at the same time that domestic civil society had become more complex and more closely linked to the state proper (Forgacs 1988: 233).

The role of liberal internationalists and the primary tasks of world organizations

Much of Gramsci's work on social orders in crisis concentrated on the role of *intellectual leadership*, the kind of leadership that liberal internationalists have attempted to provide at the international level. Thus Smith saw mercantilism, the limits imposed by narrow national markets, as a barrier to industrial innovation and recommended that the geographical scope of the social order be expanded; nineteenth-century functionalists recognized that state action and international cooperation would be needed to build the infrastructure of wider international markets; Hobson and Keynes, for slightly different reasons, both believed that policies designed to increase the wages of the working class would spur demand, and then investment, and thus resolve the periodic crises to which capitalist economies are prone; David Mitrany recognized that statism could doom an expanding capitalist economy and urged the piecemeal transfer of sovereignty to international institutions; and today's neoliberal fundamentalists and Keynesians propose alternative plans to pull the western economies out of the doldrums, spur growth in the Third World, and reintegrate the former communist states into a capitalist world order.

Intellectual leaders do more than come up with ideas about the institutions of the next world order. To go back to the image of a historical bloc as a puzzle, as Rubik's cube, or perhaps one of those older wooden block puzzles that Gramsci might have played with as a boy, those who are trying to reconstruct a historical bloc need to work on all the faces of the puzzle at once, putting together the ideology of the new order with its political institutions, defining its economic base, and, of course, the coalition of social forces that constitute the historical bloc *qua* alliance. The changing audiences to whom the liberal internationalists have addressed their appeals have been the social forces that they have hoped to bind together in alliances at the center of the new historical bloc. And the political processes in which successful liberal internationalists have taken part have been just as painstaking as the manipulations needed to solve any complex, three-dimensional puzzle.

Perhaps the architectural metaphor is even more telling. Building the international institutions of a world order in an industrial age is a bit like building a cathedral in late medieval Europe. While the aims of liberal internationalism provide designers with a single general plan, the way that the rituals of medieval Catholicism demanded structural similarity among all diocesan seats, the final form of the institutions of the prewar Interimperial Order and the postwar world order of the Free World differed as greatly as Salisbury and Chartres. Like most gothic cathedrals, the institutions of each of the successive world orders have been built sporadically over many dozens of years as the interest of the community to be served waxed and waned and as different sponsors and benefactors were found to realize one or another part of the originally imagined project. As a result, if we look closely at the completed edifices we see a host of mismatched parts. At no point during their construction did their designers have any real assurance the final structures would be as pleasing as Chartres with its mismatched but harmonious towers, or Salisbury, rising triumphantly to defy its inadequate foundations.

Initially the more successful liberal internationalist designers of world organizations have all focused on mobilizing the *political leader-ship* of national governments and powerful philanthropists willing to act as *sponsors* and *benefactors* of new international institutions.[3] The intellectual leaders have most often worked in the political space created within the institutions of international civil society estab-lished under the previous world order to push for the further devel-opment of the same realm so that it can become an effective mechanism regulating the world economy in the next industrial epoch.[4] Throughout each of the world order crises, liberal interna-tionalists have led transnational coalitions that pressed governments to call international conferences, establish international agreements, and create experimental IGOs to carry out two *primary tasks* essential to fulfilling the liberal vision.

The first has been to *foster industry* by creating and securing inter-national markets for industrial goods. International agreements de-signed to link together the transportation and communication infrastructure needed as the physical base for an international market help complete this task, as do agreements defining tradable goods through industrial standards, rules protecting intellectual property, and rules directly governing international trade.

The second has been to *manage potential conflicts* with organized social forces which might oppose the further extension of the indus-trial system promoted by the activities undertaken to complete the first task. People whose interests are tied to older industries, workers subject to the discipline of new industries, and those in the less industrialized world might be helped to adjust to the new order; agreements maintaining existing privileges might be worked out; or states might agree to use coercion to assure compliance with the new order.

After convincing political leaders to establish institutions carrying out these tasks, liberal internationalists have relied on the institu-tions to develop powerful constituencies. Experimental institutions that do not achieve this fall by the wayside. They lose their benefac-tors, typically as an economic consequence of the continuing crisis. Surviving agencies, on the other hand, usually gain the support of major investors who bet on the new opportunities created by the wider markets, and of interest groups which have come to depend on the benefits that the international institutions confer. In this way the alliance at the center of an international social order can be formed at the same time as its cooperative political institutions and the economic system that they will help establish and maintain.

A full evolutionary explanation and the secondary tasks of world organizations

The historical social orders which liberal internationalists helped to create each lasted through 20 or more years of the relative prosperity and relative peace their designers had promised. Nevertheless, so far at least, the normal development of a capitalist industrial economy has also had undesired consequences not ancipated by designers of past world orders. The boom years have always ended and a decade or more of conflict, both international and domestic, has followed.

Capital accumulation and the capacity to build a new world order   Ironically, a key power on which the liberals always relied to create new social orders – the power of private investors – has also tended to prolong world order crises even after many of these conflicts have abated. After years of war or weak profits due to industrial strife the whole capitalist class can appear to go on a gambling binge, pulling money from long-term investments and betting on short-term financial maneuvers with high stakes and little connection to the real economy of jobs and production. And when the casino economy finally goes bust, as it did at the beginning of Long Depression in the 1870s and after the crash of the New York stockmarket in 1929, a decade of unproductive hoarding – of capitalists putting their funds into precious metals, jewels, or anything rather than the more speculative long-term investment in fundamentally new industries – can follow.

Yet even during a world order crisis that has been protracted by gambling and hoarding, liberal internationalists can have a rational hope that their vision eventually will be fulfilled again. Even in the process of prolonging the crisis, capitalists prove that they still have the investment power needed to build the new industrial era of the next international social order. So far at least, each era of rapid industrial growth (with its institutions encouraging capitalists to put their money into long-term productive investments) has left capitalists, as a global class, in a better position than they were at the beginning of the era. When liberal internationalists have succeeded in convincing a bloc of "progressive" investors to lend a hand in creating a new industrial era, the larger historical process of capital accumulation has already provided them with the capacity to make the necessary contribution of investment in new industries, a power that is just as important as the ability of states to cooperate in creating the climate that convinces investors to be "progressive."

The expanding state and the reproduction of liberal internationalism Similarly, even if many of today's liberal internationalists felt isolated throughout the 1980s when liberal fundamentalism was in ascendancy, they could look to the past and feel confident not only that they would eventually find allies, but that there would still be men and women who would share their vision if there were another world order crisis a generation on. Much of the intellectual leadership needed to reform international institutions has come from intellectuals linked to the growing industrial state, the group that some scholars influenced by Gramsci have called the "cadre class" of "salaried functionaries who are in one way or another engaged in operating the reproductive and normative structures that unify... social class relations ... (state) managers, teachers, trade union bureaucrats, social workers and others" (Pijl 1990: 301; cf. Bihr 1989; Markovitz 1977: 325–41; 1987: 233–321). This state class is in no more danger of disappearing than is the growing link between civil society and the state proper within the industrial world.

In fact, international institutions have always worked to strengthen this state class. This has been a consequence of the two *secondary tasks* of global IGOs. These activities still turn out to be essential to fulfilling the liberal internationalist vision, but only because world organizations must carry them out in order to complete their primary agenda. First, because they are intergovernmental bodies serving nation-states, the UN agencies and their successful predecessors have always had the task of *strengthening states*, both directly (by encouraging cooperation in public administration and public finance) and indirectly (by facilitating the peaceful resolution of international disputes, supporting refugees, providing war relief, and aiding in postwar reconstruction). Second, in diverting opposition directed against the further development of industrial capitalism and in carrying out other functions, global IGOs are *strengthening society* in relation to the state proper. World organizations have encouraged states to be more responsive to their national societies by becoming more responsible for meeting basic needs and by respecting human rights. Both categories of secondary tasks help create international networks supporting the state bureaucracies that carry out related domestic functions. The secondary activities strengthening the state directly benefit the state class that has nurtured many liberal internationalists. Those strengthening society have created political space for the organization of social forces that might otherwise have been antithetical to further extensions of the industrial system. International workers' associations and the movements for decolonization and development are the most important historical examples. Not surprisingly, the movements which organized within global IGOs have developed agendas compatible with the liberal internationalist vision and have nurtured intellectuals interested in integrating new social forces into a liberal world order.

One step beyond the evolutionary explanation: political leaders and the role of the liberal myth

While the world organizations may have contributed to the replication of the intellectual leadership needed to keep liberal evolution on track, no unilinear, uninterrupted process of liberal learning has resulted. The critical strain of liberal internationalism – the strain nurtured by IGOs and by the state – has been preserved, but it has always confronted an equally strong strain of liberal fundamentalists who prefer a world of pure laissez faire. Liberal fundamentalists thrive in the early years of the world order crises when the power of private investors is at its peak. The fundamentalists provide the intellectual leadership needed to justify the era of gambling and hoarding; they provide justification for a kind of governance of the world economy by capitalists alone, unencumbered by necessary alliances with other social forces. As a result, the past triumphs of the critical strain of liberal internationalism should not really be understood as the result of an "inevitable" evolutionary process; they have been the particular historical consequence of social struggles which could have had very different outcomes.

This becomes especially clear when we consider the political leadership necessary to create the Interimperial Order and the Free World Order. It was very different in the two periods and neither form of political leadership can be expected today. A host of aristocratic philanthropists played the central role in the nineteenth century, and the United States government led the move toward the postwar order. Neither is available to play the same role today and it is not clear that alternative leaders have been socialized in sufficient numbers to support the numerous experiments in international organization that would really be needed for something like the "natural selection" of new institutions to operate again. But then, both at the time Keynes wrote *The Economic Consequences of the Peace* and earlier, at the beginning of the Long Depression of the nineteenth century, the necessary political leadership was slow to appear, but it eventually did. Liberal internationalists had to mobilize that leadership and they did so, in great part, with the mythic elements of their philosophy. They did so by appeals to the kind of "higher" interests about which they, as liberals, have always been skeptical.

Both at the beginning of the Long Depression and in Keynes's day many liberal internationalists were more (narrowly) "realistic" about appeals to such "higher" interests. They first turned to the top military powers to provide the political leadership to put the liberal vision into practice, and the liberals used arguments about the powers' narrow self-interest. In the 1870s they appealed to the German empire, the victor in the recent great-power wars, and to Great Britain, the dominant maritime power. In the early interwar years it was the United States, the decisive victor in the First World War, which received much of the attention.

The prestige of the victors certainly explains why they might be importuned, but their military power did not by itself provide these states with the interest in, and necessary capacities for, political leadership, nor did it preclude other governments from having that capacity. The capacity that the political leaders needed was simply the ability to convince others to join in creating the necessary experiments in international cooperation so that they could be proven in practice: While the US government eventually played a key role in providing that political leadership in Keynes's day, and (in a few areas) some officials of the German empire played a similar role in establishing the Interimperial Order, Britain played a very small role in establishing that world order, and played a much larger role in creating the Free World Order at a time when its military power was much less significant.

In the long run a predominant coalition of powerful states proved necessary to assure the survival of international institutions, but such a coalition was not needed to establish the institutions in the first place. On the military side all that has been needed to begin the process of creating a new international social order congruent with the liberal vision is a stable international balance of coercive powers and the defeat or isolation of any major powers dedicated to an alternative.

Today's neoliberal fundamentalists usually argue that at the very least there needs to be predominant *economic* power willing to initiate the political movement toward a new liberal world. Their historical justification goes back to the interwar period when a good case can be made that there were a few, very specific economic tasks needed to be performed in order to reestablish Keynes's "economic utopia," and that only one actor, the United States, happened to be in a position to carry out those tasks by itself (Kindleberger 1973). The neoliberals make a similar argument about the nineteenth century, when Britain supposedly provided a similar degree of the necessary "hegemonic stability."

In fact, while the British did carry out some key economic tasks, the same ones the US eventually performed in the Free World Order, and the British contributed to the stability of the prewar military order, in the late nineteenth century Britain was the power least interested in leading the political movement toward a more integrated world economy. Britain was the power that was the most reluctant to join the Public International Unions. The British justified their policy as reflecting their greater loyalty to the fundamentals of liberalism, but Britain's competitors also pointed out that the policy protected the interests of Britain's powerful speculators and increasingly uncompetitive industrial firms.

Nonetheless, the reluctance of the leading military and economic power certainly did not doom the liberal internationalist project in the generations before the Great War. If we accept, as Gramsci does, that the political superstructures of coherent social order always combine both coercive and permissive or consensus-based elements, then we should expect that military predominance only would be a key to establishing an order that relies mainly on coercive means. In contrast, the liberal internationalist vision has always imagined its world of prosperity and peace as relying first and foremost on consensual institutions, institutions that can best be created by leaders able to mobilize consent.

If the only means that political leaders had to mobilize consent were to assure immediate, individual economic gain – that is, side-payments to every powerful economic interest if they will support the new social order – then it would make sense, at least, that the predominant economic powers would be needed in order to offer the necessary rewards. But the slower, cathedral-building-like process of establishing a new world order assures that only a few powerful economic interests need to be paid off at a time, and even then their payoff can be limited to the benefits they can expect by joining an

experimental international institution whose effectiveness in promoting prosperity has already begun to be proven in practice.

Not surprisingly, then, both in Keynes's day and during the earlier
crisis era, liberal internationalists eventually were able to find the
necessary political leadership, but it took a great deal of time and
many of those who provided that leadership have been all but forgotten. Even when the liberal internationalists could not rely on the
preponderant powers, they could find less powerful states, aristocratic benefactors, and private philanthropists to sponsor the necessary conferences, agreements, and agencies. As outlined in the
introduction, it has always taken decades even to get international
agreement on agencies to carry out the first primary task – building
and securing a wider world market – but the process has always
begun to snowball when the clear benefits of the earliest agencies
have been proven.

The first potential political leaders to whom liberal internationalists have made *successful* appeals always appear to be responding
(either directly or indirectly) as a result of altruism, *noblesse oblige*, or
one of those other "higher" motivations that liberal theory usually
treats as so unreliable. In the nineteenth century, liberals appealed
to a sense of *noblesse oblige* on the part of princes and state functionaries. At that time, and ever since then, liberal internationalists have
argued that if capitalists could transcend their short-run individual
interests long enough to push collectively for a liberal international
order, they all would receive remarkable long-run benefits (the
mythic part of the liberal vision). Similarly, in the twentieth century,
liberals from Hobson through the authors of the Brandt Commission
reports have asked privileged industrial workers along with capitalists to go beyond their immediate economic interests and to press
governments to build a new order.

Gramsci argues that making such appeals to "higher" interests is in
the nature of what intellectual leaders do, and that, furthermore,
there should be nothing mystical or contradictory about it since these
"higher" motivations are no more or less reliable than the "baser"
immediate pecuniary interests to which liberals would rather appeal.
Gramsci accepts, as all liberals since Smith have, that every person
may have *individual* "interests" that an external observer can infer
from our position in the world of work.[5] He adds that we all also have
collective class interests and, more significantly, collective *aspirations*
to form a coherent social order under the hegemony of people who
share our position in society, aspirations whose abstract possibility an
external observer can just as easily infer from our position in the real

economy, even though their concrete form is only determined within specific political struggles.[6]

This is where Gramsci even more clearly differs from most liberals: He concludes that our actual actions are not necessarily motivated by interests and aspirations that an observer can infer; they are motivated by the concrete goals and world-views we have learned. Our interests and aspirations may shape our learning even to the extent that the different ideologies that guide us over time may asymptotically approach our interests, but narrow individual interests by themselves are not a good predictor of actions, especially since members of a class can just as "realistically" be convinced to act on the basis of their long-term, collective aspirations, motivations that might take them in a very different direction (cf. Augelli and Murphy 1988: 122–6).

While their own theory will not reveal it to them, liberal internationalists play their own role in the fulfillment of their vision not by taking interests as given, but by *shaping* their audiences' motivations, their understandings of both their aspirations and their interests. The "myths" articulated by critical liberal internationalists move their audiences to discard narrow, immediate self-interest and look to long-term, collective aspirations. The liberals need not convince all members of the classes they target to act in this way, only enough members to establish the regulatory institutions that will make further movement toward a liberal internationalist world a matter of most governments' self-interest.

These institutions also shape action, in part by shaping interests, but more by taking interests as given (cf. Keohane and Murphy 1992). The international institutions simply change the actions that powerful states, powerful investors, and others will prefer. As Keohane (1984) argues, international institutions often reveal previously unrealized ways in which congruent state interests can be served. At the same time, perhaps even more significantly, by creating new world markets and satisfying potential opponents of new industrial developments international institutions convince capitalists to invest in the economic base of the next world order.

One step beyond cooperative cosmopolitanism: tasks, means, and sites of regulation

Liberal internationalists from Kant forward have understood the power of international institutions in much the same way that

Keohane has explained it to us today. Kant saw his parliament of nations as securing a world in which men of commerce would place cosmopolitan interests above local interests. Mitrany imagined both citizens and state officials as increasingly recognizing their interests in world government. And today's global Keynesians admonish the reluctant wealthy powers to see their own interest in collective solutions to global problems. However, unlike liberal internationalists, Keohane recognizes that the tradition's preference for the most inclusive, collective solutions to global problems – its very "internationalism" – can obscure the real sites of regulation in stable world orders.

It is useful to think of the elements regulating such an order – the political institutions of a liberal international historical bloc – as being distributed along three dimensions representing the *tasks*, the *means*, and the *sites* of regulation.

On the first dimension we have the regulatory tasks that must be performed, beginning with the primary task that has always been recognized by the tradition: fostering industry through the expansion of international markets. Other necessary tasks (satisfying potential opponents of new industries, maintaining a stable balance of military power) would follow. The list of those additional tasks would be similar whether we created it inductively, by looking at the additions that later successful liberal internationalists added to the original agenda, or by deriving it from theories in the Marxist and realist traditions.

On the second dimension we would distinguish coercive means of carrying out those tasks from more consensual means. Thus, for example, one world order could be distinguished from the next by a shift in the way (say) potential opponents from the less industrialized world are regulated, coercive means (colonialism) giving way to more consensual means (mobilizing international support for the governments of "developing" countries).

Finally, the third dimension would locate where regulatory action takes place. It could take place at the global level (as in the case of some development assistance provided by IGOs and transnational associations). It could take place among smaller groups of states (as in the case of most foreign aid), or within a single sovereignty (as in the case of colonial government), or at the level of the region, industry, family, workplace, and so on, within various countries. The regulatory structure of a particular, concrete world order can involve different means at different levels. For example, the consensual international activities that constitute development assistance can support LDC governments in their coercive management of dissent against the existing world order.

The main liberal internationalist tradition focuses only on one part of this three-dimensional matrix. It is primarily concerned with the evolution of *consensual means* of regulation at the most inclusive, *global level*. There is certainly nothing wrong with that focus; any champion of democratization and wider human understanding can appreciate the reason for it. The focus only becomes problematic when this evolution is considered without considering its broader context, including the evolution of less consensual means of regulation and the evolution of regulatory tasks carried out in other sites at other levels.

Contemporary economists and political scientists of the "social structures of accumulation" and "regulation" schools, who a great deal to Gramsci, have devoted their efforts to detailing the first dimension of this matrix, the wide range of regulatory tasks that need to be carried out for capitalist industrialism work as well as it has. The lists they derive include many functions that contemporary liberal internationalists ignore. The most significant are tasks associated with managing potential conflicts over democratic control of industry – regulatory mechanisms operating at the level of industries or groups of industries – especially the Fordist bargain that allowed workers to enjoy mass consumption in exchange for acceptance of the discipline that assured mass production. Conversely, because most of this work inspired by Gramsci has focused on sites of regulation within individual nation-states,[7] it tends to ignore the key international regulatory tasks that the liberal tradition has always recognized: the tasks associated with allowing capitalist industrialism to expand across existing political boundaries, especially the task of creating and securing wider international markets to promote new industries (cf. Robles 1994).

One of Robert W. Cox's articles (1977) introducing Gramsci's concepts to English-speaking international relations scholars suggests a way to begin with the focus that the liberal internationalist tradition has always maintained, yet work toward a more complete delineation of the evolving regulatory mechanisms of successive world orders. Cox focused on the activities of a world organization that many of its original liberal internationalist promoters might now treat as an anachronism and a failure, the International Labor Organization. The original design of the organization imagined a powerful regulatory agency that would manage conflicts between workers and capitalists across the industrialized world through a kind of parliament in which both social forces would be directly represented, a body whose main purpose would be to establish authoritative global labor standards. By the early years of the Cold War the organization had become something quite different. It still created international labor standards in a semiparliamentary way, but this process was certainly not the central mechanism regulating potential conflict over the democratic control of industry throughout the Free World.

Yet Cox demonstrates how ILO activities provided clear indicators of more significant regulatory mechanisms. The deeper mechanisms included the Fordist bargain of mass consumption for mass production as well as a system for constantly replicating that bargain when conditions changed: the system of collective bargaining at an industry or shop level. As Cox moved from the international level to the lowest level on which the conflicts putatively regulated by the ILO might emerge, he was able to outline a host of elements of the postwar, historical bloc, the Free World Order. The ILO played a role. So did certain "private" voluntary associations operating alongside the ILO within international civil society: the international association of "free" trade unions centered on the American Federation of Labor and Congress of Industrial Organizations (AFL-CIO). But much of the job of regulation went on within states.

Similarly, Cox's method followed the trace of regulation from sites and times where consensual means clearly dominated to sites where coercion played a key role. Links between the AFL-CIO and the US Central Intelligence Agency; especially when operating in the Third World, showed the connections. Cox argued that his method allows us recognize the limits of the *hegemony* Gramsci saw as the ultimate glue of most of the social orders that have existed in the industrial world.[8] That hegemony minimizes the use of force. It "arises in civil society and expresses a structure of social power in which one class is dominant, but in which that class consents to concessions to subordinate classes such as to make the structure tolerable to them, thereby creating a broadly-based consensus in its favor" (Cox 1980b: 166). In Gramsci's terms, the ultimate goal of the liberal internationalists has always been one of securing the global hegemony of a particular class, the cosmopolitan bourgeoisie.

We can go even further and say that most critical writers in the liberal internationalist tradition have worked to create what Gramsci called the *ethical hegemony* of the same class, the kind of hegemony that not only minimizes the use of force, but also eschews all fraudulent ideological claims, all the hype and all the smoke and mirrors designed to secure the consent of allies who do not really benefit much from a social order under bourgeoisie supremacy (Augelli and Murphy 1988: 125). In such a social order it would become impossible to distinguish the "dominant" class from "subordinate" allies to whom concessions have to be made.

The Interimperial Order and the Free World Order were approximations, although very poor approximations, of ethical hegemony. It is in the context of this goal that the "retrograde" development of the economic nationalism underlying the welfare state needs to be understood. Liberal fundamentalists, including many of today's neoliberals, decry this and similar developments as deviations from the original liberal internationalist path laid out by Adam Smith. In one sense, they are. But in a more significant sense they have been ways to secure the hegemony of the liberal internationalist vision in a world where the growth of industry either creates or reinforces conflicts between managers and workers, between protectors of society's past and champions of the new order, between people in the industrialized world and those in LDCs, and among the various industrial states.

Ironically, the continuing historical significance of the liberal internationalist vision has depended on practical men and women whom other, more dogmatic, liberals have always derided as "statists." The liberal officers of the nineteenth-century European state played a more significant role in creating the prewar European "economic Eldorado" than any Cobdenite true believers. The Keynesians who championed the welfare state and development cooperation had more to do with establishing the Free World Order than any of the Depression-era champions of liberal orthodoxy. Similarly, we should expect that today's globalist Keynesians are more likely to carry the liberal internationalist vision forward than any of today's neoliberal fundamentalists, which is one practical lesson that this history of global governance should teach.

2

BUILDING THE PUBLIC INTERNATIONAL UNIONS

The next three chapters are about the "economic Eldorado" that Keynes believed Europe had enjoyed before the Great War. I argue that the Public International Unions worked with regular intergovernmental conferences and a host of international agreements to create the non-coercive part of the international political order that was needed for Europe to enter the Second Industrial Revolution. Ultimately, the new industrial system allowed Germany to overtake Britain's dominant position in continental markets for industrial goods. When the resulting disputes between the two powers played into existing social conflicts – especially the one between champions of the industrial system and protectors of Europe's *ancien régime* – movement toward a more liberal European social order halted and the descent into 30 years of war and economic decay began. That long crisis had barely started when in 1920 Keynes expressed his nostalgia for "the delicate organization" of international institutions that once had made a more liberal European order seem inescapable (1971: 10). This chapter looks at the design of those institutions and at the way in which they were established. Chapter 3 looks at what the Public International Unions actually did. And chapter 4 examines the impact of this prewar "world government," not only its contribution to Keynes's economic utopia, but also its unexpected contribution to the forces that would tear that world apart.

The Political Economy that Inspired the Unions

When liberal internationalists like Kant began promoting world organizations they were initially as unsuccessful as all the other western idealists who had done so since Dante. In the 1860s their luck changed. More than 30 global IGOs were founded between 1864 and the First World War. They were joined by a dozen or more regional agencies, most of them in the Americas. In some ways the global agencies, the Public International Unions, were more like the regional organizations in the Americas than the universalistic charters of the Unions suggest. Most of their members were European. That is why William T. Stead, a correspondent called by E. H. Carr (1946: 76) Britain's "most popular and brilliant journalist" of the day, could describe his 1898 visit to Berne, home of five of the most important Unions, as a journey to "the capital of the continent" (1899: 25–37).[1] Of course, the Unions reached beyond the continent simply because European states controlled much of the world. The first of the global IGOs (table 2) affected every part of the European empires, both formal and informal.

TABLE 2   World organizations in 1914 (by main area of responsibility and date of founding)

FOSTERING INDUSTRY

Infrastructure
1865   International Telegraph Union
1874   Universal Postal Union
1884   International Railway Congress Association
1890   Central Office of International Railway Transport
1894   Permanent International Association of Navigation Congresses
1905   Diplomatic Conference on International Maritime Law
1906   Universal Radiotelegraph Union
1909   Permanent International Association of Road Congresses

Industrial standards and intellectual property
1875   International Bureau of Weights and Measures
1883   International Union for the Protection of Industrial Property
1886   International Union for the Protection of Literary and Artistic Works
1912   International Bureau of Analytical Chemistry of Human and Animal Food

Trade
1890   International Union for the Publication of Customs Tariffs
1893   Hague Conference on Private International Law
1913   International Bureau of Commercial Statistics

MANAGING POTENTIAL SOCIAL CONFLICTS

Labor
1901   International Labor Office

Agriculture
1879   International Poplar Commission

1901   International Council for the Study of the Sea
1902   International Sugar Union
1905   International Institute of Agriculture

STRENGTHENING STATES AND THE STATE SYSTEM

Public order and administration
1875   International Penitentiary Commission
1910   International Institute of Administrative Sciences

Managing interstate conflicts
1899   Permanent Court of Arbitration
1907   International Court of Prize

STRENGTHENING SOCIETY

Human rights
1890   International Maritime Bureau Against the Slave Trade

Relief and welfare
1907   Bureau for Information and Enquiries Regarding Relief to Foreigners

Health
1900   Commission on Revision of the Nomenclature of the Causes of Death
1907   International Office of Public Hygiene
1912   International Association of Public Baths and Cleanliness

Education and research
1864   International Geodetic Association
1903   International Association of Seismology
1908   International Commission for the Teaching of Mathematics
1909   Central Bureau for the International Map

The Unions would have been inconceivable before the first decades of the Industrial Revolution had come and gone. The dignitaries who created the first of the world organizations learned from the experience of Germany and the United States, the major powers that first followed Britain into the industrial age. The similar German and American industrial policies provided a model of how Europe as a whole could unite and begin a new industrial epoch based on even more advanced technologies than the railroad and telegraph, the new industries that had begun to transform the few industrialized nations at mid-century.

While the key leaders who learned from this model were fascinated by the promise of industrialism, most gained their own power and prestige from the economic order that had preceded the industrial system. Much of the political leadership needed to create the Public International Unions came from aristocrats, men whose position and wealth was a result of the continuation of the *ancien régime*. Even the newer ideas underlying the Unions came from the recently acquired expertise of the aristocrats who worked along with some commoners as high state functionaries, men who gained their new knowledge as the European states tried to cope with the unprecedented problems created by the new industrial system.

International cooperation among these men was facilitated by the European conference system which had long been in existence and which had helped mute conflicts among the powers. The conferences, along with Britain's naval supremacy and its willingness to act as a balancer in conflicts on the continent, also contributed to the peace in the years when the Public International Unions got started. The peace, in turn, contributed to the development of world organizations. In this way the putative hegemon of the day played an indirect but important role in establishing the Unions, even though the British government disdained any more direct role in their creation, arguing that as the first and leading industrial power the United Kingdom would gain little from them.

The American and German roads from Huddersfield

Stead's 1899 study of *The United States of Europe* aimed to challenge this conclusion. His book was the first of a genre of first-person accounts of the activities and implications of the world organizations. One of the best is James Morris's 1963 study of the World Bank, *The Road to Huddersfield*. Morris took his title from one of the Yorkshire mill towns where the Industrial Revolution began. Of course, while the World Bank's clients still may be on the road *to* Huddersfield, Stead was writing some 60 years earlier about institutions designed to put Europeans on a road *away* from the early industrial system that Huddersfield represents.

In fact, a better place than Huddersfield to begin the story of the Public International Unions would be on the other side of the Atlantic – in Lawrence, Lowell, or Watertown, Massachusetts – the riverside mill towns where the Industrial Revolution began in the first country to follow Britain's lead. The American push into the industrial world got underway in earnest in the early nineteenth century when a few Massachusetts investors began speculating in textile mills and in the even more profitable systems for providing water-power to run them (Parker 1940: 60–7; Chandler 1977: 57–9).

American industrialization did not take under strict laissez faire. Early American industrialists pushed for protective tariffs and they blithely disregarded British patents on the machines they needed to build for the new factories. But tariffs could not protect the early American mills from becoming less profitable when domestic competition grew and the textile market in the United States became saturated. Of course, a depression in one part of an economy does not necessarily mean that profitable investments cannot be found elsewhere and by the time the mills and waterworks that powered them began to lose money many large investors had already found profitable outlets for capital in the digging of canals, and soon afterward in the construction of the much more capital-intensive railroads. Both activities were supported by the public treasuries. Some of the earliest railroads in the United States linked the inland riverside industrial towns to the older coastal cities that remained the centers of population. Other early lines linked the eastern seaboard cities to each other. Then the tracks headed west to the already populated agricultural regions along the Great Lakes and the Ohio River. There, spurred in part by the railroad boom itself, the vast expansion of the American coal, iron, and steel industries began. By the middle of nineteenth century the US had moved into a new industrial era led by these new industries.

Even though industrialization in the US had depended, in part, on illiberal economic policies, it inspired many European liberals who emphasized Adam Smith's arguments about using larger markets to encourage innovation in the technologies of production. By mid-century a European model, the German Customs Union (the *Zollverein*), appeared to repeat the American experience.

Both the Americans and the Germans made deliberate attempts to use the state to achieve prosperity. The institutionalization of what we would now call "development policy" (if we were in the Third World) or "industrial policy" (if we were in the richer capitalist states) was what really distinguished the United States and Germany from Britain in the minds of those who wrote about industry and international organization before the First World War (Zimmerman 1917: 39). Before 1850 Germany's many sovereign states and the American federal states actively encouraged development of the transportation and communication infrastructure needed to link each nation as a whole. In both countries Adam Smith's necessary "publick works" came to include massive programs of lighthouses, roads, canals, and railroads. The republican constitutions of the United States encouraged governments at all levels to respond to business demands for improved transportation and communication systems (Chandler 1977: 40). In Germany the politics of industrial policy were a bit different. The father of German statist political economy, Friedrich List, observed the early results of American industrial policy, and he carried their example home, becoming the voice of movement demanding in 1844 that German governments create the physical infrastructure of an integrated national market and that they then agree on rules to govern that trading system (List 1922). By the late 1840s the German states were competing to build new railroads, encouraged by the fact that many proved to be very lucrative, at least at the beginning (Freundlig 1983: 122).

Both the German and the American governments did more to encourage new industries than just establish the infrastructure for a national market. Both used tariffs to protect infant industries (the Americans somewhat haphazardly because the tariff remained a central issue of sectional politics), following the policy first envisioned by Alexander Hamilton (Woytinsky and Woytinsky 1955: 35–6), the policy List would later make a centerpiece of his political economy.

External tariffs, however, were not the part of the German and American models that seemed the most relevant to the nineteenth-century European functionalists who wanted to replicate the experience of these countries on a larger scale. It seemed more important that both societies also supported industry by well-developed systems of patent and copyright, policies that had to be negotiated among the several states. The German experience with the protection of intellectual property, in particular, was taken as a model by nineteenth-century advocates of wider European economic integration (Bowker 1886: 25–33; Penrose 1951: 14–15).

Of course, both the United States and Germany also ensured that the advantages of industrial innovation would be extended to the entire nation by abolishing internal tariffs and other trade restrictions. And both governments even anticipated extension of their systems beyond their borders, the Americans to the entire new world and the Germans to the entire European continent. As Alan S. Milward and S. B. Saul (1979: 372) argue, the architects of the *Zollverein* designed it to restore something lost after the Congress of Vienna, the larger continental markets of the briefly hegemonic Napoleonic system. Similarly, the Federalists, Whigs, and Republicans who sustained the nationalist economic vision in the United States from Hamilton, to John Quincy Adams, to Lincoln, always foresaw the progressive incorporation of a wider world into the new order that they were creating (Augelli and Murphy 1988: 60–6).

The persistence of the ancien régime in substance and ideology

Few of the Europeans who first promoted a continental vision were like Hamilton and Adams, men of the merchant and manufacturing classes, the classes most likely to benefit from the extension of the new industrial system. The Europeans were men of the aristocracy, the old ruling class with its interests rooted it in the land, and men of the growing state class, a class that in many countries had been spawned from the aristocracy. Together the aristocrats and the men of government helped forge a late nineteenth-century social order which served both aristocrats and the bourgeoisie, and which even promised to serve a small privileged sector of the working class, especially in Germany, where in the heyday of the Public International Unions, German socialists succeeded in moving privileged working men into the center of national political life. But, except for this very small privileged sector, European workers and peasants, and almost everyone who lived in Europe's colonies and dependencies, remained outside the social alliance at the core of the late nineteenth-century social order.

The central role of the aristocracy in creating the Interimperial Order may surprise us today unless we remember that the Industrial Revolution had caused no definitive break from the *ancien régime*.[2] Europe's rural economy remained the major employer until well into the twentieth century, and European governments reflected what Gramsci calls the "merger" between the old aristocratic ruling classes and the bourgeoisie. Aristocrats kept their privileges on the land, in the management of government, and in the military. Some, including many of the men who contributed to the design of the Public International Unions, began to become, as Gramsci argued, the new "intellectuals of the bourgeoisie" (see Augelli and Murphy 1993: 145). At the same time businessmen reinforced the prestige of the aristocracy by modelling their private lives on those of the older ruling class.

Not surprisingly then, *within* most European countries the ideological face of the late nineteenth-century social order was neither bourgeois republicanism nor the cosmopolitan liberalism of Smith and Kant. Even today the ceremonies required by that great turn-of-the-century cosmopolitan institution, the modern Olympiad, still reflect the ideological face of Europe's domestic social orders a century ago. Nationalism, not labor's democratic socialism or the industrial bourgeoisie's liberalism, became the main ideological glue of European societies in the late nineteenth century. It was a glue that Europe needed, as economic historian William N. Parker argues (1984: 230), in order to link the individual to the universal in a world which had been so rapidly changed by industry, where all the older systems for providing collective identity had been shattered – localism, fealty, and religion.

Recently many scholars have also reminded us of nationalism's radical roots. Yet even though European nationalism may have originated in movements attacking privilege and demanding popular sovereignty (Mayall 1990: 40–1), it was quickly transmuted into the defensive kind of "official nationalism" characteristic of the late nineteenth century, "a conscious, self-protective *policy*, intimately linked to the preservation of imperial-dynastic interests . . . something emanating from the state and serving the interests of the state" (Anderson 1983: 145). And even if the goal of official nationalism was to command the allegiance of the entire population to an inherently nondemocratic order (by privileging the state and, through it, the aristocracy and the other classes that the state served), the ideology also demanded that the state be paternal and that the crowned nobility who embodied the state act on the basis of *noblesse oblige*. Official nationalism encouraged Italy's King Victor Emmanuel III to support impoverished peasants, Germany's Wilhelm II to promote the welfare state, and Britain's Benjamin Disraeli to lead the party of the old order to enfranchise working-class men. In each case, official nationalism created a national community and justified a much larger, more active, and more benign state.

The origin of the disciplines of the state

Thus the aristocrats who championed the Public International Unions in the late nineteenth century found themselves engaged in a larger project of extending the powers of national government. F. H. Hinsley puts the issue in focus for students of international relations: "As a tolerably integrated, comprehensive and efficient organisation of power the state hardly existed before 1890, but wherever it did develop to and beyond this level, it then developed with formidable speed" (1963: 280). Institutionalist historians of Hinsley's generation traced the first justifications for the expansion of the state taking place in the 1890s to a growing competence in administration that began to develop at least 50 years earlier, in the 1840s, when national legislators (whether parliaments or princes) faced the fundamentally new problems generated by the Industrial Revolution. Oliver

MacDonagh (1958) observed five typical stages in the development of this competence, basing his model on the British experience.

First, faced with some fundamentally new problem, for example, the conditions of the working class as exposed in 1845 by Disraeli (1980) and Engels (1962), Parliament would pass an act, such as the first rules for humane working conditions in the new factories, without really considering how it could be enforced. When the problem continued, a second stage would ensue of appointing temporary panels of "experts" to monitor both the problem and compliance with the new regulations. While this stage may have given us the blue-book reports which allowed Marx to develop his theory of capitalism, it certainly did not solve the problem of working-class poverty. This failure was typical of second-stage policy innovations. Consequently, the new group of experts in the government would often become lobbyists for new and better legislation, a third stage. If this failed, the experts would often turn away from legislative solutions and search instead for a new "science," a new *discipline*, a new set of ideas about how the social evil could be overcome. Ultimately, MacDonagh argues, experts within government who had been involved with an issue through all these four stages would develop an ethos supporting wider and wider administrative discretion, thus establishing the ideological foundation for modern bureaucratic government (cf. Jacoby 1973; Osborne 1983).

The specific way in which a particular state's institutions emerged on top of that ideological foundation depended on the country's prior system of interest representation – the structure of civil society and the relationship of the various institutions of civil society to those of the state proper (Stone 1983). In Germany, for example, the larger state appeared to grow out of conflicts between king and chancellor in which each tried to manipulate the political space available in the Reichstag and to gain allies among business and labor (Stone 1983: 97–103; Macht 1980: 176), while in Britain government grew with the emergence of the Parliamentary Labour Party (Dangerfield 1961; Overbeek 1990: 52–4).[3] But in each case the expanding state relied on a body of expertise that could be shared throughout the industrial world, and on ideas about the need for government in an industrial society and about how to govern, and these had been concretized into new intellectual disciplines by the last decades of the century. The same expertise influenced the establishment of the Public International Unions. It helped explain the relevance of the American and German models and it added a layer of knowledge on top of the liberal internationalist world-view inherited from Smith and Kant.

The interimperial military order

We will turn to the specific content of that knowledge, the details of
the new disciplines of the state, after considering the political institutions at an international level that gave those who held that
knowledge the power to work together across the boundaries of state
and nation. Even men who shared the same expertise in dealing with
problems of the early stages of industrialism could not have created
lasting international agreements had their governments refused to
deal with one another out of jealousy or fear. While international
jealousies were prevalent in the late nineteenth century, fears were
surprisingly few. The two major wars involving the great powers –
the Austro–Prussian War of 1866 and the Franco–Prussian War of
1870 – were brief. Both the powers defeated by the Germans quickly
returned to playing that great-power balancing game that helped
keep the peace throughout the nineteenth century. Many observers
credit Britain, with its naval supremacy and its policy of never entering peacetime alliances, with a leading role in that system, a role that
continued even though the "classical" era of the balance-of-power
system ceased soon after the Prussians finally united the German
empire at the end of the war with France (Chatterjee 1975: 125).

In the "classical" era, from the end of the Napoleonic wars until the
1870s, "equilibrium" on the continent could be maintained by small
shifts in frontiers, transfers of European territory to the victors in
Europe's short wars or, more often, transfers made to avoid war. But
from 1878 to 1913 only trivial changes could be made in European
frontiers. The growth of European nationalism, with its connection
to the increasingly powerful idea of popular sovereignty, made the
old adjustment mechanism obsolete. If military conquests were
going to be sought, they had to be sought overseas, and they were
(Chatterjee 1975: 127).

Nevertheless, in most other ways the nineteenth-century military
order remained as it had been since the end of the Napoleonic era.
Britain continued to play its early nineteenth-century role as balancer. If anything, its ability to play this role was enhanced by the
shift of focus overseas because the British navy remained predominant throughout the century. Margery Perham, biographer of one of
the leading figures of British colonialism, describes the resulting
struggles among the rival empires. Europe's powers

> were not unlike a lot of greedy quarrelsome children in a school play-
> ground; none quite big enough to dominate all the others, kicking and

making up to each other, sulking, coaxing, telling each other secrets and then "splitting," combining for a moment and then breaking up. Britain was the rather aloof child in the corner, a little superior, unwilling to join wholeheartedly in the rough games, and yet warily watching lest too many of these quarrelling schoolmates combined against her. (Quoted in Gramont 1975: 302)

The late nineteenth century interimperial military order may not have had all the pomp and dignity of the intergovernmental diplomacy that created the first of the world organizations, but the protection against protracted military conflicts among the powers that this military order provided was enough to assure that such diplomacy could take place at all.

The conference system

Of course, peace among the powers in the nineteenth century was never just a matter of a crude balance of military might. Europe's quarrelsome school children certainly knew how to go inside, put on their best clothes, and practice their best manners in hopes of becoming better friends. Students in their first course in international relations are apt to learn something like this about the international institution that made this possible: for nearly one hundred years after the Congress of Vienna reestablished the continental order that had been threatened by Napoleon, Europe's monarchs and their governments kept the peace by holding regular face-to-face meetings – "congresses" and "conferences" – to try to come agreement over issues which otherwise might have led to war, issues like "Belgian neutrality" and (again and again) "the Eastern question" (cf. Hinsley 1963: 186–271; Holsti 1991: 164–74; Holsti 1992).

There are some more things that are important to know about this aspect of nineteenth-century international civil society if we want to understand the later history of the international institutions and industrial change. By getting European governments into the habit of meeting together, the conference system contributed to the further institutionalization of world politics (table 3). Ironically, it could have this effect because it was so imperfectly institutionalized itself. It was never clear who had the right to call such meetings, what topics could be broached, or which dignitaries and officials from invited states should attend. Yet the trend was always toward increasing the scope of the conference system along each of these three dimensions.

TABLE 3   European and world conferences, 1850–1914

FOSTERING INDUSTRY

Infrastructure
1857   Sound duties, Copenhagen
1861   Navigation of the Elbe, Hanover
1863   Mail, Paris
1863   Navigation of Scheldt, Brussels
1864   Marine signaling, London
1864   Marine signaling, Paris
1866   Navigation of the Danube, Paris
1878   Railways, Berne
1881   Railways, Berne
1882   Neutralization of submarine cables, Paris
1882   Technical standards on railways, Berne
1883   Navigation of the Danube, London
1885   Suez Canal, Paris
1886   Railways, Berne
1886   Technical standards on railways, Berne
1888   Suez Canal, Constantinople
1889   Maritime law, Washington
1892   Maritime law, Genoa
1897   Ocean telegraphy, Paris
1903   Radiotelegraphy, Berlin
1905   Maritime law, Brussels
1907   Maritime law, Venice
1907   Technical standards on railways, Berne
1909   Maritime law, Brussels
1910   Aerial law, Verona
1910   Aerial navigation, Paris
1910   Navigation of the Baltic, Christiania
1910   Maritime law, Brussels
1911   Maritime law, Paris
1912   Maritime law, St Petersburg
1913   Maritime law, Copenhagen

Industrial standards and intellectual property
1880   Industrial property, Paris
1884   Copyright, Berne
1885   Copyright, Berne

Trade
1853   Statistics, Brussels
1867   Monetary issues, Paris
1878   Monetary issues, Paris
1885   Commercial law, Antwerp
1892   Monetary issues, Brussels
1910   Unification of bills of exchange, The Hague
1912   Unification of the law of the check, The Hague

MANAGING POTENTIAL SOCIAL CONFLICTS

Labor
1890   Protection of labor in factories and mines, Berlin
1897   Labor legislation, Brussels
1900   Labor legislation, Paris
1905   Labor legislation, Berne
1906   Labor legislation, Berne
1906   Unemployment, Milan
1913   Labor legislation, Berne

Agriculture
1882   North Sea fisheries, The Hague
1890   North Sea fisheries, Stockholm
1908   Fisheries, Washington

STRENGTHENING STATES AND THE STATE SYSTEM

Public order and administration
1883   Exchange of official documents, Brussels
1886   Exchange of official documents, Brussels

Managing interstate conflicts
1850   Schleswig-Holstein, London
1853   Eastern Question, Vienna
1855   Eastern Question, Vienna
1856   Peace, Paris
1858   Principalities, Paris
1860   Syria, Paris
1863   Ionian Islands, London
1864   Humanity in war, Geneva
1864   Affairs of Denmark, London
1867   Neutralization of Luxemburg, London
1868   Humanity in war, Geneva
1868   Explosive bullets, St Petersburg
1869   Cretan questions, Paris
1871   Neutralization of the Black Sea, London
1874   Rules of war, Brussels
1876   Eastern Question, Constantinople
1878   Eastern Question, Berlin
1880   North Africa, Madrid
1884   Africa, Berlin
1889   Samoan Islands, Berlin
1890   The Congo, Brussels
1899   Peace, The Hague
1906   Morocco, Algeciras
1906   Humanity in war, Geneva
1907   Peace, The Hague
1908   Arms in Africa, Brussels
1908   Naval arms, London
1910   African boundaries, Brussels

STRENGTHENING SOCIETY

Human rights
1889 Slave trade, Brussels
1904 White slave trade, Zurich
1904 White slave trade, Paris
1908 Dueling, Budapest
1910 White slave trade, Paris

Health
1851 First Sanitary Conference, Paris
1859 Second Sanitary Conference, Paris
1866 Third Sanitary Conference, Istanbul
1874 Fourth Sanitary Conference, Vienna
1881 Fifth Sanitary Conference, Washington
1885 Sixth Sanitary Conference, Rome
1887 Liquor on the North Sea, venue unrecorded
1892 Seventh Sanitary Conference, Venice
1893 Eighth Sanitary Conference, Dresden
1894 Ninth Sanitary Conference, Paris
1897 Tenth Sanitary Conference, Venice
1899 Liquor traffic in Africa, Brussels
1903 Eleventh Sanitary Conference, Paris
1906 Liquor traffic in Africa, Brussels
1909 Opium, Shanghai
1911 Twelfth Sanitary Conference, Paris
1911 Opium, The Hague
1913 Opium, The Hague

Education and research
1884 Fixing the Prime Meridian, Washington

Excludes regular conferences of the Public International Unions and conferences on education and research held in conjunction with international exhibitions.

Sources: Cooper (1986); Hill (1929: 229–32); Hinsley (1963: 214); Kindleberger (1984: 66–7); Lowe (1921: 31–64); Reinsch (1911: 15–73).

The number of dignitaries who could call conferences grew right up to the First World War. While the great powers who had conquered Napoleon had set the precedent by initiating the Congress of Vienna that only one of their number could reconvene all the powers, the more conservative victors, those who believed that they had united as much against French republicanism as against French territorial ambitions, quickly accepted the principle that invitations from any of what Hobsbawm calls "the international clan of monarchs" (1987: 181) demanded attention. This applied even if the invitation came from a cousin on as minor a branch as the one ccupied by the Prince Liechtenstein, who promoted a Swiss initiative to call the first international labor conference in 1889 (Follows 1951: 122). The principle of giving this privilege to the traditional crowned heads of Europe, in turn, easily slipped over into the late nineteenth-century practice that an invitation from any head of state had to be respected, whether it came from the American President, the collective executive of the Swiss federation, or even the French Emperor Napoleon III (N. Hill 1929: 47–9).[4]

Of course, if an invitation came from the head of state of one of the republics or of the constitutional monarchies, it could be treated simply as an invitation from the government, at least in theory. In fact, though, throughout the nineteenth century the norms of the conference system provided many European monarchs (and a few remarkable lesser aristocrats) with one of the few ways in which they could exercise autonomous initiative. Germany's Wilhelm II, for example, took over the Prince Liechtenstein's role as the sponsor of international labor conferences, in part in order to maintain his independence in the delicate domestic balance of power between Bismarck's supporters and the socialists (Follows 1951: 126–8).[5] In most other cases governments appear to have acquiesced in their monarch's desire to call an international conference simply to give the prince room to ride his particular hobby-horse, or, more charitably, to express his sense of aristocratic *noblesse oblige*. This is one reason that conferences came to cover so many topics.

The practice of allowing crowned heads to call conferences on topics of interest was extended even further by the lesser nobility acting in their "private" capacity. They would convene international conferences on topics of their own interest, often acting along with peers of the same rank and with experts in and out of government and often meeting at the international exhibitions – the world's fairs – that became so popular in the second half of the nineteenth century. Baron Pierre de Coubertin created the modern Olympics in this way. Earlier, Prince Albert, Victoria's consort, was an avid sponsor of such meetings, encouraging his sons and nephews to find the issues for new conferences that would both interest them and allow them to serve their *noblesse oblige*. Such "private" meetings could result in international agreements and complicated programs involving many governments, as for example did a meeting of 1867 among Europe's crown princes (initiated, however, by Albert) to discuss exchanging plaster casts, photographs, and other reproductions of great works of art. Soon boats and trains criss-crossed Europe loaded with artifacts, some as monumental as a full-size plaster cast of Trajan's Column.

Some diplomatic historians would consider most of the princely hobby-horses that were ridden at the nineteenth-century international conferences as fairly petty issues of "low" politics, thus putting most of these conferences, even those called by heads of state, outside the "system" established with the Congress of Vienna in 1815 and which continued in all the subsequent nineteenth-century meetings devoted to issues of war and peace. But, in this case at least, the "high politics versus low politics" distinction is neither useful nor historically accurate. As Norman Hill (1929: 5) points out, even the Congress of Vienna was "not only concerned with getting rid of the arch enemy of Europe, but was also interested in the slave trade and the internationalization of rivers." A later commentator, Georges Scelle, in explaining his view on the somewhat arcane question of why some intergovernmental meetings have been called "congresses" and others "conferences," suggests that it was in the "low politics" realms that the Congress of Vienna established the precedent for all subsequent "conferences." Instead of trying to "remold completely the traditional or written constitution of a part or a whole of the international community of nations," the powers addressed the issues of navigation and slavery by the "drawing up of a system of laws or regulations . . . leaving it to national governments to ratify through conventions the results of this normative activity" (1953: 241–2). To use today's argot, the powers at Vienna established the precedent that "conferences" would propose international regimes, "principles, norms, rules, and decision-making procedures" specific to particular issues (Krasner 1982: 185). Conferences would not impose a broad new political order, the way the victors had at the Congress of Vienna.

Thus conferences became a way for national governments to explore potential common interests without necessarily committing themselves to ratify or abide by any regimes which might be proposed. This is a second reason why conferences came to cover so many topics. The tentative and experimental nature of the conferences helped minimize any domestic political costs to the governments taking part. This, in turn, encouraged more experiments with the institution itself, more attempts to see whether an international conference could reveal common interests in new regimes covering more and more aspects of life that had never before been the subject of multilateral agreement.

As the topics covered by international conferences expanded throughout the nineteenth century to include almost all those which were already the subject of domestic administration (as well as ones someone with the ear of the prince believed should be the subject of domestic administration), the personnel attending them expanded and changed as well. Often the places of heads of government and foreign ministers were taken by the ambassadors resident in the capital where the meeting was convened, and even they were likely to play only a ceremonial role. The central figures became professional civil servants from the government ministries most directly involved with the issue in question, along with private experts temporarily employed by governments to advise them and to take part in the intergovernmental discussion (N. Hill 1929: 37–43).

Taken together, these three characteristics of conferences – the relative ease with which they could be called, the wide range of topics that could be discussed, and their tendency to empower a wide range of professionals as the voice of the state – gave the conference system a striking ability to uncover previously unrecognized common interests and to generate useful suggestions for new international regimes. The conferences worked like committees within any modern complex and hierarchical organization – modern business enterprises or any of the other complex bureaucracies. International conferences, like committee meetings in a firm, provide "a forum for multidirectional communication" that otherwise would not occur,[6] and they create a temporary equality among unequals (great powers and small powers, princes and politicians, experts and ambassadors) which encourages the sort of open discussion that often gives rise to innovation. Keohane (1984) argues that international regimes make the business of international cooperation cheaper by reducing associated transaction costs and information costs. This is certainly true of the conference system, the meta-regime under which all of the specific regimes in the nineteenth century were created.

The New Knowledge of the Experts in Government

By itself, the conference system could only provide forums in which proposals for new international agreements, including those modeled on the American and German experience, might be discussed. That discussion might generate further ideas, but that would not be enough to create international agreements. Those confering needed ways to assess whether or not different proposals actually contributed to collective interests. The new disciplines created by the experts who played increasingly central roles within nineteenth-century governments provided that shared understanding. Volker

Rittberger (1973) even argues that the emergence of the modern intelligentsia based on particular disciplines itself explains much of the rise of formal international institutions. While that overstates the case, many IGO activities rely on professional and scholarly disciplines that are relatively modern.

The disciplines followed by experts advising nineteenth-century government – from medicine to statistics to public administration – were not confined by national boundaries. Disciplinary communities have always been transnational, voluntary associations linked by norms other than service to the national interest. Most of the nineteenth-century disciplines shared the Enlightenment faith in science, a confidence that the natural universe was ordered, that causes and effects could be discovered, and that rational discussion in which all available evidence was presented would yield agreement on what was the most probable explanation for any sequence of events. In the nineteenth century most disciplines also supported the rationalist project of perfecting human society, turning it into an ordered machine reflecting the order of nature, creating what Stephen Toulmin (1990) calls the "cosmopolis," where the human community would mirror the harmony of the cosmos.

This ideology can readily contribute to international cooperation. Writing about the late twentieth century Gilbert Winham argues:

> The principal problem for most contemporary negotiators is not to outwit their adversaries, but rather to create a structure out of a large mass of information wherein it is possible to apply human wit. The classical diplomat's technique of the management of people through guile has given way to the management of people through the creation of system and structure. (1977: 88–9)

These techniques of statecraft are not as new as Winham implies. They were central to negotiation within the conference system since its beginning in the early nineteenth century. Experts within nineteenth-century governments were dedicated to providing system and structure, and that dedication, along with the specific knowledge each gained from a particular discipline, contributed to international agreement.

The experts responsible for the new sciences of the state became some of the central figures at the international conferences in the late nineteenth century. Some were *experts in the applied natural sciences*, engineering and medicine, fields associated with MacDonagh's first stage of standard setting and second stage of monitoring and information gathering (Buchanan 1988; Hamlin 1988). Chemical and electrical engineers played central roles in establishing the first international industrial standards regimes (Guillame 1902), and medical professionals played such a central role in setting up the first international health regimes that in the history of those regimes can be read the triumph of the modern "germ theory" of disease, the theory that diseases were caused by invisible organisms rather than by unbalanced "humors" or bad air. (Cooper 1986). Other disciplinary experts were what the early nineteenth century called *statists*, what we would now call statisticians and statistical cartographers (T. Porter 1986; A. Robinson 1982), men like John Snow, a physician who began to map deaths by cholera across London's neighborhoods in 1855 to demonstrate that a single public water-pump carried the infection (Robinson 1982: 175–7). Operating the middle stages of MacDonagh's model, statists helped identify the "natural" systems into which the state tried to intervene. By 1910 there were a host of international conferences and a few intergovernmental agencies with essentially the purpose of gathering statistics, including the International Institute of Agriculture (IIA) (Einaudi 1910), from which the Food and Agriculture Organization of the UN (FAO) developed. Finally, there were statists who had moved on to create some of the new sciences of the state, leaving the discipline of "statistics" (information gathering for government), to become designers and builders of public system which would achieve the original aims of earlier, less successful innovations in government.

I take the notion of a nineteenth-century *system builder* from Alfred D. Chandler, Jr (1977) and Thomas P. Hughes (1989). Chandler first used the term to identify the entrepreneurs who linked separate American railroads together into a single comprehensive network. Chandler and Hughes both extended the concept to apply to those in all fields who combine innovations in management with innovations in technology to create comprehensive, purposeful systems. It was *public* system builders who most often appeared at international conferences, officials who had designed and administered public rail systems, public health systems, public relief systems, and so forth.

One of the earliest of these public systems became a powerful exemplar for international regimes: the penny post of British postmaster Rowland Hill. This was a mid nineteenth-century innovation in one of the oldest departments of most modern governments, a department that in most countries had been in place for a generation or more when the new system was introduced. The new system involved a few technical advances and a number of policy decisions, any one of which would have been wildly irrational had it been taken by itself. National governments adopting the system agreed for the first time to provide mail delivery to every place within the country, yet they also radically reduced most postal rates and drastically simplified them; a letter could pass to any point in the country as long as it had the uniform, inexpensive stamp – "a penny to any town in Britain." At the same time governments would ban most private mail carriers and establish inexpensive franchises for post offices, providing special incentives for people prepared to run post offices in the least desirable places. The result was usually an astonishingly rapid development of a nationwide communication system. The original goal of post office legislation was finally met, often with substantial reductions in cost to government due to the economies of scale achieved by greater throughput. At the same time the post office's major consumers, the most significant of which were private businesses communicating with each other and with agents throughout the country, saved through lower rates.[7] The penny post system provided the model for most of the nineteenth-century international agencies involved with transportation and communication, and even for regimes that may seem far afield, for example, those administered by the IIA.

In *Discipline and Punish* (1975), Michel Foucault outlines the broader ideology shared by the nineteenth-century public system builders,[8] the ideas encouraging professional association and friendship across national boundaries, making it easy for them to agree on international regimes. The public system builders valued *order* and control; they tried to make society more structured and predictable. They valued *economic efficiency*; the systems they proposed reduced the economic burdens of public policy, both the costs borne by any individual citizen and those borne by the state. Equally, the public system builders valued the minimization of the political costs of control, what might be called *political efficiency*, what Foucault calls the "invisibility" of power. Typically, as was the case with the penny post system, most of the nineteenth-century public systems involved a politically invisible form of redistributive taxation, with large, centrally located and, as a result, usually better-off users of the system subsidizing service to others. But this redistribution did not become a political issue when most of the systems were put in place because the systems' sponsors were able to emphasize the new or improved service that all would enjoy.

Foucault's invocation of the model of a public system provided by Jeremy Bentham's Panopticon emphasizes a second typical way of minimizing political costs. The Panopticon was a model for a prison that would require little active punishment and little active surveillance because every moment of the prisoners' day would be visible to guards who are themselves invisible to the prisoners. After the prisoners learned to understand the structure from within, they would modify their behavior to the point when an actual guard would hardly be necessary. Political costs can be minimized by infrequent but unpredictable monitoring, especially of adherence to norms that would be publicly affirmed by those served by the system, even if they might have private desires to violate the same norms. The few inspectors who randomly check to see if passengers on urban transit systems have tickets provide a prosaic example, as do the "home visitors" in many industrialized countries who monitor the provision of public services (milk, vaccinations, child subsidies), but who also use their visits as opportunities to check for signs of neglect, child abuse, and family violence.

Such systems of random monitoring work only when they are part of a system which is relatively universal, one that applies to all of those who have access to a particular government service. Not surprisingly then, public system builders valued *universality* in public services, as well as what might be called the *extendability* of a public policy. That is, in comparing two systems designed to achieve the same goal (for example, the penny post versus regulated competition among private mail carriers), the public system builders generally would prefer the one that could be extended the most easily, the one that could most easily be made universal.

While Foucault recognizes the value that public system builders placed on order, economic and political efficiency, and universality, he does not mention something else that they valued just as much, the controlled public realm itself, the *state*. And Foucault does not explicitly discuss the belief of the early system builders in *progress*. Speaking in 1935 to American graduate students in economics, the great institutionalist economist Wesley Mitchell did feel he needed to remind his audience of these things that Foucault, as a postwar French intellectual, probably took to be obvious. Mitchell pointed out that even the men who founded the American Economic Association in 1886, many of them trained in Germany, adopted the self-consciously statist ideology of the European public system builders (Gound and Kelley 1949: 120–1). Thus the first principle of the association reads: "We regard the State as an agency whose positive assistance is one of the indispensable conditions of human progress."

Mitchell also noted that this founding generation of American economists, "so thoroughly indoctrinated with the viewpoint of the German economists of the day . . . found themselves reverting to the

English tradition" of international laissez faire (Gould and Kelley: 122), but they did so without abandoning their other statist principles. This should not be all that surprising, Mitchell tells us, since *instituting* a system of laissez faire could be compatible with the "problem-solving," public system-building orientation that the American economists brought from the continent. Laissez faire was also a policy that could be justified as part of a broader system on the basis of its economic and political efficiency and its potential universality (cf. Jacoby 1973: 55–7). As Karl Polanyi concluded, even in England, "There was nothing natural about *laissez faire ... laissez faire* was enforced by the state," and its creation was part of the same movement that resulted in "an enormous increase in the administrative functions of the state" (1957: 139).[9]

The nineteenth-century public system builders who designed the Public International Unions imagined incorporating the liberal vision of Smith and Kant in the same way. They would establish international public systems (economically efficient, politically efficient, and extendable to the whole world) in order to create the larger markets in which liberal economic policies would result in improvements in the division of labor (from the global level to the factory floor), thus contributing to human progress.

Understood through the lens of the system builders' ideology, the American and German models could be combined with reflection on the developments in nineteenth-century statecraft affecting all states to make a new version of the liberal arguments about industry and international organization. A complete elaboration of the new argument appeared as early as 1851 in a tract by John Wright, an Anglo-Irish engineer who had promoted railroad development for the state of Illinois. The text was titled (without brevity or modesty), *Christianity and Commerce, the Natural Results of the Geographical Progression of the Railways, or A Treatise on the Advantage of the Universal Extension of Railways in our Colonies and Other Countries, and the Probability of Increased National Intercommunication Leading to the Early Restoration of the Land of Promise to the Jews.*

Wright proposed that the statesmen and scientists visiting London's Great Industrial Exhibition agree to create a universal rail network, a public system that would provide the infrastructure for a global market in industrial goods and the raw materials needed to produce them. The railroad would be constructed using the method then employed in Illinois (and later used throughout the United States). Governments would give land along the proposed rail lines to the private companies agreeing to build and operate them. This sort of system was economically efficient; its immediate costs to governments and taxpayers were few. It also allowed for political efficiencies; investors could be required to build rail links through less favored areas in exchange for control over highly profitable routes. And any part of the system would be extendable; the new worldwide rail network could be built through hundreds of similar projects covering short distances, the way the US rail network was, in fact, being built.

Wright, who was an ardent free trader – reciprocating the compliment of Richard Cobden, who had "speculated up to his neck in the shares of the Illinois Central" (Faith 1990: 76) – argued that when the worldwide railway system was in place Britain's Cobdenite trade policy would truly be able to assure the greatest possible prosperity not only for Britain, but for the whole world. He promised Africa, India, East Asia and Latin America that the plan "cannot fail to soon place all alike on an equality with the advanced kingdoms of the world, and in many instances, render their sources of wealth superior" (Wright 1851: 12). Finally, of course, Wright promised to usher in the millennium of peace (albeit a somewhat secularized one), even in the unstable Arab provinces of the Ottoman Empire where a new, prosperous, and independent state based on freedom of religion and freedom of emigration would replace Turkish rule and thus restore "the Land of Promise to the Jews."

Wright responded to those who would dismiss him as a utopian that the promise

> of producing such mighty results and at the same time uniting the commerce of east and west in one common bond of union may at first appear speculative, even impossible. But when we reflect how the United States, less than two centuries ago a mere penal settlement of divers European nations, has acquired a degree of power and importance, bidding fair to surpass that of Greece or Rome, and at the same time has become the grand receptacle of all nations and all creeds; while the gratifying trial has been triumphantly made of what in less than four score years since the Declaration of Independence the perseverance of man can accomplish . . . should we hesitate . . .? (1851: 13)

Abraham Lincoln, who also got his start as a promoter of Illinois railways (and who appears to have studied from the same rhetoric book), might have been able to point out some things that Wright had not learned about the American experience. Still, Wright had learned to add some new elements to the vision Kant had articulated half a century earlier. Wright understood the flexibility of the European conference system, he internalized the norms of the public system builders who were just beginning to transform the state, and from the American experience he concluded that the physical infrastructure for larger markets had to be built. Wright and fellow promoters of what would become the Public International Unions had concluded that Smith's doctrine – the extent of the market limits the division of labor – had a physical as well as a political meaning and to build the necessary public systems would require a form of world government that went beyond the universal adoption of laissez faire.

The other lessons from the American experience Lincoln might have imparted are indicative of the limited understanding that the earliest promoters of the Public International Unions had of the conflicts that could be generated by the industrial system. However, their understanding of some of those conflicts increased over time. By 1898, when William T. Stead visited the Berne Unions and traveled on to Berlin, the conflict with labor over democratic control of industry was foremost in his mind. He argued that a common market and parliamentary union of all Europe would necessitate improving the conditions of all European workers by emulating Germany's high welfare standards (Stead 1899: 56). Stead's sojourn in Germany also brought him face to face with another aspect of Germany's experience which advocates of European unity had tended to overlook a half-century before: the important role of military production in Germany's economic growth (p. 215). There had been a counterpart in the United States, where the early, state-supported firearms industry became an exemplar of efficient large-scale production (Chandler 1977: 72–5).

Of course, there would be an ominous connection between the significance of the arms industry and the growing power of nationalism when attempts were made to rewrite the German experience on the larger scale of the interimperial system. Yet throughout the age of empire liberal internationalists saw little contradiction between nationalism and their cosmopolitan vision. In the 1850s Wright wrote his plan for a world railroad system under the assumption that nationalists would embrace his design because it would glorify every nationality by giving them all the prosperity enjoyed in the first countries to industrialize. At the end of the century J. A. Hobson could still conclude that "Nationalism is a plain highway to internationalism and if it manifests a divergence we may well suspect a perversion of its nature and its purpose" (1965: 11).

The original connection between nationalism and progressive mass movements helps explain why nineteenth-century liberal internationalists saw no fundamental contradiction between their ideology and the ruling ideas of the interimperial system. Wright was a champion of the rights of what we would now call "oppressed nations," the American colonists, the Latin American republicans, the Irish, and the Jews. Hobson still connected nationalism with the movement for democracy, with the French Revolution and with Chartism.

Moreover, as E. H. Carr points out in *The Twenty Years' Crisis*, because liberals assumed an ultimate harmony of interests, they could not conceive of national identities as inherently in conflict. Mazzini, the liberal founder of the Italian nation, for example, believed that peace would prevail because each nation had a unique essence that could contribute to the whole of humanity without detracting from any other nation. Carr comments:

> One reason why contemporaries of Mazzini thought nationalism a good thing was that there were few recognised nations, and plenty of room for them. In an age when Germans, Czechs, Poles, Ukrainians, Magyars and half a dozen other national groups were not yet visibly jostling one another over an area of a few hundred square miles, it was comparatively easy to believe that each nation, by developing its own nationalism, could make its own special contribution to the international harmony of interests. (1946: 46)

Many liberals continued to hold this belief right up until the war, even though national movements were multiplying on the near periphery of Europe's industrial economy and reactionary official nationalism was hardening within the imperial centers of the industrialized core. Perhaps we should not be surprised. While today we may see only Mussolini's face whenever we think of that of Italy's King Victor Emmanuel III, in 1914 Mazzini and Garibaldi still came to mind, and while today we may link Kaiser Wilhelm II with Hitler (as militarists responsible for world wars), between 1900 and 1914 the Kaiser's name could just as easily have conjured up that of the Social Democrat, August Bebel, a stalwart internationalist, Germany's most powerful electoral leader, and architect of the welfare state that Stead wished to generalize across Europe.

By 1900 a few liberal internationalists such as Hobson could at least imagine that a "perversion" of nationalism, imperialism, might endanger the interimperial social system and the economic transformations it was creating. Most, however, simply expected a continuation of the social system until the technological revolutions it fostered would allow a rewriting of its history on an even larger scale.

Public System Builders and Other Intellectual Leaders

The earlier generation of thinkers who learned the lessons Wright learned and then went on to design the Unions were of a different, perhaps a bit more practical, sort than Hobson (an academic economist) and many of his contemporaries. Sharing the public system builders' ethos, the mid-century functionalists thought about achieving their new version of the liberal internationalist vision in small, extendable steps. Theirs was not Kant's dream of one moment of international agreement on a few definitive articles of peace that would for ever after be guaranteed by the immutable laws of nature. They believed that the institutionalization of the Unions could begin in many places, through the small actions of many people; and, of course, in part as a consequence of this belief, it was.

The establishment of an individual Union most often proceeded through four stages, three stages of building and one of maintenance. First someone had to *propose a design*, however tentative, of a new institution that could solve some perceived international problem. This had to be someone, as Winham says, who could "create a structure out of a large mass of information," someone like the new experts within government. Second, to begin a productive international discussion someone needed to *sponsor a conference*. Conferences could often lead to agreement if a single state, or even a powerful individual, agreed to *support an experimental Union*. Europe's princes often played both these roles. Finally, after the building was complete, a Union could become more permanent only when it was able to *develop a constituency* benefiting from its activities. The new knowledge of the experts in government not only explained the logic of this process, it also provided the designs needed in the first stage of building.

Experts in the applied natural sciences and statists provided part of the design of the Public International Unions. Physicians designed the early health Unions. Associations of scientists in and out of government lobbied to create the Metric Union (the International Bureau of Weights and Measures) and those for seismology, mathematics, and cartography, arguing that they were needed simply to advance the sciences themselves (Wilford 1981: 219; T. Porter 1986). Statisticians made repeated attempts to design regimes for standard trade statistics, first at their 1851 meeting (held in London in conjunction with the Great Exhibition), then at a Brussels conference in 1853. Eventually they concluded that this responsibility had to be carried out by an independent international bureau, which led to designs for the statistics-keeping functions of the Telegraph, Postal, and Rail Unions as well as those of the Tariff Union – and for the separate statistical bureau that was to have taken over those functions when the First World War broke out (J. Haas 1923: 36).

Public system builders provided even more designs. Many were based on Rowland Hill's uniform rate system for the mails and on agreements negotiated among the states of the German Customs Union. In 1862 the US Postmaster General proposed what would become the Postal Union. The American Civil War delayed any American initiative, but French and Prussian colleagues employed the design in both the Postal Union and its one major predecessor, the Telegraph Union (Sly 1907: 397). Other designers thought of applying Hill's system to some services provided by local, national, and international railroads, creating the model for some of the Rail Union's activities (US Interstate Commerce Commission 1940: 1). One of the very few designers of a Union who did not make a living by offering disciplinary expertise to government, the American businessman and philanthropist David Lubin, even imagined extending the single rate system to bulk goods shipped by rail and steamer. This, he believed, would be a way to aid farmers suffering from the uncertainties of the new international market. His plan for the IIA was less ambitious, but he still used arguments about the desirability of the single rate system to sell his second best alternative to potential sponsors and benefactors (Agresti 1941: 117).

Even when Rowland Hill's design was not the model for a new international public system, the system builders' philosophy informed the proposals for most Unions, even those that never were established. When the Marquis de Moustier opened the 1867 International Monetary Conference (held at the same Paris Universal Exposition where the princes discussed exchanging copies of art treasures), he emphasized the extendability of the Latin Monetary Union formed a few years before. The simplicity of the Latin Union's agreement on a gold standard meant that a universal union did not have to await drawn-out multilateral negotiations on cross-exchange rates, banking rules, or the organization of mints (US Senate 1879: 807). Édouard du Cpétiaux, the Belgian penologist credited by some authors with first suggesting the plan for the International Labor Office,[10] emphasized both the extendability of a system that would standardize labor legislation in industrialized states by publicizing who had the strongest and who had the weakest laws, and the political efficiency of the plan as well: rather than government letting the market encourage sweated labor and then taxing the wealthy to provide for the resulting poor, the ILO would contribute to a constant improvement in the conditions of the working class by making improved working conditions a nearly invisible condition of doing business. Not surprisingly, as chief of Belgium's prisons for 32 years, the penologist had internalized the lesson of Bentham's Panopticon; for years he had followed the Benthamite "American plan" of prison administration (Follows 1951: 53).

The career of the ILO's greatest promoter, Swiss public servant Emil Frey, illustrates the universal applicability assumed by nineteenth-century system builders for their philosophy. Although Frey had devoted his career to matters of agricultural labor, military strategy, and diplomacy, in 1899 the members of the Telegraph Union selected him to preside over its highly technical bureaucracy, arguing for the transferability of skills in public administration (Follows 1951: 90ff.).

Other careers reveal the same story. For example, Serge Yulevich Witte, who designed the Permanent Court of Arbitration (the most significant late nineteenth-century attempt to manage interstate conflict), began as a minor employee on the Crimean railroad. He rose to prominence as a systems builder as the first director of the Russian railway department, briefly ran the imperial communications ministry, and then, like the Marquis de Moustier, became his country's first minister of finance to apply principles of modern management to his state's finances. All of which combined to make him the most respected of the men relied on by Tsar Nicholas II to help him cajole Europe toward a Union for Peace (Stead 1899: 298–307).

Even though public system builders like Witte could provide designs for international agreements covering an unusually wide range of issues, they did ignore some of the issues eventually addressed by the Public International Unions. Interest groups within civil society had to be the ones to push first for the Unions dealing with intellectual property. Austria called the first global patent conference in 1873 because American firms feared that inventions they were to display at the Vienna international exhibition would be stolen (Penrose 1951: 35). Real momentum toward establishing an international regime came at a later conference, in 1878, when a major European firm, the German electrical giant Siemens, began to push for an agreement (Penrose 1951: 48–9). Similarly, the international authors' association under the presidency of Victor Hugo appears to have originated the idea of the Copyright Union, and Hugo led authors who lobbied hard for it (Reinsch 1911: 38); an American writers' petition for international copyright protection united an unlikely, broad alliance, including Henry Adams, Louisa May Alcott, Henry Ward Beecher, Edward Bellamy, Samuel Longhorn Clemens, Henry George, Bret Harte, Oliver Wendell Holmes, and Walt Whitman (Bowker 1886: Appendix).

The Radiotelegraph Union also had its origin in a dispute over intellectual property. It began as an attempt to break the monopoly of the British firm Marconi. Marconi prevented operators of its radios from communicating with sets using rival technologies. After firms using competing technologies reached an "armistice" among themselves and agreed not to make their systems incompatible, they worked with their governments to create an international regime requiring mutual recognition of different systems (Gartmann 1959: 160–1). In this case, however, public system builders were again back at the center of the story. Governments treated radio as an issue of national security and worked to build national systems which would not depend on foreign firms or foreign technologies (Headrick 1991: 116–37).

The earlier political process that led to the International Labor Office also involved public system builders working with interest groups in civil society. The original idea of establishing international agreements to secure progressive labor conditions had many sources, from utopian socialists like Robert Owen, to humanitarian conservatives like Benjamin Disraeli, who thought that legislating better conditions for labor would be the only way to unite the "two nations," the rich and the poor, created by the Industrial Revolution. If one country in an international trading bloc is alone in legislating better working conditions, firms in other countries will be at an advantage. By mid-century British legislators found themselves pressured to pass laws to eliminate medieval guarantees to labor in order to help British businesses beat international competition. Some MPs suggested that medieval guarantees should only be retained if Britain's trading partners agreed to establish equally high labor standards (Follows 1951: v–vii). This initiated a debate on the best way to achieve the desired end, whether through an intergovernmental treaty or through private agreements among progressive manufacturers (p. 24). State functionaries like Édouard du Cpétiaux and Emil Frey argued the case for treaties that would link the labor protection systems of progressive states and provide incentives for other states to adopt them as well.

The movement for "international labor legislation" only began to gather steam after it was joined by representation from industrial labor. The key shift occurred in Germany and was part of the program that united the German Social Democratic Party without leading to any coherent agreement on how capitalism might be superseded or any plan for how socialism might triumph (Hobsbawm 1987: 112–41). Georg Adler, a German academic economist, friendly critic of Marx, and long-time promoter of international labor legislation (Adler 1888), argued that the new unity of German socialists marked a historic turning point: "Henceforth, judging by all appearances, we may look to Social Democracy for straightforward cooperation in the work of social reform, even though this be never rendered on the understanding that in a perfected system of labour laws would lie the *final* aim of social readjustment for an appreciable period of time" (Adler 1891: 709). The 1891 program of the German socialists began with a ringing endorsement of the views Adler championed:

> With the expansion of world transport and production for the world market, the state of the workers in any one country becomes constantly more dependent upon the state of workers in other countries. The emancipation of the working class is thus a task in which the workers of all civilized countries are concerned in like degree. (Quoted in Steenson 1981: 248)

The first plank of the socialist platform demanded national and international legislation for minimal labor standards, including the eight-hour day, an end to factory work for children, and the two-day weekend without work.

Based on the German agreement, the new Second International, uniting Marxists and "Possibilists," put international labor laws at the top of its agenda. They became "the principal topic of discussion at the second congress of the new International in Brussels" in August of 1891 (Lowe 1921: xvii). By 1893 Bebel was on his way to convincing the Kaiser to call the first international conference (Macht 1980: 238).

In many cases the public system builders on their own were able to convince the sponsors and benefactors who were needed to establish experimental international organizations. After all, the system builders ran national systems and therefore were able to argue that they were the best placed to understand the national interest in international linkages. Moreover, often the European public system builders would themselves be members of the aristocracy, which gave them another form of privileged access to those who could call international conferences. The conference that created the International Telegraph Union was typical: at least nine of 26 delegates representing national telegraph ministries were titled (ITU 1965: 52).

But even non-aristocrats who adhered to the public system builders' philosophy could gain access to potential sponsors. David Lubin, for example, was simply a successful American businessman who made his original fortune by designing a type of canvas trousers for California gold miners, the only successful alternative to those invented by Levi Strauss. Yet Lubin was welcomed as a kindred spirit by European professors of administration, government ministers, and permanent secretaries throughout the continent.

In contrast a Persian aristocrat found very little interest among Europe's leaders in his proposals for an international tribunal to decide disputes between nations and an international police force to support its decisions. But then Bahá'u'lláh, as the founder of the Bahá'í faith, did not limit his arguments to the functionalist rhetoric of the public system builders. Tsar Alexander II, who claimed a special interest in issues of international peace, did not respond to Bahá'u'lláh's appeal. Queen Victoria was unenthusiastic, saying, "If this is of God it will endure; if it is not, it can do no harm" (Hatcher and Martin 1984: 45). But Serge Yulevich Witte's success in selling the same proposals to Nicholas II suggests that Bahá'u'lláh may have gotten further if, like Lubin, he had left God out of his argument.

The Political Leadership of Princes and States

Lubin's experience exemplifies the typical pattern in the next stage of the institutionalization of the prewar Unions. Lubin had come up with the idea for the International Institute of Agriculture by reflecting on the experience of American farmers, the kind of experience that Frank Norris had documented in his muckraking novel of 1901, *The Octopus* (Norris 1964). Despite their unparallel efficiency, American farmers faced periodic ruin because, in Lubin's view, transportation trusts and brokers took the farmers' just profits. The IIA would provide producers with market information and other support to counter the powers of those that oppressed them.

After consulting with European officials Lubin quickly realized what was needed to make his vision a reality, "He would find . . . a . . . King. [He] would place before him the idea. He would show the need of strengthening the conservative country man as a bulwark against the revolutionary progressive forces of Finance, Commerce, and Labor" (Agresti 1941: 167). Italy's Victor Emmanuel III proved to be just the man.

Sponsoring conferences

Many of Europe's other monarchs would not have been good choices. They had already worked out their roles in Europe's implicit division of labor in sponsoring conferences on international problems. The German emperor had his interest in labor as well as an interest in geodesy, the science of determining the shape of the earth (Reinsch 1911: 68). Belgium's Leopold II had a prime interest in expanding opportunities for trade, which meant both supporting trade conferences to make tariffs transparent and standardize trade statistics, and sponsoring conferences on opening Africa and other colonial sources of raw materials (Milward and Saul 1977: 175). The Tsars retained a special interest in peace conferences that went back to the beginning of the Concert of Europe, and they added a concern with the science of seismology (Reinsch 1911: 70). The Scandinavian monarchs sponsored conferences on "the living resources of the sea" as well as on hydrography, the mapping of the oceans (Peaslee 1956: 167; Reinsch 1911: 70–1). Even as minor a monarch as Prince Albert of Monaco had his responsibility: crime. He proposed sponsoring a conference in 1914 that would have created an anti-crime union, but the actual founding of International Criminal Police Organization (Interpol) had to wait until after the war (Noble 1975: 20). Even France's Third Republic retained a position in this division of labor among monarchs by continuing to sponsor conferences and Unions initiated by Napoleon III on the telegraph (Codding 1952: 5), money, and health (Abt 1933: 1).

Another European republic also played a role in this division of labor. Switzerland sponsored the conferences that led to the rail regime, a matter they saw as closely linked to vital national interests. In 1880 Switzerland was at the intersection of what appeared to be two separate international railway systems. One system was made up of German, Austro-Hungarian, and Dutch lines linked by agreements that went back to the 1840s. This was surrounded by a looser "system" covering most of the rest of the continent. It had been built largely with French capital, which provided some coordination. The private capital market had been successful in quickly eliminating unprofitable parallel routes on the surrounding system, while competition for national prestige among the various German states assured that similar routes were maintained before unification (Jeans 1887: 10; Cameron 1961: 208). French financiers were less successful in making sure that standard technologies were used from line to line, the unique wide gauge of the Russian system being a typical problem. The Swiss worked first to standardize commercial conditions across the two systems and then to standardize technologies (Wedgewood and Wheeler 1946: 1), at the same time building the alpine links necessary to connect the united continental rail system.

This Swiss experience illustrates two lessons that can be drawn from the nineteenth-century conferences. First, the powers that dominated an issue were rarely the ones who succeeded as sponsors of international agreements on that issue. The Swiss success depended on Switzerland *not* being Germany or France, with their special interests, but a power interested in French and German cooperation. The Italians were in a similar position in sponsoring the IIA: agriculture was vitally important to Italy, but Italy could be an honest broker because it was neither one of the major agricultural importers nor one of the major exporters (Agresti 1941: 186). Second, the success of the late nineteenth-century conference system in making the liberal internationalist vision a reality depended on many potential sponsors with different interests and aspirations, rather than on a single dominant power with only one set of interests. The Swiss, for example, may have ended up hosting the headquarters of the five Unions that were the most important for creating the kind of international market in industrial goods envisioned by nineteenth-century functionalists – those for the Telegraph, Post, Rails, Patents, and Copyright – but the Swiss certainly could not have been relied on to sponsor the conferences founding each of these key Unions. Switzerland had singularly little interest in the Patent Union. In the 1880s Swiss leaders perceived themselves to be in what we would now call a "newly industrializing country," like Taiwan in the 1970s or Malaysia in the 1990s; rather than being vitally interested in the international protection of patents, the Swiss wanted to give their own infant industries free access to foreign inventions, an attitude that only began change when Swiss industrial firms began to produce for the larger international market that the Unions helped create (Penrose 1951: 122).

Both of these lessons may seem strange to those of us who developed our understanding of successful international institution-building on the experience after the Second World War, when the dominant power, the United States, played such a decisive role. However, the leading nineteenth-century power, Great Britain, played no such role. Prince Albert did indeed initiate and sponsor a number of international conferences, in his own capacity, on matters of education, culture, and the new sciences of the state. But more often than not the British government did not wish to be involved in international conferences that would regulate international economic conditions, preferring instead that international economic relations be regulated by the dominant firms in each sector, firms that were often British. Not only did Britain initially oppose the Radiotelegraph Union in order to support Marconi's monopoly position, in 1899 Britain refused to adopt an amendment to the international copyright regime that protected the rights of foreign authors over those of publishers (Reinsch 1911: 39). Britain's interest lay more in protecting its publishers' desire, say, to distribute English translations of Ibsen and Björnson throughout the vast imperial market without paying royalties than it lay more in protecting Kipling's or Conrad's rights to earn royalties on translations of their works into Norwegian.

The British government also preferred to have international ocean shipping regulated by a British-dominated cartel rather than by international agreements that promised increased competition. Britain even opposed international health agreements designed to check the spread of cholera and other infectious diseases because quarantines placed an unacceptable burden on international (read "British") shipping interests (Reinsch 1911: 59; Howard-Jones 1975). The British government claimed that there was little evidence for the germ theory of disease and for the public health policy it demanded: quarantine. It may be difficult not to suspect the British of the following paranoid logic: the germ theory's greatest champion was, after all, a Frenchman, Louis Pasteur; the French certainly were interested in breaking the British hold on ocean shipping; and they had long seemed inordinately interested in sponsoring international discussions of health matters. But even though the self-interest of British monopolists certainly could lead to such a line of reasoning, it is equally true that the independent British scientific community also had doubts about the germ theory, doubts that were only very slowly allayed (Abt 1933: 2; Cooper 1986: 67, 70).

Supporting experimental Unions

The British were not alone in fearing that some proposals for international organizations were based on inadequate scientific understanding. Moreover, all European governments were a bit cautious about engaging in the fundamentally new kind of cooperation that the Public International Unions represented. As a result many of the

Unions were initially established for a limited duration and most of them were provided only with a staff seconded by the government of the state in which the Union's headquarters was located. Before the First World War Swiss civil servants ran the five Unions in Berne; Belgians staffed the Customs Bureau; Italians did the day-to-day work of IIA; the International Geodetic Association in Potsdam was administered by the Prussian government in neighboring Berlin; and the similar Seismology Association in St Petersburg was staffed by Russians (Reinsch 1911: ch. 2). This practice was so common that a contemporary observer thought it necessary to commend the "liberal spirit" of the Metric Union's French administrators because, "the bureau at Sèvre has always had some foreigners on its staff" (ibid.: 36).

In most of these cases those who staffed the Union were employed by one of the states most interested in its success. This provided an opportunity, at least in the early years of the agency, for the host government to subsidize the Union's work. Host governments also acted as benefactors by building headquarters and by subsidizing the regular conferences of some agencies.

In a few cases it was not the host government that acted as a Union's benefactor, but rather the prince who had first sponsored the Union. The Danish Crown supported the Union for the exploration and study of the sea, and Victor Emmanuel III supported the IIA out of royal funds. Long after the First World War, one observer noted that a quarter of the IIA's members were unwilling to donate as much to the organization as the average US family paid to keep up a car; the Italian King still paid one-third of the bills (A. Hobson 1931: 154–5). Leopold II of Belgium, who began his country's empire in the Congo on his own account, also contributed to the much less costly Brussels-based Unions serving the same end of expanding Belgium's trade opportunities abroad (Stead 1899: 175–9).

Even when the Unions initially received no subsidy from a sponsoring prince or their host government, most were initially financed by the states most interested in their success. When it began in 1865, the International Telegraph Union established a precedent for the finance of the larger Unions by letting members choose what their financial contribution to the agency would be, within certain constraints; the Union offered different categories of membership each associated with different dues (ITU 1965: 312). Implicitly, and sometimes explicitly, such category schemes also determined how much power different members would have over the workings of a Union; those choosing low contributions would have less influence than those choosing high ones. The next major Union to be formed, the Universal Postal Union (UPU), adopted the ITU precedent and it continued to be adopted by the larger Unions until the 1907 establishment of the last major Union, the International Office of Public Hygiene (Abt 1933: 4).

The International Railway Congress Association and the International Labor Office illustrate another way in which experimental institutions could be established and supported. Both institutions were established as what are now called "quangos," quasi-nongovernmental organizations. In both cases founders established the organizations as private associations in order to avoid political problems that might arise if a formal treaty had been written and made subject to ratification. In the case of the Railway Congress Association the problem was one of some governmental agencies fearing a rapid move toward what could be a costly new international bureaucracy at a time, the mid-1880s, when a long period of slow economic growth advised caution. The original ILO was set up as a quango in order to sidestep that debate over whether international labor legislation was best established through an intergovernmental treaty or through private agreements among progressive manufacturers.

Both organizations, despite putatively being clubs of private associations, had governmental agencies as their major members, national rail authorities and the national "friends of labor legislation," who usually just happened to be public system builders running European labor ministries. The Railway Congress Association was soon able to spin off a more significant, fully intergovernmental bureau, the International Union of Railway Freight Transportation (Reinsch 1911: 30–1), later more commonly known as the Central Office for International Railway Transport. The Labor Office ran as a quango until after the First World War, with most of its funding coming from voluntary state subventions, in a manner very similar to all the other major Unions (Lowe 1921: 40).

The history of the changing sources of funding of each of the Public International Unions reveals a great deal about their institutionalization. The benefactors, sponsors, and designers of Unions all hoped, and expected, each of the Unions to develop its own constituencies of state members and citizens willing to make the contributions necessary for the organization's long-term survival. The sponsors of conferences and the princes or states who acted as benefactors of the Unions simply gave the institutions time to prove the value of their activities in practice. Therefore, to understand why most of the Unions succeeded, and a few significant ones failed, we need to turn to tasks the Unions took on and the ways they performed them.

3

THE UNIONS' WORK AND HOW IT WAS DONE

This chapter outlines the activities of the Public International Unions, distinguishes those that regulated the interimperial world economy from those that are simply signs of regulation achieved by other means, and explains how the Unions, as fundamentally cooperative institutions of international civil society, were able to "regulate" at all.

First, we need to put to one side those Unions that played no substantive role in the Interimperial Order simply because they failed to mobilize sufficient support. Most of the Unions faced moments of crisis when they could no longer rely on their early sponsors and benefactors. Napoleon III's defeat in the Franco–Prussian War created the first such crisis, and the International Telegraph Union was left strengthened and more independent. Fiscal crises throughout the Long Depression from the mid-1870s to the mid-1890s created problems for the first of the railway agencies, for the Metric Union, and for the intellectual property unions. They survived, but one of the minor unions, the International Meteorological Committee, had to become a private association (Daniel 1973: 9). A third of the Unions failed to survive the First World War. Only one, the International Labor Office, was absorbed into a stronger successor, the postwar International Labor Organization.

The surviving Unions all had powerful constituencies that included relevant ministries within member governments as well as powerful, and increasingly transnational, coalitions of interested social forces, beneficiaries of the Union's activities. The experience of the education and research Unions illustrates the importance of government support. As table 4 illustrates, the Geodesy, Seismology,

Meteorology, and Cartography Unions each had significant professional constituencies, but in 1919 only one of these sciences, cartography, had long and deep connections to the state (Robinson 1982; Konvitz 1987; Buisseret 1990), and only cartography survived as a focus of intergovernmental cooperation. Similarly, the crown princes' pact supporting the exchange of plaster casts of great works of art did not survive the Long Depression.[1] One of Prince Albert's other hobby-horses, the mathematics IGO, had a similar fate. It did not survive the brief recession after the First World War.

TABLE 4 World organizations abolished before 1920 (with disposition of activities)

MANAGING POTENTIAL SOCIAL CONFLICTS

Agriculture

International Sugar Union	ceased in World War I

STRENGTHENING STATES AND THE STATE SYSTEM

Managing interstate conflict

International Court of Prize	ceased in World War I
Permanent Court of International Justice	most functions to International Court of Justice

STRENGTHENING SOCIETY

Human rights

International Maritime Bureau Against the Slave Trade	some functions to League then to UN

Relief and welfare

Bureau for Information and Enquiries Regarding Relief to Foreigners	ceased in World War I

Health

Commission on Revision of the Nomenclature of the Causes of Death	most functions to League then WHO
International Association of Public Baths and Cleanliness	ceased in World War I

Education and research

International Geodetic Association	privatized in World War I
International Meteorological Committee	privatized in the Long Depression
International Association of Seismology	privatized in World War I
Central Bureau for the International Map	most functions to League then UN

In addition to their constituencies within states, the surviving Unions had the support of private interests they had helped to create: firms shipping goods along the European rail network that had be linked by the Rail Union, that communicated with agents and suppliers through the networks created by Telegraph and Postal Unions, and that depended on the industrial standards established by the Metric Union and on the protection of intellectual property

Primary Tasks

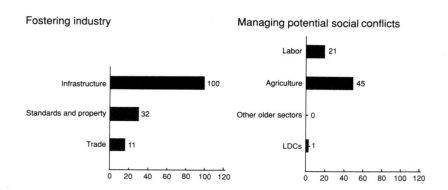

Secondary Tasks

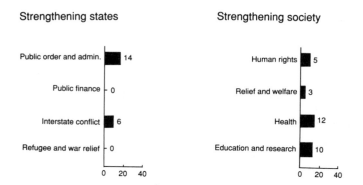

FIGURE 2 Tasks being carried out by Public International Unions in 1914 (derived from a study of their regular activities, 1911 to 1915, see appendix, pp. 286 ff.)

supplied by the Patent and Copyright Unions. Many of the same firms employed the industrial workers who most benefited from the international labor standards promulgated by the Labor Office, and they even had an interest in supporting the Health Union's activities because they helped assure that trade would not be impeded due to fear of infections inadvertently spread by ship and rail.

Figure 2 provides a more detailed breakdown of the activities carried out by the Unions in 1914, after all the Unions had been established but before the outbreak of the war. The *regular activities* enumerated are ongoing tasks, such as: "establishes international postal transit charges based on distance" or "arbitrates disputes among members." I collected the data on the prewar Unions for five-year periods from 1861–5 to 1911–15. (The appendix provides details about the complete data set that goes through 1985–90). The number of activities an agency carries out correlates with the size of its staff and with its budget. To have some sense of the scale of the Public International Unions consider the agencies in Berne (the Telegraph, Postal, Rail, Patent, and Copyright Unions). At the outbreak of the First World War they engaged in some 88 activities, one-third of the total. Their combined annual budgets came to a modest sum, about $100,000,[2] and they employed only a few hundred people, many of them civil servants seconded by their benefactors, especially the Swiss government.

Fostering Industry

Yet even with so few employees the Berne Unions were effective in carrying out two of Adam Smith's essential functions over a vast new trading area. They completed the necessary public works of a continental market, and by protecting intellectual property they helped establish a coherent civil order among conflicting interests that would operate in that market. Numa Droz, the director of the Railway Union and Switzerland's chief delegate to the first of the peace conferences (the one championed by his professional colleague, the Russian rail system builder, Serge Witte) summarized the problems the Berne Unions alleviated:

> Letters used to pass from one administration to another, by each of which a tax was imposed, and this caused expense and delay. It was the same with telegraphic messages. There was no international protection for inventors, proprietors of trade-marks, or authors. And with regard to railway transport, new regulations were found at every frontier, the times of delivery were

not the same, indemnities in case of loss or damage depended on the
caprice of officials; it was impossible to discover who was in fault, or against
whom a charge could be made. It was the most utter juridical confusion.
(Quoted in Stead 1899: 29)

Droz argued that the Berne Unions could overcome those problems
with so few resources simply because they served a natural urge to
truck and barter:

For the most part, trade asks little from the State, as it is accustomed to
settle its own difficulties in its own way, and the State rather hinders it in
its movements. But there are two things which it needs most certainly and
most imperatively: one is rapidity and exactitude in its relations, the other
is legal security. (In ibid.: 28)

The Unions could provide these without deploying many resources,
even though, as Droz quickly discovered in his role as Swiss delegate
to the Tsar's first peace conference in 1899, Unions modelled on
those in Berne would fail when the impulse to trade was dominated
by a nationalism that served the preindustrial order.

Infrastructure for a European market

The Berne Unions helped change the economic base of European
society. The ITU, as the first of the transportation and communication Unions, provided the model for all the rest. Functionally, a
telegraph is any mechanism that sends messages over long distances
in real time. At the beginning of the nineteenth century, governments used flags and towers to communicate with distant armies
(Headrick 1991: 11–12). Merchants soon realized the advantages of
this "optical" or "visual" telegraph as a conduit for market information (Harlow 1936: 32), but in countries that feared their neighbors
the telegraph remained a government monopoly even after the introduction of electrical systems in the 1840s (Brock 1981: 136, 139).
Even in the relatively secure United States the high initial cost of the
electrical telegraph network convinced Samuel Morse to try to sell
his invention to the state (ibid.: 61), but the federal government
showed little interest.

In security-conscious Europe, before the ITU, long-distance telegrams faced innumerable delays. Printed messages had to be walked
across the frontiers separating one national telegraph administration
from the next (Pelton 1981: 233). Bearing security interests in mind,
the ITU established and maintained an international telegraph
regime requiring its members to accept all international messages

and to link the wires of the separate national systems into a single network. The Union periodically set rates for international telegrams, following a slightly modified version of Rowland Hill's single rate system (ITU 1968: 312; Codding 1952: 65), and the ITU maintained a system for clearing the international accounts of different telegraph administrations (Reinsch 1911: 15). The Union established a regular system for gathering and distributing information about new telegraph technologies, comparative operating costs, and the effect of rates on demand for service, thus making it possible for national telegraph administrations to see new ways in which they could cooperate (ibid.: 15–19).

As the public systems builders expected, the volume of international telegrams rose dramatically after the ITU was formed, while rates fell. This result convinced Emil Frey to trumpet the ITU as the model for international cooperation long before he became the Union's chief in 1899 (Follows 1951: 158). The Telegraph Union, he argued, showed how states could support cosmopolitan interests without sacrificing national security or the internal revenue benefits of a government-owned monopoly. After all, the Union allowed government to delay international messages during military crises to check for breaches of security, as long as there was prior notification so users could expect the delays and calculate their cost (Reinsch 1911: 19). In the 1890s, when it had become common practice for firms to try to reduce the cost of telegrams and prevent industrial espionage by sending messages in private codes, the ITU established a system for approving codes and a multilingual dictionary of "official" telegraph words as a way to eliminate this threat to revenue (Codding 1952: 68).

The ITU's European regime ended up being applied relatively universally. Although the United Kingdom and the United States initially remained outside the Union because their telegraph systems were in private hands, their companies were always subject to the ITU convention when they established offices in foreign countries, even if these were at the ends of undersea cables that the British or Americans had laid themselves. Firms in the nonmember states quickly came to recognize the advantage of using the ITU's rules as a guide for all of their international service (Nagle 1923: 23).

The rapid success of the telegraph regime brought many of the same representatives of national telegraph and postal administrations back to the negotiating table in 1874 to create the Universal Postal Union (UPU) (Codding 1964: 26). The Postal Union became a clearing house for information on national postal systems as well as the agency managing the international postal regime and setting international rates (Reinsch 1911: 24; Codding 1964: 41). The UPU also established an international reply coupon service enabling correspondents to overcome any national currency restrictions (Sly 1907: 439); it balanced the international accounts of national postal administrations (Reinsch 1911: 25).

In the 1880s and 1890s some UPU administrators and supporters imagined that its functions could grow even greater, spilling over into related areas and becoming the seed of an eventual world government. The UPU established an international identity card service that might have served to replace national passports with an international travel document (Sly 1907: 439), but a late nineteenth-century movement to abolish passport controls within Europe made the need for this service much less compelling (Mance 1947: 231–2). W. T. Stead wrote that by 1899 the tourist or commercial traveller experienced "no more inconvenience in passing from France to Germany or from Belgium to Holland, than he would in passing from New York into Pennsylvania or from Illinois into Minnesota . . . This passport – a nuisance at one time almost universal – has gradually retreated eastward, until now no one ever asks to look at your passport outside Russia and Turkey" (1899: 9). And one of the things Keynes missed most about Europe before the Great War was the ability to "secure forthwith, if [one] wished it, cheap and comfortable means of transit to any other country of climate without passport or other formality" (1971: 11).

The UPU also extended its reply coupon service and its system for balancing the accounts of postal administrations into a universal postal currency linked to a system for authoritatively determining exchange rates, all of which some imagined would become the beginning of a sort of global central bank (Sly 1907: 441). Again, this turned out to be a sign of effective international regulation that was exercised elsewhere. It was the international adoption of the gold standard, not the UPU, that made Keynes able to continue his reflections in 1920 by rhapsodizing that a comfortably well-off man

> could despatch his servant to the neighboring office of a bank for such supply of the precious metals as might seem convenient, and could then proceed abroad to foreign quarters, without knowledge of their religion, language, or customs, bearing coined wealth upon his person, and would consider himself greatly aggrieved and much surprised at the least interference. (1971: 11–12).

The UPU's real contribution to this unified world was the same one that the penny post had made within countries. The UPU allowed international postal rates to fall, once again aiding those businesses that were the largest users. At the same time, the international regime helped governments keep their subsidies to national mail services low, in part because the flow of international mail increased to the point that new economies of scale could be achieved, but also by limiting a government's responsibility for lost or damaged mail.

Ironically, the revenue interests of European postal administrations help explain the one way in which the Public International Unions failed to develop all the possibilities for low-cost communication throughout Europe. Neither the UPU nor the ITU developed an international telephone regime until after the First World War. There was little demand for one because Europeans had so few phones. In 1910 the continent had only one-tenth of the telephones, per capita, that were in service in the US (Webb 1910: 12). The entire phone system in Europe was relatively undercapitalized; national postal and telegraph administrations did not want to build networks they believed would compete with their own services, and the private firms willing to build phone systems were all foreign, which raised issues of national security and national pride (ibid.: 18, 56–60).

In contrast, the other late nineteenth-century invention that revolutionized communication – radio – quickly became the topic of an intergovernmental agency and an international regime. Radio's most important role before the war was to make it possible for ships to communicate with each other and with stations on land. Britain's ocean supremacy gave it an incentive to try to impose a global radio monopoly. The Radiotelegraph Union (RTU) was set up in 1906 to support competitors to the British firm Marconi (Mance 1944: 10; Tomlinson 1938: 12–13). The Union established the principle of nondiscrimination among radiotelegraph systems using different technologies, set technical rules for linking coastal radiotelegraph stations to inland wired telegraph systems, and established a set of priorities for radiotelegraph messages to assure that messages affecting maritime safety were given priority (Reinsch 1911: 20). While Britain had initially been reluctant to take part in the RTU, the Titanic disaster of 1912 – which might have been diminished had RTU conventions been universal – proved to the British government that the narrow interests of the Marconi patentees should be subservient to those of British liner companies who benefited from the regime of nondiscrimination (Tomlinson 1938: 29).

Radio's prewar role in overseas communication was analogous to that played by the telegraph within Europe. Both communications systems provided special services to one mode of transportation system, radio to ocean liners and the telegraph to the railroads. The telegraph and railroad worked together to create the most important infrastructure for a continental market in industrial goods. Goods travelled on rail. Telegraphed orders preceded them. Sales agents who traveled by rail sent those orders. And it was often market information reported on the wire services that first brought the agents to their destinations.

The international railway Unions began with the aim of creating this European market. The International Railway Congress Association and the Central Office for International Railway Transport are both ostensively open to all national railway administrations, but in practice their membership has always been limited to the European continent plus those Asian and African states whose rail systems are linked to systems on the continent. John Wright's vision in the 1850s of a world united by a global rail network proved to be a fantasy. By the end of the nineteenth century, continental Europe was the only place where railroads constantly crossed national boundaries. Britain, British India, and the United States all became as railway-rich as the continent, but their systems could be regulated by national laws that covered many of the same issues as the "universal" regime. In all cases regulation was designed first and foremost to link together a freight network among different operating companies and then to regulate freight shipping in the interests of those who used the service.

The Railway Congress Association continues to be an information-gathering and deliberative body with no oversight or enforcement powers, but early railway congresses established a regime for freight railroads, standardizing rolling stock and providing a basic formula for agreements among different rail companies to use each other's carriages and vans. These agreements were very similar to the private arrangements among US rail companies that allow freight cars to be used efficiently throughout North America (Wedgewood and Wheeler 1946).

The Central Office's original purpose was to further lower freight costs by dealing with governmental issues, including customs documentation, exchange rates, and the transfer of funds from one national railroad administration to another. The Central Office continues to maintain the long-standing continental freight regime that required members to accept all freight going from one point on the network to another, even if the freight was only passing through the country. The Union also established liability and safety rules for

shipping dangerous goods and fragile items and helped freight hand-
lers collect from one another, and even arbitrated disputes among rail
lines. Perhaps most significantly, it enforced a system whereby a
single bill of lading – a single set of documents – can be used by
shippers throughout the network, making the paperwork needed for
a shipment of steel from Sweden to Turin almost as simple as the
paperwork needed for a similar shipment from Alabama to Detroit
(Reinsch 1911: 29–30).

When turn-of-the-century European manufacturers ordered materials other than steel or coal or other products of the continent, they
would receive them by the mode of transport least affected by the
Public International Unions, ocean shipping. This was another case
where the work of the Unions only points to effective regulation
carried out by other means. British firms controled the shipping
business until well into this century. As a result it was British law, not
international agreements, that set standards for safety on board ships
(Mance 1945: 37). Britain also played a central role at the nine
international maritime conferences securing the general freedom of
commercial navigation that the British felt their vast navy was
needed to protect.

The British government did not, however, exert downward pressure on ocean freight rates, nor did it do much to rationalize the
overseas transport network or the techniques of shipping. Since 1869
ocean freight rates have been set by "liner conventions," cartel
arrangements supported in the era of the Public International Unions
by the putatively liberal British government for the same reason that
it supported Marconi's attempt to establish a radiotelegraph monopoly, for reasons of national security and because most of the firms
involved were British (ibid.: 95; Abrahamsson 1980: 2). Yet even
without intergovernmental regulation, overseas shipping rates fell
(Zimmerman 1917: 256), because tramp freighters – ships following
no predetermined routes – remained outside the liner conventions
and larger and faster freighters became much easier to build. States
had some voice in price setting at intergovernmental conferences
held from 1905 onward at the same time and place as the meetings of
the liner cartel, but extensive intergovernmental action remained
limited to helping rationalize international shipping practices through
the Permanent International Association of Navigation Congresses,
created to exchange information about navigation and the construction of ports (Reinsch 1911: 34).

Eventually the similar Permanent International Association of Road
Conferences, the Road Union, would have a greater impact on the

transportation of goods, but the real challenge of long-distance trucking to the railroads would not come until after the Great War. Before the war the Road Union exchanged information and held meetings of national road administrations to discuss technical standards for vehicles as well as roads (League of Nations 1929: 163). The Union created a road regime that unified national traffic codes, established an international system of road signs, and created the international system for registering automobiles, licensing drivers, and freeing tourists and temporary residents from paying taxes on vehicles they imported (League of Nations 1930: 222; Mance 1947: 16; UN 1968: 250). A British commentator at the end of the Second World War wrote that the road regime, unlike the rail regime, had always been truly universal (Mance 1947: 5). There is a great deal of truth to this – despite the British habit of driving on the wrong side of the road or the peculiarity of American road signs. From its beginning the Road Union has helped make automobiles, trucks, and buses relatively standard products that competent operators can use anywhere.

Rules encouraging investment in industry and trade in industrial goods

The Road Union was not the only prewar intergovernmental agency that set standards for some of the new products of the Second Industrial Revolution. The Chemistry Bureau played the same role for the new packaged-food industry by sharing information about additives and means of preservation and by setting up a foodstuffs code that eliminated the need for national inspection of all packaged foods brought from abroad (League of Nations 1929: 80). The Bureau continued one type of work initiated by the most significant of the prewar standards agencies, the Metric Union.

The major role played by the Metric Union was not, as might be assumed, promotion of the metric system. With the important exception of Britain, all Europe's industrial nations had adopted the system before the Union was founded (November 1877), while LDCs like Spain and Portugal which traded heavily with both Britain and the rest of the continent maintained standards that were similar to the British but were shifting to metric (Halsey 1919: 3–4). The Union's more significant role was scientific and technological, aiding the burgeoning fields of chemical and electrical engineering by maintaining measurement standards, carrying out the research needed to establish physical constants, and constantly adding to the international system of units as new, measurable natural processes were discovered (Guillame 1902; Reinsch 1911: 35; League of Nations 1929: 71; Wilford 1981: 219).

The chemical and electrical engineers served by the Metric Union developed many of the products of the Second Industrial Revolution, everything from the synthetic dyes that would give their name to Germany's chemical giant, I. G. Farben, to the electric elevators that let Parisians see their city from the top of Alexandre Eiffel's tower. The chemical and electrical industries were served by the regime that economic historian William N. Parker describes as "Not monopoly, not pure competition, but the uneasy monopoly in a competitive world [which] offered the economic – as distinct from the sheer intellectual – stimulus to invention" (1984: 38), the modern patent system.

The Patent Union collected and disseminated information on patents and trademarks (Reinsch 1911: 37), held conferences to reform the international patent regime (Ladas 1930: 118), and required its members to recognize the patents and trademarks of others (McClure 1933: 58). The European patent regime did not turn inventions into an absolutely protected form of alienable property, something that could be freely bought and sold anywhere in the world, even though the states where the greatest technological breakthroughs were taking place at the turn of the century – the United States and Germany – wanted such a system (J. Brown 1936: 159; Penrose 1951: 201). International agreements could only be reached on a regime that allowed members to demand that foreign patents be worked in order to be valid: Edison could not stop a Danish firm from making something like his light bulb in Denmark unless he was willing to start production there himself. This rule created a system of preferences for less industrialized members of the Union. The very least industrialized were effectively exempt from the patent system, which is perhaps as it should be if the benefits of the industrial economy are to be spread as widely as possible, as Edith Penrose, one of the leading postwar analysts of the patent system and the modern industrial firm, argues (1951: 233). Yet the more industrialized a state became, the more it had an incentive to join the system and enforce the international regime in order to protect its own industries' inventions.

Encouraging invention and establishing international standards for similar products would not, by themselves, assure either increased trade in industrial products or the kind of growth-inducing industrial innovation that Smith identified in his pin factory. Analysts at the turn of the century did not even agree that Europe was experiencing trade-related economic growth. An American advocate of protection, George Boughton Curtiss, confidently wrote that it was a general climate of protection that had led to further industrialization throughout Europe after 1879 (1896: 557). However, he was writing at just the moment when the long slump in trade and industrial production was ending. Other writers would look back to the mid-1890s as a time when trade liberalization pulled Europe out of the Long Depression. But even the critical liberal internationalist John A. Hobson argued that, over time, trade would become less and less correlated with growth (1904: 5–11). He believed that as incomes increased, a greater proportion of wealth would be put into transport-ation and communication, the fine arts, recreation, amusement, and other services, all of which he considered to be inherently local products. Trade might grow, but it would not keep pace with the economy as a whole. However, the two exceptions Hobson allowed to this rule proved significant from the mid-1890s until the war: trade could lead to industrial growth immediately after new markets had been opened through international agreement, and at any time that new manufacturing methods allowed greater economies of scale and, thus, sale of more goods abroad. The latter could not happen in a highly protectionist environment, and there certainly was a protec-tionist surge in Europe during the economic crisis of the 1870s and 1880s. But many restrictions on trade in manufactured goods eased from the late 1880s onward. Those that remained became much more straightforward and transparent; governments gave importers a clear idea of what restrictions they could expect and when laws might change.

Liberalization had been encouraged by wider knowledge of exactly how much trade was going on, making governments less insecure about how much they would gain or lose under a new trade regime. European commerce ministries had repeatedly attempted to agree on standard trade statistics since the early statistical conferences in London in 1851 and Brussels in 1853. The Brussels-based Tariff Union would finally succeed and even spin off a statistical agency, the Bureau of Commercial Statistics. Not surprisingly, it was the statistical activities of the ITU, the UPU, and the Rail Union that finally made agreement possible; data on the value of posted parcels and of rail shipments under the single bill of lading assured that much of the work had already been done (J. Haas 1923: 36).

The Rail Union of 1890 was also responsible for the first major break in the protectionist wave by abolishing transit duties on goods shipped by rail (McPherson 1910: 142). The Brussels Tariff Union, which also began in 1890, made the remaining restrictions transparent by publishing a regularly updated list of tariffs in five languages, the first time that such information had been made widely available (Reinsch 1911: 42; League of Nations 1929: 67–8). The Tariff Union also held conferences promoting further trade agreements. It was not successful in encouraging broad multilateral agreements like those engineered within the GATT after the Second World War, but Europeans did agree to liberalize in the 1890s and the Tariff Union helped governments take timely actions to extend and enforce those agreements – for example, Serge Witte's "tariff war" of 1893 that aimed at extending Germany's more liberal trade policy of 1891 – events that are key markers of the move to a more open European market. In the end, despite Witte's attack on Germany, agricultural Russia along with Spain and Portugal maintained relatively closed economies until the First World War. At the other extreme stood Belgium, the Netherlands, Norway, Sweden, and the UK, whose economies had remained open even in the Long Depression (Woytinsky and Woytinsky 1955: 251–2). Germany, Austro-Hungary, Italy, and France followed mixed strategies that reflected the overall European picture. While they maintained tariffs protecting peasant agriculture, they did not protect new manufacturing industries. From the turn of the century onward at least half the imports into Germany, Europe's largest market, entered duty free. German liberalism covered tropical goods as well as industrial products; after 1902 even sugar, derived from both tropical cane and European beets, became the subject of a liberalizing regime, the International Sugar Union (Reinsch 1911: 50).

In reflecting on the regime that began in the 1890s a survey commissioned in the early 1950s to support the new GATT concluded, "Thanks to the system of trade treaties, the world as a whole was never closer to the freedom of . . . traffic and trade than on the eve of World War I" (Woytinsky and Woytinsky 1955: 11).

The Interimperial Order's predictable, if far from completely liberal, trade regime complemented Europe's increasingly integrated commercial banking system, which allowed businessmen and tourists to make withdrawals from deposit accounts or lines of credit through checks, bills of exchange, and circular notes. Intergovernmental regimes regulating these instruments had been established through bilateral discussions and a major multilateral conference in 1885, and they were further solidified in two conferences in Hague in the decade before the war. The results seemed so remarkable that

W. T. Stead, like Keynes, also saved his most purple prose for a panegyric to the prewar private banking system:

> You give no notice, but simply walk into the office, announce that you want so much money . . . In five or ten minutes the money is handed to you . . . and you depart, feeling impressed with the perfection of organization of credit by which at a thousand different points in your journey, not in Europe only, but on other continents, you can convert a bit of paper, valueless to anyone else, into gold . . . If, after the fashion of Orientals, you converted your cash into precious stones, you would only be allowed to enter the country after having paid tax and toll to the custom house; but . . . you can snap your fingers at this institution, and cash your notes in a kingdom where no custom-house office can interfere. (Stead 1899: 12–13)

Stead was a journalist, not a banker or an economist. He did not worry about how this financial system worked, only cared that it did.

The fact that it did was not the mystical result of an enlightened policy of laissez faire that let banks everywhere operate under a "natural" gold standard; the global financial system was actively managed by the central bank in the country with the greatest financial resources, Britain, even if it was not, as some contend, simply a "sterling standard."[3] Moreover, even though world organizations may not have been needed to maintain the gold standard, international institutions had played an important role in its development.

Agreement on the gold standard as a universal monetary system originated in the Latin Monetary Union among Belgium, France, Italy, and Switzerland (Kindleberger 1984: 65–7). The French called the Paris Monetary Conference of 1867 in order to extend the Union to other countries. Before that conference the gold standard had been only a matter for academic discussion in Germany, the most significant trading partner of many in the Union. The Paris Conference converted the skeptics among German economists and led German commercial interests to push for the system for the first time. In 1868 the Ninth Congress of German Economists endorsed the gold standard and "Its action was ratified soon afterwards by the united commercial bodies of the North German Confederation, and would have been carried into effect at once but for the war with France. The event postponed the reform for one year" (White 1893: 15–16).

With Germany adhering to the gold standard its other major trading partners felt they had to follow suit. In terms of international trade in industrial products the most important of these (and formerly the most reluctant) was the Netherlands, which adopted the standard in 1875 after a royal commission reporting on consequences of the

German decision had recommended a series of "temporary" suspensions of the coinage of silver (ibid.: 25).

The international monetary conferences after 1867 had a different purpose. They were called by a silver-rich United States interested in establishing a global bimetallic standard (US Senate 1879, 1893). Populists, who represented the small farmers of the American West, argued that coining silver would have shortened the nineteenth-century Long Depression (anticipating the way Keynesian policies of credit expansion worked to ease recessions under a very different global monetary system after the world wars), but financial interests, commercial interests, and governments were all satisfied enough with the working of the gold standard that no real change occurred until Britain could no longer play its central role in the world financial system.

Supporting Farmers and Workers

The Populists never convinced European governments to abandon the gold standard in favor of a more welfare-oriented monetary system even though social forces underlying the movement were potentially quite powerful. As Arno Mayer (1981) argues, while agriculture, small-scale manufacturing of consumer goods, and local commerce may not have been the sectors that led European economies into the twentieth century, they still accounted for the bulk of production and employment before the First World War. In the case of agriculture this economic presence translated into political power, at least for large owners if not for the typical populist constituency. In 1889, 30 per cent of the French parliament gained their livelihood from the land. Even in the oldest industrialized state, Britain, 23 per cent of members of parliament had the same kind of personal interest in farming in 1900, more than a generation after the Corn Laws had been abolished (Peterson 1980: 121).

Nineteenth-century European farmers had reason to fear extension of the industrial system. They saw the Long Depression as triggered by a dramatic fall in the price they received for grain, a consequence of improvements in ocean shipping and the completion of both the European and the American rail networks. As one scholar puts it, steamships and the railroads placed France's towns closer to North America's much more cost-efficient farms than they were to France's traditional agricultural villages (Tracy 1964: 64). Those who have read Marcel Pagnol's *Jean de Florette* and *Manon of the Springs* will understand; those stories take place in a farming village less than twenty miles from Marseilles, yet traditional attitudes and bad roads meant that residents

> saw "foreigners" only rarely . . . Before 1914 it was still possible to find old people on the farms who spoke nothing but the Provencal of the hills; they would make the young people who came from the barracks "describe Marseille," and they were amazed that it was possible to live with so much noise, to brush with people in the streets whose names one did not know, and especially to meet policemen everywhere! (Pagnol 1988: 4)

David Lubin's plan for the IIA assumed that such farmers, armed with extensive, reliable, and up-to-date market data, would rapidly learn to adjust their methods of cultivation and the products they raised in order to meet the new demands of a global market. That is why most of what the IIA bureaucrats did was simply gather and report information (Reinsch 1911: 54; A. Hobson 1931: 101). In fact only one European country, Denmark, adjusted (Tracy 1964: 14). Even in Italy, where there was a "modern" class of landowners – the *borghesia* of bureaucrats, professionals, tradesmen, and skilled artisans who had become semi-absentee owners of *latifunda capitalistico* – a class that might have been expected to welcome the plan of Lubin and their king, the needed adjustment was never made. For the *borghesia*, "Land-owning was only marginally considered to be an economic stake. Its social and political implications were of overriding importance" (Peterson 1980: 166). They invested their profits outside the rural areas. In Italy, as everywhere else in Europe except Denmark, protection substituted for adjustment, and in that the liberal internationalists of the IIA played no role.

Unlike the IIA, the ILO played a real role in discouraging political opposition to Europe's new industrial system. The ILO took on the tasks of studying the conditions of industrial labor worldwide and collecting labor statistics (Follows 1951: 155–61). It also studied existing national labor protections and social security systems (Lowe 1921: 125), prepared the international conferences on labor legislation, and drafted domestic labor legislation and labor treaties (Follows 1951: 155; Reinsch 1911: 49), including two major multilateral labor conventions signed before the war.

One of these became the model for most subsequent labor and environmental treaties. It ended the production of matches using white phosphorous, a chemical linked to degenerative disease. To make the ban work not only meant ending the practice in the major match-producing countries – Britain and its newly industrializing competitors, Sweden and Japan – but it also meant assuring that new competitors did not spring up in other countries once production had stopped. States with as yet no white-phosphorous match industry found it easy to sign and enforce the convention. Japan did not enforce the agreement before the war, but it lost much of its overseas market. Britain and most other European states and their colonies adhered to the agreement. Sweden simply banned the sale of these matches at home. Nevertheless, the sum of these varying responses to the convention was enough to make match manufacturers quickly depreciate older factories and invest in new production processes (Lowe 1921: 123–31).

The ILO was also involved with the 23 bilateral labor agreements before the First World War that standardized some labor laws from the Pyrenees to the Balkans and from Stockhom to Sicily (Lowe 1921). The details of those treaties reveal the limited group of workers invited into the overall European social pact of which they were a part. The treaties explicitly *do not* cover workers in colonies, those in some relatively low-tech industries like open-pit mining or sugar refining, those in older industries like wool spinning and weaving, or even most manual workers in newer chemical and electrical sectors. The treaties simply provided reciprocal pension rights and rights of workers' compensation to foreign skilled workers in the newer industries where these rights had already been extended to nationals. These beneficiaries were the workers that Lenin would call "bourgeoisified" and the "labour aristocracy" (1970: 14) in 1920, the same year Keynes lamented that Europe's prewar economic Eldorado had done so little for the common man.

Strengthening both State and Society

The ILO was not the only Public International Union that directly contributed in some small way to domestic social orders. In the course of building the world organizations to carry out the liberal internationalists' primary tasks, the designers, sponsors, and benefactors of the Unions also strengthened the coercive apparatuses of their state members and helped protect domestic social orders from disruptive interstate conflicts. At the same time, however, the political space opened by the primary activities encouraged social movements demanding that governments protect human rights and assure the satisfaction of basic human needs. In a few cases these movements also succeeded in establishing world organizations, which, as a result, strengthened civil society *vis-à-vis* the state proper.

Strengthening the state proper and the state system

After 1910 European governments had an institution for sharing information about the most efficient ways to carry out and further extend the expanding functions of the state, the International Institute of Administrative Science. The institute built on the experience of one of the oldest Unions, the International Penitentiary Commission, which continued to share information on penal law, prison administration, the reform of criminals, and the prevention of crime (Reinsch 1911: 57; League of Nations 1929: 115). The Commission was an institution concerned with strengthening Gramsci's "political society," the state proper. It helped national governments make the most efficient use of all those gendarmes and constables that Pagnol's peasants were surprised to find in big cities like Marseilles.

However, most of the prewar instances of inter-European cooperation aimed at strengthening the nation-state did not focus on the kind of crimes that might be encountered in Marseilles or Liverpool. Instead, cooperation focused on the kind of opposition governments found in places like Dakar or Mombasa, where the relevant crimes were likely to be committed by other European powers. From the mid-1880s onward the European conquests of Africa and the Pacific became the central topics of international conferences aimed at reducing tensions caused by conflicting colonial claims. The world organizations that grew out of those conferences reflected the regulation exercised there, even though the IGOs themselves eventually failed to perform the tasks they had been given.

This is not the place to go deeply into the debate over the sources of this new wave of imperialism in great detail. Suffice it to say that in every colonial state the initial political decisions to pursue new claims in Africa and the Pacific (and to allow other European states to pursue such claims) served more than one purpose. Certainly the perception of easy economic advantage – new sources of raw materials, new markets, protected trade routes, and outlets for "surplus" population – played a role, something even the sharpest critics of purely "economic" explanations of imperialism have always acknowledged (Usher 1918: 37; Fieldhouse 1966: 210–11). Nevertheless, many of those initial decisions were also aimed at enhancing the power of the colonizing state *per se* (Schumpeter 1955: 96–8; Fieldhouse 1966) and at keeping the nineteenth-century system for managing international conflict operating under fundamentally new conditions. By 1870 most of Europe's small states had been eliminated with the consolidation of the Italian and German nations (long before the next wave of nationalism would threaten to split up older empires in the east), while industry had made the weapons of war much more destructive, as had been proven in the Crimean War and even more dramatically in the American Civil War. Both factors made the old classical balance-of-power game much more difficult to play (Chatterjee 1975: 135–52).

Nonetheless, European conferences succeeded in defusing most (but certainly not all) of the interimperial conflicts that appeared for 30 years after the 1884 Berlin Conference partitioned Africa. As a result, non-European colonies became part of the currency of power within the state system, even though the economic logic of maintaining, extending, and deepening the control of colonies diminished after 1890 as the Second Industrial Revolution took hold and pulled the European economy out of the Long Depression. Profitable investment opportunities appeared throughout the metropoles. Colonies that provided raw materials essential to Europe's new lead industries (cocoa, coffee, copper, palm oil, rubber, and tin) remained vital, but those that appeared to function only as outlets for "surplus" population and capital became less important, at least until the very end of this prewar era when core consumer markets again threatened to become saturated and the prospect of declining profitability in core industries again appeared on the horizon.

J. A. Hobson's 1902 contribution to our understanding of the new imperialism can be understood in this light (Hobson 1965). He explained the economic logic of one wave of imperial investments that probably peaked at the beginning of the Long Depression, and was only secured by the extension of European *political* control in the 1880s and 1890s. At the same time he anticipated another period when the economic logic of imperial investments would again be great, a period of saturated European consumer markets when investments at home would again appear less promising.[4] Hobson believed that the tenacity of the new imperialism was ultimately linked to the low wages paid by turn-of–the-century industrialists. An alternative path of economic development – a proto-Fordist one based on high levels of production and high levels of consumption at home – had so far been foreclosed, although Hobson hoped that the nascent continental social pact reflected in the early twentieth-century international labor agreements would again make it possible.

In the meantime, he blamed the "underconsumption" by underpaid turn-of-the-century workers for what he considered to be the perfectly rational conclusion of many investors that they might make bigger profits on colonial enterprises than they could make if they put their money in building more industrial capacity in Europe. At the same time, underconsumption fueled working-class aspirations for the better life promised in settler colonies overseas. Given the possible ways in which workers and large investors could develop imperialist aspirations, those with such aspirations could often build coalitions and develop unusual political clout.

Throughout the last quarter of the nineteenth century, intellectuals linked to colonial interests and to the imperial aspirations of champions of the *ancien régime* began to articulate social Darwinist theories justifying militant imperialism as a necessary reflection of European superiority over the "backward" races (Hobson 1965: 223–84). The focus of these theories sometimes shifted and *European* targets of "necessary" military action were placed alongside the recalcitrant non-European natives. Any power which might keep one's own nationals from increasing their grip on the foreign lands deserved a similar fate.

Much to the dismay of Hobson and other turn-of-the-century liberal internationalists, official apologists for the new imperialism helped design the IGOs that had been meant to improve on the conference system's mechanisms for managing interstate conflicts, the Permanent Court of Arbitration and the International Court of Prize. The former was established at the Tsar's peace conference of 1899. The latter was established by a convention signed at the Second Hague Conference in 1907 but never ratified (Hudson 1944: 165–6). The Permanent Court was meant to facilitate immediate recourse to arbitration in international disputes and it actually heard fifteen cases between 1902 and 1920 (ibid.: 7). Its bureau in The Hague was also supposed to establish international commissions of inquiry and circulate their reports (Scott 1917: 32–42). The Court of Prize was a specialized spin-off designed to assess claims for damages made by neutral states against belligerents (Scott 1911: 305). Had the Court of Prize been working during the Great War, Woodrow Wilson would have been able to make claims for the loss of American life and property suffered as a result of German submarine warfare. Instead Wilson could only seek redress for the sinking of ships in the Atlantic by joining the war in 1917. Of course, had the Court of Arbitration been working the way it was meant to in 1914, at the beginning of war, the issue would never have come up.

These ineffectual international courts had, in part, been the brain-child of a legalist branch of liberal internationalism, a movement that aimed to find "constitutional principles" for a general international organization that could assure world peace. David Mitrany and other functionalists would later criticize this "international law move-ment" both for its naivety about power and for its lack of attention to the concrete workings of modern industrial societies (Mitrany 1948: 356–8), but in 1899 and 1907 functionalists accepted the help of the International Law Association and the Institute for International Law in setting the agendas of the conferences, and sympathetic international lawyers served on national delegations.

However, they were always outnumbered by delegates from the military (Scott 1917: 14–20, 205–14), who had a strong claim to functional expertise on the main topic of the conferences; in addi-tion, the ideology that had begun to dominate military thinking at the turn of the century devalued the kinds of peacemaking preferred by the international lawyers. The ideas of Captain Alfred T. Mahan, delegate plenipotentiary of the United States to the First Hague Conference, reflected the least bellicose end of a spectrum of milit-ary thinkers. Mahan was a social Darwinist who championed "the Anglo-Saxon race" and his popular history of naval power (1898, its fifteenth edition) was becoming the intellectual foundation for America's new imperialism. Mahan remained sympathetic to the version of international arbitration proposed by the functionalist Serge Witte, who wanted agreements to arbitrate concrete disputes arising among industrial powers, not the international lawyers' ab-stract constitutional principles.

At the other end of the spectrum were the members of the Ger-man and Austro-Hungarian high commands who represented their governments at the Second Hague Conference, members of what Kalevi J. Holsti calls the "redemption-through-war-school" (1991: 163). They devalued the efforts of both the international lawyers and the functionalists and viewed war much more positively than Mahan. "War," one of them would argue in 1914, could "promote the progress of mankind" by furnishing Germans with "enlarged poss-ibilities of expansion and widened influence" (Bernhardi 1918: 22). Not surprisingly, when the conference finally turned to spec-ifying Witte's concrete functional areas in which arbitration should be mandatory, the Austrians and Germans objected (table 5), doom-ing any hope for institutionalizing better ways to manage con-flicts among the industrial powers and foreshadowing the coming crisis.

TABLE 5   Opposition to compulsory arbitration, 1907 (proposals made at the Second Hague Conference)

AUSTRIA AND GERMANY ALONE	JOINED BY OTHER POWERS
Infrastructure	**Infrastructure**
Collisions at sea	Post, telegraph, and telephone [Great
Measurement of vessels	Britain]
	Dock, lighthouse, and pilot fees
	[Great Britain]
Standards and property	
Weights and measures	
Intellectual property	
Trade	**Trade**
Equality of foreigners in taxation	Monetary systems [Italy, United States]
Private international law	General pecuniary claims [Great
Civil and commercial procedure	Britain]
Customs tariffs	
Right of foreigners to hold property	
Regulation of companies	
Claims for damages	
Labor	
International protection of workmen	
Wages and estates of seamen	
	Agriculture
	Epizootics [Italy]
	Managing interstate conflict
	Claims arising from acts of war [Great
	Britain]
Health	**Health**
Reciprocal free aid to the indigent sick	Sanitary regulations [Italy]

Source: Scott (1917: 407–10).

Extending human rights and expanding the state's role in meeting basic needs

While this fundamental failure of the Hague conferences meant that the European conference system remained the only international institution on which the powers could rely to resolve conflicts short of war, another institutional spin-off of the peace conferences was a success: the International Maritime Bureau Against the Slave Trade became the first major global IGO with a mandate to end abuses of human rights around the world. This Anti-Slavery Union originated as an act of interimperial cooperation – cooperation among the "civilized" nations against Arabs and Africans. The Union was to enforce regimes regulating the sale of firearms and liquor to African natives, and it sanctioned the practice of forced labor in African colonies. Nevertheless, Europe's century-old anti-slavery movement was able to use the opportunity created by international debate over creating the Union to convince colonial powers to adopt the kind of strict regulation of the east African slave trade that would eventually assure its end (Reinsch 1911: 64).

A similar move to connect further extensions of human rights to issues that were already the subject of international cooperation helps explains the creation of an international anti-prostitution regime to deal with what was called "the white slave trade" (ibid.: 65–6). A 1910 conference extended the regime to the publication and sale of pornography. Both efforts remained fairly inconsequential before the war. So did a similar attempt to extend the Hague Conference principle of providing relief to disabled prisoners and foreign neutrals caught in war to try to create a general international relief regime administered by the International Bureau for Information and Enquiries Regarding Relief to Foreigners (League of Nations 1929: 65).

The International Office of Public Hygiene reflected a much more successful attempt both to support human rights through international agreement and to extend the state's responsibilities for fulfilling basic needs. The Office's original functions derived from quarantine regulations in the shipping and rail conventions; it was the place for registering the diseases cited in international conventions and for identifying their characteristics, and it was to monitor the application of international sanitary conventions (Abt 1933: 83). But to carry out those functions it had to become a pool for general epidemiological information, and it rapidly became a source of information on effective means to curb infectious diseases of all kinds, as well as a promoter of the domestic public health policies that appeared to be the most effective (Reinsch 1911: 58; League of Nations 1929: 133).

Promoters of the Cartographic, Geodetic, Mathematics, and Seismological Unions argued that these organizations would support public education in the same way that the Health Union supported public health (League of Nations 1929: 82), which was a hard case to make since the earlier conferences had only been directed toward adepts in the various fields. And, as we have seen, unlike the Health Union, the Unions in education did not become sites of expanding intergovernmental activity.

In sum, the tasks that the Public International Unions carried out most effectively remained those associated with creating and regulating a European market for industrial goods. The success of the Health Union and the Anti-Slavery Union correlated with the success of the communication and transportation agencies, as well as with that of the agencies defining industrial standards, protecting intellectual property, establishing rules of trade, and promising to benefit one very privileged group of workers.

Of course, even in the field where the first of the world organizations were the most successful, other institutions – a unified monetary and financial system and a coherent shipping regime linking European industries to overseas sources of raw materials – were needed to complete the regulatory tasks suggested by liberal internationalist theory. In other cases – responding to the hardship that farmers faced with the extension of the industrial system, and managing interstate conflicts – the activities of the first global IGOs were also, at best, signs of regulation accomplished at other sites and by other means.

Using Information to Create Order

In those realms where the Unions contributed to substantive regulation of the European economy the indirect evidence of their effectiveness is straightforward and compelling. Telegrams, letters, and packages flooded the international networks at the end of the nineteenth century. The tonnage of goods – especially of industrial products – shipped a long European railways and roads constantly increased. National courts defended foreign holders of copyrights, patents, and trademarks. Producers increasingly employed the same standards. The benefits received by Europe's most privileged workers converged. The slave trade waned. Fewer epidemics crossed national frontiers.

Yet we can still question the degree to which the activities of the world organizations influenced these changes. Could it really have been something about the *Unions'* activities that convinced governments to keep the infrastructure linked, give rights to foreign holders of intellectual property, and converge on some similar labor standards? Was it really something that the Unions did that convinced private firms to sell in many markets and employ similar industrial standards? After all, the Unions were second-order institutions, clubs of jealous sovereign states that liked to keep the world organizations in close rein. And the IGOs were poorly funded, collaborative associations with no direct material incentives to offer and no coercive sanctions they could use, or at least this is the image that most texts on international organization present.

Only the second half of this image is really accurate. The first half, the part about the tight constraints placed on the agencies by their state members, is more true in theory than it was in fact, and perhaps more true of the world organizations at the end of this century than of those at the end of the last. In fact, functionalists have always argued that the limits governments place on intergovernmental agencies can actually contribute to their effectiveness. National governments are not apt to see limited organizations as potential rivals and therefore members will give such IGOs the autonomy they need to do their jobs. The Public International Unions reflected this logic. None, with the exception of the ineffectual Court of Arbitration, had a general mandate, and almost all acted with a great deal of autonomy, even though the constitutions of the agencies make some look much more autonomous than others.

As figure 3 indicates (based on data explained in the appendix), if we look at the more "official" histories of the Unions we learn that they carried out only about 13 percent of their activities without official oversight from their members states. More typically, the constitution of the Union would require that all activities be carried out under the oversight of a governing board elected by members and ultimately reflecting a principle of majority rule.

Most often this was not exactly what happened. Member governments rarely appointed permanent representatives to the Unions. In some cases the resident ambassador in the capital nearest the headquarters of an agency might be given responsibility for overseeing its activities, but those delegates could only expect to discuss the Union's activities with other representatives at the periodic intergovernmental conferences that could be biennial, triennial, or even less frequent. In most of the Unions, most of the time, the chain of command ended with the chief executive officer, often with a man like Numa Droz, a former Swiss civil servant somewhat detached from the machinations of the powers themselves.

To explore why members might allow (or be forced to allow) the Unions to act autonomously, I have made a checklist of means of

How Members Controlled Organizations

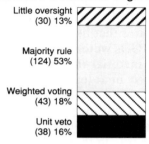

Little oversight
(30) 13%

Majority rule
(124) 53%

Weighted voting
(43) 18%

Unit veto
(38) 16%

How Organizations Influenced Members

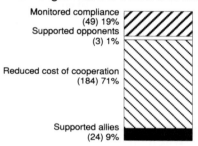

Monitored compliance
(49) 19%
Supported opponents
(3) 1%

Reduced cost of cooperation
(184) 71%

Supported allies
(24) 9%

FIGURE 3 Formal controls by member states over Public International Unions and means used by Unions to influence their members, 1914 (regular activities, 1911–15, see appendix on data)

influence available to unions and then used them while collecting data on the activities of the Public International Unions and their successors. The results for the world organizations in existence when the First World War began appear in the second part of figure 3.

Services strengthening the state, cosmopolitan interests, and the links between them

In 9 percent of the cases of tasks undertaken by the Unions, the organization did nothing more than provide a *service to domestic or foreign allies* of its state members. But, in most cases, these activities indirectly served to strengthen the state (often quite a bit more effectively than the services of IGOs designed to strengthen the state more directly). In some cases the Unions gave governments a way to provide services that no single state could provide by itself: an efficient international postal system or a means of allowing private businessmen to learn about rapidly changing markets abroad. In many cases, creation of a new international service defused a hot domestic political issue and immediately increased the allegiance of one part of the citizenry to the national government. For instance, businesses relying on information about foreign markets had demanded that governments connect the telegraph network across frontiers with something better than runners or homing pigeons (Headrick 1991: 12–13). Similarly, companies that already sold goods abroad before the 1890s demanded a unified, efficient European freight system.

The Rail Union further strengthened some member governments by providing them with new ways to manage domestic conflicts that grew out of earlier attempts by the Belgians, Dutch, French, and Germans to each boost their own national steel industry by using freight rates, terminal charges, and complex systems for documenting and classifying raw materials and finished products to favor their own producers, ports, or cities at transfer points (Meyer 1905: 21–38). This was one consequence of the Unions' ability to influence members simply by allowing them to perceive common interests. In Keohane's (1984) terms, the Unions reduced the "information costs" and the "transaction costs" of intergovernmental cooperation.

All the agencies that helped harmonize national laws and national business practices – the ILO, the industrial standards and intellectual property Unions, and even the Sugar Union – worked in similar ways. They let governments see their collective interest in regulation, and once again in the process they indirectly strengthened the state. The international body became a new site for what had formerly been a purely domestic conflict over regulation of the economy. As is often the case in politics at all levels (Schattschneider 1975: 60) the change in forum influenced the resolution of the conflict, favoring some groups over others. The change to an international forum, for example, would almost always favor social forces depending on international commerce. It is important to recognize that this shift in the site of regulation was rarely "necessary," if by that we mean that the parties to the conflict demanded it. Some of the social forces to which the ILO appealed to help resolve conflicts between employers and workers would have been just as satisfied with purely domestic regimes. Consider those generous employers who served only a domestic market, men like Charles Dickens's liberal and jolly Cheeryble brothers who introduced Nicholas Nickleby into the world of commerce; for them, protectionist legislation that would keep cheap goods produced by sweated labor out of Britain would have been quite satisfactory. Similarly, provincial publishers and writers with no international reputation did not need international agreements as a basis for resolving any conflicts they might have over copyright. And most European sugar beet farmers would certainly have preferred to operate under the typical domestic agricultural regimes of protection and subsidy rather than under an international system whose ultimate purpose was to reduce the bounties paid to sugar growers to zero.

Of course, the Unions served these parochial interests well enough: sugar beet farmers still received their subsidies, even if they had to plan for the day that they would end. National copyright laws which had been harmonized with international agreements still defined and protected the rights of even the most provincial publishers and authors. And the few real-world employers at the turn of the century who were as generous as the fictitious Cheeryble brothers (perhaps Britain's Quaker chocolate manufacturers: Cadbury, Fry, and Rowntree) were apt to be supporters of the movement for international labor legislation anyway.

Yet it is still critical that the Unions served others, those involved in international commerce, even more effectively: the owners of a fleet of freighters that brought sugar cane to refineries in Bromley and Hamburg; the workers at the Swiss firm Nestlé, a liberal employer whose small domestic market already forced it to ship milk and chocolate around the world at the turn of the century; and the writers like Ibsen and Tolstoy, with readers in every part of the world.

In a number of cases a Union could not satisfy major interests within its member countries, yet the Unions still indirectly strengthened the state by helping members manage a domestic conflict by aiding the state's key allies. When Britain joined the Radiotelegraph Union, Marconi was certainly not satisfied with the outcome. But the existence of the RTU regime allowed the British government to treat the issue as one of public safety and international responsibility. As such, the issue was closed. In effect, adherence to the RTU regime became a weapon that the General Post Office used in a battle with Marconi for control over the new technology (Headrick 1991: 185).

The Public International Unions also provided some services that indirectly strengthened their state members simply by removing potential sources of international conflict. Again, most were examples of activities that can be thought of as reducing the costs of international cooperation. For example, the communication and transportation unions balanced the accounts of different national service providers, determining how much each owed for service provided by others. This would not have been a difficult task if each national service provider had kept relatively good books, but most did not. Given the astronomical growth in usage of all of the networks – international telegrams increased from 5.7 million in 1868 to 82.2 million in 1905 (Reinsch 1911: 18) – the sums involved became quite large and Unions quickly had to resort to sampling (for instance, weighing a week's mail) in order to assess fees. With presumably impartial civil servants carrying out these tasks, few problems arose. When they did, most of the transportation and communication Unions provided systems of arbitration for resolving any differences. These systems provided an inducement for members to take part in the regime, but they also created a potential constraint on state action should arbitrators rule against them. That constraint is reflected in the 1 percent of the cases where the Unions could be thought of as *supporting opponents* of their state members.

Disinterested inquiry and consensual norms

The Unions did more than perform services that usually strengthened the state and cosmopolitan forces. The first global IGOs also influenced the agenda of world politics by activities designed to uncover previously unrecognized collective interests. Most of the men and women who worked for the Unions spent their time gathering and disseminating information on the issues within their agency's bailiwick. IIA clerks were supposed to have their eyes locked on the printing telegraphs that reported the latest market information and their hands flying across keypunches that spat out the cards from which tables of statistics could be calculated. Similar data-gathering by the communications unions, the Rail Union, and the Tariff Union had all led to new multilateral agreements before the war.

In fact, governments would often only focus on the information collected in preparation for the periodic conferences that governed the Unions. By 1910 conferences called by global agencies began to outnumber those called at the invitation of individual heads of state and their governments. This was perhaps the most important institutional innovation engineered by the Unions, and ironically most state members did not expect it to have the effect it did. After all, most members saw the periodic conferences as a way to oversee the work of the agencies. Yet the necessary preparation for these conferences would gave IGO functionaries power over the agenda of world politics. By 1910 the global agencies themselves were playing the roles that used to be played by the foreign ministry or personal attendants to the monarch of a hosting country: sending out invitations, deciding on a venue, negotiating a preliminary agenda, arranging for transportation and housing of some delegates, preparing meeting rooms, performing conference services (including translation, editing, and copying) and following up on the conference by publishing and circulating documents, circulating conventions for signature, and keeping track of ratifications.

The conferences called by the Public International Unions continued to contribute to international cooperation by providing forums for multidirectional communication that otherwise would not occur, just as the older kind of international conferences had. But simply by their greater regularity, the Unions' conferences contributed more to the development of international civil society than had the *ad hoc* conferences out of which they grew. Governments and private associations regularized their own work to match the Unions' conference schedule. Informal professional networks of experts, government officials, and representatives of private interests developed among those who attended a series of conferences. As a result, when research and debate led to new perceptions of shared interests, it became much easier to turn that possibility of increased international cooperation into a reality.

The ITU played this role of nurturing a transnational professional network that facilitated further international cooperation particularly effectively. Although the Union began as a club of nationalized telegraph administrations, it always opened its conferences to representatives of private firms and government regulators in countries where the telegraph was in private hands. The ITU's first meeting convinced conferees from national postal administrations, which often controlled the telegraph, to begin discussing and planning the Postal Union. Later conferences became the places where governments and businesses concerned about Marconi's monopoly could find allies and devise a strategy. And finally, when the RTU was formed as a separate agency – so that non members of the ITU could be part – RTU members did not bother to create their own central office; they simply voted to increase the ITU's budget by about half and give the same men and women in Berne the job of collecting and distributing information on radio, along with, of course, the job of preparing and staffing further RTU conferences (Reinsch 1911: 20).

The Unions' professional staffs even designed many new international agreements. By 1890 international civil servants provided as much of the intellectual leadership needed to establish new international institutions as did professionals within national governments. The ILO even had this as its primary function, although it was the ITU that had initiated the practice of having the professional staff of the unions draft members' proposals for changes in the regime (ibid.: 15). The Postal Union staff initiated all of the proposed extensions of its own work, including those that had the UPU inching toward becoming a global central bank. The staff of the Metric Union initiated its own programs in response to the needs of the scientific community. And the Chemistry Bureau, one of the last of the prewar IGOs, drafted changes in the international foodstuffs code necessitated by new chemical preservatives and additives (League of Nations 1929: 80).

Promoting norms and monitoring compliance

In each case the staff's presumed professional neutrality gave it the authority needed to design agreements and promote them to members, first and foremost by appealing to their rational self-interest. The Rail Union's Numa Droz and his countryman Emil Frey were particular masters of this rhetoric (see Stead 1899: 25–37). Yet even while making appeals to their members' self-interest, they – and the heads of other agencies – also used the whole panoply of psychologically effective rhetorical ploys to promote the international regimes in their bailiwick. They appealed to the "higher" interests of national altruism and the global good, used bandwagoning arguments to support regimes that many states had joined, and also the contradictory argument that a convention was "exclusive" when it had few ratifications. They made appeals to end "international lawlessness" and to fulfill the responsibilities of "civilized" nations. They used the foot-in-the-door technique of encouraging states to ratify conventions, even with added reservations, as a way of getting commitment to the process of negotiating international agreements in new areas like labor legislation or pure food standards. Then they used the old haberdasher's trick of immediately bringing out small items (shirts, gloves, ties) after commitment to a big item (a coat or suit) has been made: with the Public International Unions the "big" items were agreements in principle on an international regime or a major extension of an international regime (such as the translation, publication, and prior dissemination of all laws that might restrict trade), and the "small" items were things to make the regime "work effectively" (an agreement to simplify trade restrictions by relying increasingly on tariffs and further agreements to collect comprehensive trade data so that tariffs could be set "fairly and rationally").[5]

This kind of rhetoric, and the normal psychology into which it plays (a psychology of which liberal fundamentalists often seem ignorant), not only allowed the Unions to promote and extend international norms to states that might not yet see that the regimes were in their interests, it also provided one way to deal with the free-rider problems that arise when parties have an interest in the provision of some collective good but no individual incentive to make a contribution or the sacrifices needed so long as the collective good is already being provided by others.

Publicizing failures to live up to commitments provided another method of persuasion, which is why some Unions had the job of monitoring compliance with previous agreements within their area of competence (a characteristic of 19 percent of the Unions' activities). In most cases the Unions simply circulated reports submitted by members. In one case, that of the Slavery Union, a separate bureau did more active policing of the slave trade regime (Reinsch 1911: 64).

The significance of monitoring to the success of the Public International Unions fits with the conclusion of British social theorist Anthony Giddens (1981) that "surveillance" has become a central mode of regulation within modern societies. Giddens, like Foucault (1979), emphasizes the way that the structuring of social relations by the promulgation and promotion of "consensual" norms, followed by the construction of institutions to monitor compliance, quickly becomes an invisible and seemingly benign form of social control. We have seen Foucault's powerful image of this new mode of regulation, his equation of the modern state and corporate institutions with refinements on Bentham's Panopticon prison. The convex mirrors placed in shops to deter shoplifters, the customer service managers' random monitoring of calls answered by staff, and the private firms that establish individual credit ratings for each of us who has ever paid a utility bill or used a credit card are all based on the Panopticon principle. It is the *sine qua non* of political efficiency, a way of husbanding power, a way of gaining maximum compliance from a minimum of inducements or coercive sanctions. If, as in the case of the Public International Unions, the Panopticon principle is linked to prior public agreements on norms and to systems aimed at promoting such agreement by using all the more benign psychological means (analogous, perhaps, to the programs for "reforming" criminals that typify modern penal systems), the overall control system can become quite effective.

When intergovernmental agencies employ the Panopticon principle, the norms they promote are readily apparent, as are the inducements to follow those norms (enlightened self-interest), as well as the systems used for monitoring adherence to them; but the means of punishing those who violate international norms is much less visible than it is even in Bentham's prison. The successes of the Public International Unions certainly depended on extensive information gathering, discovery of shared interests, and norm setting, but there was also rule enforcement going on. It might not have been visible very often, and it was not carried out by the same people who gathered the information and set the norms, but it was, nonetheless, quite real.

Sources of enforcement

The tools available to a Public International Union for encouraging compliance with international norms would have been inconsequential if most states had not already agreed to comply with the regimes it administered. Most often, the Unions simply needed to identify free-riders and then rely on other members to bring them in line. But even when states had not originally agreed to comply, or when their interests in complying had fundamentally changed, an international regime could become a significant restraint on action. To understand how this might happen it may be useful to look at an example of the power of rules in everyday life. When we are conscious of a rule – for example, the rule to drive on one particular side of the road – or, to be more precise, when we are conscious of a *sign* of the rule – the line painted down the middle of the road – it can remind us of *all* the following reasons to obey: our environment could punish us in that we might run into an oncoming car; others might observe us and punish us; we might feel bad, assuming we do not think of ourselves as the sort of people who break traffic laws; moreover, if we are observed, others might no longer consider us law-abiding; we might even encourage others to break this and other rules, and we certainly would not want to live in a world of lawless drivers.

Each of these reasons reinforces the others. Some rely on public systems of monitoring. Some do not. Only one relies on a special institution of punishment. (I have deliberately made the source of that punishment ambiguous; a driver may have to worry about highway patrols and traffic courts, but national governments violating international agreements are more likely to find themselves punished by other governments or by their own people.) More significantly, all of these reasons for obeying only need to come into play when we are not in the habit of following the rule. Most of the time we follow rules simply because we are habituated to them.

In normal times, in periods when stable world orders – stable international historical blocs – have been formed, international and transnational relations are just as habit driven as our everyday actions. Intergovernmental agencies constantly provide signs of international agreements, but these signs are of the greatest importance for those states not yet habituated to the rules embodied within them. Sometimes the key to habituation is simply growing recognition that the physical environment will become a bit more benign if the agreement is followed. Adherence to the early international health conventions arose primarily from this consideration. As the germ theory of disease gained increasing acceptance, governments recognized the value of quarantines and the even greater value of attempting to contain epidemics anywhere in the world. In other cases the key may be those who are ready to punish the states that do not follow the norms. For example, Eric Schiff (1971: 23, 94) argues that the pressure the Patent Union placed on Switzerland to adhere to the patent regime only bore fruit when Germany, the largest customer for Swiss chemical products, threatened to ban their sale. Schiff contrasts the Swiss experience with that of the Dutch, who faced no such threat to important Dutch markets, but who finally adhered to the patent regime due to a lingering feeling of "international lawlessness" (ibid.: 79).

Finally, there are cases like that of British adherence to the ban on production of white phosphorous matches. The British government was not under overwhelming domestic pressure to sign the agreement, no other state had the power to force British compliance, and Britain, at the time, was quite willing to be in a minority of one when it came to new international agreements. Yet the British government signed the agreement, even without being assured that it would be enforced universally, simply because it was committed (for domestic political reasons) to the larger principle of establishing international standards for labor, and the treaty had become a test of whether universal international agreements would ever be possible.

From members' habits to effects on industrial society

The Unions had their greatest impact in cases when adherence to the consensual norms they promoted and monitored became so habitual that regular state action based on these norms came to shape the expectations of private citizens and of other governments. The habits states develop within international civil society became part of what Daniel Little (1986) calls the *institutional logic* within which other social actors pursue their interests and aspirations. The most significant effects of international institutions on industrial change appear only when we look for ways in which they conditioned choices made by those whose actions were the proximate cause of such change – inventors, entrepreneurs and investors (whether private or public), industrial workers, and consumers of industrial products. The significance of these choices, and of the institutional logic by which the Unions helped assure they were constrained, are the topics of the next chapter.

Of course, the Unions did not always succeed at the tasks they were given. Where they were less successful – establishing the same conditions for industrial work around the world, helping farmers adjust to a global free market in agricultural goods, and managing interstate conflicts – the immediate problem was always similar. The problem was not so much one of enforcing international norms as as it was of having uncovered very few norms about labor, agriculture, and managing international conflict that all the prewar powers were willing to affirm. The ILO had been successful in getting two multilateral agreements and a number of bilateral ones, but very little time elapsed between the first multilateral labor agreements and the outbreak of the war. The IIA appeared only after the protectionist policies of the Long Depression created powerful domestic interest groups opposed to adjustment and free trade in European farm products. And the Austrian and German objections to mandatory international arbitration – the only new means of managing interstate conflict explored by the promoters of the Hague Court – doomed that international effort at the same time that the techniques of the old European concert of powers were becoming less effective.

Where the Unions were the most successful – establishing international communication and transportation networks, industrial standards, rules for intellectual property, trade in nonagricultural goods, and a public health regime – every part of the formula for success came into play. The Unions provided services to domestic interests –

everything from the international telegraph system to means for identifying infectious disease. They discovered, promoted, and monitored compliance with norms to which almost all European states were willing to adhere – everything from the rules that limited the liability of national postal systems to those that defined the form in which trade statistics should be collected. And, as a result, state action in accordance with those norms – everything from operating national railroads as part of the continental network to rigorously adhering to published tariffs schedules and customs formalities – shaped the expectations of the industrialists and investors who ushered in the Second Industrial Revolution.

4

THE SECOND INDUSTRIAL REVOLUTION AND THE GREAT WAR

Keynes's contemporary, Rose Macaulay, shared none of his nostalgia for the prewar world. In *Told by an Idiot* (1923), her novel of middle-class life from the 1880s to the 1920s, her narrator complains that the years before the war "are now generally thought of as gay, as very happy, hectic, whirling butterfly years," but "this is a delusion. Those years only seem especially gay to us because, since July, 1914, the years have not been gay at all" (Macaulay 1983a: 263). Nevertheless, Macaulay's ironic portrait makes it clear that even if the years before the war were far from utopian, they were not quite the run of "quite ordinary years" that her narrator recalls. The period was one unprecedented invention, both technological and institutional. Giant industrial firms and huge state bureaucracies first appeared both in Europe and the United States. In Europe they were joined by the Public International Unions, the institutions that had been inspired by the earlier American example.

Nevertheless, Europe after 1880 did not follow the same path that the United States (or Germany, for that matter) had used to enter the railway age. The continent did not become a cohesive economic union under a sovereign central government. Yet Europe did experience the next industrial transformation, the Second Industrial Revolution, marching in step with the more united continent across the Atlantic. But Europe's lack of unity assured that the continent would end this new industrial era in a conflict even more brutal than the American Civil War.

From the Railway Age to the First Age of Mass Production

In the United States the next industrial wave, the Second Industrial Revolution, depended on two things that the railroads had helped provide: a readily accessible continent-wide market, and the modern form of professional, bureaucratic business management (Chandler 1962, 1977; Yates 1989). The firms that best exploited the new continental market were those with the highest rates of *throughput*, the conversion of raw materials into sold products. To maximize throughput a firm needed complex systems for learning about the changing local markets for the products it sold and for the materials it used. Not surprisingly, the firms that led the US into the Second Industrial Revolution had agents and buyers throughout the country (and, later, throughout the world) telegraphing reports and orders back to their home offices. Those firms employed the most sophisticated means of production available, continuous processes, like the meat packers' "disassembly lines" (Chandler 1977: 241; Hounshell 1984: 217–61). Many of those firms produced branded consumer goods – processed foods and household items – for mass markets (Chandler 1962: 24–7). By the turn of the century the industries that began America's Second Industrial Revolution had some of the most profitable investments around. Although the railroad boom continued after the Civil War, capital had started to move toward the newer industries before the end of the Long Depression. Chemical, electrical, and petroleum-based companies providing cheap dyes, soap, medicines, light, and fuel grew alongside the firms that processed food and tobacco.

The companies that dominated these fields were so heavily involved in processing market information and internalizing sales and service functions that they grew to an unprecedented size, comparable only to the armies and state bureaucracies of historical empires. There are some fairly straightforward economic reasons why the continental market knit together by the railroad and the telegraph provided the perfect medium for the growth of these more hierarchical institutions rather than leading to a concomitant increase in reliance on markets for coordinating economic transactions (Yates 1986); there were significant economies of scope and scale associated with every attempt to gain information about all the local markets opened by the new transportation and communication networks' and the significant economies of scale that could be achieved through mass production required huge initial investments. Large firms facilitated both.

Europe's prewar industrial system developed along similar lines. But in Europe, unlike in America, international agreements had been needed before continental rail and telegraph systems could operate and Europe's hodgepodge of trading communities – each with its own industrial standards and rules protecting intellectual property – had to be rationalized. The Public International Unions allowed European firms to expand into the large markets needed in the age of the chemical and electrical industries and even laid the groundwork for Europe to join the United States in the industrial transformations of the mid-twentieth century that created what Emma Rothschild (1973) calls the "auto-industrial age," or what many of us as children learned to call, just as appropriately, the "jet age."

Allowing the most efficient plants and firms to produce close to capacity

The major effects of what world government there was a century ago took place in two stages. The first had more to do with shaping the expectations of consumers and with *existing* industries. The second had more to do with shaping the expectations of investors who created *new* industries. Although the second of the two effects was more important in ushering in the Second Industrial Revolution, the first effect was more what John Wright and other mid nineteenth-century functionalists had expected.

I call the effect that Wright anticipated the "Owen effect" after British economist Nicholas Owen, whose 1983 study of the impact of the European Common Market on three of today's "older" industries (automobiles, trucks, and large household appliances) demonstrates the kind of welfare benefits from market integration that liberal economists have long predicted: as markets get larger, existing industries should realize greater economies of scale and costs to consumers should fall (Teitel 1975). Owen isolates the specific mechanism that realized these welfare advantages after the Treaty of Rome came into force in 1960: the most efficient firms within the European Community, those with the greatest capacity and the lowest costs, were able to supply more of the market.

Something similar happened in Europe between 1885 and 1900, beginning as soon as the physical infrastructure of the European market was in place (McPherson 1910: 143), and gaining momentum as the network of bilateral, multilateral, and, finally "global" agreements on rules of trade grew. The first evidence of this nineteenth-century Owen effect appear in the reports of disturbing new developments sent back to London by British trade consuls in the mid-1880s. This one from Palermo at the end of 1885 is typical:

> German and Swiss goods introduced through the northern land frontiers of Italy are being brought into competition with our direct trade with this island. The opening of the St Gothard tunnel [through the Alps] has facilitated German transportations which may, in the course of time, materially injure British trade, and if the Germans, by a better system of education of the lower classes and harder labour, can produce the same article cheaper than we can, the facilities of transit being equal, our trade must necessarily give way to theirs, particularly when it is fostered by commercial travellers who frequent the place. (Quoted in Hoffman 1933: 311)

Historian Ross Hoffman found 72 similar reports from British trade consuls from 1885 and early 1886 alone. France, Belgium, and the Netherlands appear along with Switzerland and Germany as countries whose products were "taking away" English markets, but more often than not Germany is singled out as the culprit. The markets most often mentioned as in jeopardy are those for iron and steel goods (43 percent of all products mentioned), key products of the railway age. Textiles, products of an even earlier era, are also significant (29 percent), as are those of other older industries that began in Britain, including railway equipment, pottery, and refined sugar.

The trade consuls sometimes mention discriminatory laws that aided Britain's competitors. Much more frequently the reports simply comment on the improving transportation links, the competitors' willingness to employ agents who know local conditions and who keep in touch by telegraph, and, most significantly, the fact that the competitors can deliver similar goods for lower prices due to their use of more efficient production processes. Many of the reports sound like the ambivalent responses of American business leaders to the Japanese penetration of US markets in the 1970s and 1980s, or, as Owen would note, like the complaints that relatively inefficient firms made to their governments after the Common Market was formed. In the nineteenth-century reports the Germans are even treated as "great imitators" who once made somewhat shoddy products based on English models, but who now, some consuls noted, made much higher quality goods, equaling or bettering anything produced in Britain. There is a lot of respectful praise of the competitor's education system and industrial discipline along with criticism for engaging in an unsportsmanlike level of state-supported competition.

Surprisingly, the consuls pay little attention to some of the key sources of German "success," the more mundane "advantages of backwardness" that Thorstein Veblen was to outline in his explanation of German economic development some 30 years later:

> Having no obsolescent equipment and no out-of-date trade connections to cloud the issue, they were also free to take over the processes of the new industry at their best and highest efficiency, rather than content themselves with compromises between the best equipment and what used to be best a few years or a few decades ago. (See Veblen 1966: 193–4)

On average, German plants in the older industries were simply more efficient than their British counterparts. That is why, other things being equal, the Germans (and the other late industrializers) could sell similar products for less. Similarly, Owen points out that the successful, welfare-enhancing firms within the Common Market tended to be those with significant recent investment in larger, more efficient plants.

The British trade consuls saw the result as an overall "loss" from Britain to Germany and the smaller industrial states of the continent, but trade statistics, and economic logic, would suggest that this was a very temporary problem. The prices of the British goods facing increased continental competition fell, but the volume and total value Britain's exports eventually grew. In 1885 the trade consuls only knew that their exports were slumping (W. Lewis 1949: 153). But between 1895 and 1913 world exports would expand at about 5 percent per year, a great increase over the much slower annual rate of about 1 percent from 1865 to 1895 (Woytinsky and Woytinsky 1955: 39). British trade grew along with the world trend. Firms that briefly enjoyed the advantages of backwardness certainly did unusually well. The iron and steel industry, for example, grew dramatically in Germany, the Low Countries, and France from 1880 to 1913 (W. Parker 1984: 59). But, the more significant to the Owen effect were the firms and private citizens who were given access to these firms' products by Europe's new infrastructure and trade regimes.

Encouraging investment in new production processes and new industries

The new larger market area also made it profitable to invest in new industries manufacturing fundamentally new products. Toward the end of the Long Depression European capital began to move from the textiles, railroads, and steels to chemicals, electrical goods, and branded consumer products – the new leading sectors of the next industrial era. As soon as the main arteries of European commerce became those that crossed national borders (even for a somewhat protectionist state like France), trade, economic growth, and the new industries became inseparable.

Alfred Chandler has long argued that the prospect of new markets provided the key incentive to invest in the new technologies and management practices that created the Second Industrial Revolution (1962: 15). Chandler links his argument to Simon Kuznets's (1971) demonstration that the leading manufacturing industries of different industrial eras make a disproportionately large contribution to economic growth (Chandler with Hikino 1990: 3–4) and to Joseph Schumpeter's theory of industrial development in which innovation holds a pride of place (see Schumpeter 1934). Like all those who have been influenced by Schumpeter (including W. W. Rostow as well as many of the economists of the social structures of accumulation and regulation schools), Chandler argues that the periodic emergence of fundamentally new lead industries has been a key dynamic of industrial societies.

Those who follow Schumpeter the most closely see periods of economic stagnation, including the Long Depression of the late nineteenth century, as points when innovation has been stymied. They note that in the depressions of 1825, 1873, and 1929 businessmen complained of a lack of useful inventions (Mensch 1979: 4). Chandler's work is agnostic about the origin of crises in capitalist economies; it is, for example, perfectly compatible with those empirical studies showing little relation between the frequency of inventions and the end of periods of rapid economic growth. Chandler's contribution has more to do with the beginning of new eras of growth. He helps explain when and why capitalists turn inventions into new products by demonstrating that the firms that introduced the new products of Second Industrial Revolution were able to do so due to the larger markets originally created by the railroads and the telegraph (Chandler 1977: 8).

The roots of Chandler's argument are as old as Adam Smith's "the Division of Labour is limited by the Extent of the Market." As larger markets are brought within the reach of individual centers of manufacturing, it becomes increasingly rational for investors to risk the large amounts of capital needed to establish new industries. Big investments finance the research and development needed to use new technologies of production and enable firms to establish and maintain the marketing and servicing departments needed to convince consumers to want and use fundamentally new products (Pinder 1965: 246). Chandler calls those who initially see the rationale for these necessary big investments "first movers" and he shows that they are apt to gain enormous competitive advantages over any firms entering a new industry later. First movers tend to dominate new lead industries for as long as they provide a major impetus to economic growth (Chandler with Hikino 1990: 34–6).

When larger markets convince first movers to create new industries we have what I call the "Chandler effect." International institutions can contribute to the Chandler effect by linking transportation and communication networks and by breaking down those legal barriers between countries that would make it difficult to realize profits in the new industry. The Public International Unions did both these quite successfully.

Late nineteenth-century Europe was a place of massive investments in new, capital-intensive enterprises linked to international trade (Zimmerman 1917: 92; Lippincott 1936: 11; Caron 1974: 110), although some of this new investment went into overseas enterprises that made little contribution to the Second Industrial Revolution. Woytinsky and Woytinsky provide an illuminating caricature of the proclivities of the different national communities of overseas investors at the turn of the century (1955: 189–94). French financiers preferred colonial enterprises that promised immediate and high returns, like the Congo River ivory trade depicted in Joseph Conrad's *Heart of Darkness* of 1899. The British put their money in overseas projects with greater long-term potential, like the railroads and water projects they built in the Andes and the American West. Germans bought the government bonds of neighboring nations and invested in their infrastructure in order to develop markets for German industrial goods. The Americans, however, concentrated their multinational investment in manufacturing itself, and much of that investment was in Europe.

A few American firms – notably the sewing machine manufacturer Singer, and the innovator in canned milk and processed cheese, Borden – became models for some of Europe's first movers (Chandler 1980; Schiff 1971: 101–2). In fact, the European food processors that arose to serve the continental market – like Switzerland's Nestlé, founded in 1878, Maggi founded in 1883, and Knorr, founded in 1907 – proved more successful than their American model.

Most of Europe's first indigenous multinational firms also arose to serve the new continental market, firms like Unilever, formed by the merger of two Dutch margarine firms with the British Lever Brothers

(Chandler 1976: 44–5). Strikingly, the "British" firms that were the most successful in the new turn-of-the-century industries were those worked in partnership with owners on the continent, including Shell, the British-Dutch petroleum firm, and Nobel Explosives, which joined four German firms in 1886 to form the Nobel-Dynamite Trusts (Chandler with Hikino 1990: 271).

In contrast, firms beginning with fewer transnational links led the Second Industrial Revolution in Germany. But, as Chandler argues,

> By the 1880s German industrialists, like those in the United States, enjoyed the benefits of a new transportation system that permitted the movement of materials and goods and messages with unprecedented regularity and speed over a continental area – the essential precondition for achieving the cost advantages of the economies of scale and scope inherent in capital-intensive high-volume technologies of production. The continental railway network . . . gave German entrepreneurs a readier access to the industrial markets of Europe than British or even French manufacturers had. (ibid. 414)

Germany's greatest advantage over the other large European industrial powers was its central location in the continent, an advantage it shared with its smaller neighbors, Switzerland and the Low Countries. Like Chicago and other cities of the upper midwest in the United States, the cities along the Ruhr and Rhine held a central position along the arteries of commerce through which the goods linked to the new industries flowed.

Not surprisingly, Germany, more than any other European power, developed along the same lines as the United States at the turn of the century (Chandler 1984: 473–503).[1] The German economy was led by the new industries that maximized throughput and by firms producing standardized products, often for mass markets. They included the electrical giants, Siemens and AEG, and the chemical companies whose "first-mover advantages gave the Germans domination of European and global markets" (Chandler with Hikino 1990: 485) in dyes, pharmaceuticals, fertilizers and other branches of the industry, as well as those firms in the older machinery and metals industries that adopted new production techniques like the electrolytic processes making it much less costly to produce aluminum, tin, copper, lead, zinc, and nickel.

The market linked together under the European transportation and communication regimes even proved important to the economic vitality of those major continental economies that were less dynamic at the turn of the century, Austria-Hungary, France, and Italy. In those countries older sectors operating in the narrower national markets remained significant sources of national wealth until the First World War (Pavan 1972; Dyas and Thanheiser 1976: 175). But those few Italian and French firms that became leaders of the newer industries – including the Italian automobile giant, Fiat, and Michelin, the French firm dominating the tire business – were even more cosmopolitan than their German, Dutch, or Swiss counterparts. And the few industrial centers of the Austro-Hungarian empire operated in the continental market through their close links to Germany (Milward and Saul 1977: 316; Katzenstein 1976: 92).

By the end of the first decade of the twentieth century every industrialized country in Europe had become home to Second Industrial Revolution firms that depended on the continental market in industrial goods created and secured by the Public International Unions. Thus in the end it was through the Chandler effect that the Unions helped create their most important constituencies within civil society: the private firms that would not have existed without the services the Unions performed. It was also through the Chandler effect that the Unions did most of they did to fulfill the liberal internationalist vision. The new industries changed the European landscape and transformed everyone's life. Electricity extended the day. Chemicals controlled disease and eased pain. Mass-marketed foods and other branded consumer products transformed the home as much as the continuous production processes transformed the workplace. And in the 20 years before the First World War all the European economies grew right along with European trade in manufactured goods, which meant they grew as rapidly or more rapidly than they ever had before (Lippincott 1936: 51; W. Lewis 1949: 153; Woytinsky and Woytinsky 1955: 39–40).

Were the Unions Really Necessary?

In sum, turn-of-the-century Europe followed the same path as the US because international agreements designed to secure a more cosmopolitan civil society extended the market in which private firms could operate. Profit-seeking capitalists, realizing the potential of new markets, invested in new plants, new production processes, and new industries that would not have been profitable if they had been confined in the smaller national or regional markets. The size of the market changed industry, it changed the division of labor within factories, regions, and the world, and it lead to unprecedented prosperity. Or did it?

The size of markets might not matter

To those of us who first learned something about economics in the 1960s or 1970s Chandler's argument that market size played a key role in the Second Industrial Revolution initially may seem surprising. For quite some time economists neglected the role that market size or economies of scale at the level of the plant, the firm, or the industry might play in significant economic changes, despite the fundamental role attributed to larger markets and to the increasing efficiency of technologies of production (especially the division of labor within factories) by Adam Smith. Paul Krugman, one of the trade economists who have recently revolutionized the field by developing ways to incorporate assumptions about increasing returns to scale into mathematical models of trade and the diffusion of industry, believes that the main reason for this neglect was that such effects are "difficult to model formally. Since economics as practiced in the English-speaking world is strongly oriented toward mathematical models, any economic argument that has not been expressed in that form tends to remain invisible" (Krugman 1990b: 3)

If the problem were only one of ideas that could not be expressed the way academic economists like to hear them, it should not detain us. Unfortunately, at the same time that the limitations of their models made it hard for economists to say much about the effects of scale, important empirical work appeared that cast doubt on Smith's original conclusion.

The relevant studies usually focused on policy questions about the size of nations and economic development. Would a widened Common Market be necessary for Europe to "catch up" to the United States? Must the less industrialized countries have a certain market size (larger than most now have) in order to have certain industries? A symposium conducted by E. A. Robinson (1963) on the economic consequences of the size of nations did not support various arguments about the benefits of large nations or customs unions. Robinson argued that outside of a few exceptional industries, most technical economies of scale that engineers can identify are exhausted by plants of a very small size (p. xvii). Similarly, in a 1976 discussion among business historians who were familiar with the economists' findings, Jeremy Atack reported findings that economies of scale at the plant level may have played no role in the development of the businesses that contributed the most to American economic growth, at least in the 1850s and 1860s (Weiss 1976), that is, before the Second Industrial Revolution.

Nevertheless, at the same workshop Mary Yeager pointed out that a great deal of the economists' research did not bear on the business historians' arguments. The historians were searching for correlates of "bigness" of a variety of sorts: big companies, big plants, big investments, all of which came together in the Second Industrial Revolution. Chandler's argument about growth industries in the Second Industrial Revolution was ultimately one about big investments, the investments of the "first movers" in new industries who exploited all the opportunities available within the markets. Many of the industries of the Second Industrial Revolution turn out to be among those "few" that the Robinson symposium indicates require a fairly substantial plant to achieve all the possible engineering economies of scale, and thus they require a very large market in which to sell the abundance of goods that the plants could create. But it is even more important that *all* the industries of the Second Industrial Revolution required substantial initial investments – not just in plants, but in suppliers, service, marketing, and research and development. Success in any of the industries of the Second Industrial Revolution required maximum throughput in order to pay off the large initial investment. That is what made market size so important.

Not surprisingly, then, for every empirical study that indicates some aspect of the argument linking market size to economic growth through economies of scope and scale, there is at least one that leads to the opposite conclusion. Preinvestment studies indicate that significant economies of scale typified the lead industires in the United States from 1890 until at least 1958 (Brown and Popkin 1962). Empirical studies investigating the effect of the size of the domestic market on the presence of *advanced* industries almost always find a strong relationship (Chenery 1960; UN 1963; Carnoy 1972); Jamaica may be able to have profitable knitting mills, but an automobile made for the Jamaican market alone would be absurdly expensive. Even in quite old and highly protected industries such as textiles, costs in a country with a small domestic market, like Canada, are much higher than they are in the much larger US (Scherer et al. 1975: 51). Similarly, a significant econometric study designed to explain world trade flows (Linneman 1966) – a study that ignored the formal trade theory of the day and tried instead to operationalize the trade and growth theories of Adam Smith, Kuznets (1971), and the political modernization theorists, Karl Deutsch and Alexander Eckstein (1961) – concluded that for advanced industries to evolve in a small country there must be access to a large international market, something that could be achieved through membership in a trade community.

Finally, to return to Europe at the end of the nineteenth century, it is important to remember that recovery from the Long Depression began only after the European market for industrial goods had been created. Some governments initially adopted policies aiming for recovery within the narrower confines of the national market, protection of agriculture and promotion of investment in new imperial domains, but these policies failed. High rates of growth were restored only in the mid-1890s, after the transportation system was linked and liberalization of trade in manufactured goods had begun.

Capitalists could have formed the European market by themselves

Even if the European market knit together by the Telegraph and Rail Unions was an essential precondition for the Second Industrial Revolution, it is not clear that this had to be brought about by the Unions or by any activities of government. After all, earlier in the century private capitalists had done much of the work of creating an international rail network; French financiers operated throughout the continent and British capitalists operated along the borders where the French were more reluctant to invest, creating the railways of what is today northwest France as well as the rail links between the Ruhr, Alsace, and Belgium (Henderson 1965: 54–76).

Yet private investors could not have created a European market for industrial goods by themselves. They would have failed for the same reasons that French financiers failed to standardize the rail lines they built, because national governments were already involved and they treated the issue as an issue of state. This was the case most clearly with the telegraph, which, unlike the railroads, had almost always begun as a government monopoly, something built as part of the national defense system, long before any concrete discussion of an international network emerged. As Kevin Nier and Andrew Butrica argue, even though "the world economy, to the extent that it was a unit, quickly became coordinated through the telegraph," and "market structure became essentially a telegraphic matter," the system could not have been created by the market alone. National governments could always block the building of international telegraph links if they considered them a threat to national security, "and most lines were not private in any case . . . even the British government paid for uncommercial lines in the name of defense, imperialism, and public welfare" (Nier and Butrica 1988: 216, 221). As a result, intergovernmental agreements provided the only way to coordinate an international telegraph service.

Bilateral agreements might have worked

Even if intergovernmental cooperation had to play a role in creating the European market, governments might have avoided using the fundamentally new mechanism of intergovernmental agreements administered by international bureaus. After all, some of the most important rules for operating within the continental market created by the telegraph and rail networks were negotiated bilaterally and enforced that way. For example, there was no Public International Union given the responsibility for lowering tariffs on industrial goods. Instead a series of bilateral agreements, extending back to a British-French tariff reduction agreement of 1860 (Woytinsky and Woytinsky 1955: 267), accomplished something of the same purpose in the earlier period that preceded the Long Depression.

However, in the last quarter of the nineteenth century even bilateral tariff agreements were beginning to have a significant multilateral element with the adoption of most-favored-nation (MFN) principles. When two states extend MFN status to each other this assures that any tariff concession granted to a third country is also granted to the party in the original agreement. As result, even Britain, Germany's rival, benefited enormously from Germany's 1891 decisions to adopt a conventional tariff system and to negotiate more liberal trade regimes with Austria-Hungary, Belgium, Italy, Romania, Russia, Serbia, and Switzerland. Britain had already made a series of MFN trade deals with continental governments and thus received the same concessions given to the Germans. This series of agreements provided the final innovation in international civil society needed to trigger the recovery of European trade (which had been relatively stagnant throughout the Long Depression) and the beginning of the years of unprecedented economic growth (Hoffman 1933: 103–4).

The harmonization of tariffs encouraged by MFN principles provided another way to deal with those deeper issues that gave rise to the Public International Unions and, even earlier, to the vast extensions of the European conference system. The integration of

European commerce, including links established long before the Telegraph and Rail Unions, combined with the constantly expanding scope of national administration, assured that European governments kept having more and more business to do with one another. While it is conceivable that this business could have been conducted using nothing more than the means available to Renaissance princes, the process would have been both cumbersome and costly. Even if we leave out Luxemburg, the semi-independent Nordic countries (Finland, Iceland, and Norway), and the near peripheries of Europe's industrial economy (Romania and the Balkan and Iberian peninsulas), Europe at the beginning of the Second Industrial Revolution was home to 11 industrial or industrializing powers: Austria-Hungary, Belgium, Denmark, France, Germany, Great Britain, Italy, the Netherlands, Russia, Sweden, and Switzerland. It would have needed 55 bilateral agreements to do the work of one agreement hammered out at an intergovernmental conference.

The great powers could have done it by themselves

Of course, pre-nineteenth-century tools of statecraft can lead to harmony without the bother of formal bilateral or multilateral agreements. It can be imposed by a great power. We have seen that British safety standards governed most ocean freighters and that British financial regulations played a central role in the international financial and monetary systems. Similar public–private arrangements might have unified the telegraph and rail networks and established the necessary rules for commerce in industrial goods. After all, many of the technical standards eventually employed by telephone companies around the world were those negotiated between the US's main telephone company, AT&T, and the American regulatory agency, the Federal Communication Commission (Mance 1944: 32).

Similarly, Germany played a leading role in extending the intellectual property regime to Switzerland, and Germany became the major promoter of the metric regime in the years immediately before the war by requiring the metrication of any products that entered the vast German domestic market (Halsey 1919: 150). In the early 1890s Germany also took over Britain's leading role in the negotiations to liberalize trade that finally secured the continental market.

Nevertheless, the creation of the continental market was not a matter of Prussian supremacy, nor could it have been. Germany did not take the lead in establishing the telegraph and rail regimes, even if both regimes relied on models from the *Zollverein*. And Germany could not have succeeded in imposing regimes on most of its continental partners. France may have been defeated in 1871 but it remained a continental power and one deeply distrustful of the Germans. The French moved toward linking their rail system with Germany very slowly, initially entering the rail pacts through bilateral agreements with Belgium (McPherson 1910: 144). The international character of the transportation and communication regimes, and the fact that they provided for impartial arbitration of specific disputes were necessary preconditions for French involvement.

If Germany had been a truly predominant power it would have been able to impose a continental market on the other ten key states. The Unions allowed the market to form in the real world, where the powers were more evenly balanced and suspicious. The Unions encouraged international agreement without a clash of wills. Reluctant states (France relative to the rail regime, Switzerland relative to the patent regime, Britain relative to the communications regimes) could remain outside the agreements at the beginning, but later enter when they became convinced that the agreements were in their interests. Occasionally, as in the case of the Swiss and the intellectual property regimes, an important neighbor might help convince the reluctant state that it was in its interest to be involved, but this was much more the exception than the rule.

To recap, international civil society, the realm of voluntary institutions that includes agreements among states, had to develop in order to establish and maintain a continent-wide market for industrial goods. To some extent private agreements, short of innovation-stifling monopolies, could have accomplished things that were accomplished by intergovernmental agreements. But to the extent that state interests were already involved in an issue, as in the case of the telegraph or of tariffs, intergovernmental agreement became essential. Moreover, because the nineteenth-century state fostered both the intellectual leadership and the political leadership that was needed in order for new institutions of international civil society to evolve, it is not surprising that so many of the institutions essential to Second Industrial Revolution were intergovernmental rather than private.

The similar American experience

Contemporary developments in the United States, the only other place where the Second Industrial Revolution arrived before the

First World War, help confirm that the Unions played an essential role in forming the continental market of Europe and encouraging the types of firms that made this industrial transformation possible. In the United States itself, the mix of public and private forms of regulation – the roles of those new institutions of civil society that were juridically embedded within the state and those standing outside it – differed, and intergovernmental agreements played a small, perhaps inessential, role.

In the US, private firms built the continental telegraph and rail networks. Although the telegraph network quickly became a monopoly coordinated by a single firm, Western Union (DuBoff 1983), the many separate private rail lines had to negotiate agreements on technical standards and the sharing of rolling stock similar to those brokered by the International Rail Congresses in Europe. Eventually those predictable consequences of self-regulation by businessmen that had worried liberals all the way back to the days of Smith and Kant appeared in the American rail industry. In 1887, in response to the failure of state regulation of railroad rates and services, the federal government stepped in, establishing the first major national regulatory institution of the United States, the Interstate Commerce Commission (Kolko 1965; McCraw 1984: 61). The similarity between the regulatory regimes that then developed in the US and Europe was so great that a 1910 study could conclude that their influence on rail traffic was "entirely analogous" (McPherson 1910: 147–8)

In United States, as in Europe, systems establishing industrial standards, rules of intellectual property, and rules of commerce were needed to make the transportation infrastructure useful to business. Most of these systems were simple to create in the US, where a patent system, a free internal trade regime, and the beginnings of a single monetary system had been created by the constitution of 1789. Private associations did most of the work of setting industrial standards in the US, and even if government became involved, private groups could lead, as they did in establishing a standard national time system in 1883 (Stephens 1985: 113). It took until 1918 for the Congress to pass a law endorsing the system as part of a package of measures to boost wartime efficiency.

The federal government did not even have to play much of a role in linking the US to its less industrialized trading partners in Latin America and the Pacific. American, British, and local Latin American trading interests were close enough for private businesses by themselves to assure that most of the New World adhered to the Anglo-

American system of weights and measures until the First World War (Halsey 1919: 38). The US government did take the lead in intellectual rights by promoting the inter-American patent treaty, which, not surprisingly, worked in the same way as national or imperial patent laws did in the European empires. Unlike the Berne patent regime, the inter-American treaty did not require owners of patents to work them in each country in order for them to be valid; it assured that owners (most often US firms) had complete control of their inventions throughout the New World (J. Brown 1936: 162; Ladas 1930: 756–804). For similar reasons of US predominance, the Pan-American Sanitary Organization developed a different regime for dealing with the spread of infectious diseases from the tropics than the one designed by the International Office of Public Hygiene, although the original aim, facilitating commerce, was the same (Reinsch 1911: 77).

The juridical form of the institutions encouraging the Second Industrial Revolution in the United States and Europe – whether public or private, domestic or international – turns out to be much less important than what those institutions actually did. In both Europe and the United States new institutions emerged within civil society to establish and secure larger markets for industrial goods, and they in turn encouraged the investments needed to begin the Second Industrial Revolution. Where formal empires had developed to link industrial metropoles to dependent peripheries, as was the case with the empires of European powers, national law could provide some of the necessary links, these links had to be provided by international agreements in the more informal empire of states dependent on the United States, whose empirical sovereignty ranged from that over protectorates such as Cuba (taken from the Spanish in 1898) and Panama (created in 1904 so that the US could build the canal) to the much larger, more distant, and quite independent states of the southern cone (which some economic historians would argue were part of the European trading area). Conversely, within Europe international agreements to form the market for industrial became essential; but they were unnecessary within the US. The Public International Unions became necessary to the further development of capitalist industrialism in late nineteenth-century Europe simply because the market required by the industries of the Second Industrial Revolution was larger than the domestic market of any single industrial country except the United States, and in Europe an international market of that size could not be created by private initiative alone.

Industry and the Breakdown of the Interimperial Order

Contemporary champions of the Public International Unions believed that inventions of the Second Industrial Revolution would
make an even larger market possible. Radio, the Zeppelin, and
the airplane held out the promise of rapid intercontinental trade
and a new industrial era. Liberal internationalists began anticipating
this possibility long before the new transportation and communication technologies were much more than science fiction. In the
1880s, well before Marconi discovered the principles that made
ground-to-air communication possible (1895), and well before Zeppelin launched his first rigid airship (1900) or the Wright brothers
made their first flight at Kitty Hawk (1903), the International Law
Association began designing an international air regime (Colegrove
1930: 42).

The first air conference followed the same pattern as discussions
about a radio regime. Britain refused to accept international regulation, but in 1913 Germany and France found a way to work out an air
agreement (ibid.: 50–1). Optimists imagined fulfilling Tennyson's
vision of

> the heavens filled with commerce, argosies of magic sails;
> Pilots of the purple twilight, dropping down with costly bales,
>
> . . . .
>
> the war drum throbbed no longer, and the battle flags were furled
> In the Parliament of man, the Federation of the world.

Unfortunately, business and governments were more interested in
using radio and aircraft as a part of imperial policy, as a way to
increase the value of distant possessions, and as a way to prepare for
war with other empires. In 1913 more ominous lines of *Locksley Hall*
would have been more apropos

> the heavens filled with shouting and there rained a ghastly dew.
> From the nations' airy navies grappling in the central blue.

Tennyson proved a better prophet than his contemporary, John
Wright of *Christianity and Commerce*. Most nineteenth-century liberal
internationalists could not imagine that intractable conflicts would
be generated by the wider world markets they championed. Yet
those conflicts were as much a product of the Interimperial Order as
economic Eldorado that would be mourned after the war.

Raimo Väyrynen (1983) argues that great-power wars should be seen as a converging effect of changes in economic structure, material conditions, and the cultural sources of national decision-making within a particular historical distribution of power among states and within the constraints of a particular historical system for managing great-power conflicts. In Gramsci's terms, great-power wars represent one way in which a multinational historical bloc can break down: conflicts generated by converging changes at the economic base and in the ideological superstructure (Väyrynen's "cultural contexts") lead to war when the political superstructures of the international historical bloc (the overall distribution of power among states as well as the formal and informal institutions for managing international conflict) fail to prevent it.[2]

The Second Industrial Revolution either created or exacerbated all the conflicts that led to the Great War. The dynamism of Europe's industrial economies began to threaten the old social order at the same time that the new economy created resentment on the near periphery of Europe's industrial core and uneven development among the industrial powers. All these conflicts combined to ensure that a competitive kind of official nationalism would arise in place of the benign nationalism anticipated by nineteenth-century liberals. As Europe hardened into two competitive blocs, the nineteenth-century institutions for coping with international conflicts became ineffective. Most of the cooperative institutions of international civil society simply were not designed to manage a world in which inherent conflicts of interest replaced an implicit harmony of interests; thus the Public International Unions could do little to avert the final crisis.

Lateral pressure, crises, and the arms race

The rapid economic growth that followed the Long Depression generated new demands for resources and markets, in part simply as a consequence of the greater economies of scale achieved in the new industries of the Second Industrial Revolution (cf. Gilpin 1981: 70). When French economist Henri Hauser set out in 1916 to explain the origin of the conflict among Europe's industrial powers, he began with a list of factors that could just as easily explain the Second Industrial Revolution: the rise of giant firms and the scientific organization of standardized, mass production (1918b: 17–30). Hauser's catalog of the unfortunate consequences of economic growth mirrors the list of the components of lateral pressure set out by Choucri and North (1972: 90–1): Europe's industrial powers looked outside their borders for new markets, new sites for investment, and new sources of raw materials. As the European empires extended "their interests and psychological border outward . . . the opposing perimeters of interests" began to "intersect" (ibid.: 95), both at the borders of their overseas empires and much closer to home.

At the core of the European industrial economy, and along its closest peripheries, the industrial powers came into conflict over markets for industrial goods. The Public International Unions defused some of these conflicts. For example, in the early 1880s British trade consuls frequently heard the complaint that competitors tried to pass off "low quality" continental "imitations" as "high quality" British brands (Hoffman 1933: 46–7), but that practice virtually disappeared when the trademark regime went into effect. Unfortunately, international institutions needed to manage other conflicts over markets for industrial goods had not been created. One conflict was especially severe. British and French firms persistently accused German manufacturers of dumping, of selling goods at less than a fair market price in order to drive competitors out of a market (Hauser 1918b: 85–94; Zimmerman 1917: 136).

In retrospect it seems that German dumping played only a minor role in the changing pattern of European trade before the First World War (see Hoffman 1933: 286–8), but this would have been a difficult case to prove to the British traders at the time. The kind of data they would need to accept such conclusions did not exist until after the war. Economists, industrialists, and policymakers did not agree about what constituted "dumping," or even whether such a phenomenon could exist in theory. Some of the economists who were the most critical of German trade practices, including Hauser, still suspected that many complaints about dumping could be explained by the failure of British and French competitors to adopt the management practices that had allowed large German firms to sell things so cheaply.

The International Bureau of Commercial Statistics planned to establish an authoritative definition of dumping and gather the relevant data. Unfortunately, governments only set up the bureau in 1913 and, if economists like Hauser were right, something more would have had to have been done to eliminate the source of British and French resentment. Their manufacturers would have had to learn to follow their competitors' practices of studying local preferences, employing agents who spoke local languages, and providing easy credit and reliable service after the sale (Hauser 1918b: 148–59, 188–96; Hoffman 1933: 77–93), things that British businesses, at least, had never had to do before.

The industrial nations not only competed for control over markets in which they could sell their goods, they competed over raw materials. A few sources were very close to home, for example, Spain and Sweden, major sources of iron and coal (Zimmerman 1917: 44; Milward and Saul 1977: 27). Most were more distant. By 1900 the near periphery of the European industrial economy became a site of concessionary investments – local monopolies granted to particular firms or trusts to mine resources, purchase crops, or to build railroads, roads, telegraph lines, and water systems serving the raw material exporters. At the outbreak of the war Stanford political economist Alvin Johnson (1914) argued that more than 20 years of repeated international squabbles over such concessions in North Africa, the Middle East, China, and the Balkans had doomed Europe to fight. Decades later his successors at Stanford, Nazli Choucri and Robert C. North, used more precise language to describe the general pattern these crises reflected: "Competitions and conflicts between two or more high lateral pressure countries frequently lead (through colonial or client wars, or through some combination of local and more diffused conflicts) into arms races and crises" (1972: 95).

As early as 1899 W. T. Stead had worried about British disputes over rail and road concessions with the French in North Africa and with the Russians in China. Similar logic led one of the British Foreign Office's leading experts on the Balkans and the Near East, George Young, to argue in 1913 that the Balkans would not be the site of the international crisis that would lead to war: Austria had been forced to allow Anglo-Russian support of Balkan nationality movements and that eliminated any threat posed by Austrian and German economic penetration from the peninsula. Nevertheless, he still worried about conflicts in other parts of the world, and about the effects of the Anglo–German arms race that had been fueled by years of similar crises and had been given a major boost by the Balkan wars (Young 1918: 41–2).

Rose Macaulay peppers *Told by an Idiot* with the statistics of the ever larger and more expensive battleships at the center of the British–German arms race. She has her irreverent narrator think about the appropriateness of the biblical verses used to send the British ships on their way, "They that go down to the sea in ships and occupy their business in great waters . . . reel to and fro and stagger like a drunken man: and are at their wits end" (Macaulay 1983a: 229).

Germany's decision to build a navy equal to Britain's came in the middle of a series of strategic crises over concessionary interests far from the core of the European industrial economy. Germany's decision, in turn, led to Britain's entente with France and Russia, which ended the nineteenth-century system of flexible alliances. This ensured that Austria-Hungary and Germany would be suspicious of attempts to further institutionalization of the liberal internationalist vision at the Tsar's 1907 Hague Conference. Eight years later the American journalist Walter Lippmann, then a very young utopian socialist on his way to becoming a bitter political realist, would write:

> Let me make myself clear: I do not think that Europe is fighting about any particular privilege in the Balkans or in Africa. I think she is fighting because Europe had been divided into two groups which clashed again and again over the organization of the backward parts of the world. Those clashes involved prestige, called forth national suspicions, created the armaments, and after a while no question could be settled on its merits. Each question involved the standing of the Powers, each question was a test of relative strength. Since no question could be settled, every question continued to pour its poison into the European mind and made European diplomacy incapable of preserving the peace. (1915: 125)

Liberals sometimes caricature socialists as believing that all the world conflicts can be reduced to purely economic matters, and especially to conflicts between labor and capital. Yet, as Lippmann's summation suggests, it is hard to explain the First World War in those terms alone. But it is equally hard to explain the war without thinking about interests and aspirations that originate in the world of production. While labor's struggle for democratic control of the industrial system may have played only a minor role in the etiology of the war, other conflicts – especially the conflict between the industrial system and the *ancien régime* and the conflicts associated with the uneven development of the industrial powers – played a fundamental part in the events that led to the First World War.

The ideological counterattack by the old order

Schumpeter may have overstated the case when he claimed as late as 1919 that "while the bourgeoisie can assert its interests everywhere, it 'rules' in exceptional circumstances, and then only briefly," because the state class and the old aristocracy remained one, but he hit the mark more precisely when he argued:

> Whoever seeks to understand Europe must not overlook that even today its life, its ideology, its politics, are greatly under the influence of the feudal "substance" ... This [aristocratic] quality of possessing a definite character and cast of mind as a class, this simplicity and solidity of social and spiritual position, extends their power far beyond their bases, gives them the ability to assimilate new elements, to make others serve their purposes – in a word gives them *prestige*, something to which the bourgeois, as is well known, always looks up, something with which he tends to ally himself, despite all actual conflicts. (Schumpeter 1955: 92–3)

Arno Mayer (1981: 277–8) concurs and further argues that the Long Depression convinced Europe's landed classes to choke the liberal movement in order to stem the rising powers of the industrial bourgeoisie and the working class, or at least to deflect them from a course that would inevitably lead to the end of the old order.

If we accept Mayer's view, then the titled nobility who worked to perfect the industrial system by sponsoring the Public International Unions have to be considered as atypical. Perhaps the more accurate way to look at it, and one that preserves the force of Mayer's argument, is the way the popular historian Robert Massie (1991) does in a recent account (though, unfortunately, he sometimes seems to reduce the Great War to a battle of wills between the British and German kings). Massie is very perceptive in his depiction of the battle between liberal and reactionary forces *within the minds* of men like Kaiser Wilhelm II, an aristocrat trained *both* in the cosmopolitan liberalism that made him champion the ILO and in the archaic version of nationalist *noblesse oblige* that, when combined with a very modern social Darwinism, made him glorify battle to protect his realm. As Gramsci would argue, we should not be surprised when, over time, the ideology of a person or of a class comes to converge with the interest given by the realm of production, especially when a corps of intellectuals is available to demonstrate that interest. Thus we should not be surprised that in Wilhelm, and in the European aristocracy in general, the ideology supporting the old order ultimately gained more and more of their allegiance as the industrial order increasingly threatened the *ancien régime*.

Although aristocrats certainly failed to stem the tide of industrialism and some even contributed their prestige to the creation of the continental economic system in which industry flourished, the champions of the old order did succeed in forging the coalitions blocking adjustment of European agriculture to the realities of the new technologies. Perhaps more significantly, in their own role as "intellectuals" of the bourgeoisie/aristocratic order within European states in the decades before the war, aristocrats lent their prestige to ideas that justified the continuation of their power: official nationalism and social Darwinism.

While a straightforward connection exists between official nationalism and defense of the old order, the strong link to social Darwinism may not be that clear at first glance. In the hands of turn-of-the-century apologists for the old order, Herbert Spencer's ideas provided a biological justification for social inequalities congruent both with aristocratic claims to rule through merit and with the reality of the power of blood within the old order. At the same time, social Darwinist arguments about the need to demonstrate the superiority of races and nations in international combat could justify arms races and the military services, a place where scions of the old order could still perform something akin to their old social function.

Perhaps somewhat surprisingly, many liberal internationalists embraced both social Darwinism and the official nationalism, failing to see either as ideas that "embodied and fostered the recomposition of those conservative forces in the *ancien régime* that were determined to block all further liberal and democratic advances" (Mayer 1981: 290). Thus, E. H. Carr can find Bagehot, the voice of the Cobdenite London *Economist*, arguing, "Conquest is the premium given by nature to those national characters which their national customs have made the most fit to win in war, and in most material respects those winning characters are really the best characters" (Carr 1946: 48).

Unlike Bagehot, liberal internationalists of a more critical persuasion, and Hobson in particular, recognized the economic advantages of imperialism as one source of the acceptance of social Darwinism by the bourgeoisie. Hobson anticipated Carr's argument that social Darwinism gave business interests a ready explanation for the "unfit" victims of capitalist excesses, whether abroad or at home. More recently Charles A. Jones explained the phenomenon in Britain this way:

> Cobden's dream . . . became a nightmare toward the end of the century as new attitudes toward colonial empire, enthusiasm for tariff reform, [and] mounting expenditure on armaments . . . coincided with amalgamations, concentrations of capital, the ennoblement of leading businessmen, their extraordinary prevalence among the companions of Edward VII, [and] their increasing hostility toward labour. (1987: 14)

The institutions of prewar international civil society, more especially the world organizations, did nothing to undermine the ideologies used to buttress the old order. On the contrary, as arenas in which Europe's crowned heads could exercise their *noblesse oblige* the Public International Unions simply reinforced the prestige of the old ruling elites while the rituals of international civil society – the flags, the protocol, and the nationalist pomp of every international conference – reinforced the prestige of the old order and the men who embodied it. In a world in which prestige gave power to many ideas designed to buttress the older order, champions of the new industrial system could easily lose sight of their interests, including their collective interest in averting international conflicts that would bring on a European crisis.

Resentment on the periphery

Europe's industrial core was not the only place where some elites grew resentful in the boom years before the First World War. Social movements protesting inferior treatment grew up among native business, cultural, and political elites in Ireland, Iceland, Norway, Finland, the Baltic states, Poland, the Czech and Slovak nations, Hungary, the Balkans, Persia, Armenia, Anatolia, the Arab lands, southern Italy, and Catalonia, in fact all around the core of the European industrial economy. The nationalisms that developed on Europe's near periphery became the ideologies of popular mass movements. The movements might be led by native members of the commercial bourgeoisie or, more frequently, by teachers, doctors, lawyers, and other professionals, but they reached far down into society, proclaiming an aspiration to statehood for a community that was not limited by class. In that sense, they were similar to earlier popular nationalist movements that had developed at the core of the European empires.

These movements grew out of the fundamental conflicts that emerge with the geographical extension of the industrial system, sometimes uniting social forces protesting the loss of the preindustrial social order with elites resenting the incomplete penetration of the new order. In some cases the movements on the periphery protested use of the region as a pawn in great-power games involving concessionary interests. Perhaps even more often, the movements themselves attempted to become clients of one of the industrial powers as part of a strategy of national liberation, helping provoke many of the crises between 1890 and 1914 (see Johnson 1914). This continued a pattern typical in Europe throughout the entire century after the Napoleonic wars, when conflicts over state creation were a major proximate cause of small wars among the great powers (Holsti 1991: 145–7).

Those nineteenth-century social analysts who were the most deeply indebted to Adam Smith had a great deal of difficulty understanding why this happened; they constantly anticipated the end of petty nationalism and treated it as a throwback to an earlier social form. Marx and Engels, who fully embraced Smith's view of the interconnection between advances in the means of production and the creation of larger and larger economic units, wrote contemptuously of "small 'would-be' nations like the Danes, the Dutch, the Belgians, and the Swiss" (Kissin 1988: 14), let alone the Norwegians, Czechs, Slovaks, or Serbs. On the right, Gustav Cohn, a follower of List (a man who, of course, agreed with Smith about the limited economic viability of small, closed nations), wrote in 1885 that eventually a single global economy would be necessary in order to realize all possible economies of scale, but that "everything to which humanity aspires . . . is at this point already [*zunächst einmal*] achieved for a significant fraction of humanity, i.e., for 30–60 millions . . . it follows that the future of the civilized world will, for a long time to come, take the form of the creation of large states [*Grossstaatenbuilding*]" (quoted in Hobsbawm 1990: 31). For those of Smith's followers who clove most closely to his original liberal line, nationalism, as benign as it might be, was merely a temporary "phase in human evolution . . . from the small group to the . . . unified world of the future" (ibid.: 38).

Nonetheless, not even Europe's largest nations fulfilled the liberal promise. Uneven development within and across nations highlighted older geographic boundaries of privilege. Norwegian businessmen or Irish teachers could easily come to imagine a better future within the boundaries of their ancient, almost mythical,[3] nations than the one promised to them as citizens of Sweden or the United Kingdom, no matter how industrialized and prosperous the larger state became. In Czechoslovakia or Catalonia the issues were a little different; there regional leaders could imagine surging ahead of other parts of the empire if they could build closer links to Europe's dynamic industrial centers, links prevented by the archaic governments in Vienna and Madrid. In either situation, the aspiration to national liberation was far from unreasonable, even if it was only a second- or third-best alternative to the global economy anticipated by liberal internationalists as well as by many of their critics on both the right and the left.

In many ways the institutions of turn-of-the-century international civil society reinforced the new nationalism along Europe's near peripheries. As new nation-states appeared, their citizens and leaders found recognition and welcome in international conferences, international exhibitions, and the modern Olympic movement. Formal diplomatic recognition was hardly a prerequisite for recognition of nationalist movements by private international associations. For example, in order to increase the interesting diversity at the 1900 Paris Exhibition the organizers invited pavilions from a host of nations that were not yet independent, requiring only that the pavilion be designed by local architects in the "national style." In fact, Finnish architects created the most celebrated building, and in designing it they solidified the "national romantic" style, an architectural movement that became a focal point of the Finnish nationalist agitation (Hausen et al. 1990: 32–3). The Nobel prizes to Norway's Björnstjerne Björnson in 1903, Poland's Henryk Sienkiewicz in 1905, and India's Rabindranath Tagore in 1913 played a similar role; the Swedish Nobel committee even rather pointedly passed over the more radical and internationalist Ibsen in favor of the more romantically nationalist playwright from their neighboring dependency.

Of course, few of the conflicts on the near periphery of Europe's industrial empires were resolved as amicably as the one between Norway and Sweden. The conflicts to the south and east contributed to international crises, to the interimperial arms race, and, ultimately, to the Great War itself.

Uneven development and growing resentment among the powers

There is no inherent reason why crises and arms races should inevitably lead to war or even why they should when champions of an older, threatened order that glorified battle are placed in positions of prestige and power in all the states involved. However, the crises preceding the First World War occurred in a context in which the leaders of Germany, "an aspiring, but still somewhat weaker or less prestigious power," became convinced that the country was " 'encircled' by rivals" (Choucri and North 1972: 95). The underlying structure of power within the European system had changed. Germany's more rapid industrial growth gave its leaders a rational incentive to try to change the rules of the continental political system (Gilpin 1981: 156–210; Väyrynen 1983: 398–401). At the same time, Germany's relative rise made Europe's other great industrial powers, the

British and the French, equally resentful and firmly committed to the status quo.

Economic historians describe prewar Germany as dominating most of the leading sectors of the Second Industrial Revolution. By 1913 the two German electrical giants held impregnable positions in electrical manufacturing (Milward and Saul 1977: 36). German chemical firms controled most branches of that industry. In the newest machine-based industries (producing automobiles, airships, etc.), Germany faced stiff competition and market restrictions as competing states tried to protect their own infant industries (ibid.: 40). But it was only in the mass marketing of processed foods and domestic products that Germany played a clearly subordinate role.

In terms of the etiology of the war what matters most is that Germany rather suddenly replaced Britain as the major trading partner in Europe's industrial core (see figure 4). German exports gained a decisive edge in the Low Countries, in Russia, and in Scandinavia between 1895 and 1900. By 1906 Germany sold as much as Britain did to Italy and by 1910 Germany equaled Britain's exports to France. Even in the much less important markets on the immediate periphery of industrial core, German competition was stiff. German exports to the Balkans began exceeding those of the British in 1903 or 1904. Only in the Iberian peninsula, with its long dependence on British manufacturing, were the Germans unsuccessful (Hoffman 1933: 120, 130).

Germany's relative success was in part the legacy of List's nationalist industrial policy.[4] Italy, Europe's other large, recently unified, centrally located, and late industrializing nation did not have a similar mercantile era and failed to enter the Second Industrial Revolution as quickly or as completely. After forming a customs union in 1861, Italy maintained a low tariff regime until 1878. Milward and Saul argue that "misguided political liberals" kept the country relatively backward, although short periods of high tariffs and strong internal policies promoting industrialization led to spurts of industrial growth (1977: 252). Chandler's former student, Robert Pavan, agrees, but argues that Italy's brief periods of nationalist economic policy between 1878 and 1898 made it possible for the major firms in steel, machinery, chemicals, and automobiles to establish themselves. They grew in response to continental demand under the post-1898 free trade policy and then flourished after 1914 (Pavan 1972: pt 2, 11–13).

France, Germany's only other potential rival as the leading industrial economy on the continent, followed policies that would have been more effective for Italy. France had already passed through that

To Belgium and the Netherlands

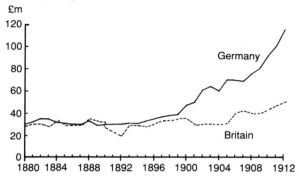

To Russia and Scandinavia

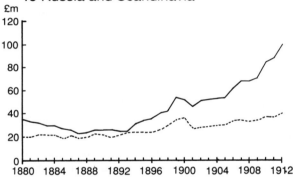

To France and Italy

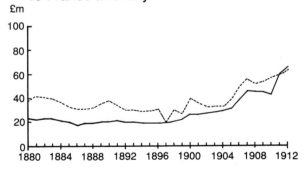

FIGURE 4 Germany surpasses Britain in the export trade (exports for consumption in importing country, 1880–1912; data from Hoffman 1933: 115–35)

early stage of industrialization when List's economics seems to be the most appropriate. Nonetheless, French leaders believed that this kind of policy was essential because the Franco–Prussian war had deprived the country of its industrial base (Lippincott 1936: 157). At the start of the Long Depression, France had retreated behind tariff walls and the government initiated a national economic policy supporting cartels and a "negotiated market" system which did not encourage firms to develop the kind of marketing, purchasing, research, and product development capabilities that characterized the Second Industrial Revolution corporations in the United States and Germany (Dyas and Thanheiser 1976: 175, 264). Before the war French exports remained focused on colonies and other markets where they faced little competition. The new industries of the Second Industrial Revolution that France did develop were ones where firms embraced the competitive continental market (Milward and Saul 1977: 124) and followed modern business practices similar to those used by their foreign competitors. These companies may have led France out of the Long Depression (ibid.: 79) but, as Henri Hauser lamented, such firms were the exception rather than the rule. The reliance of most French firms on the national and colonial market made it possible for Germany to displace France as the most powerful continental economy between 1870 and 1914, and for average incomes in Germany to top those in France as well (ibid.: 17).

British industry followed a similar trajectory. Patrick McGowan, following Eric Hobsbawm, argues that when the world economy shifted in an increasingly competitive direction in the 1890s British capitalists had two possible ways of responding. They could renovate their industrial plant and meet the Germans head-on, or they could redirect investment toward the colonies and other areas where Britain's historical advantages still counted (McGowan with Kordan 1981: 56). Derek Channon, who completed the first comprehensive study of British industrial development following Chandler's methods, demonstrates that British firms tended to follow the second strategy by expanding trade in Britain's dominions and colonies, where German firms could not compete, but where British firms could not learn the lessons that were important to the Second Industrial Revolution (1973: 19).

Hobsbawm explains that British capitalists were in an enviable position in responding to the German challenge. They "did not have to compete but could evade" competition and still profit for decades (quoted in McGowan and Kordan 1981: 56). In a habit-driven world, that possibility in itself is enough to explain Germany's relative rise:

Capitalist economies do not have an automatic bias toward innovation. They have a bias only toward profit and will continue along well-known paths if such a strategy continues to yield satisfactory profits. The formal and informal British Empire of the 1870s made such evasion possible. The Empire expanded after 1880 as well, in our view, to permit continued evasion. (McGowan with Kordan: 1981)

McGowan's empirical work supports Hobson's original argument about "the economic taproot of imperialism" and its continuing significance in Britain even after the post-Depression boom opened alternative sources of remunerative investment. The dean of British business historians, Leslie Hannah, even repeats Hobson's conclusion to explain why German and American capitalists (who should be just as habit driven as the British) would find it easier to invest in the new industries of the Second Industrial Revolution: the history of relatively high wages in the US and the rising trend of wages and the expansion of the welfare state in Germany made large investment in the production of goods for mass consumption appear more rational there (1976: 200). But it is equally true that German and American firms did not have the same access to captive markets that the British had: German Tanganyika hardly provided the same sorts of opportunities for trade as British India.

Even if we can explain Germany's relative rise as an aggregate consequence of a large number of perfectly reasonable decisions by European investors, it did not seem that way to many Europeans at the time, especially to those French and British firms that felt they had lost "their" markets. Most contemporary observers wanted to assign blame for the outcome and few followed the examples of the British trade consuls and Henri Hauser in criticizing the practices of British and French firms as well as those of their German competitors. The memory of half a century of German economic nationalism, as well as the continuing reality of a German commercial policy that was a good deal more coherent than that of its European competitors, gave British and French industrial associations and their popular press all the grounds they felt they needed for arguing that Germany's rise was the consequence of a venality inherent in the German state and the German people.

The Failure of Global Governance

In 1906 the London *Times* supported the entente with Russia and France with social Darwinist arguments and with the geopolitical theories of America's Captain Mahan: it had become a matter of life and death for Britain to retain its one remaining sphere of economic supremacy, its "preponderant maritime commerce," which was threatened by the German decision to expand its navy (Hoffman 1933: 301). A year later *The Times* would call the Second Hague Conference "a sham" and hope that there would be "no repetition of the strange and humiliating performance just ended," a view that the chief American delegate found "mysterious" (Choate 1913: 55–6). German officials saw no enigma. German rejection of attempts to extend compulsory arbitration along with most other intergovernmental means to resolve its increasingly frequent disputes with Britain was simply a necessary response to Britain's militant defense of its economic supremacy. In 1910 the German trade representative in London reported that "anti-German feeling is so strong that it is scarcely possible to discuss matters with one's oldest friends because the people over here have turned mad and talk of nothing but the next war and the protective policy of the future" (Hoffman 1933: 292).

The same could have been said about anti-British feeling in Germany. Even German liberals like Max Weber began to write about the international system as a site of unrelenting Darwinian struggle (Mayer 1981: 297–8). It became commonplace for German intellectuals to assume that Britain had only professed belief in international laissez faire when it suited British interests; that is, in cases where Germany could not compete. By early 1914 the less liberal men than Weber who were the ideological voice of the old order were arguing that Germany was "compelled" to force open "markets for our growing industries" because it was surrounded by economic and moral inferiors, especially the British, who "may not yet have made the decision to attack us; but it doubtless wishes, by all and every means, even the most extreme, to hinder every further expansion of German international influence" (Bernhardi 1918: 24).

This was not the atmosphere in which agreement on new international institutions for managing great-power conflict was likely. None of powers were anxious to attend a third Hague Conference, planned for 1914, and nongovernmental peace movements proved just as unsuccessful. Uneven development ultimately assured that even the most powerful labor movements would join the clamor for war, reversing decades of strict internationalism. In 1870, August Bebel's labor internationalism had been so strong that he opposed the Franco–Prussian war even though Marx and Engels still sided with "progressive" Germany (Macht 1980: 73). But by 1914 Bebel, and the vast majority of Germany's parliamentary socialists, had come to equate the fate of socialism with that of their nation; both had to be saved from "tsarist Russia . . . the greatest of all possible evils for world socialism" (Kissin 1988: 169). As Martin Peterson demonstrates, in country after country nationalism gained command over labor due to fears about one particular enemy (1980: 67): Russia (for Germans and Austrians) or Germany (for the Belgians, British, and French). Labor leaders argued that the enemy state was "subject to barbarian rule" and, should it emerge victorious, it would wipe out labor's gains in the vanquished nations. These antagonistic mirror images doomed the years of effort to avert the conflict by labor's international peace movement and the efforts of its allies in the women's and businessmen's peace movements that had emerged right before the war.

Even if the newer peace movements had begun their work years earlier, a final consideration of the American case suggests that they may not have been able to establish international institutions in which the underlying conflicts of the Interimperial Order could have been resolved short of war. Richard Bensel (1990) argues that a dominant theme in American political history has been the competition between the Boston–New York trading area and its rival, a trading area that originated in the cotton and tobacco regions of the American South. The conflict might be considered analogous to the rivalry between the early-industrializing Atlantic-oriented British economy and the later-industrializing, continent-focused German economy. Between 1890 and 1945 the American division created a regionally structured party system, shaped the Populist response to the Second Industrial Revolution, and lay just beneath the surface of the fragile New Deal coalition. From 1914 to 1945 the analogous European division split the continent apart.

The American international lawyers who attended the Hague Conferences and later promoted the League liked to argue that the difference between the American and European responses to the pressures of the Second Industrial Revolution was mostly a matter of the sagacity of the American federal constitutions, a view that overlooked the comparatively recent horror of the American Civil War, a true war of the industrial age and the only real prototype for the world wars. It may be wiser to look for the explanation for the relatively calm American response to the Second Industrial Revolution in one of the outcomes of that war, the defeat of the economic system championed by the American Confederacy and the subsequent reconstruction of a unitary industrial economy, which is the focus of Bensel's analysis.

The military defeat of the South ended an economy that had grown alongside the industrial order and had challenged its domination just as the world wars ended Europe's old order. Of course, the slave economy of the American South and Europe's *ancien régime* were hardly the same. If nothing else, the *ancien régime* was never confined to one part of the continent. Moreover, its ultimate champion, Germany, was also the site of what was arguably Europe's most advanced industrial order. Nonetheless, both the slave economy and Europe's old order were coherent economic systems with their own dominant classes and ideologies that differed from, and ultimately were antagonistic to, the dominant classes and ideologies of the industrial system. Both in Europe before the world wars and in the US before 1860 the dominant class of the preindustrial economy was powerful enough to have to be included in the alliance at the core of any stable social order. In hindsight, the great wars of the industrial age appear to have been about destroying that power. Even if not by the original design of the leaders of the Union, the American Civil War defeated the slaveholders of the South and destroyed the slave economy, just as, even if not by the original design of Britain and her allies, the First World War destroyed the material base of Europe's old order and the Second World War destroyed the power of its ideas.

In both the European and American cases, the peace created the first opportunity for the absolute supremacy of the industrial system. In the American case, reconstruction involved the building of a powerful continental state and the further articulation of the myriad connections within civil society that would link North and South and transform a fundamental, organic conflict between different economic systems into the more manageable conflict that continues between two economic centers of a unified industrial order. The victors in Europe – Britain and her allies – were not in a position to create such a state, yet they had to pull together an even larger world, one that included the United States, the greatest victor in Europe's civil wars. Lincoln's successors – Wilson, Roosevelt, and Truman – faced a task that was even more daunting than his. To succeed, they had to combine the tools he had used with those advocated by his old colleague, the early functionalist John Wright. And the result was a closer approximation to a full realization of Wright's vision than anything the builders of the Public International Unions had achieved when the similar task was theirs.

5

LIBERAL LEARNING AND THE
FREE WORLD ORDER

In April of 1917, Woodrow Wilson – moved by elite sympathy for Britain and by a wider public's outrage over German attacks on civilian ships – sent his armies to break the European stalemate. The US replaced Russia – already in the midst of its year of revolution – as Britain's key ally, joining the Entente with Belgium, France, and Italy, tipping the balance against Germany to such an extent that the president was soon on his way to Versailles to make the imperfect peace.

Books on international organization often make too much of the result. They reflect the promise of the League of Nations that brought millions into the street of London, Rome, and Paris to hail Wilson as "the Prince of Peace." While political scientists may make too much of both the initial hope and the later disappointment of the League era, economic historians are apt to pay it too little attention, treating it as an unimportant interval between the liberal hegemonies of Britain and the United States. But we are bound to misunderstand the postwar world order if we try, as William Parker puts it, to "remove the interwar decades like a piece of leaky pipe from the plumbing of history" (1984: 11).

The interwar period was one of frenzied economic speculation and then the Great Depression, a time both of radical politics and of uncommonly conservative governments. At the international level it was a time of experiments, a time when governments tested new forms of imperial conquest and multilateral cooperation, and a time when governments had to learn to let world organizations do more than they ever had before.

That learning continued into the Second World War and throughout the UN era, at least until the early 1970s, when another world order crisis began to loom. A catalog of the agencies of the League and

UN systems tells part of the story (table 6). Many of the major world organizations of 1970 were the successors of failed agencies of the League era. In other cases the global IGOs of 1970 carried out tasks that were not even discussed at Versailles: supporting economic development and facilitating international cooperation in public finance.

TABLE 6 New world organizations of the League and UN eras (established from 1919 through 1970)

FOSTERING INDUSTRY

Infrastructure
1919   Commission of Aerial Navigation
1920   International Institute of Refrigeration
1925   Telegraph and Telephone Consultative Committee
1926   Committee of Experts on Air Questions
1927   Radio Consultative Committee
. . . .
1944   ICAO
1947   International Frequency Registration Board
1948   International Maritime Consultative Organization
1957   Consultative Council for Postal Studies
1964   Intelsat

Industrial standards and intellectual property
1926   Federation of Standardizing Societies
1934   International Commission for Food Industries
. . . .
1944   UN Standards Committee
1946   ISO
1952   International Copyright Committee
1955   International Organization of Legal Metrology
1961   Union for Protection of New Plants
1962   FAO/WHO Codex Alimentarius Commission
1967   WIPO

Trade
1919   International Institute of Commerce
1931   International Exhibition Bureau
. . . .
1948   GATT
1950   Customs Cooperation Council
1964   International Trade Center

Management
1925   International Management Institute

MANAGING POTENTIAL SOCIAL CONFLICTS

Labor
1919   International Labor Organization
. . . .

1959   Occupational Safety and Health Centre
1960   International Institute of Labor Studies
1963   Center for Vocational Training

Agriculture
1924   International Office of Epizootics
1924   International Vine and Wine Office
1939   International Cotton Advisory Committee
. . . .
1944   International Rubber Study Group
1945   FAO
1947   International Waterfowl Research Bureau
1947   International Wool Study Group
1946   International Whaling Commission
1948   International Rice Commission
1948   International Sericultural Commission
1949   International Wheat Council
1950   International Olive Oil Council
1951   Council for Appellations of Origin of Cheeses
1958   International Sugar Organization
1962   International Coffee Organization

Other older sectors
1956   International Tin Council
1959   International Lead and Zinc Study Group

LDCs
1945   World Bank
1946   UNICEF
1955   Economic Development Institute
1956   International Finance Corporation
1957   Special UN Fund for Development
1958   Center for Preservation of Cultural Property
1960   International Development Association
1962   International Secretariat for Volunteer Service
1963   World Food Program
1964   UNCTAD
1965   UNDP
1966   Center for Settlement of Investment Disputes
1966   UN Capital Development Fund
1967   UN Industrial Development Organization
1968   WHO Center for Community Water Supply
1969   UN Fund for Population Activities
1970   International Investment Bank

STRENGTHENING STATES AND THE STATE SYSTEM

Public order and administration
1923   Interpol
1926   International Diplomatic Academy
. . . .
1963   UN Institute for Training and Research
1968   Council for Data Processing in Government
1968   UN Social Defense Research Institute

Public finance
1930   Bank for International Settlements
. . . .
1945   IMF

Managing interstate conflicts
1920   League of Nations
1920   Permanent Court of International Justice
. . . .
1945   UN
1945   International Court of Justice
1956   IAEA
1970   International Nuclear Information System

Refugees
1939   Intergovernmental Committee on Refugees
. . . .
1943   UN Relief and Rehabilitation Administration
1946   International Refugee Organization
1950   UN Relief and Works Agency (Palestine)
1951   UNHCR
1951   Intergovernmental Committee for European Migration

STRENGTHENING SOCIETY

Human rights
1926   International Institute for Private Law
. . . .
1945   UN Human Rights Commission
1967   UN Center Against Apartheid

Relief and welfare
1927   International Relief Union
1931   International Civil Defense Organization
. . . .
1950   International Children's Center
1963   UN Research Institute for Social Development

Health
1919   International Commission for Military Medicine
. . . .
1946   WHO
1955   UN Protein-Calorie Advisory Group
1961   International Narcotics Control Board
1965   International Agency for Research on Cancer

Education and research
1921   International Hydrographic Organization
1925   International Bureau of Education
1925   International Institute of Intellectual Cooperation
. . . .
1945   UNESCO
1946   World Meteorological Organization

1951   UNESCO Institute for Education
1960   International Oceanographic Commission
1963   International Institute for Educational Planning
1970   International Center for Theoretical Physics

Ellipses divide the League from the UN era.

The new functions reflect five deeper lessons that had to be learned in the creation of the Free World Order. First, governments had to learn to trust new intellectual leaders, not the liberal fundamentalists who were in ascendance in the 1920s, but intellectuals who continued the critical tradition of which the public systems builders had been a part. Second, these intellectual leaders had to learn to work for a social order that was more *inclusive* than both the failed Interimperial Order and the world envisioned by the liberal fundamentalists of the 1920s, a social order that included both the working class within the industrial world and mobilized LDC elites. In contrast, third, the architects and builders of the postwar world also had to learn to be more *exclusive* than the interwar liberal fundamentalists had been; they had to exclude the ideas underlying the fascist world order. The failure to contain fascist expansion in the 1930s gave rise to the fourth and fifth lessons that needed to be learned before the Free World Order would stand. Unlike so many of the intellectuals who backed the League, the designers of the postwar world order were obliged to temper their idealism and accept that there was much that world organizations could not accomplish. And, finally, the new intellectual leaders also learned to mobilize a different kind of political leadership; rather than relying solely on the philanthropic urges of individual statesmen and private citizens that had typified the political leadership of the League era, the UN's designers turned to powerful states and to the world organizations themselves.

From the League's Fundamentalists to the UN's Keynesians

Since the early 1970s many of us have come to expect that the greatest supporters of world organizations will be somewhat on the left. This was not always true. When Theodore Rossevelt proposed a League for Peace in his 1910 Nobel Prize address he energized social movements across the political spectrum. On the right were the liberal fundamentalists of the businessmen's peace movement who convened international meetings of national chambers of commerce before the war (Ridgeway 1959: 22–4) and formed national groups like the American League of Nations Association under William Howard Taft (Northedge 1986: 26–7). On the left were Britain's Union of Democratic Control of Foreign Policy led by John Hobson (D. Long 1991: 290), Leonard Woolf's Fabian Society (Woolf 1916), and the international women's peace movement led by American social activists including the pioneer of social work, Jane Addams, and Wellesley College economics professor Emily Greene Balch (Addams, et al. 1915; Balch 1918). The movements on the left shared many views with scholars who were deeply skeptical of the result at Versailles, including Thorstein Veblen and John Maynard Keynes. Keynes would become one of the most influential architects of the world organizations created after the Second World War and Balch would receive the 1946 Nobel Peace Prize for the prescience and steadfastness of the movement she had led for 30 years. But, in 1919, governments did not listen carefully to critical views like theirs.

The businessmen's peace movement

Statesmen were more apt to care about the views of fundamentalists who affirmed a simple version of the liberal myth about industry and international organization. "Awake!" one of the Boston-based World Peace Foundation's pamphlets proclaimed, "If businessmen would say the word there would be no more wars." The foundation's main benefactor, publisher Edwin Ginn, argued that it was just a matter of agreement among the men "who have shown great originality and executive ability in carrying on large business enterprises" that they are "the best of the race" (World Peace Foundation 1985: 9).

When the League of Nations first met in 1920, Social Darwinism, international law, and laissez faire remained the creed of its supporters on the right. An official history of Ginn's foundation notes that American businessmen in the 1920s believed that Herbert Spencer's theory, "in which a laissez-faire system allowed the best of the race to rise to positions of leadership and guaranteed continuous progress," had been proven in the US. Global peace and prosperity simply required institution of the American system of laissez faire on a global level, along with a world legal system like the United States's permissive constitution, "in order that Spencer's social Darwinism not simply be the struggle of the jungle" (ibid.: 13; cf. Carr 1946: 51).

Woodrow Wilson sympathized with this somewhat humanized version of the very ideology used to justify Germany's militarism. It was consistent with these views for him to veto a Japanese proposal at Versailles for a League ban on racial discrimination (Northedge 1986: 44–5) and to agree to a mandate system that distributed the German and Ottoman dependencies among the victorious powers based on the long-standing European and American "hierarchy of races" that correlated with industrial development.[1] The least "advanced" peoples, the "Bantus and Bushmen" of Africa, were deemed unlikely ever to become competent enough to govern themselves, while an "advanced" Christian, Europeanized, white business community like that of Lebanon was assumed to be almost ready for self-government.

Not surprisingly, many of the liberal fundamentalists of the 1920s believed the greatest resistance to their plan for peace would not come from disappointed peoples on the periphery of the world's industrial economies, but from the appeal of Bolshevism to the naive working-class men and women at the core who were being newly enfranchised as a partial back-payment for their sacrifices in the war. A few members of the businessmen's peace movement were so concerned that they rejected liberal fundamentalism and proposed letting the International Labor Office regulate the world economy, because, as Henry M. Robinson, president of First National Bank of Los Angeles, argued, it would be "one of the best ways of holding back Bolshevism and various forms of socialism" (Perigord 1926: xxv). Robinson typified the businessmen who would eventually be at the core of the Free World historical bloc after the Second World War. Like fellow Californian David Lubin, and unlike most of the fundamentalists, Robinson appealed more to businessmen's aspirations to lead a stable, long-lasting world order than to their immediate interest in profit.

Some influential British supporters of the League believed international institutions could be used to dampen the fire of the masses in a different way. When Gilbert Murray, one of the League's staunchest champions in Britain, became chairman of the League's Committee on Intellectual Cooperation he filled it with people who saw "parliaments, popular voting, and public opinion" as the principal sources of political disorder. These included Walter Lippmann who, having lost his youthful socialist ardor, was eager to promote the kind of mass education that would convince the general public to leave problems of state to the experts. Perhaps not surprisingly, the only member of the committee who regularly commented on the naivety of this plan was the Bengali Nobel laureate, Tagore, a man very familiar with the similar ideas underlying Britain's colonial education policies (Kolasa 1962: 45).

Failed plans for reconstruction

While the victors in the Great War accepted the new roles for multilateral cooperation to deal with dangers of democracy, they were skeptical when it came to the economic issues that had been the central concerns of the Public International Unions. Convinced by the liberal fundamentalism of their day, the Entente governments gave American, Belgian, British, French, and Italian business leaders responsibility for deciding on postwar transportation, trade, and monetary regimes at a 1919 international trade conference in Atlantic City. Even George Ridgeway, a very sympathetic chronicler of the progressive businessmen's organization eventually formed by many of those at the conference, the International Chamber of Commerce, was struck by the greed of the European conferees and the simultaneous "superficiality of early American conceptions" of reconstruction (Ridgeway 1959: 35). European plans were predicated on a "colonial-style" exploitation of the defeated powers, an idea endorsed by the 1916 intergovernmental conference that had been held before the US entered the war (ibid.: 29–34). Although the American businessmen did not accept this idea, a similarly narrow self-interest motivated what they considered essential: (1) elimination of the threats of socialism and Bolshevism; (2) abolition of European restrictions on business (in order to encourage American investment); (3) improvement of European business attitudes toward American investment; and (4) European adoption of the rational management procedures that had typified American (and German) industry before the war. In addition, most of the Americans took a fundamentalist attitude toward free trade, rejecting any compromise of international laissez faire.

A few Entente officials recognized the shortsightedness of the businessmen's prescriptions. They included Keynes and the American tariff commissioner W. S. Culbertson who noted that even the most progressive idea proposed in Atlantic City – the American proposal for strict international laissez faire – failed to address the different rates of development that had helped trigger the war. (1923: 144). Culbertson argued that national regulation of trade and investment was needed to "equalize conditions" of production even in the most modern industries where competition was certainly fruitful. Because he remained committed to Adam Smith's conclusion that trade encourages gains in productivity, Culbertson argued for international regulation to ensure that the national policies needed to equalize conditions did not just become another source of conflict, and he feared that the results of Atlantic City would be even worse than the self-interested American proposals. European plans for reconstruction won out and they would do nothing to eliminate uneven industrial development. At most, they would just reverse the order of the leaders and the laggards (Culbertson 1923: 346–8).

Keynes had even graver doubts, especially about the reparations demanded from Germany, which the European powers needed to pay back war debts to the US. The only way that the complex game of postwar sovereign debts could be ended, he argued, would be for the US to complete the circle by putting into German hands by making massive foreign investments there or by buying massive quantities of German goods. The Germans could then pay the reparations they owed to Britain and France, who would then have the money to pay the US (Kindleberger 1984: 301–9; Ridgeway 1959: 51–82). As complicated as this sounds, there was an even stickier part of the problem: the Germans were not only responsible for monetary debts, they also had to provide "reparations in kind" – specific goods that Keynes was convinced it would be physically impossible for them to produce.

Early confirmation of Keynes's fears came in 1922 when the Germans fell behind in shipping trainloads of telephone poles and coal to the European victors. In January of 1923 Belgian and French troops occupied German factories along the Ruhr to try to force deliveries. German workers went on strike and the Weimar Republic's democratic socialist government tried to help them by printing money for strike benefits, leading to an unprecedented hyperinflation.

In August of 1923 a new German chancellor, Gustav Stresemann – a business-oriented liberal – called on the French to recognize the futility of the occupation, just as he had recognized the economic hopelessness of the workers' resistance. Stresemann succeeded in bringing the French to the negotiating table by invoking a favorite solution of the League's supporters on the right: creation of an "international committee of businessmen" to decide the issues on the basis of "business principles" (Ridgeway 1959: 74–5).

Charles G. Dawes, a Chicago banker and chair of this committee, Owen D. Young, president of General Motors, Alberto Pirelli, the Italian tire magnate and a long-time leader of the International Chamber of Commerce, and others met for months and heard hundreds of suggestions. Keynes proposed that all German reparations be monetized and the US simply guarantee payment, nearly giving apoplexy to one J. P. Morgan banker (Kindleberger 1984: 302).

Ultimately, the 1924 Dawes Plan and its successor, the 1929 Young Plan, involved debt forgiveness and a substantial loan to Germany, subscribed by both public and private bankers. Under the Dawes Plan France and Belgium withdrew their forces, the German currency stabilized, and a brief economic boom and briefer era of good feeling in world politics ensued.

Unfortunately, businessmen did little to sustain the boom. Instead of making long-term productive investments, many continued to try to grab quick, easy, and ultimately unsustainable profits, a tendency not altogether surprising in the decade after a major war, when new outlets had to be found for the capital of the many private businesses that had been supplying powers. With no institutions existing to encourage investors to look to the long term, the decade after the Great War became one of widespread speculation, a decade of what Susan Strange (1986) called "casino capitalism" when referring to a similar pattern in the 1980s.

Interwar governments missed their one chance to create such institutions. The League's first economic conference in 1927 tried to convert tentative unilateral and bilateral steps toward liberalization into a treaty for multilateral tariff reductions under the most-favored-nation principle (Chalmers 1953: 23–32; Ridgeway 1959: 83–106), but the treaty received too few ratifications to come into force (Northedge 1986: 171). Some governments felt it was of little value because the US, with its many leading manufacturing industries, did not need to reduce protection as substantially as many of its potential trading partners in order to get the tariff concessions it wanted. Others wanted to continue to pursue restrictive trade practices for political reasons: the successor states east and south of Germany-aiming for economic autonomy (Berend 1974: 180), Mussolini's Italy (Pavan 1972: pt 2, 13), and the Entente governments, still hoping to gain from a predatory economic alliance against Germany.

That hope was very slow to die, as a codicil to the 1929 Young Plan on civil aviation illustrates. In a last unsuccessful attempt to reverse Germany's first-mover advantages, Entente members forgave German debts in exchange for the transfer of some German aircraft and routes to France and Belgium (Colegrove 1930: 25). Earlier the victors had barred Germany from intergovernmental air agreements and required the destruction of thousands of aircraft. But Germany still started the world's first scheduled commercial air passenger service (Gartmann 1959: 118), set up critical international routes outside the agreements, and regained its position as Europe's leading air power by 1928 (Colegrove 1930: 13, 27). Ironically, Germany's defeat had made it more able to pump money into profitable routes than the Belgians, British, French, and Italians, who continued to build money-losing links to their colonies (Thornton 1969: 8–9).

The Young Plan not only failed to cut Germany's lead in aviation, it failed to end the debt crisis and the divided market that had restricted European investment. Nevertheless, the plan did secure Keynes's reputation as a prophet. The Entente had reduced its demands for reparations to the level that Keynes had considered reasonable a decade earlier. In 1929 it was still too much, because the Great Depression had begun. With no institutions in place to encourage greater commitment, the Roaring 'Twenties could be stopped just by bursting a few speculative bubbles. The largest of these, the run-up of the New York stockmarket to the October crash, had drained savings away from capital-starved Europe at the moment when the Young Plan's tenuous system for assuring the payment of sovereign debts had required the injection of American funds (Papi 1951: 40–52).

The crash put any discussion of a larger European trading area on hold, and one American reaction, the Smoot-Hawley tariff, made new world markets even more impenetrable. The president of the German central bank, Hjalmar Schacht, resigned in 1930, protesting that world economic conditions had again made the allies' conditions unbearable. He began organizing bankers to finance the Nazis (Sampson 1981: 64). Germany defaulted in 1931, a wave of economic nationalism followed, and Hitler came to power in 1933.

Robert Lekachman pays Keynes the ultimate compliment by arguing that the rise of German fascism was a consequence of the failure to heed his advice throughout the 1920s: "Weimar democrats were saddled with the ... perpetual financial wrangle over reparations," becoming "targets of popular German dissatisfaction" when "Allied protectionism," encouraged by the plan to rely on reparations for reconstruction, and allied "economic mismanagement led directly to the huge depression which opened the doors to the Nazis and their business and military allies" (introduction to Keynes 1971).

The Depression and the ascendancy of the critical tradition

The Depression convinced the allied powers to begin accepting Keynesian advice. In doing so they delegitimated the liberal fundamentalism of the 1920s and made the critical tradition in liberal internationalism the logical place to turn for ideas about how to recreate a liberal order after the Nazis' defeat.

In the wake of the stockmarket crash financiers became even more wary of long-term commitments, but they lost their taste for speculative short-term investments, turning the 1930s into a time of hoarding – of accumulating gold, jewels, land, and risk-free securities. It became a decade of few large investments in productive enterprise, of joblessness, and that very real sort of "underconsumption" that filled the soup kitchens and lengthened the welfare lines.

Keynes decried the capitalists of the 1930s and looked for ways to convince reluctant investors to restart the idle factories, employ the idle workers, and develop the new inventions that would make it possible for mankind to be "freed of the morbid love of money to confront deeper questions of human existence – how to live wisely and agreeably and well" (Keynes 1932). The same logic that led him to propose ending the game of interwar sovereign debts by having the US guarantee German repayment, also led him to propose the "Keynesian" macroeconomic solution to the Depression: lowering interest rates and increasing government spending to spur demand and thus convince the hoarders that productive investments would be profitable.

Public system builders of the nineteenth century would have admired Keynes's proposals for both their economic and their political efficiency. Although Keynes proposed the pledging of huge sums of money to the welfare state, his proposals rarely had immediate costs. His proposals for counter cyclical macroeconomic policies relied on what Marx called "fictitious capital," credits that governments would bet on production that did not yet exist.

Marx, of course, doubted that any program for regulating the hydraulics of capitalism by priming the pump here and bleeding the excess there would work in the long run. Marx's view rested on his assumption that money ultimately had to rely on something of concrete value, a commodity like gold. Those who controlled the production and distribution of that commodity would have an incentive to undo the various financial manipulations of governments and cooperating banks no matter how public-spirited they might be, and in the end the money holders would have the power to do so as well (Harvey 1989: 107). In contrast, Keynes assumed that the value of money ultimately rested on the coercive powers of the states that enforced obligations within societies and between them. Of course, Keynes understood that there were some obligations that no level of coercion would be able to enforce, debts that were physically impossible to repay, like those imposed on Germany at the end of the Great War. But, within that constraint, Keynes and other economists of the 1930s still believed there was wide room for governments to create an institutional framework in which private capital was encouraged to move into long-term, socially productive investments.

Although subsequent events have given a great deal of credence to the Keynesian arguments, it is not difficult to understand why they were originally ignored by those who would have had to act on them in the 1930s. The liberal fundamentalist financial orthodoxy endorsed by major banks – public and private – was antithetical to the Keynesian prescriptions. Moreover, key governments initially could not act on them even if they wanted to. At the beginning of the Depression, American President Herbert Hoover complained that the US central bank, the Federal Reserve, was only a "weak reed for a nation to rely on in a time of trouble" (Greider 1987: 299). At the same time, because the US had become the world's major creditor, the responsibility for the stability of the international financial system had fallen on the US, into the laps of private American bankers, to be precise. But, as William Parker argues (1984: 221), the American banking system was not up to the global task, simply because it had evolved after the civil war to serve the national market. For more than two generations the most successful American banks had insulated themselves from overseas financial shocks. The move from that historically proven defensive strategy to the untried one of the activisim took time, and it took the shift of responsibility for the financial system from private buisness to government.

The Dawes Plan and the Young Plan were small steps along the way, but even they were still guaranteed by American private banks, not by government. Franklin Delano Roosevelt's response to the Great Depression was more significant because it signaled acceptance of government responsibility not only for the financial system, but for the health of the economy as a whole. By 1944, when the Bretton Woods Conference was convened, the US was ready to lead its allies in establishing a system of intergovernmental cooperation to forestall any cycle of grabbing and hoarding that might threaten to follow the Second World War. Keynes and Harry Dexter White of the US Treasury, true descendants of the nineteenth-century experts in government designed the Bretton Woods institutions to bolster governments carrying out Keynesian policies by insulating them from international financial shocks and loaning them the money they would need to weather some short-run challenges to an expansionary macroeconomic course.

The wartime governments all recognized that even with extensive cooperation in public finance, expansionary national macroeconomic policies would be incompatible with a world trade system organized under a fundamentalist version of laissez faire. The experience of the Depression on top of the Great War led the welfare states to accept the formula that had been proposed by Wilson's tariff commissioner: global management to harmonize national regulation of trade. Disagreement remained over the ultimate goal of global regulation, with the US State Department and some key wartime academic analysts (Mander 1941; Doman 1942) arguing Commissioner Culbertson's position that the kind of control and direction of national economic life found in the new welfare states was compatible with a predominantly laissez faire world economy (cf. Murphy 1984: 13–28).

The idea of international development assistance

Cooperation in public finance, support for refugees, and support for LDCs are three areas of activity for the UN that do not have a precedent in the Public International Unions. The fields are historically linked and Keynes's economics also inspired key innovations in supporting the LDCs, although some members of the businessmen's peace movement anticipated UN activities better than anyone in the critical tradition. While Emily Greene Balch had conceived of the idea of a "trusteeship" (rather than the idea of "mandate") as a way to pusch colonial powers toward granting independence (Abrams 1988: 143–4; Balch's 1946 Nobel lecture, see Balch 1972: 348–9), she did not treat colonial underdevelopment as a major problem. J. A. Hobson recognized the problem, but thought there was a simple solution: combine popular sovereignty with universal free trade (1915: 124).

David Lubin's long connection with the IIA gave him much more practical experience in the LDCs. He doubted that international laissez faire would be enough and advocated international assistance to industrialize nonindustrialized countries, arguing that manufacturing countries would ultimately gain from the increased demand for industrial products because prosperous agricultural nations would then be able to afford them (Agresti 1941: 193, 245, 287). Another American, William Coyne, made a similar argument for a scheme of massive loans to reconstruct Europe and develop South America. Writing in 1921 to Owen Young's predecessor as president of General Motors, Pierre S. du Pont, Coyne suggested waiving the principal when the proposed loans came due, but argued that the interest payments received and the markets for industrial goods thus created would assure that the US would be "immeasurably better off than we are today with idle farms, idle factories, idle railroads, idle shops."[2]

Neither of these businessmen's proposals had any immediate impact even on American policy. Mainstream interwar business leaders like du Pont and Young simply ignored them. The liberal fundamentalist Republican administrations of the 1920s under Warren G. Harding and Calvin Coolidge opposed any expansion of intergovernmental economic cooperation on principle. Coolidge's much more sympathetic successor, Herbert Hoover, who had organized one of the earliest international programs for reconstruction and development in the war-ravaged Soviet Union, had no room in his Depression-strapped budgets for kind of program that Coyne and Lubin proposed.

Intellectual leaders of the critical tradition revived the idea after the Second World War. One of the most prominent figures in the postwar Third World movement, Argentine economist Raul Prebisch, embraced Keynesianism in the 1930s, wrote one of the early Keynesian texts in Spanish, and convinced his government to adopt counter cyclical policies that allowed Argentina an unusual degree of industrial development throughout the Depression (Love 1980: 50–2). In the 1940s Prebisch formulated his concepts of the "core" and the "periphery" of the industrial world economy and argued that differences in the power of economic actors in the North and South would assure that an increasingly laissez-faire world economy would let the North continue to enter new industrial epochs but leave the South further and further behind (Cardoso 1977: 12–13). To counter this tendency, Prebisch argued that LDCs should be granted temporary exceptions from global liberalism (a position consistent with the long tradition that went back to Alexander Hamilton) and be given international assistance to encourage investment in industry.

The UN Relief and Rehabilitation Administration (UNRRA), the wartime IGO for refuges and the reconstruction of liberated areas, and later the Marshall Plan, provided models for such aid. In 1946 the UNRRA director, New York liberal Republican Fiorello La Guardia, urged that when European reconstruction was completed, the UN should turn its focus to the areas of the next greatest need (the war-ravaged areas of Africa and Asia), and then move on to industrializing the less industrialized regions whose poverty would remain a global problem. Echoing the interwar businessmen's peace movement, La Guardia argued that such a system would always be in the enlightened self-interest of the more advantaged nations because it would assure that there would always be new markets for the goods of the most productive, capital-rich countries. A UN development assistance system would both expand global welfare and help avoid the crises of overproduction that many still feared (Murphy 1984: 30–1). La Guardia noted that Harry Dexter White had made a similar argument about the original design for the World Bank (officially called the International Bank for *Reconstruction* and *Development*), but that final plans for the bank offered little hope to LDCs, who needed the kind of grants, low-interest loans, and technical assistance that UNRRA provided, not the bank-rate loans to be provided by the new agency (Oliver 1975: xvii).

La Guardia's grand vision never became a reality, but the rapid emergence of a Third World voting bloc within the UN and the desire of the US in the 1950s and early 1960s to keep Latin America allied in the automatic majority against the Soviet bloc assured that Prebisch would have a place to develop the intellectual leadership of the Third World movement, the UN Economic Commission for Latin America (ECLA). From ECLA and other centers within the UN system, Third World leaders proceeded to design the institutions that would fulfill part of La Guardia's vision, providing technical assistance through the UN Development Program (UNDP), creating a development wing of the World Bank – the International Development Authority (IDA), and linking issues of development and trade in the UN Conference on Trade and Development (UNCTAD), founded in 1964 – the second and last UN agency that Prebisch would design and then direct, and one of the key institutional actors in the early years of the world order crisis of the 1970s and 1980s.

A More Inclusive Social Order that Excludes Illiberal Societies

Although the Third World had to struggle for inclusion in the Free World Order, it was aided by a new bias toward inclusiveness. The capitalist victors in the Second World War reintegrated defeated societies into the liberal order instead of planning for their exploitation the way the 1919 Atlantic City conference had, and the industrialized countries institutionalized the new inclusiveness at home in the new economic system of mass consumption and in the welfare state. By 1944 all had embraced one or another version of the new "Keynesian" orthodoxy in the process of constructing new national historical blocs in response to the Depression.

A new kind nationalism linking labor and capital and a larger role for the state characterized all of the new domestic social orders.

William Parker even argues that by intensifying economic nationalism the newly powerful labor movements of the 1930s made it harder
to create a new *global* order by prolonging the Depression and de-
laying American acceptance of the role of stabilizer of the international financial system (Parker 1984: 222; cf. Borkenau 1942: 24).

Gramscians would interpret the same evidence differently: the
business-oriented liberal internationalists who had been ready for the
US to embrace global responsibilities at the beginning of the Depression needed to form a social coalition powerful enough to wrench
the government away from interests satisfied with operating within
the confines of America's smaller, post-Civil War market. Privileged
sectors of labor eventually became part of that coalition, and they
eventually embraced the internationalist vision, but they first joined
the historical bloc *qua* social alliance to secure the welfare state
policies and the concomitant economic nationalism that Parker sees
as "prolonging" the Depression (cf. Rupert 1990).

Those business-oriented liberal internationalists who anticipated
the Free World historical bloc, like the Californians Lubin and Robinson, and the prominent political scientist and early management
consultant Mary Parker Follett (1918), had emphasized the need to
balance the interests of business with those of labor. The reformed
ILO of 1919 appeared to them as a harbinger of the eventual democratic parliament of nations. Ordinary men and women, represented
by their labor federations, would have a direct voice in international
affairs. It was written into the ILO rules that women be given an
equal voice whenever issues affected them (Perigord 1926: 114). In
Geneva the headquarters of the ILO and the League were neighbors, housing staffs of comparable size (Northedge 1986: 179), sym-
bolizing this promise that the aristocrats and militarists who had led
Europe to war would be replaced by working men and women in the
social alliance with progressive capitalists that could secure a liberal
world order.

This promise would remain unfulfilled as long as labor leaders
played only a small role in designing national industrial policies.
Lubin's close friend, the American labor leader Samuel Gompers,
was able to get US legislation that reduced labor's resistance to
liberalized trade by restricting immigration in the 1920s, but little
more (Borkenau 1942: 15). The French socialists played a larger part
by helping to usher in the brief period of inter-European good
feeling in the mid-1920s, but they were given the opportunity to do
so only with the defeat of the Weimar socialists in Germany in their
attempt to aid workers who resisted the French occupation of the

Ruhr. In Britain the late 1920s boom was a time of intense industrial disputes, including the 1926 General Strike with its portent of social revolution, which solidified bourgeois opposition to the left. In Italy the boom years were marked by Mussolini's decision in November of 1926 to end the pretense of parliamentary government by banning the opposition parties and arresting Communist MPs, including Antonio Gramsci.

Fordism and the Free World

Throughout the next decade, when he was forced to be a theoretician and not an activist,[3] Gramsci pondered the ways that workers might enter the historical blocs within contemporary capitalist societies. He correctly anticipated one prospect in the system of production that was beginning to be introduced in the United States, the system he called "Fordism." Henry Ford required workers to submit to unprecedented domination by machines, something that conceivably could lead to the kind of neurotic defiance displayed by Charlie Chaplin in *Modern Times* (released in 1936). In exchange Ford paid his workers much more than competitors, whose operations were not as large, productive, and rationalized. Gramsci reflected:

> It seems possible . . . that the Ford method is [truly] rational, that is, that it should be generalised; but that a long process is needed for this, during which a change must take place in social conditions and in the way of life and habits of individuals. This, however, cannot take place through coercion alone, but only through tempering compulsion (self-discipline) with persuasion. Persuasion should also take the form of high wages, which offer the possibility of realising a standard of living which is adequate to the new methods of production and work which demand a particular degree of expenditure of muscular and nervous energy. (1971: 312)

Gramsci doubted that the interwar capitalism of grabbing and hoarding would make it easy to win the high wages and increased leisure needed to make the Fordist system a success. Nevertheless, he argued that when Ford's innovations could be generalized they would solve one of the problems that led capitalists to try to lower wages and lengthen the working day. Ford intended his wages to be high enough that his relatively unskilled workers could afford the automobiles they were making; Fordism meant both mass production and mass *consumption*. It was a solution to the problem of underconsumption that Hobson (along with a number of Marxists) had seen as the source of the earlier Long Depression and of the new imperialism.

In the 1920s and 1930s Fordism might have been a way to help sustain the brief economic recovery by averting a crisis of underconsumption, but the growing chasm between labor and capital and between left and right hardly portended an era when industrialists would learn to "temper compulsion . . . with persuasion" in order to establish a new social order. Eventually that did happen through the reinforcing moves establishing the welfare states and the many policy shifts solving the social puzzle and establishing the new national historical blocs: the victories won by wage workers in the industrial disputes of the late 1930s, the support given by Fordist industrialists to Keynesianism in order to encourage the mass consumption on which they relied, the new economic nationalism encouraged by policies aimed at protecting societies from external economic shocks, the reinforcement of that nationalism by governments trying to mobilize citizens against the fascist enemy, and the greater social cohesion demanded by the attempt to prevail in a total war.

In the United States one consequence was a shift of conservative opinion away from the hands-off attitude toward government and intergovernmental cooperation of the 1920s. By 1940 even many stalwart Republicans had embraced the idea of establishing an inclusive world social order modeled on Roosevelt's New Deal. The American journalist Clarence K. Streit found he could even enlist Henry Luce, the conservative publisher of *Time* and *Life*, behind a planned federation of "democracies" that would join the US, the British, French, Dutch and Belgium empires, Switzerland, the Nordic countries, Canada, Australia, and New Zealand (Streit 1940: vii–viii). Tens of thousands of ordinary citizens also pledged their support by sending in the postcards that Streit included with his books promoting the plan. And the Republican presidential nominee that year, Wendell Willkie, made a vision of an inclusive liberal world order the center of his campaign.

In 1943, in a clear sign of how broad-gauged the American internationalist movement had become, a group of publishers created a one-volume edition of works promoting postwar world organizations (canby 1943), covering the political spectrum from Herbert Hoover and Hugh Gibson's *The Problem of Lasting Peace*, to Willkie's more moderate *One World*, to *The World of the Four Freedoms* by Sumner Welles, who reflected the position the Roosevelt administration, to *The Century of the Common Man* by Henry Wallace, who saw himself as reflecting the progressive interests of America's industrial unions and the unemployed.

Welles (1943: 423) gave the name to the world that the wartime
leaders all hoped to create, the "Free World – the world of the Four
Freedoms" enumerated by Roosevelt in his 1942 State of the Union
Address, where he outlined the goals of the antifascist alliance, the
wartime United Nations: "Smashing ... militarism ... liberating the
subjugated nations ... and securing *freedom of speech, freedom of religion, freedom from want, and freedom from fear everywhere in the world*"
(quoted in Stern 1975: 232). In 1943 Welles continued in the same
vein, describing the kind of postwar order that Gramsci would say is
characteristic of hegemony rather than domination: "the extent prac-
ticable, the essential principles of international political and economic relations in that new world order must be agreed upon in
advance and with the full support of each of the United Nations'
(Welles 1943: 423). When the wartime allies met in the same year to
discuss postwar plans for a reformed IIA and ILO, the 1919 Atlantic
City conference's presumption in favor of business control of the
world economy had long been discarded. Initially Roosevelt conceived of the ILO as the international coordinator of macroeconomic
policies simply because its tripartite structure made it the most
democratic of the global IGOs.

The US eventually abandoned that plan in an attempt to bring the
Soviet Union into the postwar order; the USSR opposed both collective bargaining, which was championed by the interwar ILO and the
non-Communist trade unions that dominated the organization
(Luard 1982: 71; Russell with Muther 1958: 73, 170, 307–8). Contemporary functionalists, including David Mitrany and Mary Parker Follett, pointed out that in any event Roosevelt's original plan would
have required the kind of centralization that they believed had
contributed to the ineffectiveness of the League. But an ILO that
stuck to its narrower original purpose could operate on the basis of
western consensus about collective bargaining and the welfare state
and leave the coordination of macroeconomic policy to an agency
that the Soviet Union would be willing to join (Luard 1982: 38).

Given the shift away from the vision of the ILO as the Free World's
primary international economic coordinator, the 1944 Bretton Woods
Conference on cooperation in public finance became the forum in
which that inclusive organization would have to be created. There
the US began advocating a powerful economic council of technical
experts "to keep the varied international economic activities consist-
ently in line with policies conducive to sustained and high levels of
economic activity – a more accurate terminology than 'full employment' " (Russell with Muther 1958: 313). This shift in language was

significant. As Charles Maier (1977) argues, the design for the industrial world that American planners ultimately embraced was not one
requiring constant renegotiation of corporatist bargains between workers and capitalists. Instead, a permanent Fordist bargain – high
wages in exchange for high productivity – was meant to do the trick.
Capitalists could control the workplace and get as rich as they wanted,
as long as they assured growing incomes to everyone else. This,
many Americans had come to believe, was the real lesson of America's economic success in the later years of the Roosevelt administration, and thus the model for the world (ibid.: 609).

Leaders in the industrial world who held on to more corporatist
views – those who wanted to retain the direct representation of interests that the ILO structure would have allowed – criticized the global
IGOs that institutionalized this Keynesian-Fordist vision from the
beginning. In 1947 a young member of the British parliament writing
under the pseudonym "Cassius"[4] complained to colleagues
throughout the empire about in a pamphlet called *The Bretton Woods
Plan for World Domination by the USA*. The key to the plan, Cassius
argued, was an American interest in increasing exports, the same goal
pursued by the American businessmen at Atlantic City in 1919, and
something that was even more important in 1946 because massive
exports would be needed to maintain the productivity-based domestic class compromise worked out in the US during the war. Cassius
warned that the US would not be interested in increasing imports
from and production within the war-torn countries for many years.
Instead it would balance its payments with other industrial societies
by exporting excess capital, thus increasing the global reach of the
Americans.

Yet, as Michael Hogan emphasizes in his history of the Marshall
Plan and its consequences (1987: 429), the self-interestedness of
American postwar policy did not make it incompatible with the
interests and aspirations of most European workers and industrialists. Without American goods and capital, Europe's recovery would
have been much less rapid. In Gramsci's terms, the establishment of
American supremacy at the core of the Free World was a matter of
hegemony, not of domination.

Excluding illiberal societies

The core of the Free World never covered the whole industrialized
world. As early as 1949 the phrase could no longer conjure up Sumner

Welles's vision of the universal extension of the New Deal from its core in the wartime antifascist alliance. "The Free World" had become the anti-communist alliance. By failing to join the Bretton Woods institutions in 1946 and by using force to sustain the Soviet hold on states occupied at the end of the war, Stalin signaled his intention to remain independent of American supremacy by building an alternative international social order. The West's response, "containment," was not simply a consequence of the persuasiveness of Winston Churchill's 1946 "iron curtain" speech in Fulton, Missouri (one conventional marker of the beginning of the Cold War) or of George Kennan's "long telegram" from Moscow detailing the supposedly inherent expansionist tendencies of Soviet society (which is often credited with giving Truman the idea of containment). The policy also came from reasoning by analogy with the failed interwar attempts at cooperation with fascist Italy and Nazi Germany by businessmen as well as by governments and, through that analogy, to another lesson learned by those within the critical tradition of liberal internationalism.

The social Darwinism embraced by the businessmen's peace movement created a wide bridge to fascism that worried interwar intellectuals on the left. For many interwar champions of the critical tradition, the other side of the lesson that former adversaries should be reintegrated into the liberal order was that they should be forced to make a decisive break with the antiliberal ideas they had embraced. Thorstein Veblen, for example, argued that Germany should be forced to surrender unconditionally at the end of the First World War, the way the South had in the American Civil War (1917: 238–40). This would let the Entente powers transform German society from within. With typical irony Veblen called this an argument for the "elimination of the unfit," and extended the case to Japan's imperial militarism, an equally "unfit throwback," which would have to be eliminated if the world were to advance toward perpetual peace.[5] Unfortunately, he suspected that Entente captains of industry would reject his argument and turn the peace into nothing more than a "program for uniting Germany and her allies in a holy war against Russian atheistic Communism" (Lekachman in Keynes 1971: xxxiii).

While Veblen was wrong about the sympathy that Entente businessmen would feel for Germany, he was right about the continuing power of the old order's ideologies to unite some capitalists behind governments antithetical to liberal internationalism. By the early 1930s even the American businessmen who supported the social

Darwinist World Peace Foundation had learned that lesson firsthand from trying to collaborate with fascist business leaders to establish and maintain the International Management Institute (IMI), an offshoot of the ILO created in 1925 to promote scientific management to European industrialists, one of the goals of the American businessmen at Atlantic City.

The institute's intellectual mentors included the management consultant Mary Parker Follett, and it attracted a group of supporters which reflected the relative prestige of scientific management in different countries before the war. Aside from the "Entente fascists" especially the Italian businessmen who supported both Mussolini and Fordism, the supporters came from interests that would later be part of the social coalitions that would underlie the welfare states. Edward Filene, the liberal Boston retailer, was a major American backer. Seebohm Rowntree, one of Britain's progressive Quaker chocolate manufactures, was the IMI's most active British benefactor, paying for the institute's British office and seconding one of his executives to run its central administration. A group of successful Italian industrialists tied to Adriano Olivetti, Secretary General of the Fascist Industrial Federation, also joined the movement, as did a few Belgians with similar convictions. The French were less active. The ILO's socialist director, Albert Thomas (hardly a captain of industry), became the main supporter from France. The Germans were at first excluded, as they had been from almost all the interwar global agencies. When they were invited to become active members in 1930, a consequence of the Young Plan, the director of the German association for scientific management responded that his organization, the most extensive national agency for modern business methods in Europe, did not need the international association.

This German pronouncement played into an ongoing battle within the IMI between the American and British benefactors and conservatives from Italy and Belgium; the latter, as the executive seconded from Rowntree argued, "believe in Scientific Management, but merely as an employer's instrument to lower costs. They don't believe in the further essential conceptions of either lower prices or higher wages" (Wrege et al. 1987: 13). Subsequent attempts to contain fascist influence within the IMI failed. Liberal internationalists who hoped for social compromises benefiting working people pulled the institute one way while the fascists pulled it the other. The ILO pressured the IMI to study only the "*social* aspects" of business rationalization (that is, ways to maintain full employment and keep wages high), at the same time as the association of British employers (where progressives like Rowntree were still in a minority) began to see merit in Olivetti's argument that the institute should be used only to help firms combine against the wage demands of labor. In 1933 Filene caused the IMI to disband by withdrawing financial support. He lamented that there was no longer any way of "enlisting the interests of businessmen" to support international cooperation (ibid.: 17).

Over the next decade progressive businessmen like Filene became key supporters of the vision inspired by the New Deal of a postwar world order. They took with them the lessons they had learned in their failed experiment in cooperation with the fascists. Their own enchantment with the ideologies of the old order ended and they became convinced by Veblen's argument that the enemies' ideology had to be rooted out along with the personnel of the militarist states and the illiberal economies on which it was based. When the Soviet and British governments demanded unconditional surrender by the Axis powers, they found a great deal of support within the Roosevelt coalition (Köhler 1991). Unconditional surrender allowed the allies to reconstruct the Axis social orders along liberal lines. The new postwar global IGOs played a part. The first work of UNESCO, the successor to the Gilbert Murray's elitist interwar education IGO, the League Committee on Intellectual Cooperation, included helping Germans revise generations of textbooks reflecting the divisive theories of the Nazis and of the *ancien régime* (Laves and Thompson 1957: 238) and leading an international campaign against social Darwinist ideas and the concept of racial superiority (Sewell 1975: 184).[6]

Soon American statesmen would reason that the same logic that called for the unconditional surrender of societies organized along illiberal, fascist lines also demanded confrontation with societies organized along the illiberal lines that Stalin proposed for the postwar communist order. Initially, at least, this reasoning did not simply reflect the fulfillment of Veblen's fears about businessmen leading a holy war against communism; it was not just a matter of the liberal fundamentalism of some political conservatives. It was a reaction to Stalin's rejection of US and British designs for a world economy programmed to become increasingly open over time.

That rejection actually surprised some of the designers. After all, the Bretton Woods agreements welcomed and would have supported a Soviet Union whose firms were government owned and whose central authorities had instituted a variety of controls on external economic relations in an attempt to isolate the economy from external shocks, because this latter set of policies simply mirrored similar controls instituted by all of the liberal powers to protect the welfare state. But, as Cassius's critique of Bretton Woods recognized, the designers of Bretton Woods were not prepared to support any state that attempted to establish an alternative, and potentially threatening, world order, a social order outside the Free World (cf. T. McCormick 1989: 58–69; Nau 1990: 101–4).

Recognizing the Limits of World Organizations

The resulting Cold War ended any hope that a world organization would be at the center of the postwar system for managing conflict among the great powers. Yet, disappointing as this was to many liberal internationalists, their acceptance of this conclusion reflected the most important lessons learned in the interwar years: there were some things that world organizations could not do, and the UN Charter recognized it. The Security Council, led by the three major allied combatants (Britain, the Soviet Union, and the US) and their two putatively "great power" allies, France and China, required the kind of great-power consensus that had existed under the nineteenth-century European conference system (Luard 1982: 3–63; T. McCormick 1989: 40). By 1949 it was clear that it would not re-emerge after the war. Stalin had militarized his defensive perimeter of captive allies and then blockaded the western sectors of Berlin in an attempt to consolidate Soviet rule over all of eastern Germany. The response of the West to the blockade initiated the pattern of using escalating threats of military confrontation to manage conflicts between East and West. The UN system came to play a number of subsidiary roles in this deterrence system, and it would sometimes be relied on to help manage militarized conflicts within the Free World, but the veto power granted to the five powers by the UN Charter assured that the Security Council would not intervene in the conflict between world orders.

In accepting the power of the veto, the UN's champions discarded a utopian hope reflected in the League's more ambitious programs. The League tried to contain the kind of nationalist resentment that had emerged in the ethnically divided states of the Balkans during the Second Industrial Revolution by guaranteeing the rights of minorities in multinational states. Unfortunately, the League ended up protecting only people of the formerly dominant nationality of the old empires who now lived in successor states where they were a minority, especially Germans living outside the centers of the old German and Austrian empires (Mair 1928). Similarly, the League failed to secure disarmament by considering the problem as the uncontrolled growth of one particular function of government, a problem that could be countered by a "rational" international measures: governments simply had to be convinced that the functions served by large military expenditures might be more effectively served by the collective security provisions of the League and by its systems for arbitration, conciliation, and judicial settlement of international disputes.

F. S. Northedge remarks that the story of the League's drawn-out attempts to achieve disarmament "has a tragic quality about it, but also a certain tediousness" (1986: 115), especially given the ultimate futility of the whole effort, which lasted from 1920 (when the League first met) through 1932–4 (the years of the World Disarmament Conference). Suffice it to say that League members each saw their own defense needs as greater than those of any potential adversary. By the time the Disarmament Conference finally met, the arms race was already on again, despite the tremendous efforts expended in the previous decade. Aristide Briand, the French social democrat who had almost convinced his people to accept Germany as a partner in the peace in the few prosperous years before the Depression, even pushed the most utopian of the interwar treaties simply as a means to the unrealized goal of banning weapons. Accepting the argument that no government would give up arms unless it were confident that peace could be kept by other means, Briand concluded that confidence in the League's conflict resolution mechanisms could be built if all the powers signed "a pact against war," with "Germany [acting] willingly and on the same footing as all others" (Thomson 1930: 305); hence the 1928 treaty promoted by the idealistic Briand and a more cynical US Secretary of State, F. B. Kellogg, to "outlaw war."

Even Woodrow Wilson's original vision had not been quite as utopian. Of course, under the Covenant of the League of Nations members had pledged that they would not initiate war until a whole series of international attempts at fact finding, mediation, and adjudication had taken place, but the Covenant did not try to ban war altogether. Instead, as E. H. Carr argues (1946: 29–31), the original idea was for the League to be a sort of giant "card-index" of possible international crisis "situations," each of which could be linked to the appropriate means of conflict resolution in the same way that medical doctors index the symptoms of disease and cross-reference them with pharmacopeia to tell them what to prescribe for each disorder. Unfortunately, even after the League did nothing effective to counter Japan's seizure of Manchuria in 1931 and Mussolini's annexation of Abyssinia in 1936, many of those who believed in the League most deeply still imagined that its index of symptoms would always lead to un ambiguous diagnoses and its pharmacopeia would always hold the remedy even when the "disease" was the existence of states that simply did not share the principles on which the League was based.

Carr's account makes the League's system for managing international conflict sound like something designed by a nineteenth-century public system builder who was having a particularly bad day. The League's designers had the same rationalist faith in the application of the methods of science to statecraft, but they did not share the nineteenth-century concern with political efficiency. Rather than struggle to make power invisible, the successors of the nineteenth-century statists and system builders often seemed to ignore power.

Arguably, this was a consequence of the fact that the League's designers were much less familiar with the ordinary work of government. The very success of the nineteenth-century statists and public system builders had helped to create a new stratum of independent professional intellectuals, men and women trained in the academic disciplines that grew out of the older practical activities.[7] The intellectuals of the League movements did not gain the ear of the prince by proving their abilities in the day-to-day affairs of state. They gained their influence as intellectual mobilizers of social movements. Carr argues that almost all the men and women who designed the League had very little sympathy for the "practical affairs" of government (1946: 18). The movements led by the professional economists Hobson and Balch even blamed war on the bureaucrats, diplomats, and professional military officers who were just as much descendants of the nineteenth-century statists and public system builders as any academic economist or political scientist.

As a result of this antagonism between "intellectuals" and "bureaucrats," Carr argues, the League and its sister organizations developed something of a self-defeating detachment from, if not always an aversion to, the state *per se*. This is one reason that the League era institutions never developed the same capacity as the Public International Unions to influence the global political economy by shaping the goals and expectations of state officials. Moreover, given the antagonism between the League intellectuals and government functionaries, the League never internalized one important lesson that most government experts on security and diplomacy knew, that the ideological or moral consensus governing an international social order had to reflect its balance of coercive forces. It did no good to outlaw war if some states with the capacity to begin wars did not go along with it; it would just make those states that had agreed look foolish when they, of necessity, began to fight the war-makers.

To put the issue more generally: many of the intellectuals who designed the League seem to have forgotten the lesson of Bentham's Panopticon. They rarely concerned themselves with political efficiency. The League intellectuals did not see cooperative political institutions as husbanding inducements and coercive power. In trying to regulate geopolitical rivalries, they designed something like the cells and corridors of Bentham's prison without providing for its guardhouse and its guards.

This does not mean that the League's designers added nothing to the understanding that had been developed by their less "academically professional" predecessors. If nothing else, the League's designers were more conscious proponents of the self-correcting practices of "science" that held out the promise that liberal internationalists could learn what they did not know without the tutelage of another world order crisis. This was the hope that even Carr, one of their sharpest critics, was willing to share.

Still, it was a very long and harrowing tutelage. The world order crisis that had begun with the Great War did not end with the Depression. To the dismay of many League intellectuals, the bureaucrats, diplomats, and military officers were unwilling to rely on the League's unproven collective security system to counter the Japanese, Italian, and German advances throughout the 1930s. The French and British mixed policies of coercive sanctions and appeasement. Stalin plotted a short-term alliance with the fascists. In the end, the antifascist United Nations could only solidify their military alliance after all the powers – China, France, Britain, the Soviet Union and the United States, in turn – had been attacked.

That alliance itself became central to the victors' plans for a post-war global security organization. When the alliance broke apart along the fault-line created by the Soviet decision to pursue building an alternative to the Free World Order, the allies still retained their understanding of the lessons of the interwar period. They did not try to rely on the new world organization to do something it was not suited to do.

Mobilizing New Sponsors and Benefactors

The UN's designers were just as realistic about creating world organizations, recognizing the League's over-reliance on private philanthropy to provide political leadership. After the war the allies divided
the responsibility for sponsoring the conferences where the UN
system was formed, began funding experiments in international organization based on the ability to pay, and gave the leaders of the
new organizations the power to act sponsors and benefactors of further innovations. The greater realism in evidence in the UN's system
for creating world organizations did not make it a matter of energiz-
ing narrow self-interest; UN intellectual leaders, like their League-
era predecessors, continued to call on sponsors and benefactors to
look beyond short-run local interests and toward their more global,
long-run aspirations.

The League's sponsors

The League had relied on hegemonic aspirations, but also on the
idealistic motivations often affirmed by interwar statesmen. League
intellectuals expected government leaders to give substance to their
stated faith in public diplomacy, international arbitration, the power
of the market, and the rule of law in international affairs by sponsoring the international conferences needed to reform the Public International Unions and take on new responsibilities.

Some statesmen did. Woodrow Wilson, of course, provided the
political capital needed to establish the League, and American officials continued to sponsor key international agreements, even
though the US remained outside the League itself.[8] Perhaps most
significantly, Americans sponsored and financed the renegotiation of
reparations and European financial cooperation. French leaders
played as active a role, especially in the 1920s. In 1924, after a new
government came to power supporting mass education, France put
the question of unifying and expanding the educational, scientific,
and cultural activities of the Public International Unions on the table
at the League. The result was Gilbert Murray's Committee on Intellectual Cooperation (League of Nations 1930: 316–17), albeit a group
that did not share its sponsor's faith in the masses. Nevertheless, the
French socialists ensured that the committee would be tempered by
a bureaucracy, the International Institute of Intellectual Cooperation

(IIIC), underwritten by France and operated from a headquarters building in Paris donated by the government (Northedge 1986: 184).

For a few years after the establishment of the IIIC, France's Aristide Briand seemed to have taken over Wilson's role as the most visible promoter of international institutions. He not only pushed for the Kellogg–Briand ban on warfare and for the League disarmament conference, he joined the US as a major sponsor of the intergovernmental economic conferences designed to end the Depression and reverse the turn to protectionism it had encouraged. As early as 1929 Briand wanted to hold negotiations on a "United States of Europe" similar in scope to the Common Market of the 1960s (Chalmers 1953: 51).

Briand and Wilson both believed that the end of the *ancien régime* made it the obligation of democratic governments to sponsor international cooperation, a view that David Lubin had begun to expound somewhat earlier. The old order was dead. Princes could no longer be trusted to serve the global interests. History had passed the task on to those now most likely to act on the basis of *noblesse oblige*, the popularly elected leaders of the republics (Agresti 1941: 330).

Nevertheless, in the interwar years at least, it would be hard to argue that all democratic statesmen took to this task as well as their aristocratic predecessors had. Interwar leaders failed to work out a division of labor to cover all global issues yet assure that no one bore too much of the burden of promoting international cooperation. The few regular sponsors of interwar conferences often seemed perversely jealous of others who followed their example, while other democratic statesmen felt that they should play no role because they agreed so wholeheartedly with the liberal fundamentalists who argued that it was best to keep most of the international agenda out of government hands. Those regimes taking on most of the burden suffered from the problem that confronts democratic leaders whenever they push for dramatic changes in world affairs: they could not promise that even their own governments would follow through with the necessary level of commitment. This was certainly Wilson's tragedy after Versailles. It was also the tragedy of the American and French sponsors of the final attempts to reestablish the prewar European social order a decade later. The Depression had made new American financial contributions to the settlement politically impossible at the same time that Germany's rearmament and turn to the right had soured the French to Briand's hope that the old enemies might become partners in a united Europe.

Private philanthropists as agitators and benefactors

While interwar democratic statesmen may have been dilatory and ineffective sponsors of international cooperation when compared to their nineteenth-century predecessors, the other representatives of the new bourgeois order who became political leaders in the League era showed more zeal, although it was often based on an unrealistic idealism. Individual philanthropists like David Lubin and the Norwegian polar explorer Fridjof Nansen (the man who dragged the League's refugee agencies into existence) became benefactors of social movements that worked together to push governments to expand intergovernmental social programs. Nansen's refugee relief movement, for example, was aided by the success of the private International Red Cross under the ambitious Giovanni Ciralo, who wanted to provide disaster relief and basic public health services throughout the world. Interwar governments created the International Relief Union and the League of Nations' Health Committee in part as an attempt to gain control over such growing private efforts (Gorgé 1938: 22), and also because a number of governments oriented to laissez faire feared the precedent that would be created by agreeing to Nansen's or Ciralo's demands to turn private voluntary associations like the Red Cross into public agencies (Greaves 1931: 88). Both the Relief Union and the League's Health Committee may have done less than had been hoped for by the interwar movements, but the intergovernmental agencies did institutionalize international programs that became a regular part of many national budgets and, thus, less vulnerable to financial crises than they might have been as strictly charitable efforts.

Nonetheless, in the interwar years governments were often less reliable than private charities. Private foundations established to distribute the fortunes of successful industrialists played a key role in sponsoring innovations in international cooperation throughout the League era. A 1945 Carnegie Endowment study of what the UN could learn from the League (Ranshofen-Wertheimer 1945: 158) even argued that the organization had become too dependent on a small group of philanthropists. The Rockefeller Foundation, for example, had covered nearly half the cost of the League's health programs and nearly 10 percent of the secretariat's economic programs. The Carnegie Endowment, Twentieth Century Fund (supported by Edward Filene), and Edwin Ginn's World Peace Foundation also made significant contributions.

These philanthropists typically had quite utopian expectations. Ginn, for example, anticipated the day when the work of his foundation would be complete and instructed his trustees to shift its income then "to his other favorite cause, Charlesbank Homes, a housing project he had established in Boston for the poor" (World Peace Foundation 1985: 14). Similarly, when Andrew Carnegie established his Endowment for International Peace he imagined that war would quickly be abolished and that the funds would then be used to eradicate "the next most degrading remaining evil or evils whose banishment would advance the human cause" (Fabian 1985: 43).

In contrast, when it came to matters of the management of world organizations, the philanthropists proved quite hardheaded. They struggled to make the international agencies just as efficient as the most advanced private companies. Filene, for example, accustomed to the speed of transactions in an up-to-date department store, with all its intercoms and pneumatic tubes, wanted to speed up business in the League's committees, where delays in transcribing and translating slowed everything to a crawl. To solve the problem Filene commissioned the first system for simultaneous translation, later improved by IBM with the financial help of Filene's colleague in the businessmen's peace movement, Thomas J. Watson (Ridgeway 1959: 115).

Filene's promotion of the tools of modern management extended to joining the Rockefeller Foundation in funding the IMI, which disappeared when their philanthropy ended. The failure of the IMI's state members to pick up the organization's tab followed a general interwar pattern of stinginess toward the world organizations. Of course, governments could justify their tightfisted policies by citing the antigovernment philosophy promulgated by liberal fundamentalists in the businessmen's peace movement itself, but the consequence was the kind of managerial inefficiencies that the fundamentalists considered typical of the most backward national administration. Northedge argues that the League always operated "in an atmosphere of continuous carping about money," and with a necessary parsimony that "had hardly any parallel within the administration of its member-states" (1986: 70–1). Often League officials would have to cover their own fares to and from Geneva, or chip in to pay for paperwork. That they did so right through the Second World War was a testament to the power of an idea.

Greater realism in creating the UN

The men and women who designed the UN system did not rely on private philanthropy to provide the political leadership to create new world organizations. The wartime UN allies divided responsibility for the conferences needed to reform what world government there was at the end of the League era. They also agreed that the costs of multilateral cooperation should be assessed on all governments according to their ability to pay, the principle reflected in the UNRRA precedent of having each of the UN allies contribute 1 percent of their national income for the immediate reconstruction needs of the liberated nations (Murphy 1984: 54).

A similar principle influenced the division of responsibility for the postwar conferences. It placed greater responsibilities on the more powerful, who thus, also gained greater influence on the shape of the most significant postwar world organizations. The US took charge of the conferences concerned with managing potential conflicts generated by the industrial system (Russell with Muther 1958: 66–8) and with multilateral means to strengthen the state and the state system, especially the Bretton Woods conference and those creating the UN itself. Moscow called the preparatory conference of the big five to reform the ITU (Codding 1952: 197–206) and Britain took charge of civil aviation (Schenkman 1955: 63). The powers that had been occupied during the war had to be content with sponsoring conferences that strengthened society. France called the UNESCO meetings and later used her position as the patron of international intellectual and cultural cooperation to fend off a US effort to turn the organization into an agency dispensing anticommunist propaganda (Sewell 1974: 163–6). China's job was the World Health Organization (WHO); it was joined by Brazil (Jacobson 1974: 158), the largest of the noncombatant United Nations and a country that the US at one time had argued should join the five as a permanent member of the Security Council.

Even with governments having a more realistic attitude about supporting experiments in world organizations, plenty of room remained for private philanthropists. The drawn-out debate over the location of the UN headquarters ended when John D. Rockefeller offered the site on New York's East River (Luard 1982: 84). Similarly, religious charities and private foundations played critical roles in the long process that resulted in the founding of the UN High Commission for Refugees (UNHCR) in 1951, simply because the private groups were willing to foot most of the bills for relief efforts (Holborn 1975: 124, 134, 370–1).

The UN as sponsor and benefactor

By 1951 the Cold War and the emerging North–South conflict dramatically reduced the number of national governments that could be relied on to support experiments in world government. The 1949 Maoist revolution isolated both China and the USSR from the UN because the Soviets could not get the organization to recognize China's new regime. Britain and France spent much of their time in the 1950s fending off attacks on their colonial empires that began whenever they appeared in organizations where all states were represented.

The French and Chinese roles in dealing with issues of human rights and basic needs were soon taken over by the agencies, on their own or in combination with the US government, a pattern that was also followed when it came to development issues. La Guardia's vision of world organizations permanently redistributing part of the world's wealth spurred the first experiments with taking IGO funds accumulated by one agency and using them to underwrite the experimental institutionalization of new agencies or programs. When the wartime allies wrapped up UNRRA, as each of the Cold War superpowers took over reconstruction in its own sphere of influence, the agency's remaining funds were transferred to the relief programs of the new Food and Agriculture Organization (FAO) as well as to the "temporary" International Refugee Organization (IRO) and the UN Children's Emergency Fund (UNICEF) (see UNRRA 1948: 45). The FAO was able to fulfill part of La Guardia's original vision when it took over UNRRA's fledgling programs for relief of some of the non-European areas torn by war, Ethiopia and China, the first victims of the fascist alliance (Hambidge 1955: 73–4).

In the five years of the IRO's operation from 1946 to 1951, UN members became convinced of the need for a more permanent organization that would rely on private charity, hence the Office of the UN High Commission for Refugees. Similarly, while UNICEF was still using UNRRA funds its managers developed the organization's unique system of seeking private donations to fund its programs. Given their relative independence from wealthy donor nations, it should not be surprising that the UNHCR's and UNICEF's changing priorities have mirrored La Guardia's hopes about the development agenda of the UN as whole; they have moved from concentrating on the postwar European problems that most interested the US government, to worldwide problems of refugees and development whether or not they are of special interest to the most powerful governments.

The more typical pattern of sponsoring and underwriting new world organizations since the Second World War has relied on both the General Assembly's power to create new UN agencies (Peterson 1986: 149), and sometimes on the willingness and the ability of the supreme power, the United States, to deflect any radical attempts to redefine its hegemony. In the General Assembly each member has an equal vote and LDCs have controled the Assembly since the early 1960s, when most African states became independent. In the late 1950s and the 1960s the LDCs used the General Assembly's powers to create the Special UN Fund for Economic Development (SUNFED), UNCTAD, the economic commissions for all the developing areas, the UN Institute for Training and Research (UNITAR), the UNDP, the UN Capital Development Fund, the UN Centre against Apartheid, and the UN Industrial Development Organization (UNIDO).

The executive heads of UN agencies have also used their capacity to establish and underwrite additional experiments in international organization. In 1969, for example, UN Secretary General U Thant created one of today's most significant development agencies, the UN Fund for Population Activities (Salas 1979: xx, xxiv). Similarly, the World Bank itself has spun off a number of agencies, including the Economic Development Institute (to train Third World development professionals) and the International Center for Settlement of Investment Disputes (to protect foreign investors in the LDCs), as have the ILO and UNESCO.

By the early 1970s the UN system had thoroughly demonstrated its ability to provide the political leadership to sponsor and underwrite experiments in international organization demonstrating an unprecedented capacity for self-transformation that made predictions about an eventual emergence of a "real" world government seem quite sensible. Observers at the turn of the century had seen a similar capacity for self-transformation in the Public International Unions. Although the Unions did not have the UN's capacity to act as benefactors of new international agencies, they had become major sponsors of the international conferences that established experimental international programs. Yet, at the point when their capacity for self-transformation appeared to be the greatest, the Unions descended into their worst crisis. And a similar fate awaited the UN.

6

THE WORK OF THE LEAGUE AND THE UN SYSTEM

Between 1914 and 1971 world population doubled, the number of states quadrupled, and the work of the world organizations increased more than tenfold. While the Depression and the Second World War ended a few experiments in international organization – the IMI and the League's protections for minorities – postwar expansion into the fields of development, public finance, peacekeeping, and human rights assured that the UN system would soon dwarf the Public International Unions. These four new fields have so dominated UN activity that it would be easy to forget that the primary tasks performed by the prewar Unions – fostering industry and managing social conflicts in the industrial world – remained the foundation of global governance.

Despite the UN's new activity, the world organizations remained clearly of secondary importance when it came to the management of interstate conflict and the protection of human rights. At least until the late 1980s the bipolar balance of power, and not a multilateral security regime, remained the military face of the postwar world orders, while many of the global human rights norms were honored only in the breach.

Nevertheless, despite the League's spectacular failure to avert the Second World War, and even with the rapid dissolution of the great-power alliance on which the Security Council was based, most of the interwar pharmacopeia of remedies for international conflict survived. After all, for all their faults, the League agencies had used them to resolve an array of international disputes (Q. Wright 1942: 1429–30; Coplin and Rochester 1972; Holsti 1991: 210). Of course, the UN's capacity to manage international conflicts was inherently restricted by the Cold War division of the wartime allies. Two tightly connected communist world orders – the Soviet bloc and China – existed alongside the much looser "Free World," with its close economic bonds and sieve-like net of overlapping military alliances in which the majority of LDCs could remain officially "nonaligned" either to the West or to either of the communist worlds.

Struggles between the nonaligned and the core of the Free World and struggles among the nonaligned themselves became the main focus of UN conflict management (Zacher 1979: 68–80). Early on the world organization proved useful in the first Arab–Israeli war in 1948 and the Kashmir crisis of 1949. The UN security regime survived the organization's involvement in the Korean war (1950–3). A Soviet walkout over the UN's nonrecognition of China's revolutionary government had given the US the opportunity to gain Security Council support for American forces. Soon after that war ended, the UN proved useful in helping protect some of the nonaligned from Free World allies in the Suez crisis of 1956, when France and Britain (with the help of Israel) had tried to take the Suez Canal from nonaligned Egypt. Eventually even the Soviet government would recognize the usefulness of multilateral agencies when dealing with conflicts that could arise with and among the nonaligned. The USSR worked with the US to create the nonproliferation regimes of the International Atomic Energy Agency (IAEA), which offers non-nuclear states access to nuclear technology for peaceful uses (IAEA 1977).

Meanwhile, the UN continued to develop the "peacekeeping" role it had pioneered in 1948, using the standard tools of the world organizations – observation and reporting – to maintain ceasefires. The partial success of peacekeeping in Kashmir, the first two Arab–Israeli wars, Lebanon in 1958, the Congo in 1960, West New Guinea in 1962, Yemen in 1963, Cyprus in 1964, the Dominican Republic in 1965, and again between India and Pakistan in 1965 explain why states at war increasingly turned to the UN throughout the 1950s and 1960s (Alker and Sherman 1980: 39–40; Wilkenfeld and Brecher 1984). It also explains why the UN's peacekeeping mechanism survived the 1962 announcement of its early benefactor, the United States, that it planned to reduce its support to the level that would be required if the traditional UN "ability to pay" standard were used. As Ernst Haas notes, by most measures the UN's effectiveness in dealing with international disputes actually increased for a number of years after the American decision (1983: 230,1; cf. Luard 1989: 443–66).

League and UN activities providing war relief and supporting refugees followed a similar trajectory. In the 1920s the League helped feed, protect, and relocate refugees of the First World War, the

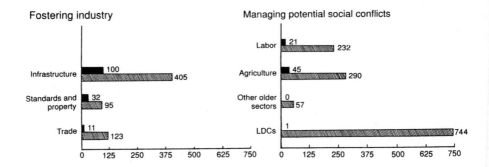

Primary Tasks

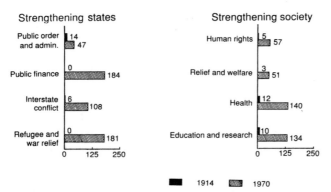

FIGURE 5 A comparison of the tasks being carried out by world organizations in 1914 and 1970 (regular activities, 1911–15 and 1966–70)

Russian Civil War, and the conflicts in the East – including Turkey's war against the Armenians. In the process the League created most of the mechanisms still used to support the stateless, including the "Nansen passports" that give refugees the right to move from country to country, a right that many countries suspended during the Depression in response to public demands to exclude foreigners who were competing for jobs (Holborn 1975: 13). The League's failure to protect refugees from xenophobia induced by the Depression culminated in the completely inadequate response to the Holocaust by the

Intergovernmental Committee on Refugees (ICR), the first successor to Fridjof Nansen's office (Gordenker 1987: 22).

As soon as the wartime UN antifascist alliance solidified, the ICR's own successors proved more successful, at least in the areas liberated from the Nazis. Nonetheless, the UN's leaders remained deeply divided about refugees. Some of the wartime allies wanted to give refugees the right to live anywhere, but the Soviet Union demanded that they all be repatriated, especially those who had used the fog of war to flee communist rule, while the US refused to change the restrictive immigration policies it had set up after the First World War. Instead it sponsored the Intergovernmental Committee for European Migration to help resettle refugees in other countries (Holborn 1975: 115). The US also championed the UN Relief and Works Agency for Palestinian refugees (UNRWA) and hoped to "run the show" to avoid the East–West battles that were plaguing the ICR's immediate successors, UNRRA and the International Refugee Organization (ibid.: 59).

The Americans soon decided that UNRWA should not be a precedent, at least as long as the US was the UN's major benefactor. Unlike any of the other world organizations that have supported refugees, UNRWA actually provided (and continues to provide) education, housing, and health care to its clients. The others act as coordinators of private philanthropic efforts, a much less costly business for the governments that foot the bill.

In 1951 US Ambassador Eleanor Roosevelt proposed this voluntarist design of the Office of the UN High Commissioner for Refugees (UNHCR), which has since remained the primary coordinator of international war relief, often moving into new conflicts much more rapidly than UN agencies concerned with managing interstate conflicts. The UNHCR also became the model for the Office of the UN Disaster Relief Coordinator (UNDRO), which coordinates private relief from natural disasters.

Eleanor Roosevelt also led the movement to give the UN responsibility for defining human rights and monitoring their enforcement. Of course, even though the UN's human rights agenda has vastly increased since the 1948 Universal Declaration of Human Rights, and even though the Human Rights Commission has had some monitoring powers since the 1970s (Donnelly 1986), most monitoring is still done by nongovernmental organizations such as Amnesty International, except in two of the Free World regions – Europe and the Americas – where regional intergovernmental organizations have had more extensive rights to monitor human rights since the mid-1970s.

The early refugee regimes also influenced the UN agencies that have done the most to satisfy basic human needs. The World Health Organization evolved from the prewar Health Union into a vast, decentralized system for sharing medical information and for administering a few basic public health programs in much of the Third World. The UN usually highlights the eradication of smallpox as the model of what the WHO can do (UN 1986: 411), although its programs to immunize infants against preventable childhood diseases and to promote simple means for controlling infant diarrhea have probably saved many more lives. Similarly, some of UNESCO's least flashy and apparently least newsworthy field programs to support basic education contributed to the rises in literacy that sometimes began with decolonization. Moreoever, as A. F. Robertson (1984) argues in a telling study of the entire "development" system – from donor states, to intergovernmental intermediaries, to Third World governments, to the ultimate clients – the typical postcolonial state has come to legitimize itself through "development" as a populist program, a program designed to give citizens what they most want: longer lives, better health, and more chances for their children. Life expectancy, diets, and literacy levels in the Third World all showed dramatic improvements in the heyday of the Free World Order (UNDP 1992: 14) and the basic needs programs of the UN system have played a key part in achieving these goals.

Promoting the New Industries of the Automobile and Jet Age

In contrast to the achievements above, the ostensible goal of the development IGOs – tremendous increases in Third World output – have remained elusive. Yet the postwar world organizations have still had a profound impact on industrial change, at least in the regions where it has been most pronounced: western Europe, the United States, and Japan. The League and UN systems replicated the attempts of the Public International Unions to link the physical infrastructure of an expanded world market, define intellectual property and industrial standards for the new industries that might be created within that market area, and allow the increasingly free exchange of industrial goods that would encourage investment in those industries.

Linking infrastructure for a Free World market

The first of the twentieth-century infrastructure technologies to be regulated by international agreement, radio, has remained crucial for ocean shipping and air transport, and it has become crucial for point-to-point international communication through telephones and satellites. This new role would have been impossible without international agreements on radio's other major use, broadcasting: agreements to divide the radiospectrum and establish standards for equipment. Getting those agreements was far from easy. A few interwar governments wanted to focus on banning propaganda from the international air waves, including the "tasteless commercial propaganda" that offended elitist British supporters of the League like Gilbert Murray (Mance 1944: 33–40). However, most interwar governments only wanted to protect the frequencies used by major shippers and broadcasters, even that meant banning the amateur "spark" radios that used to be assembled by Boy Scouts (Codding 1952: 265).

Ultimately, the radio regime reflected the interests of large users and service providers who wrote the first modern international radio regulations (Tomlinson 1938: 293). Continuing close ties between business and government later encouraged the establishment of the International Telecommunications Satellite Organization (Intelsat) as the first "internationalized" public service corporation, with shareholders (the operators of national telecommunications systems) who are also its major customers (Snow 1976: 47).

A similar pattern of close relations between business and government typifies global governance of civil aviation, where the IGOs have always been as much a sign of regulation carried out by a private cartel as they have been sources of substantive regulation themselves. British, Dutch, German, and Scandinavian air carriers (some of them government firms) created the nongovernmental International Air Transport Association (IATA) in 1919 to regulate routes and fares, following the model of the liner conventions (Colegrove 1930: 119). For a few years IATA competed with the intergovernmental International Commission of Aerial Navigation (ICAN), but the two agencies soon worked out a clear division of labor: ICAN would deal only with safety and with sovereign rights, including the right to land.

During the Second World War the United States proposed doing away with the noncompetitive aspects of the IATA while the sponsors of the International Civil Aviation Organization (ICAO) conference, the British, "favored a world system of regulation in opposition to unfettered competition" (Schenkman 1955: 71–5). Canada achieved a compromise by making it clear to US carriers that "freedom of the air" would also mean opening their lucrative domestic air routes (90 percent of their prewar business) to foreign competition. The ICAO replaced ICAN, but a division of labor between IATA and the key intergovernmental agency was restored – this time IATA was restricted to dealing with rates and proposing treaties to restrict airline liability. The ICAO became the first of the postwar global agencies and it was the first of the world organizations to have its headquarters outside of Europe, in Montreal, a location that recognized the Canadian role in arbitrating the British–American dispute, fulfilled the American intention to move the center of world government across the Atlantic, and encouraged Canada to continue to act as the agency's main benefactor by providing its initial secretariat (ibid.: 108).

Today the ICAO is the most active of the IGOs promoting industrial commerce, with more extensive obligations than its predecessor for setting standards for safety, navigation, and personnel, and for drafting and enforcing conventions on liability for air accidents. Like ICAN, the ICAO has tended to favor those it regulates, often getting involved in a safety issue only after a crisis has occurred and sometimes exonerating firms that have built and maintained unsafe aircraft (Golich 1989). In addition to its safety work, the ICAO has financed international air navigation networks, including the one used across the north Atlantic, the world's most traveled route (Schenkman 1955: 287). It proposes and enforces customs rules for air freight, thus simplifying global air shipment in the same way that similar rules for railways simplified the fastest means of trade a century ago. And the ICAO enforces rules on duty-free airports and duty-free zones. In an attempt to lower costs of air transportation to all users, the agency monitors the subsidies paid to national airlines and makes that information available to states negotiating exchanges of air rights. Finally, the ICAO maintains a relatively complex system for resolving air disputes to help ensure that international incidents do not slow air commerce (Schenkman 1955; Kihl 1971; UN 1986: 418–19).

Even though much of the international air network has been in place since the mid-1950s, and even though the proportion of goods shipped by air has constantly grown, surface transportation has remained crucial to the Free World economy, as the Japanese cars rolling off ships in every US port, the constant stream of Indian Ocean oil tankers, and the endlessly expanding port of Rotterdam attest. The compromise between government and the interests of private business reflected in the radio and air regimes was difficult to reach in the shipping industry, long dominated, as it was, by a British cartel opposed to competition and uninterested in innovation. In the interwar years the International Chamber of Commerce first proposed something that would eventually become a key factor in the trade of industrial goods throughout the Free World: intermodal "containerized" shipping in standard bins that could be moved earily from freight trains to motor trucks to ships (Long 1935: 247). It was a cooperative solution to competition among different modes of transport which reflected the new management philosophy that Mary Parker Follett had helped introduce. But the ocean freight industry was not interested in amending traditional practices. It took the growing pressure of competition and the demands of labor to change that.

Both came in the 1930s when Britain lost her ocean supremacy: US tonnage grew eightfold, while both Japanese and Italian tonnage doubled, but British capacity barely expanded at all (Mance 1945: 67). Thriving American companies began registering ships overseas – typically in Liberia and Panama – to escape the Roosevelt administration's costly safety regulations. American unions pressed for international agreements to achieve the same ends. One result was the postwar International Maritime Consultative Organization (IMCO). By the mid-1960s it had set standards for ports and personnel, established global navigation systems, regulated containerized shipping, and standardized shipping documents (Silverstein 1978: 3–4).

To placate the shipping industry the IMCO's charter prevents it from addressing costs and prices. However, since 1964 the UNC-TAD has provided an intergovernmental forum that attempts to lower the price at least of the bulk shipments of raw materials along north–south routes (Juda 1981). Otherwise, postwar intergovernmental regulation of ocean shipping resembles that of radio and civil aviation: the IGOs have focused on linking the industrial centers of the Free World and have relied on technological development, not competition among service providers, to lower costs to consumers (cf. Cafruny 1985). In doing so, they have attempted to rewrite the story of the prewar rail and telegraph unions on a larger scale.

A few world organizations also continue to try to improve the older continental infrastructures of trade by encouraging the application of the new technologies. Electromechanical refrigeration has proven to be one of the most important of these, and since 1920 it has been regulated by the International Institute of Refrigeration, which proposes rules for the safe and efficient shipment of chilled goods, but leaves enforcement to refrigerator manufacturers, shipping companies, food processors, or national governments (League of Nations 1929: 115).

Of course, the greatest impact of a new technology on the older systems came from the automobile industry's shift toward mass production. This led to greater cooperation among rail companies, both public and private, which is why even though a 1923 attempt to create a much more powerful rail union had failed, by 1933 Europe's rail companies were ready to form a cartel-like association (Wedgewood and Wheeler 1946: 8, 13).

Significant international regulation of road and rail has remained at the continental level throughout the UN era. Decolonization encouraged the formation of regional organizations in Africa and Asia, at the same time that it made Europe's historically important rail organizations into similar, continental associations, and the UN has limited its role to serving as patron of postwar agreements on international standards for roads signs and drivers' licenses (UN 1968: 250).

Protecting intellectual property and setting industrial standards

Unlike the Rail Union, the Public International Unions concerned with defining industrial products have not been transcended. Even though the copright and patent Unions expanded very slowly during the League era, they grew again after the Second World War as governments regularly updated global intellectual property agreements to cover new developments in technology. In 1967 the UN's World Intellectual Property Organization (WIPO) consolidated older Unions, combining them with agencies establishing intellectual property rights for plant breeders, vintners, and cheese-makers. UN agencies also continued to maintain standards for these and other food products, another task of prewar world organizations.

The work of UN-era agencies in standardizing other industrial products has gone far beyond anything done before. The International Standards Organization (ISO), a quango modeled on the more strictly nongovernmental prewar International Electrotechnical Commission, has brought together producers, users, governments, and the scientific community to prepare standards in practically every area of technology. The ISO grew out of the International Federation of National Standardizing Associations, an organization formed in 1926 during the brief era of good feeling following the Dawes Plan. That agency did little due to the changes in attitude that came with the Depression and were exemplified in the breakdown of the International Management Institute. In 1942 the organization finally became operational as a center for standardizing war goods exchanged among the antifascist alliance. The wartime agency was transformed into a UN agency in 1944 and then into its postwar form in 1946, when it also took over the Electrotechnical Commission (UN 1965: 33–4; ISO 1977).

The ISO establishes standards through technical committees that tend to represent the major firms in the industries in question. When 60 percent of the committee agree on a standard, it is published, becoming a recommendation that national governments may incorporate into law. Many actually do. ISO standards have become particularly important for relatively large international contracts between purchasers and suppliers in different countries (R. Crane 1979: 28–9), and in the information processing fields where the ISO's international standard book and serial numbers (ISBN and ISSN) and conventions for representing and storing computer data are ubiquitous (ISO 1977).

Encouraging trade in industrial goods

The charters of the infrastructure, intellectual property, and industrial standards organizations of the UN era all anticipate a world in which free trade in manufactured goods has become the rule. This world certainly did not exist at the end of the Second World War, nor did all the Free World allies think that it should exist. Nevertheless, the wartime supporters of free trade were able to bias postwar trade agencies in the direction of the traditional liberal international vision.

Initially the Allies' plan had been for a powerful International Trade Organization (ITO) to carry out the welfare states' new orthodoxy of regulating national regulations of trade, but protectionist forces in the US and elsewhere pushed their legislatures to kill the organization, fearing the powers it had been given to force international competition and break global cartels (Rothstein 1979: 4). What the Free World got instead of the ITO turned out to be even worse for protectionist interests. The General Agreement on Tariffs and Trade (GATT) began as a temporary expedient, a way of encouraging reciprocal, multilateral reductions in tariffs under the most-favored-nation principle in order to boost the trade that would be needed for reconstruction before the ITO pact could come into force. When the US Senate rejected the treaty in 1950, GATT became a permanent organization, existing under the legal fiction that it was the staff of the yet-to-be-ratified ITO. In reality, the

GATT became the secretariat for a series of multilateral "rounds" of trade negotiations which, by 1973, had made barriers to trade on the goods of newer industries inconsequential, at least among the Free World's wealthier states.

Of course, this liberalization took time. It took until 1961 before the core of the Free World trade system was as open as it had been in 1924, at the beginning of the brief interwar era of good feeling, or after 1904 under the Public International Unions.[1] It was not until the GATT's "Tokyo Round," which began in 1973, that the governments of Free World industrial states considered liberalizing trade in their own agricultural products, and even then they did so only in minor ways and only after agreeing to treat agricultural and industrial goods very differently (Winham 1986: 166). Similarly, liberalizing postwar world organizations have played no role in regulating trade in the products of many older industries like textiles – the industry that brought the industrial revolution and one in which newly industrializing countries tend to have an advantage. Postwar governments have regulated the international textile and clothing trade through multilateral agreements whereby Third World producers "voluntarily" restrict sales to older industrialized nations (Lenway 1985: 93–124).

The protectionist politics of textiles is easy to understand: the more powerful states that have large but politically divided consumer markets and a small but united older industry can impose quotas on more efficient producers and yet have it look like a simple, reciprocal multilateral agreement. The politics of the GATT's *liberalizing* mechanism may be a bit harder to follow. GATT provides governments committed to freer trade with three arguments to use against protectionist interests: (1) the government cannot impose the protection desired by industry simply because it has previously agreed not to; (2) GATT provides an "antidumping" mechanism that allows governments to impose tariffs if businesses can prove that their foreign competitors are selling below cost in order to boost their market share; and (3) if a business persists in its demands that its government abrogate its agreements on the relevant tariffs, the government can insist, quite honestly, that any attempt to save one firm, or even one industry, is just not in the national interest, because if they do so they threaten the whole interconnected structure of GATT obligations, and potentially threaten many other firms and industries. Thus, once GATT liberalizations are in effect, they shape government perceptions of the national interests, biasing them in a liberal direction. Moreover, the liberalizations negotiated under

GATT have come to shape the perceptions of business, becoming a predictable part of the business environment (Lenway 1985: 1–15; Peterson 1986: 6; Krugman 1991: 26–31).

Managing Social Conflicts at the Core of the Free World

Other aspects of Free World global governance counter the GATT's bias toward openness by maintaining boundaries of privilege that separate well-off workers and farmers in Europe, Japan, and North America from those everywhere else.

The ILO and the welfare state

In 1933, at the height of the Depression, American scholar and diplomat James T. Shotwell could write that most of labor's original goals for the ILO had been achieved (1934: 189, 214). He was not being ironic. Laws then on the books in most industrialized countries mandated the eight-hour day, limited child labor, allowed unions to form, and required reasonable wages, weekly days of rest, equal treatment for foreign workers, equal pay for equal work, and government safety inspections of workplaces. This record is impressive, especially when we consider that those labor goals of 1919 that had not been met by 1933 still have not been met today: freedom of migration to seek work, international protection for migrant workers, universal public health care, uniform workers' compensation laws, full employment guarantees, adequate unemployment compensation, prohibition of home work, and truly international unions.

Those who advocate increasing the enforcement powers of international institutions often credit the ILO's early successes to the constraints it could put on its members. It required them to report on why they had not adopted international labor conventions, and it solicited citizens' reports about violations of those conventions that had been adopted (E. Haas 1964: 356). It sent these reports to its members and expected them to reply (Perigord 1926: 131), often following up with commissions of inquiry which produced published reports (Wilson 1934: 69). It even appointed independent experts to evaluate the reports that governments were required to submit (Landy 1966: 19). Finally, early ILO leaders readily criticized members for failing to fulfill their obligations (Wilson 1934: 233).

A few governments responded well to this sort of scrutiny: modernizing autocracies like that of Japan, self-important colonial administrations like that of British India, or pluralistic democracies where parties competed on the basis of their ability to provide for public welfare like that of Chile (Perigord: 177–8). When a government's self-image offered no such leverage the ILO could suggest that other members sanction those who defaulted on their obligations (Wilson 1934: 69; Johnston 1970: 99). This did not assure that all countries followed ILO rules. Observers in the 1930s noted that many of the countries that were just beginning to industrialize did not adhere to international labor conventions. Most Latin American countries, most of the successors to the Austrian and Ottoman empires, the Iberian countries, China, Persia, and South Africa all ignored ILO agreements (Shotwell 1934: 498; Wilson 1934: 16), which led some observers to conclude that the apparent power of the new ILO was merely the reflection of the new power of labor, which was substantial in some industrialized countries, but much less in those that were just beginning to industrialize (Perigord 1926: 129).

Instead of becoming the enforcer of global labor standards imagined by those who concentrate on the ILO's coercive powers, the organization actually became one of the midwives of the welfare state, a politically efficient mechanism for maintaining and husbanding the alliance of industrialists with those more conservative elements of the workers' movement rejecting the promise of the Russian revolution. One business-oriented interwar American analyst put it in the following this way. Short of a workers' revolution, relations between labor and employers had to be regulated by some combination of legislation, collective bargaining, and company-level personnel management. Businessmen preferred personnel management for its efficiency (and because it was "the 'American' way"), but labor leaders usually prefer the guarantees provided by national legislation, the "German" or democratic socialist way. The ILO process led to a compromise, albeit one closer to the "German" view (Wilson 1934: 24–8).

The compromise might differ from country to country based on national culture, the relative power of labor and capital, and the relative success of fascism. In the US the compromise might really be between the American Federation of Labor's desire for "unrestricted" collective bargaining (Perlman 1928: 265) and the industrialists' urge to impose a different, putatively benign regime of "scientific" personnel management at each workplace. In Japan the compromise might be secured by a paternalistic, and even militaristic ideology – the desire to protect "mothers of the country's soldiers" (the rural women working in textile factories) that had led to the country's first factory Act (Yoshiro 1968: 74–5). In Europe's smaller industrialized countries the need to develop a social partnership in order to have any hope of adjusting to the buffetings of the world economy might provide a special incentive (Katzenstein 1984: 27). But in each case the norms promulgated by the ILO, which reflected the results of similar battles over the control of labor throughout the world, gave domestic labor movements foreign models and international allies, as well as some guarantee that most reforms would continue even when times got tougher.

The success of the various national social pacts formed in the 1930s combined with the even greater social unity demanded by the Second World War to diminish the relative importance of the ILO as part of the social adhesive in the industrialized world. After all, one of the things that the ILO of 1933 could not provide – full employment – was more important to the cohesion of postwar industrial capitalist societies than the improving conditions for the employed that the world organization has assured. The promise of mass consumption, the national macroeconomic policies of the welfare state, and the compromises worked out by national employers' and workers' federations all played more significant roles. The UN labor agencies became "services institutions" to the "neocorporatist power structures of the national states" (Peterson 1980: 21).

More than anything else, the international labor standards promulgated by the ILO became substantively significant signs of the boundary between the Free World's "North" and "South," the line between the world where industrial labor was relatively privileged and the one where it was not. In the mid-1960s Africa, most of Asia, and much of Latin America stood out as regions where national labor legislation did not conform with ILO norms (Landy 1966: 11). The boundary of privilege separating labor at the core of the industrial world from Third World workers represented the ultimate achievement of the class compromise that conservative labor leaders like Samuel Gompers and progressive business leaders like David Lubin had first envisioned during the Great War.

National policies – especially restrictions on immigration – helped maintain that boundary, but even within the core many unprotected workers would remain, mostly in fields in which the ILO had no relevant "industrial committee." These less privileged workers included homemakers, those self-employed in dead-end fields, and immigrants employed in jobs that few northern citizens were willing to fill (Harrod 1987: parts 2 and 3). Northern workers in all these fields shared the Third World workers' limited chances to organize and limited access to the technologically-specific skills that protected high-wage workers (Doeringer and Piore 1971: 13).

Core farmers and other privileged producers of raw materials

The world agriculture organizations followed a similar trajectory. International agreements supporting raw material producers at the core of the Free World Order began to work alongside the indirect aid to OECD farmers that came from keeping agriculture out of the GATT.

The League had initially attempted something very different. Instead of slowly increasing free trade in agriculture and providing information and incentives to encourage farmers to adjust to new international competition – the way David Lubin had hoped the IIA would – the League briefly promoted the liberal fundamentalist idea of rapidly eliminating all agricultural subsidies and all restrictions on trade in agricultural products (McClure 1933: 287). But the Depression intervened and governments returned to the old policy of raising tariffs as the farmer's first line of defense against falling prices (Tracy 1964: 12). When this failed to prevent cascading prices, legislatures turned to interventions in the domestic market. Some of these interventions required international collaboration. In the 1930s such collaboration led to an unsuccessful agreement to fix the international price of wheat by withholding supplies when prices were too low and selling from the resulting stocks when they went too high (ibid.: 147). The agreement failed simply because the steep economic downturn meant that world wheat prices fell faster than impoverished governments could purchase a buffer stock, yet governments could not get farmers to withhold wheat from the market themselves. Many of the more successful Depression-era innovations (the egg marketing convention sponsored by the IIA is one example) operated at the level of smaller, regional markets where it was easier to identify and isolate those who broke the agreement (IIA 1942: 18). Global agreements were only successful when they turned agricultural products into a form of intellectual property, which was the strategy of the International Wine Office – created to boost wine consumption in response to the US experiment with Prohibition (Railhac 1928) – and the IIA cheese convention (IIA 1942: 20).

These institutions codified the now-familiar systems of varietal names and appellations of origin.

Europeans involved in planning postwar agricultural institutions learned from the failure of the interwar wheat agreement. They envisioned creating an international food board with a common fund to support a wide range of commodity agreements (Peterson 1980: 179), under the assumption that the price cycles of different food-stuffs would differ enough for the proceeds from sales needed to lower the price of one to be used to offset the cost of purchases needed to raise the price of another. The US vetoed the idea, preferring David Lubin's kind of information-gathering agencies that might help farmers adjust to competition from more efficient foreign, often American, farmers.

Of course, this did not mean that postwar US farms operated under laissez faire. One prominent economic historian calls the American system prevailing since the Depression, "a public center with a private periphery" (Averitt 1968: 161). Government effectively sets farmer income through a complex system of loans and transfer payments. When the food board became a dead letter, the other industrialized nations quickly reestablished and strengthened their own national systems of transfer payments, price supports, and bans on the importation of foreign agricultural products. In the early 1960s, when the US put agriculture on the agenda for the Kennedy Round of GATT talks, the European Community responded by creating a unified system of farm supports, the Common Agricultural Policy, designed to prevent the Americans from playing one Community member off against another (Tracy 1964: 321; Peterson 1980: 238).

Agriculture thus remained outside the purview of the GATT. This created a minor problem for the US government; it had to maintain its costly welfare programs for farmers who, conceivably, could have survived in a liberal world agricultural order. The problem faced by Third World farmers was larger. Those whose products competed with core producers continued to be denied access to OECD markets, while producers of tropical products (coffee, cocoa, tea, etc.) usually faced all the vicissitudes of the free market, something that was equally true of other Third World raw material producers. This made Asian, African, and Latin American governments active supporters of the kind of commodity pricing agreements that the Europeans had mooted in the 1940s.

Three commodity agreements aiding LDC producers (of coffee, sugar, and tin, respectively) were in place by 1970. These pacts did not change the overall picture of agriculture within the Free World

Order. Domestic and international regulation ensured that the producers of products unique to the temperate core of the Free World rarely faced a global free market. By not equally privileging raw material producers in the less industrialized world, world organizations helped draw the line between North and South that divided the Free World from its beginning.

Supporting the welfare state through cooperation in public finance

The financial demands of the northern welfare states – from the subsidies paid to farmers to the costs of countercyclical government spending – assured that their governments generally played a larger role in their economies than governments did in the South. In the early 1970s the government of a typical LDC (Ghana, for example) would spend one-fifth of the country's gross national product, while the government of Great Britain (a typical industrialized county) would spend one-third (World Bank 1985: 224–5). Both First World and Third World governments often had to borrow a great deal of money in order to maintain their part of the national economy, especially during business slumps when tax revenues were down. While the social order in both a country like Ghana and one like Britain might, as a result, be threatened by collapse of the global financial system, governments like Britain's may actually have been more vulnerable simply because its citizens expected more from it.

Both John Maynard Keynes and Harry Dexter White wanted the Bretton Woods system to protect the new welfare states from financial crises. And while the designers of the IMF and World Bank certainly feared that some governments would be tempted to print money to aid their political allies – the way the Weimar Social Democrats had tried to support the Ruhr strikers – a greater fear was that capitalists would trigger financial crises by using open markets to flee taxation in the welfare states, at the same time pulling investment toward less socially productive uses (Helleiner 1992: 14–15; cf., Ikenberry 1992; Nau 1990: 81–4).[2] Keynes and White also worried that a laissez-faire monetary system would encourage currency speculation, leaving huge amounts of capital tied up in the socially unproductive business of trying to gain profit from minute changes in the relative value of each country's money (Horie 1964: 176–7). But the traditional "orthodox" alternative, the gold standard, would eventually restrict international trade and therefore threaten the creation of new industries, the advantage that both continued to see as a sure result of a liberal trading order (Russell 1977: 110–11), unless, of course, gold was discovered as trade expanded, as had been the happy coincidence during the boom years before the First World War.

Interwar IGOs had been designed to cope with only the first of these problems. The League organized reconstruction loans in exchange for anti-inflationary fiscal and monetary policies (League of Nations 1930: 184–8) but could not martial sufficient resources to keep all the new states from instituting inflationary monetary policies or from borrowing beyond their means. Many governments searched for, and found, easier terms through private banks whose requirements made League conditionality seem unnecessarily doctrinaire. For example, the League required Estonia and Bulgaria to denationalize banks even though the link between that action and the goal of avoiding regional economic collapse was far from clear (Einzig 1930: 14).

League conditionality reflected the views of central bankers for whom it acted as broker. The reconstruction loans and the standards the League set for central bank statistics (Greaves 1931: 52) encouraged cooperation among central bankers that quickly became much more important than League agreements themselves (Einzig 1930: 12). This cooperation was institutionalized within the Bank for International Settlements (BIS), set up to administer the Young Plan by acting as trustee for war debts, supervising deliveries of reparations in kind, and working to shift Germany's debt from a few sovereign lenders to many private investors (ibid.: 34–5).

The BIS quickly became a forum where central bankers met, a place where they could ask each other to lend funds greatly in excess of those they made available to the BIS itself. It promised to become an informal multilateral clearing union, inspired, not surprisingly, by the Universal Postal Union's old system for clearing the accounts of different national postal administrations (Dulles 1932: 15), but it could not solve the structural problem: Germany still could not raise enough money to pay all its debts and the one country that had the money, the US, would not. Even under the Young Plan, the US government still considered debt relief to be primarily a matter for private markets. It even gave its seat on the BIS board to the private lenders who had subscribed to the Young Plan loans. Frequent meetings of central bankers, all of whom shared the fundamentalist orthodoxy that many economists thought had contributed to the mess, may only have encouraged speculators (Einzig 1930: 22). Moreover, because an association of private banks, rather than the US Federal Reserve, held the US seat in the BIS, the meeting did not even give other countries the opportunity to use moral suasion to convince the US government to open its markets and provide international liquidity and a steady flow of capital – the roles that Charles Kindleberger (1973) argues that a lead country always needs to play in order for the world economy to be stable. In fact, the interest of the American subscribers in the survival and profit of their firms were not necessarily congruent with the interest of the Hoover and Roosevelt administrations in establishing and maintaining a stable and prosperous domestic and international order (New York University Institute of Finance, n.d.: 7–10).

Keynes had originally hoped that the Bretton Woods Conference would replace the BIS with an agency that would be able to expand international liquidity as trade grew, help governments maintain fixed exchange rates between their currencies, support them when they attempted to control capital flight, and control inflation by making its loans conditional on adopting the rational economic policies proposed by the organization's independent – but, Keynes imagined, pro-welfare state – professional staff. Keynes's colleague, League economist Richard Stone, had already begun designing the basic tools that would be needed by the global professional staff (and national welfare-state managers), a standardized System of National Accounts providing "a comprehensive and detailed framework for systematic and integrated recording of transaction flows within a (market) economy" (Kanninen 1989: 4).

The IMF never became exactly what Keynes had envisioned. The Roosevelt and Truman administrations were leery of giving it the power to expand the global money supply; instead, the US government became responsible for expanding international liquidity by printing dollars whose value was secured by an American promise to redeem them for gold at a fixed rate. Without the power to issue any new kind of international money, the IMF's basic assets consisted of reserve deposits from its member states. These soon proved inadequate for the loans needed by governments trying to maintain the value of their currencies. In 1961, when both Britain and the United States needed such loans, BIS-style central bank cooperation came to the rescue. Recognizing the likelihood that similar crises would recur, the ten major capitalist states established the General Agreements to Borrow (GAB), partially outside the framework of the IMF (Strange 1974: 270–1). From that point forward, the central bankers' old club itself, the BIS, took on an increasingly significant role in

Free World cooperation in public finance, and maintained it even after the 1967 IMF agreement to create Special Drawing Rights (SDRs), the kind of international currency that Keynes had hoped for from the beginning.

One of the other "politically efficient" ideas of the Keynesians came up in the SDR debate: Keynesians had long argued that if new international reserves were issued they could be allocated to governments on the basis of some measure of economic need, thus creating an "SDR–aid *Link*," a way of increasing funds for Third World development without having to raise them by taxing the reluctant citizens of the wealthiest countries. The idea appealed to most Third World governments, many of whom did not necessarily go along with the related notion that only LDC governments with a demonstrated capacity to deal with macroeconomic problems should be rewarded with Link funds (Ferguson 1988: 107–26).

Unfortunately, at least for supporters of the Link, in order to get the US to agree to the SDR in 1967, the other IMF members had to accept that SDRs would be issued to members in proportion to their share of existing IMF reserve quotas, which meant that the US and UK (the original main contributors) would receive the lion's share of any new issue. The Fund's Australian director said this amounted to "rewarding the improvident" because it would allow the two major economic powers that chronically ran balance-of-payments deficits to mount them even higher and thus export their own inflation – their dollars and pounds that could buy less and less – to the rest of the world (Vries 1976: 218). But other observers noted that even before the SDR the IMF had no power to check the US government's ability to pay its bills by simply printing more dollars; the only thing that stopped it was the US commitment to convert dollars to gold.

While the conditionality that the IMF could place on its wealthiest members was both small and diminishing in the 1960s, the demands it made on its poorest members had become more significant and more stringent. In those relationships the IMF adopted the bankers' orthodoxy that had typified the League's operations in public finance. The IMF's supporters justified its conditionality by arguing that it was always inflation that got LDC governments into trouble. When, as result, their national currency was less valuable in real terms, their citizens had to send more of it abroad (often illegally) to buy the goods they wanted. This created balance-of-payments deficits and thus forced LDC governments to borrow from the IMF. Since the IMF had so few funds, and since its job had always been to deal with short-term problems, it had to demand that inflation be controled very rapidly. To do that meant cutting any growth in the national money supply and it meant eliminating government deficits, usually by diminishing the role of government in the national economy – which, from the liberal fundamentalist point of view underlying the bankers' orthodoxy, was all to the good, anyway.

Thus, even before the postwar monetary system collapsed in 1971 – when the US decided to abrogate its commitment to discipline its own inflationary tendencies by being willing to convert dollars to gold at a fixed rate – the IMF had begun to present two very different faces. From the one side it could be seen as a sign of an ongoing system of cooperation in public finance among the major capitalist states, a system involving both formal and informal arrangements to borrow from one another to support the fixed exchange rates of their currencies, a system designed to support both the expansion of trade in industrial goods encouraged by the GATT and the maintenance of the welfare state that the world organizations for labor and agriculture supported and had helped establish. From the other side, as seen by states that did not have access to these less institutionalized arrangements, the IMF remained a substantive regulatory agency of central importance, a lender of last resort who made the traditional bankers' demands to diminish the role of government in the economy in exchange for its help.

Encouraging Decolonization and Development

By the early 1970s the governments that most often turned to the IMF were not the welfare states at the core of the Free World but the development states on its periphery. To many of their leaders the IMF's policies were just another example of the double standards applied to them by the world organizations. Yet, looked at another way, in the League and UN era world organizations have always been allies in the Third World's struggle to gain the advantages that accrued to industrialized countries.[3]

Certainly the story of the world organizations and development is so bound up with that of the Third World nationalist movements that academic historians have been tempted to think of the UN system as essentially an elite matter, as a meeting ground for the western-educated upper circles of native societies in Africa and Asia, and as their special tool. Nevertheless, as C. L. R. James, argues, even in those colonies where decolonization appeared to be the nonviolent transfer of authority from Europeans to an Europeanized native elite, popular mass movements both forced the hands of the colonial governments and provided the native elite with the legitimacy it needed to rule (James 1977). The League and UN systems helped native leaders build an international coalition among their own mass movements and the geographically separated anti-imperial forces in other colonies and in the North. This coalition, in turn, assured decolonization.

The same coalition also pushed the world organizations to take on their many development tasks. The coalition's strategy resembled that of the movement for international labor legislation at the turn of the century. Supporters of development attached their programs to the liberal internationalist vision by demonstrating that the acquiescence of the social served by "development" would be needed in order for the liberal vision to be fulfilled.

The goals the industrialized countries served by supporting the world organizations' responsibilities for decolonization and development can be grouped under-five headings: (1) establishing a world order based on "ethical" hegemony; (2) assuring access to necessary raw materials; (3) insuring the global financial system against a string of Third World defaults; (4) containing antisystemic movements; and (6) what might be called "greenlining," that is, the identification of regions soon to be successfully incorporated into the expanding industrialized core of the Free World Order – the opposite of the "redlining" that occurs when lenders decide to make no further loans to projects in neighbourhoods that they regard as being on their way to becoming slums.

In contrast, while southern governments have accepted that "development" has been designed to serve these purposes, they have been more interested in ways the world organizations have been able to strengthen the Third World state, not so much by giving governments a greater capacity to coerce and defraud their citizens, but more by contributing to the populist project of improving the lives of the masses who gave many Third World nationalists their legitimacy in the first place. The closer we get to the ultimate clients of "development," the more prominent these purposes – which remain compatible with the various northern goals – become.

The legacies of the League: the quest for ethical hegemony, access to raw materials, and insurance against financial collapse

The mandate system gave the League responsibility for overseeing the German and Ottoman overseas territories ceded to the victors in the First World War. The system reflected liberal internationalist aspirations going back as far as John Wright's promise of 1851 that free trade and the Rail Union would put Africa, Asia, and Latin America "on an equality with the advanced kingdoms of the world" (Wright 1851: 12), the promise that any coercive rule existing under a liberal world order would be temporary, a station on the way toward an ethical kind of hegemony of the cosmopolitan bourgeoisie under which people everywhere would enjoy the riches – and the political voice – of the citizens in the powerful republics. This vision was certainly embraced by the critical voices in the League campaign, by Emily Green Balch, John A. Hobson, and Leonard Woolf, but it was also embraced by more conservative figures in the League movement, like the IIIC's Gilbert Murray and South African statesman Jan Christian Smuts, the man who had the most impact on the design of the mandate system (Northedge 1986: 34–8).

Like the ILO, the League's Mandates Commission was able to place a few constraints on national governments. It could accept petitions from natives, examine the annual reports that the mandatory powers had to submit, take the mandatory powers to the International Court if they violated League norms, and suggest modifications of their mandates (Factiri 1932: 87; Hall 1948: 198; League of Nations 1930: 332, 341; Q. Wright 1930: 105, 147–9). The ILO itself cooperated in investigating forced colonial labor by adopting conventions to combat it (Gibberd 1937: 74, 81; Landy 1966: 214).

The IGOs promoted a much broader social agenda as well. In the mandates religious tolerance was to be practiced (League of Nations 1930: 334–6), public health systems improved, public education expanded (Q. Wright 1930: 257), and native cultural treasures studied and preserved (Greaves 1931: 120). Perhaps as a result the mandates soon enjoyed more than just the rapid increases in foreign trade and investment that are the boon (or misfortune) of every productive colony. Their populations grew and they became healthier and better educated (Q. Wright 1930: 560–3). A more benign form of colonialism seemed to take hold under the League's gaze; Kipling's India rather than Conrad's *Heart of Darkness* became the rule. The Mandates Commission even began to fulfill John Wright's aspiration for the *"Early Restoration of the Land of Promise to the Jews"* when it required that Palestine be made ready to become a Jewish national home (League of Nations 1930: 337). Outside the mandates the IIIC helped the Chinese modernize their system of public education (IIIC 1946: 167), and the League secretariat provided technical assistance to Latin American governments when they needed new economic policies to adjust to the Depression (M. Hill 1946: 87). The League even experimented with conditional economic assistance by loaning money to Liberia in exchange for domestic civil reforms (Walter 1957: 570).

Of course, the IGOs did not forget the economic interests that the imperial powers had in their colonies. The League's brief attack on all intervention in markets for agricultural products complemented a much more aggressive campaign to give all industrialized countries equal access to raw materials. Throughout the 1920s those colonial powers that were rich in raw materials had imposed export duties on the sale of goods outside their empires, thus limiting economic growth in the resource-poor industrial states like Japan and giving them an impetus for a new round of imperialism. The League secretariat responded by studying the impact of such monopolistic practices and promoting a treaty that would have ended export restrictions on all raw materials (Kopp 1941: 35; Greaves 1931: 52).

The treaty-making effort failed, but other League attempts to give industrial powers more equal access proved successful. The League helped renegotiate the Anglo-Persian oil concession, which ended the British monopoly and favored American petroleum interests (Walter 1957: 572). It also pressured native leaders in the new states created from the Ottoman empire to end monopolistic foreign mineral concessions (M. Hill 1946: 40) and banned them entirely in the African mandates (League of Nations 1930: 335). The League also required gradual change to a system of private ownership of land in the mandates (Q. Wright 1930: 256) and the IIA set up a kind of shoestring international agricultural extension service for export farmers in the LDCs (A. Hobson 1931: 111); both of these programs encouraged entrepreneurs to invest in growing tropical agricultural products. Postwar world agencies, especially the IMF and the World Bank, have maintained the League's interest in ensuring that the Third World remains the site of farms, forests, and mines feeding northern factories.[4]

Finally, League-era institutions also initiated continuing practices designed to protect world financial markets from the effect of a massive default on obligations by developing nations. Depression-era defaults on bonds issued both by Latin American governments and by the successors to the defeated empires threatened many private fortunes in the industrial world. To combat the problem the BIS began aiding newly independent countries in establishing central banks and following orthodox credit policies.

After the Second World War the World Bank took on and expanded this insurance function. It has always required that its clients join the IMF and accept its orthodox advice (Mason and Asher 1973: 162). The Bank also closely oversees its own loans and the overall development programs of the countries to which it lends, even requiring that autonomous authorities be set up to administer projects (ibid. 190) and that the Bank has seats on their boards (Payer 1982: 133). Before 1970 the Bank had also become the coordinator of all western aid to ten of the largest aid recipients,[5] which allowed it to decide how much development debt each could carry (Poats 1985: 201–2; Lewis and Kapur 1973: 89).

Northern concerns with insulating the financial system, protecting access to raw materials, and promoting a more ethical western hegemony continued to operate throughout the heyday of the UN. Immediately after the war the US played a key role by lending "support at the United Nations to third world states in their campaign to speed up the process of decolonisation, and to extend the principle of international accountability from the trusteeship territories to the remaining colonial possessions of the European powers" (Mayall 1990: 116; cf. Toussaint 1957: 241; Bailey 1964: 105; Sears 1980: 7–8). Initially, of course, the US rejected extending economic aid to the new nations of Asia and Africa, in part because American policymakers were convinced that those regions would be flooded with investors interested in exploiting their raw materials (Wood 1986: 43).

Goals of the UN era: containing communism and greenlining

US views changed as a result of the Cold War. Both Truman and Eisenhower saw limited foreign assistance to the Third World as a technique for fighting communism (Augelli and Murphy 1988: 82–6), while W. W. Rostow describes John F. Kennedy's 1957 legislative initiative, the first of the large western aid programs, as well as Kennedy's inauguration of the UN Development Decade and his advocacy of the UN's 1 percent aid target as motivated almost entirely by his anti-communism (1985: 3, 13–17).

Some of the Third World goals that Kennedy failed to embrace also influenced the UN's expanding role in development. Beginning in the early 1960s the South pursued a larger say in the governance of the international financial system as well as exemption from global liberalism for LDC producers by creating new UN agencies such as

UNCTAD where southern demands could be aggregated and pressure placed on the North.

Both proposals to increase the Third World say in the IMF and proposals for international commodity agreements or other exemptions from liberalism challenged the boundary of privilege surrounding the welfare states, which may be the reason that powerful northern states have been so opposed to them. Yet states at the core of the Free World, and the global IGOs they dominate, have always treated that boundary as porous. They hold out the hope that eventually all countries will enter the core of the Free World. World Bank officials speak of the moment of "graduation" when LDCs are no longer poor enough to receive the concessionary loans provided by the IDA (Elbialy 1963: 73). For the GATT, "graduation" is the point at which an LDC should no longer enjoy the system of trade preferences for some Third World products worked out as consequences of the move to create UNCTAD (Gosovic 1972: 92).[6]

Of course, in a world order that maintains a boundary of privilege between rich and poor countries the "graduates" will have to be helped across, which is where greenlining comes in. Those on the privileged side have a self-interest in the process, for the reasons first discussed by the interwar businessmen's peace movement and later picked up by Fiorello La Guardia: the world's new manufacturing regions can constantly provide the most developed regions with new markets for the higher technology goods that only they can produce. In the 1950s Japan's growing economy might not have provided markets for the early industrial products of the Europe or the United States – textiles, shoes, furniture, etc. – but Japan did become a major consumer of machine tools, electrical equipment, and chemicals for decades before it became a partner and a major competitor in the products of the automobile age. The same, the argument goes, would be true of the next group of manufacturing countries, one good reason to help their development in the same way that reconstruction assistance had helped Japan.

We should not be surprised that some of the economic miracles of the early 1990s – Hong Kong, Malaysia, Singapore, South Korea, Taiwan – were each receiving around 4 percent of their GNP in official development assistance in the 1960s, while today's development disasters – the Sahelian states – were receiving less than 0.5 percent of their GNPs. Nor should we be surprised that South Korea, by far the most populous state to enter the high-income world after Japan, was receiving fully 6 percent of the aid allocated in 1960, when its population was less than 1 percent of that of the Third

World as a whole (Poats 1985: 121). In the successful countries, aid funds were used to build up local industry at the same time as the approval signified by such relatively large resource transfers from western donors encouraged foreign investors to risk long-term commitments to these countries. That is the logic of greenlining.

Strengthening Third World states and the Free World Order

The logic does not work everywhere. Consider India and Pakistan, the countries that received most of the IDA's credits in the 1960s and fully 60 percent in 1971 (Ferguson 1988: 130). As a percentage of GNP, or of GNP per capita, India and Pakistan received much less than Japan or Europe after war, and than South Korea did in the 1950s and 1960s, but in absolute terms the subcontinent did very well. Most of the aid may have been used just as wisely as the aid going to the countries that eventually entered the core. But in the Indian subcontinent, with a population nearly double that of the expanded European Community and the US combined, the idea of everyone entering a world of mass production and mass consumption was absurd.

Instead, the Indian government, and governments in countries with similar economic conditions, used aid to fulfill that populist agenda identified by A. F. Robertson (1984). The world organizations have played a central role in providing Third World governments with that capacity ever since the UN established the regional development commissions and began programs of technical assistance in the 1940s. In addition to providing training and funding needed to carry out education, health, family planning, and social service programs, the world organizations have provided technical expertise and financial backing that have given millions access to running water and electricity for the first time. This has been one of the major tasks undertaken not only by the World Bank but also by the International Atomic Energy Agency, electricity being the benefit gained by Third World peoples in exchange for not developing nuclear weapons (IAEA 1977: 48). Finally, the world organizations have played a key role as a propagandist for the least advantaged in the poorest countries – for children, the handicapped, rural people, traditionally excluded minorities, and women. The World Bank, for example, rightfully claims some credit for dramatizing the condition of Indian farmers to the Indian government and thereby fostering the political climate that made the green revolution of high-yield agriculture possible (Lewis and Kapur 1973: 92).

Robertson notes that the real successes of development populism – longer lives, better diets, greater literacy – are hardly as glamorous as the utopia of mass consumption promised by postwar liberal internationalists, or the even more glowing utopias promised by the now widely discredited alternatives promoted by China and the Soviet Union (1984: 221). But, unlike those grander utopias, development populism's were at least obtainable.

Robertson also argues that the organizations playing the most central role in assuring this outcome were relatively autonomous, those subject to control from many sources which could be played off against one another by the agency's staff (ibid. 131). Thus UNICEF, with its independent sources of funding, might be more significant than the high-profile UNCTAD, directly controlled by Third World governments, or the IMF, where the few richest capitalist powers could almost always set the agenda.

If we look at the development activities of the world organizations as a whole they sometimes appear remarkably decentralized and incoherent, following no simple guidelines and no single development doctrine. Moreover, the world organizations involved with development are only one part of a much larger, and seemingly even more incoherent network in international civil society consisting of the myriad bilateral relations between donor and recipient countries and hundreds of private voluntary agencies like Catholic Relief and Oxfam.

At one level, all these agencies appear to do the same things. They provide advice and they fund development "projects" – everything from opening a cooperative store in a rural village to building a dam to provide electricity for a half-dozen nations. But they do so with very different, often contradictory goals, and with very different constituencies in mind, as those who work for the agencies will readily tell you.

In 1986 I went to find out how contradictory they were by interviewing officials in the head offices of the FAO, UNDP, UNICEF, World Bank, the development units of the Canadian, Italian, and US governments, the similar office of the European Community, and two private voluntary agencies, Oxfam and the Unitarian Universalist Service Committee. Seen from the various headquarters, "development" meant everything from supporting social revolution in the Third World to preventing it, and people at the top of the development network were very clear, and often antagonistic, about the goals other agencies were trying to serve.

This diversity of goals leaves the global governance of development as something like Robertson's autonomous agency writ large.

Taken together, all the different agencies are fairly effective at pursuing the few goals they have in common, which turn out to be those populist concerns he identified, directed at improving the basic quality of life within the Third World.

At the same time the various development agencies, particularly the world organizations, tend to end up strengthening Third World states. Critics of the world organizations often concentrate on the less progressive ways in which that happens. After all, what development assistance amounts to is a transfer of funds to government officials who, therefore, do not have to raise the same funds through taxes.

The significance of that transfer varies. By the 1970s it had become fairly low in relation to India's national budget, but in quite a few countries it remained equivalent to virtually everything the government spent (Cassen et al. 1986: 29). Moreover, there is a band of countries around the world – from the shores of the Caribbean, across most of Africa, into the Middle East with states like Jordan and Asia with Bangladesh, and then across the Pacific – where governments are all deeply aid-dependent, where annual net aid receipts are equivalent to a quarter or more or the national budget and, often more significantly, where net aid receipts amount to more than the hard currency that governments gain through tariffs and other taxes (OECD 1989). Critics point out that these independent sources of funds sometimes allow Third World governments to become authoritarian and technocratic. They are able to bypass democratic decision-making and their accountability to their people is weakened (Laar 1980: 35). The world organizations can even help LDC governments fraudulently maintain whatever popular legitimacy they need by providing a venue where they can blame the North for their internal problems (Brown 1980: 216).

There is truth to these criticisms, but they do not identify what is probably the primary way that development assistance strengthens the Third World state. Robert Cassen, a long-time World Bank advisor and one of the intellectual forces behind the later reports of the Brandt Commission, argues that the fungibility of aid funds (the ability of governments to do other things with taxes because they have received money from donors) is easily overestimated. In many cases governments would not have undertaken development projects without aid. Cassen argues that, on the whole, while some aid expenditure

> may be of questionable priority, the bulk goes to support basic infrastructure in power, transport, health, and education. Without such spending, the social structure is not likely to hold together, let alone develop. Reductions in public expenditure may bear disproportionately on the poorer people.

> Social programmes are particularly vulnerable, because the proportion of recurrent expenditure tends to be high, and the potential losers have little voice in policy decisions. (Cassen et al. 1986: 21)

Aid expenditures most often enhance the authority of LDC governments simply by making their citizens more dependent on the central authorities for basic social services (cf. Gitleson 1970: 174).

Third World citizens are very aware of this. Robertson reproduces a chart of hypothesized "attitudes of three levels of officials of a development organisation" toward each other and toward their clients (1984: 156). The most striking part was the last line where "the people's" attitudes toward the agencies at all levels was listed as simply "government," for better or for worse. In 1986 I attempted to check these hypotheses by following the different development agencies whose officials I had interviewed from the headquarters to the field in Cape Verde and Senegal, two of the Sahelian countries where aid agencies were then most active.[7]

As I moved through the development agencies from headquarters to the field the views of what "development" was all about began to converge. The field officers all treated their headquarters staff as "distant . . . unrealistic . . . and ill-informed," just as Robertson would expect, while their local colleagues from agencies supposedly pursuing radically different development doctrines were considered sensible professionals with realistic aims. When I finally got to the clients, the confirmation was even more striking. For good or for ill, all projects were treated as the work of the government, even those that private voluntary agencies back in Oxford and Boston considered examples of "people-to-people" cooperation with African grassroots movements.

One long conversation with an older woman outside Cape Verde's capital was particularly striking. We talked about the local birth control clinic, which had been built by the Swedes and supported by the UN; the project was extolled to me by the women's association of Cape Verde's anticlerical governing party – " 'n supô governu" ("I surmise it's government") was my informant's predictable designation of responsibility for the project. Then we talked about a Catholic clinic for pregnant women, run by the government's only serious opponents and extoled by fundraisers in the US as an open challenge to all the evils allowed by country's Marxist bosses, " 'n creditâ governu" ("I believe it's government"). After all, she said, the same party official who had wanted me to know so much about the family planning clinic had been on hand to open the Catholic alternative and claim it for the state. Robertson's picture of "development" as the key "populist" project of the Third World state was confirmed.

More broadly, "development," a paradoxical, top–down process whose centers of power are literally half a world away from its clients, has helped incorporate the Third World masses into the often disappointing political systems that they or their parents fought to create. It has done so both by a successful appeal to interests – Third World governments *have* provided resources to lengthen lives, improve health, and improve the chances of the next generation – and by shaping aspirations: "development" has partially succeeded in turning the Third World masses into a cadre fulfilling a world-historical project, John Maynard Keynes's project and John Wright's project, the project of making all people "secure of the comforts and necessities of the body" (Keynes 1971: 10) and all nations "on an equality with the advanced kingdoms," (Wright 1851: 12).

In shaping aspirations toward the project of material prosperity and equality with the "advanced" states, Third World governments, and the allies they have made within international civil society, have succeeded in emphasizing particular lines of political conflict while obscuring others. The promoters of "development," like all successful political leaders, have been able to obscure the lines of conflict that are most threatening to their own interests. In sum, as James Mayall argues (1990: 103), the development system helped remove the threat to the liberal world economy posed by imperial trading blocs and the raw materials problems of the interwar period. And as Robert H. Jackson argues (1990: 112–18), the international redistribution facilitated by the development agencies helped assure the stability of most post-colonial states.

Relying on Civil Society

The large funds administered by intergovernmental development agencies illustrate a basic difference between the UN system and its predecessors: A few UN-era agencies have significant powers to reward, and therefore to sanction, their state members, powers never granted to the Public International Unions. Moreover, the average UN agency has a bit more autonomy than its nineteenth-century predecessors; its officers can wield their powers with a bit less attention to the immediate demands of members. Yet this increased autonomy and these increased material capabilities may be less important than the UN's new relationship to other parts of civil society. The UN is open to other essentially noncoercive institutions, it relies on private agencies to carry out much of its work, and it encourages the expansion of the realm of voluntary associations, especially the creation of international communities of policy-oriented intellectuals who can provide the intellectual leadership needed to reform world organizations and perhaps even to design a new world order.

Influence and autonomy

The most significant of the day-to-day sources of influence of the world organizations created in the mid-twentieth century remain their capacities to encourage interstate cooperation by holding regular meetings, providing information, and monitoring prior agreements (figure 6). In one sense, the agencies' new capacities to lend funds to members simply changed the way in which the IGOs typically supported the domestic and international allies of members. However, the ability of the IMF and development agencies to cut off funds on which a member has come to rely created a fundamentally new capacity to impose sanctions, even though the interwar charters

How Members Controlled Organizations

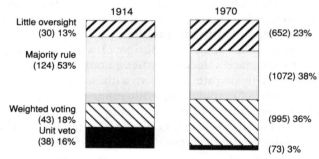

How Organizations Influenced Members

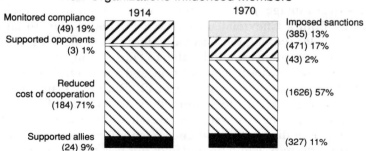

FIGURE 6   Formal controls by member states over world organizations and means used by the organizations to influence their members, 1914 and 1970 compared (regular activities, 1911–15 and 1966–70, see appendix on data)

of the ILO and the League anticipated this power when they required members to retaliate against those in violation of prior agreements, as determined by the agencies.[8]

The interwar experiments in increasing the capacities of global IGOs encouraged contradictory trends in the relative autonomy of the most powerful world bodies. Some of their activities became very independent of all their members while others almost became tools of their most powerful states. Both trends diverged from the original vision of the League. Reflecting the liberal fundamentalism of the 1920s, the League's architects had hoped for a very limited global administration subject to the rule of the majority. The limited administration was to be very efficient. According to conventional administrative doctrine of the 1920s, that meant it had to be highly centralized. But by the late 1930s centralization had gone so far that some League advocates complained that it had become inefficient and argued that the separate agencies and committees should be given more autonomy (Burton 1941: 84–5). Mary Parker Follett had always advocated such an approach, to the private firms she advised as well as to the public agencies she supported, and David Mitrany's functionalism responded to this problem.

The new arguments about the design of world organizations reflected what took place a decade earlier among advocates of systematic management in private industry, with some still championing the giant, centralized corporation, while others advocated the kind of divisional structure that had been adopted by industry leaders like Du Pont, General Motors and I. G. Farben (Yates 1985). The downside of the multidivisional corporation and the functionally separate system of world organizations was the same: to some extent "customers" would be able to use competition among the divisions to their own advantage. Just as potential North American car purchasers could go from a Chevrolet dealer, to a Pontiac dealer, to an Oldsmobile dealer seeking the best value for their money, diplomats or private interest groups would be able to "forum hop" in order to find the organization whose "composition and traditions" would most support their position (Peterson 1986: 42). But the advantages of the functional structure to the shareholders of General Motors or the state members of the UN system outweighed these drawbacks. Competition among divisions could encourage efficiency, and it assured that *more* customers would be satisfied; this was especially true in the field of development. Moreover, the functionally divided system was better able to respond to a changing environment; parts of the system could be reformed without having to rework a hierarchical whole.

The interwar urge to find the most efficient organizational structure combined with a related urge to move away from inefficient and ineffective ways of making collective decisions and overseeing the work of the agencies' professional staffs. By the early 1930s most of the League's committees had abandoned the cumbersome practice of allowing any member to forbid a proposed action (the system of the unit veto) in favor of systems of majority rule (Burton 1941: 157). Similarly, despite the lack of realism evident in much of the activity of the interwar agencies, there was a usually quite realistic move toward governing those activities by systems of weighted voting or by committees reflecting the relative power of the states most involved in the issue.[9] And there was a related move toward eliminating unnecessarily intrusive oversight of the activities of the League system's staff by limiting members to programmic control of the agencies' activities and even, in a few cases, allowing staff to undertake experimental programs on their own initiative.

The movement in both directions continued in the UN era, especially within the most influential agencies. Thus, for example, while the IMF's formal voting procedure allows the organization to be used as a tool of the foreign policies of the most economically powerful of the industrial states (Lister 1984), and while it certainly has been used by the US and its allies to sanction regimes with which the US is in conflict, in practice most decisions by the Fund's governing body are made by consensus. This gives the managing director an unusual degree of latitude to make decisions by interpreting ambiguous guidelines (Ferguson 1988: 65; Gold 1969: 516). This effective transfer of significant legislative power to the managing director, combined with the governing board's tendency to shy away from controversial issues in order to preserve unanimity, gives the IMF staff a great deal of autonomy not only in designing specific conditions to be placed on member states, but also in creating many of the IMF's most important new programs, from providing technical assistance to issuing SDRs (Horsefield 1969: I, 471–2; Vries 1976: 147).

Openness to civil society, program administration by institutions of civil society, and encouragement of social movements

Of course, the programs designed by the IMF's relatively autonomous staff do not emerge *sui generis* within the walls of its Washington headquarters. They reflect the changing orthodoxy of the transnational intellectual community from which the organization draws its personnel, economists trained primarily in Britain and the United States. Critics of the Fund from both the right and the left often (quite reasonably) blame policies that they do not like on changes in fashion within the transnational community by which the Fund is so thoroughly penetrated. Thus opponents of the SDR charge that it reflected the triumph of " 'deep' Keynesian solutions" (Nau 1990: 138, 149–50), while those who regret the human cost of the IMF's austerity programs of the 1980s see the hand of "monetarism" (Augelli and Murphy 1988: 157, 184). Others point out that the Fund goes further by underwriting the education of Third World officials in the economic orthodoxy of the day, thus producing a network of LDC officials that appear to be subject to the Fund's influence (Strange 1974: 269).

However we assess the validity of these differing explanations of changes in IMF policy, they all reflect a broad recognition that the UN-era agencies are unusually open to other institutions of international civil society simply because they rely on them to help do the work of global governance. In many cases this openness and reliance is formally recognized. The ISO and its predecessors work by empaneling engineers and business groups with governments in order to create industrial standards. The relief agencies, the WHO, and many of the development agencies rely on private voluntary organizations to carry out the work that the IGOs coordinate. The ILO has always been governed by unions and employers' associations as much as by governments. The interwar ILO, with its power to demand that members report on the status of all labor conventions, and the League, with its power to investigate social conditions of protected European minorities and of natives within the African and Asian mandates, even demonstrated that international institutions could empower citizens and transnational human rights movements relative to the nation-state. The UN's work on decolonization and human rights has continued the pattern.

Moreover, the expanding roles of the intergovernmental agencies, in and of themselves, have provided further political space for non-governmental groups to organize and press for wider recognition of human rights and for more secure provisions for basic human needs. Recall that under the Public International Unions such groups were successful only when they tied their goals to core issues of the liberal internationalist agenda. Thus the international regime regulating slavery grew out of the antislavery movement's ability to tie the issue to agreements regulating the scramble for Africa, and the first international health regime grew, in part, to prevent disease from interrupting international shipping. The vast expansion of the primary activities of the global agencies since then has provided many more opportunities for similar linkages to be made.

The paradigm case began in 1920 when the League asked Fridjof Nansen to help devise a system to repatriate the hundreds of thousands of war refugees scattered throughout Russia (Northedge 1986: 77). Many had been prisoners of war, making this an issue of state, an issue central to the fundamental purposes of the League. For Nansen this was the beginning of a long crusade to establish an international system serving civilian refugees as well as military prisoners. Nansen organized a social movement pushing for refugee rights and, eventually, for the extension of the League's role to the provision of all forms of disaster relief and the protection of all human rights, a movement whose many lineal descendants – from Amnesty International, to Cultural Survival, to Médecins Sans Frontiers – thrive in great part due to their many connections with the UN system, just as many private voluntary agencies involved in economic development have grown and prospered because governments and IGOs pay them to carry out programs (B. Smith 1990: 4, 74–5).

Transnational intellectual communities and the increased capacity for self-transformation

In administering programs the UN relies on and supports private agencies, and it has a similar relationship to the intellectual communities that have provided most of the ideas for expanding or reforming the world organizations in the twentieth century. The IMF's relationship to orthodox Anglo-American economics, Richard Stone's role in creating national accounts statistics, and Raul Prebisch's connection to the critical economic traditions that focus on the Third World are far from unique. The League and the UN have nurtured many of the intellectual leaders who designed later international institutions. Professionals within the world organizations often become part of what Peter Haas (1992) – borrowing from Foucault – has called the "epistemic communities" that reflect on different issues of international public policy. Such communities also include academics and professionals in national governments. League intellectuals of the 1930s began the practice of promoting regular contacts among all three groups, in part as a way of fostering their "professionalism" against the "political" demands of government (Dubin

1983: 489–93), and some of the most widely applauded UN agencies have made the relevant intellectual communities integral to their day-to-day work (Jacobson 1974; Haas 1990).

The role of the League and the UN in supporting transnational intellectual communities concerned with particular issues of public policy goes far beyond that played by the Public International Unions. The first-generation agencies certainly fostered a professionalism within their staff, and that in turn encouraged governments to allow staff members to design some institutional reforms, but the UN agencies have gone much further, funding research and training, often as part of the technical assistance the agencies provide to LDCs, in every field in which world organizations operate. The result has been the establishment of vast transnational intellectual communities standing outside the world organizations but ready to contribute their expertise, their intellectual leadership, to problems of reforming the international institutions touching on their field.

The UN system's support of these communities, combined with its own capacity to provide the political leadership needed for reform – its ability to sponsor the necessary international conferences and underwrite experimental organizations and programs – accounts for the most striking difference between the work of global IGOs after the world wars and their prewar activities. The postwar UN system has had a much greater capacity to grow and transform itself in response to new global problems than the Public International Unions had.

This may have been a mixed blessing. On the one hand it may help explain why the heyday of the UN system was a bit longer than that of the Public International Unions. On the other hand, it certainly did not ensure that the eventual crisis of the postwar Free World Order could be avoided, and it may have helped ensure that, when the crisis came, the world organizations would enter a period of pointless growth; they continued to expand their purview and constantly transform themselves even though the puzzle of how to build a new international historical bloc remained unsolved.

7

PROSPERITY AND DISAPPOINTMENT

Of course, it had taken more than twenty years to solve the puzzle of the Free World historical bloc. As late as 1950 Rose Macaulay could still write to her friend Gilbert Murray about searching for the first fruits of the new world that he and other backers of the League had tried to create. She wrote of how she could find hope just walking through the wreckage in the center of London and looking for the small signs of returning life: weeds blooming, birds nesting, and even vagrants sifting through the rubble to make temporary homes in the wilderness left by the bombs (Macaulay 1983b: xii).

Macaulay made it clear that neither Murray's elitism nor his grandiose idealism of the 1920s were needed by those doing the actual work of reconstruction. Yet her own egalitarian irony would have provided too weak a foundation of myth for the postwar world. It took a writer of the postwar generation, David Hare, to explore the history of the myth that actually provided the foundation for the Free World. His 1978 play *Plenty* traces the disillusion and corruption of postwar British hopes by moving backward from the violence and hypocrisy of the late 1960s, past the rise of a complacent, bloated welfare state (in pointed contrast to the mere "600 men" needed to run the empire), past the Suez debacle and other attempts to resuscitate an even more corrupt colonialism, to a gloriously sunfilled Normandy field on V-E Day when the play's protagonist, an idealistic English girl, promises a broken old French peasant that things will quickly change: "We have grown up. We will improve the world. . . . There will be days and days like this."

And there were at least 25 years of plenty after 1945. All the sifting through the rubble of interwar institutions and all the postwar building created an international social order in which rapid economic growth was again possible, and in which the benefits of that growth were spread more widely than they had ever been before.

The GATT, the Bretton Woods organizations, and the other institutions of the UN system finally began doing what the League never did. The ICAO and the expanded ITU helped link the physical infrastructure for the world market that came to knit the wealthy OECD countries and the dependent capitalist states of the Third World into a single world economy. The organizations that eventually became the WIPO and the ISO provided the rules defining industrial products and property, and the GATT created the framework for limiting restrictions on trade in industrial goods. Some of the major new functions taken on by the world organizations helped satisfy those who would not necessarily gain from a new wave of industrial change. The GATT allowed industrialized states to maintain systems aiding their own farmers, which the FAO also supported. The International Monetary Fund worked to ease the kind of fiscal and monetary "debt crises" that had undermined interwar attempts to establish welfare states. The ILO encouraged the collective bargaining systems that secured the Fordist compromise between industrial labor and capital in the OECD countries, the bargain in which the discipline of mass production was exchanged for the economic benefits of mass consumption. And the UN system created political space for those in the less industrialized world to push for decolonization and development assistance – even though, for most states and peoples, these seemed to come in lieu of incorporation into the system of privileged economic development that gave the OECD countries the 25 years of postwar growth that even surpassed Europe's growth in the 20 years before the First World War (UNIDO 1982: 3).

The postwar world organizations even began to prepare the ground for the industries of the "information age" by encouraging all of the advances in telecommunication and business equipment that some believe will soon usher in a "third industrial revolution." But that revolution has not yet arrived, nor is it likely to arrive until the conflicts generated by the postwar world economy – the contradictions that eventually destroyed the hopes of 1945 – have been confronted and resolved.

Since the early 1970s both the world economy and the world organizations have been having a very rough time. Many wage workers in the industrialized countries have seen no real increase in compensation for 20 years, even though their productivity has increased a great deal; the postwar Fordist bargain has been broken. Very few countries have entered the privileged industrialized world since 1970 (South Korea being the only one with a substantial population). In the impoverished and despoiled less industrialized world, conditions have been much worse. Much of the Third World experienced a more serious depression in the 1970s and 1980s than the 1930s.

Meanwhile, the global IGOs have been in turmoil. The IMF had to be totally restructured in the early 1970s to deal with the *fait accompli* of a new world monetary system created on principles antithetical to those agreed on at Bretton Woods. The Fund and the World Bank then had to transform themselves almost every few years to try to cope with the constantly mutating debt crises in eastern Europe and the Third World. At the same time, the central agencies of the UN have been teetering on bankruptcy, in great part because they have been under the pressure of a US government bent on undoing the meager results of the Third World's movement to create a New International Economic Order (NIEO). This has left the world organizations with few resources to encourage economic transformations of any sort, let alone those needed to foster another industrial revolution.

From the Generalization of Fordism to the Information Age

If and when a third industrial revolution begins it will begin in a world economy that has become more truly global than ever before. The Free World Order united the turn-of-the-century Interimperial Order with the American system and then expanded to include Japan. One sign of the increasing unification of the two older systems can be seen in the growth trends of intracontinental and intercontinental shipping. Both increased from the end of the war until the early 1970s, but intercontinental freight shipped by sea and air grew about four times as rapidly as intracontinental rail freight (Knudsen 1973: 1; Pillai 1969: 1), with trade across the Atlantic accounting for much of the greater growth.

Transoceanic shipping had also grown quite rapidly between the First World War and the Second World War, when the first seeds of the Free World Order were being sown and when the expansion of merchant fleets controlled by Americans had signaled the end of Britain's maritime hegemony. At the same time, American manufacturers began linking the industrialized world.

American companies began to cross borders and decentralize their marketing in order to exploit advantages over somewhat less efficient European firms. In the 1920s a host of US companies producing products of the Second Industrial Revolution entered the European market. Firms producing packaged consumer products, such as Kellogg's and Coca-Cola, began by exporting their trademarked goods and then quickly moved into overseas production. The electrical appliance and equipment companies – producing everything from elevators to office equipment – and American automobile companies did so as well. Automobile suppliers – tire manufactures like Firestone and petroleum companies like the ubiquitous Standard Oil of New Jersey (Esso) – soon followed (Wilkins 1974: 62–78). And all the American companies involved in the North–South trade in raw materials to fuel these industries began to invest in their own, non-European, suppliers (ibid. 98).

In the interwar years few European firms could make the large overseas investments of Esso, Firestone, or Ford, simply because the Europeans lacked the US's large home market and the productivity it encouraged. In the article on "Industrialism" in the 1935 edition of the *Encyclopedia of the Social Sciences* Leonard Woolf's Fabian colleague, G. D. H. Cole, explained that new engineering economies of scale meant that the "optimum" size of plants in all the newer industries had constantly grown ever since Henry Ford introduced his moving assembly line in 1913. While most of the plants producing for the US market were able to approach optimum size (Sands 1961: 366–8), Europe's many postwar markets did not allow firms to adopt the new economies to the same extent. The greater productivity of American firms at home, in turn, gave them more to invest abroad. Even though Esso or Firestone could achieve no greater economies of scale in its European plants than any of its local competitors, the American companies were able to take advantage of scale economies in purchasing oil and rubber for all their processing sites around the world, and they were able to take advantage of economies of both scale and scope in their unified research departments and at least part of their marketing operations.

New American overseas investment shrank after the 1929 stock-market crash, and then Hitler's rise to power convinced many American firms to sell their overseas holdings (Wilkins 1974: 170, 184). But the first seeds of the unified postwar industrial system had been sown and the Second World War, with its investments by the Allies in perfecting radio and high-speed ships and aircraft, would plant the rest. Wartime German investment in rockets and the Allied counter-investments in the technologies that would become electronic computers[1] would spawn the next generation of lead industries, industries that illustrate how the very success of the postwar world order would eventually contribute to its end.

Today we commonly hear about "the internationalization of production," the emergence of "the global factory," and "a new international division of labor" in which Fordism is no longer possible due to the shift of industrial production from the core of the Free World to low-wage LDCs (Fröbel 1980). Space-based telecommunications systems and modern information processing have made global coordination of production possible. UN agencies tend to refer to these technological revolutions as the rise of *telematics* – the marriage of *informatics* (computer science and information technology) with rapid long- distance communication using satellites (McLaughlin and Birings 1984: 30–1). Nevertheless, despite more than a decade of hype about the globalization of production, the primary consumers of telematics services in the 1980s and 1990s have been financial companies that send massive amounts of data through the satellite-based telecommunications network. These have created global markets in currencies, shares, commodity futures contracts, and every other financial instrument, markets that may have encouraged investors away from the more long-term commitments required for building a new generations of factories, "global" or not. The potential of the telematics industry for encouraging both other electronic markets and the coordination of global production may be staggering, but so far we have only barely entered the "information age" (Beniger 1986; Saxby 1990). We certainly have not yet seen a third industrial revolution to match the transformations that began one and two centuries ago. Nor have we even seen the kind of rapid increases in productivity that typified the postwar boom.

Promoting investment in greater productivity: the welfare state, reconstruction, American transnational corporations and the Chandler effect

Those productivity gains reflected the Chandler effect of wider markets encouraging investment in productive new technologies. Renewed American investment in postwar Europe and Japan introduced new technologies to these markets. Initially that investment did not reflect the impact of the world organizations that helped create the physical infrastructure of a new intercontinental market, but international reconstruction assistance and the new international institutions that encouraged cooperation in public finance did play a role. The removal of the Nazi threat, the reintroduction of convertible currencies, and the promise of mass consumption under the postwar welfare states encouraged American firms to continue what they had begun in the 1920s (Wilkins 1974: 375–95; Chandler 1977: 480; Wee 1987: 195). Coca-Cola even prepared for its postwar globalization by building bottling plants immediately behind the advancing front line of American troops (Tedlow 1990: 64). After the war the hundreds of thousands of American troops permanently stationed in Europe, Japan, and Korea, along with their families, became the advance guard of consumers for every American product that followed Coca-Cola into the new markets, evangelists for the mass-consumption lifestyle the US had pioneered.[2]

In the course of investing in potential mass markets overseas, American companies brought both innovations in management as well as new processes of production to Europe and Japan (Wee 1987: 198; 221–5). This encouraged local competitors to purchase American (and later European, Japanese, and Canadian) know-how through patents and licenses-to-produce (ibid.: 211). The same trend had also been supported by the Marshall Plan, fiscal incentives provided by European and Japanese governments, and the international patent system. While the patent regime favored the large transnational firms that could afford huge budgets for research and development (Firestone 1971), those companies still had to work all their patents throughout the Free World's industrial core in order to keep legal control of this intellectual property, and that in turn kept the technology flowing (Penrose 1951: 207), which is why Raymond Vernon (1966) cites patent rules as the first of his "noneconomic" explanations for the postwar explosion of firms manufacturing in more than one industrialized market.

As a consequence of both transnational investment and the sharing of technology, not only did the fixed investment per worker and the rates of productivity begin to converge throughout the core of the Free World, but national structures of industry, the number of firms dominating most industries, and even the timing of technological innovations by the most productive firms all became increasingly similar across the OECD. Some of the supporters of the interwar International Management Institute who had blamed the First World War on the backwardness of British and French firms lived to see them evolving along much the same lines as the German and American companies (Hannah 1976: 185; Dyas and Thanheiser 1976:

165). Finally, perhaps most significantly, incomes began to converge throughout the western world. The entire OECD enjoyed the consumer revolution that marked the years of plenty.

That revolution was not just a matter of the cars and refrigerators and washing machines and televisions that every family came to expect. It was also a matter of needing to work fewer and fewer hours to buy the same items. The postwar boom created leisure and it fostered industries to serve it. By the end of the 1960s jet-age tourism accounted for 10 percent of global trade (Pillai 1969: 1), while the revenue of the air transport industry was equal to 10 percent of the world's industrial production (Kihl 1971: xi).

Promoting trade in Fordist manufactured goods: competition and the Owen effect

When the first large intercontinental civilian jet aircraft had appeared in the 1950s, the formation of a single Free World market for industrial goods had begun to appear inevitable. Civilian aviation not only created the physical infrastructure of that market, airlines purchased the jets that were the first major new industrial product designed from the beginning to be sold throughout the Free World.

Much of the initial investment in civilian jet aircraft took place alongside investment in ships, docks, trucks, and rail cars needed to carry goods across borders. This first burst of private interest in contributing to the infrastructure of international trade came as soon as GATT rules had made the trading system as open as it had been before the First World War. Of course, even before the early 1960s, some trade, especially the sale of American goods to Europe and Japan to fuel recovery, had already played a role in the postwar economic miracle. That expanding intercontinental trade, along with the commerce within western Europe and between the US and Canada, convinced champions of the liberal internationalist vision to declare that it had been fulfilled. The cover of the 1967 GATT annual report made the point with its graphs of trade and production since 1953; both rise dramatically, with trade leading the way (see p. 284).

Nonetheless, some of the GATT's liberalizing effects occurred in ways that many liberal fundamentalists found perverse. The Kennedy Round in the early 1960s, for example, encouraged western European governments to protect their continental market even as they linked it more closely than it had been in the days of Keynes's prewar "economic utopia." One aspect of the new push for European unity was the creation of a unified system of support for farmers within the economic space that the six original members of the European Community (France, Germany, Italy, and the Benelux countries) had begun to create in the 1950s. A second was the push to expand the Community (Denmark, Ireland, and the UK joined in 1972) and to establish stronger free-trade agreements between the Community, the European Free Trade Area (the less ambitious association created in 1960 to abolish restrictions on trade in industrial goods among Europe's other industrial nations), and other traditional trading partners including former colonies and East Germany (Wee 1987: 364–9).

A few of the contemporary European arguments for expanding and deepening continental links even more rapidly than the GATT was liberalizing intercontinental trade emphasized the Chandler effect: Europe needed the larger market in order to ensure that some its firms would emerge as leaders in the newest industries of the late 1960s, especially aerospace, telecommunications, and atomic power. But, even more frequently, the advocates of greater European unity emphasized that it would encourage productive competition among what were already the leading industries of the automobile and jet age. In 1965 one prominent British proponent of the Community noted that Britain's national "market has become or is becoming too small to combine modern technology with healthy competition in sectors such as cars, refrigerators, washing machines, television sets – in fact the bulk of consumer durables" (Pinder 1965: 249). Later, Nicholas Owen (1983) would demonstrate that it was precisely in these typically Fordist sectors that the benefits of European integration were clearest. The wider market gave the most efficient companies and the most efficient plants in these sectors the opportunity to produce to capacity, allowing Europeans to pay less for the major products defining postwar consumer society.

The GATT process also contributed to the Owen effect as trade barriers fell and automobiles from Japan's more efficient factories flooded into the United States and as producers of the more specialized goods typical of the Fordist era – from car radios to electric typewriters – were able to sell in all industrial markets. Nevertheless, until well into the 1970s the intra-European impact of the Owen effect was undoubtedly more significant than any OECD-wide impact. Even as late as 1976 nearly half (45 percent) of the exports of the industrial areas (including eastern Europe) went from western Europe to western Europe. US and Canadian exports to each other and to the rest of the world accounted for another 24 percent, and Japanese exports only 10 percent (GATT 1978).

Assessing the results

In the Free World Order the sequence of the Owen effect and the Chandler effect was the reverse of that under the Interimperial Order, perhaps only because the Second World War devastated Europe and Japan but spared the United States. In western Europe and Japan the first round of benefits of new investment in the more efficient processes of production preceded the benefits of competition among more efficient and less efficient firms. Nevertheless, the social classes and the ideas that formed two sides of the Free World historical bloc – the coalition between cosmopolitan, progressive capitalists and relatively conservative associations of industrial workers and their Fordist and Keynesian ideology – were just as well served by this sequence as the interimperial liberal internationalist coalition was served by the reverse.

Reconstruction assured that in the US Charles Maier's "politics of productivity" could be an immediate success as high-wage workers supplied the many needs of overseas allies; a postwar crisis of surplus capacity was avoided, just as Cassius, the British critic of the American design, had predicted. Throughout the rest of the core of the Free World, workers in the brand-new postwar factories – operating under managers who were rapidly adopting the most efficient of American techniques – were able to replicate Fordism, maintaining the high wages demanded by the welfare state, yet producing goods so efficiently that, for the first time, most of the Europeans building automobiles and other consumer durables (and, only slightly later, the Japanese) could afford the whole panoply of products that they made. From its very beginning the Free World Order realized the hope that the Interimperial Order had only offered (Keynes 1971: 21): in the industrial core, most of the "overwork, overcrowding, and underfeeding" that had the typified life of the working poor since the Industrial Revolution really did "come to an end."

Preparing for a new industrial era?

Since the mid-1970s the Chandler effect has continued to contribute to the growth of new industries, while intercontinental competition among firms producing both older and newer industrial products has continued to increase. Japan's more efficient, but still relatively high-wage producers who have so worried both Europeans and North

Americans since the early 1970s have been joined by a host of manufacturing concerns both from the relatively successful newly industrializing countries (NICs) of east Asia, where mass incomes have been growing along with exports, and from the export-oriented manufacturing of the more populous, seemingly less successful NICs like Brazil and Mexico, where average wages remain quite low. These new industrial competitors have convinced many analysts that we are entering an era of truly globalized production.

Yet, perhaps surprisingly, it is far from clear that this globalization would fulfill the liberal internationalist vision, especially when looked at from the point of view of many working people within the OECD. They can expect welfare advantages from the relatively lower prices of consumer products produced in the low-wage NICs, but they have to weigh these advantages against the danger that the capital needed to employ them in the North will flee to the lower-wage South. Herman van der Wee, echoing Albert O. Hirschman (1958), argues that in the long run the welfare advantages of more globalized production can only be assured if high rates of OECD investment in new productive technologies continue at home (Wee 1987: 198–9). As parts of older industries become more globalized and move abroad, there must be new industries to take their place. In the terms introduced here, in the long run the Chandler effect of any move toward a larger liberal world order will be more important to the welfare of working people than the Owen effect. In the industrialized world, at least, the welfare impact of some of the most important of the newer industries encouraged through the Chandler effect has, so far, been unclear, as the story of the impact of the first of the "third generation" world organizations, Intelsat, and related transportation regimes, illustrates.

OECD citizens of the playwright David Hare's generation are apt to remember the day in 1962 when the American Telstar satellite provided the first live television broadcasts across the Atlantic, Pacific, and the non-Free World expanse of Chinese and Soviet Eurasia. Telstar grew out of a US government response to political rather than market incentives, but private investors soon dominated the satellite communication business, even though nationalized telecommunications firms would take most of Intelsat's shares when it was created two years later. One peculiar American firm, Comsat, still controls the largest bloc of votes (Goldman 1985: 61): AT&T, the private company that then had a legal monopoly over telephone services throughout much of North America, dominated the government-sponsored Comsat, and Comsat actually ran Intelsat's day-to-

day operations until 1976. At that time the typical period of experimental operation (in this case, under the patronage of the US)
came to an end and a workable system of fees for satellite services
was achieved (Snow 1976: 10; J. Cole et al. 1977: 20).

Despite AT&T's initial advantages through Comsat, its monopoly
on satellite communication services quickly disappeared. Even
though the investments needed to create a satellite system are (if
readers will excuse the pun) astronomical, parts of the telematics
industry rapidly became more competitive than either the European
railroad industry had been a century before, or than the automobile
industry was in the first two decades after the Second World War
(Pelton 1981: 40). In 1970 there were nine other providers and by
1980 more than 60 additional companies had joined the business,
most of them, like Comsat, private firms championed by national
governments who had hoped to establish a monopoly over some part
of the telematics business (Cole and O'Rourke 1983: 19). As a result,
Intelsat's role became less that of a monopoly provider of services
and more like that of the Radiotelegraph Union earlier in the century. Intelsat became a center where different service providers
coordinated their activities to assure the effective operation of a
global network. It remains a standard setter and a link between
national satellite communications systems, international regional
systems, and its own system, which fills in gaps in service globally
(Galloway 1986; Pelton 1981: 199, 230).

As Comsat's competitors multiplied so did the services provided by
the telematics industry. Companies involved in remote sensing –
satellite photography – serve users as diverse as property developers
trying to spot urban patterns and oil companies searching for new
drilling sites (Goldman 1985: 80; Hargreaves 1985). But the major
consumers of telematics services have always been firms that have
built and maintained flexible global databases for the finance sector
(providing everything from global systems for checking consumer
credit to the 24-hour currency and securities markets that emerged
in the early 1980s), the travel industry (with its global reservation
systems for airlines, automobile rentals, and hotels), and more traditional "information-based" organizations such as libraries and publishing houses.

Today, contracts for putting huge databases into electronic form
(computerizing the card catalog of a major research library or the
records of a giant insurance firm) are apt to go to companies that have
located most of their labor-intensive operations where the wages of
skilled workers are relatively low, whether that is western Kansas or

Kuala Lumpur.[3] After all, Intelsat makes it easy to link remote terminals staffed by low-wage keypunchers to the high-wage cities like Berlin, New York, or Tokyo, where the consumers of their services/products are apt to be found. In this way some companies actually have created a kind of "global factory," an assembly line whose stations are separated by thousands of miles. They were able to do so because world organization began to put the necessary global communication infrastructure in place almost 30 years ago.

Some might argue that investment in the transportation infrastructure needed for a world in which most assembly lines crossed national borders also began before 1970. New investment in the infrastructure of containerized shipping accounts for some of the rapid jump in intercontinental shipments of industrial goods between 1965 and 1970 (Abrahamsson 1980: 5, 146; Fröbel 1980: 178). Similarly, around 1970 growth in air freight revenues started to outstrip air passenger revenues because the introduction of larger, more efficient jets started to lower the cost of sending manufactured goods from one part of the globe to another. And, of course, the jets achieved speeds closer to those of a geographically fixed assembly line than anything that can be achieved by ships.

Yet even the most efficient assembly line relying on transoceanic aircraft would still be very slow, as well as remarkably costly; that is why the air freight revolution has created few real global factories even though telematics services allow the complex orders needed to run such a factory to be sent anywhere. Instead, aircraft are used to ship perishable goods (fruit and flowers) and manufactured products that are relatively expensive and relatively light (electronic components and personal computers), often from low-wage countries, while multimodal containers have become especially important to the transport of clothing and other lighter, relatively inexpensive manufactured goods from low-wage countries. In both cases, the indirect effect of the private transportation and communications industries fostered by the world organizations has been to threaten wages in certain sectors throughout the industrialized world (Ross and Trachte 1990: 70–1), which eventually may thwart the promise of liberal internationalism rather than fulfill it.

Was Global Governance That Important?

Even if working people throughout the OECD may have reason to doubt that the most recent impact of the Chandler and Owen effects has been positive, in the 1950s and 1960s the benefits were clear: for most people, life got much better after the war. Yet few would have recognized the role of the world organizations, and of the larger system of governance they reflected, in establishing and maintaining the social order responsible for the postwar years of plenty.

It may even have been easier to recognize the role of what Kees van der Pijl (1984) calls the new "Atlantic ruling class" that managed the giant Fordist firms and the welfare states and shared the ideas that Henry Nau calls the "postwar policy triad" (1990: 101–6). This was made up of the traditional liberal internationalist desire to expand and deepen global free markets, along with the two most prominent lessons of the interwar period: the desirability of excluding illiberal societies – what Nau calls the "limits of community" recognized by the containment policy – and the need for more inclusive domestic social orders within the liberal community (even though, as Nau points out, those social orders were to be held together by relatively "conservative domestic policies" designed to serve free enterprise economies and not to transform them).

The dominance of this class, and of these ideas, had not been inevitable. In country after country, the Atlanticists had to secure their hegemony by defusing other (often imperialist) tendencies among the wealthy and the powerful, by building alliances with privileged workers, and in some cases, by forcibly excluding advocates of more radical social programs from the national political debate. Perhaps only if citizens focused on the process of securing the postwar hegemony would the role of the world organizations come to mind.

The US did it alone

In the 1950s and 1960s most people in the OECD recognized that the incentives the US had provided through the Marshall Plan and through its administration of Japanese reconstruction had helped assure the victory of the postwar social coalitions and their ideas (cf. Pijl 1984: 138–77; Nau 1990: 110–26). This does not necessarily imply that the postwar order was the result of the diktat of the most powerful capitalist state. In 1948 the European powers had options other than entering what was becoming an anticommunist Free World Order; the timing of the decision to launch the Marshall Plan, coinciding with the postwar Italian election in which Gramsci's equally realistic Communist colleagues had forecast victory, is evidence enough of the alternatives that existed (Wood 1986: 39–40).

Ironically for the Italian Communists, the Marshall Plan provided as perfect a demonstration of Gramsci's formula for securing hegemony as you could ever find (see Gramsci 1971: 161). The Truman administration made seemingly altruistic "sacrifices of an economic-corporate kind," in order to serve the "interests . . . of the groups over which hegemony is to be exercised" and thus pursue its larger aspirations for establishing a secure international historical bloc, the Free World Order.

Yet the key part that American reconstruction aid played in establishing the Free World Order, and the key roles the US continued to play in the postwar order, does not preclude important, independent functions for the world organizations. Even if we treat the postwar order as one of "American" or "Atlantic ruling class" hegemony, we must recognize three related tasks of the world organizations. They (1) tempered American inclinations to seek domination rather than hegemony; (2) helped assure that liberal internationalist tendencies continued to dominate United States policy; and (3) helped foreclose Europe's "imperial option" which would have remained open had decolonization and development not proceeded as quickly as they did.

Even though the American Marshall Plan can be seen as a perfect tactic for seeking Gramsci's kind of consensual hegemony, the Roosevelt and Truman administrations occasionally followed policies that Gramsci identified with the pursuit of narrower "economic-corporate" interests, a strategy of seeking domination, not hegemony (cf., Augelli and Murphy 1988: 117–37). In part, this was a legacy of the liberal fundamentalism that had energized the businessmen's peace movement in the 1920s. For example, when it came to establishing a civil aviation regime, the US proposed basing it on the principle of "freedom of the air," thus hoping to let US firms dominate all routes. When it came to reestablishing the international patent regime, the US proposed that the requirement to work patents be dropped (Penrose 1951: 126). When it came to funding its innovative proposals for promoting human rights and aiding refugees, the US wanted to rely solely on volunteerism. When it came to extending aid to LDCs, the first official American reaction was always, "No, the funds are needed elsewhere."

Roosevelt, Truman, and Eisenhower moderated US positions on each of these issues, allowing effective international regimes to be established or maintained, in part simply due to the American commitment to a consensual postwar world order – the requirement that, as Sumner Welles's put it, "the essential principles of . . . that new

world order must be agreed upon in advance and with the full
support of each of the United Nations" (1943: 423). As a result, in
these and many other cases the final design reflected much more
than the original American sketch. The Americans certainly did not
do it alone. A bit of doggerel that captures the frequent division of
labor between US political leadership and intellectual leadership
nurtured outside the American policy milieu has it that:

> In Washington Lord Halifax
> Once whispered to Lord Keynes
> It's true *they* have all the money bags
> But *we* have all the brains.

Not only the governments of the British empire, but also the world
organizations, the League and the early UN, nurtured the designers
of the postwar economic order, and in that way played a role in
cementing a wider historical bloc.

The world organizations could play that role, in part, because the
US government rarely spoke with one voice, a fact highlighted by
critics of the simplistic argument that the postwar liberal order was
just a matter of US supremacy.[4] The Roosevelt administration's
advocacy of "freedom of the air," for example, was the "moderate"
position between conservative Congresswoman Claire Booth Luce's
vision of unilateral American domination of the air and Vice-Presi-
dent Henry Wallace's plan for creating a single "internationalized"
UN civil aviation corporation, along with a UN air force (Schenkman
1955: 63). The administration was able to assure both extremes that
the "demands of international cooperation" required a different approach, even if it had to be the ICAO approach rather than the more
laissez faire approach that the US had originally proposed.

Similarly, international trade agreements allowed successive US
administrations to shore up the originally quite weak elite consensus
supporting tariff reductions. Congressional rhetoric remained surprisingly mercantilist throughout the 1950s and 1960s, and it became
even more so in the 1970s. But the increasingly liberal trading system
remained inoculated against such protectionist sentiments, in great
part because the elected representatives could satisfy most of their
constituents by having them turn to the administrative system for
dealing with violations of GATT "fair trading" rules (Nelson 1981).
Many deviations from international laissez faire certainly persisted
as a result, but they ended up working to preserve the system's
liberal intent.

Yet perhaps the most important role that the world organizations played – and that the US government on its own could not play – had to do with overcoming illiberal forces overseas. Belgian, British, Dutch, and French colonialism did not die in 1945, and the US government was not its consistent opponent. John Foster Dulles's anticommunism convinced him to support European colonial interests opposing "radical" nationalists in Asian and African colonies and to nurture alliances between neocolonial business interests and the most reactionary native social forces in the already independent new nations like India and Indonesia. Mason Sears, who served the Eisenhower administration as its UN representative on matters of trusteeship and non-selfgoverning territories until fired by Dulles, argues that despite this brief American change of heart, the UN continued to ensure that the anticolonial alliance of Third World nationalists, the Soviet bloc, and anticolonial forces within the Atlantic bloc would be successful.[5] At the same time the UN and the World Bank helped Nehru's India demonstrate that LDCs did not have to rely on investment from their former colonial masters, which, in turn, encouraged European investors to pull out of imperial enterprises and invest in Fordist industry at home instead.[6]

American leadership certainly played a central role in creating and maintaining the Free World Order, but the US government was neither unified nor consistent enough to do so by itself, nor was it always immediately ready to make the sacrifices demanded of a hegemonic leader. The world organizations, and the larger process of multilateral consultation they reflected, tempered the forces within the Free World social coalition that might have diverted it from the liberal project or might have convinced the US to play a domineering, rather than a hegemonic, role.

It was all a matter of the market and of domestic politics within OECD countries

The argument that the Free World Order was the result of US dominance is not the only one that minimizes the role of multilateral institutions in the Free World Order. A more sophisticated position has it that while the GATT was important, to the extent that it helped liberalize trade, the institutions of global governance designed to manage social conflicts were not. This is not to deny the importance of those conflicts. It is simply to argue that they were actually managed in other ways: *domestic* social compromises between labor and capital provided the foundation on which Fordist mass production and mass consumption could be generalized throughout the Free World.

Yet those domestic compromises could not have been established and maintained without the interwar ILO as a conduit of labor cooperation and without the international monetary system and habits of cooperation in public finance established at the end of the war. The importance of these postwar activities became abundantly clear after the system of fixed exchange rates broke down in 1971. Since then we have had a system characterized by what Michael Stewart (1984) calls "cascading monetarism." When any OECD power tries to expand government spending in order to protect and extend the welfare state, the capital flight allowed by a system of floating exchange rates soon pulls them back in line with the most conservative of OECD governments. Today, long after the welfare state has been established, this may only mean, as Henry Nau would argue (1990: 102), that governments of rich countries are kept to the kind of "conservative domestic policies" that typified the US in the heyday of the Free World Order. Nevertheless, if today's system of free trade in currencies had existed 30 or 40 years ago, governments would never have been able to institute the wage, pension, and social service legislation needed to secure the original domestic compromises, let alone engage in the kind of Keynesian countercyclical spending they also required.

Something more than domestic social compromises within OECD states had to underlie other essential, "nonmarket" aspects of the Free World Order as well. International cooperation was needed for all of the various functions that multilateral development assistance has fulfilled for the West: assuring access to raw materials, protecting the global financial system against Third World defaults, containing antisystemic movements, "greenlining," and, perhaps most fundamentally, providing legitimacy for Third World governments and for the Free World project by serving the populist "development" agenda.

Finally, neither the market nor domestic policies could replace the important role that the world organizations played in managing the boundaries between the Free World and the alternative social systems led by the Soviet Union and China. While nuclear deterrence may have "contained" communism, the world organizations facilitated important forms of cooperation across the ideological divide. They allowed the superpowers to work together to minimize nuclear proliferation and to contain some of the violent conflicts in which they backed opposing sides. The UN system also helped the global adversaries use common global resources – the oceans, the radiospectrum and outer space – without coming to blows. Finally, the global IGOs facilitated trade and social cooperation between the systems, tasks largely undertaken by the now much-maligned UNCTAD and UNESCO. The experience of that cooperation, the real antithesis of deterrence in the postwar dialectic, partially explains how East–West tensions could disappear so magically at the end of the 1980s when the former Soviet bloc came to embrace ideals akin to Roosevelt's "four freedoms." Theodore H. Von Laue argues that the United Nations has always served "as an Agency of Westernization" *vis à vis* the Third World, even when the UN nurtured the Third World movement which pushed for economic and political equality and exemplified what he calls "the dynamics of anti-Western Westernization" (Von Laue 1987: 317, 321). Undoubtedly the same can be said of the UN system's role in socializing those completely outside the Free World.

Vietnam, the Arms Race, and the Crises of Fordism

The crisis of the Soviet world order, and the resulting shortlived sense of western triumph, led some Free World pundits to forget the less dramatic, but equally significant problems of their own international social order. Like the Soviet Union, the western industrialized countries also suffered from the unprecedented cost of "security" in a bipolar world with nuclear arms. But in most other ways the sources of the Free World crisis bear little resemblance to the challenges that broke up the Soviet bloc and that still face China. Perhaps the sharpest contrast has do with mass consumption, something the Soviet order could not provide, yet something that was disappointing to many of those in the West to whom it became commonplace.

Harbingers of the Free World's crisis appeared in the 1960s when the United States had to add the costs of the Vietnam war to defense budgets already bloated by an unprecedentedly expensive technological arms race. At the same time the political space opened by the postwar welfare state, the unprecedented empowerment of common people that it allowed, meant that the American government was faced with constant temptations to expand its role in order to foster a more equitable society. By the late 1960s the abstract categories of men and women who were "less privileged" by Fordism, those with "limited access to the technologically specific skills that protected high-wage workers," had become concrete social movements demanding an end to the concrete grounds for their exclusion from all realms of social power. Both Lyndon Johnson and, to a lesser extent, even Richard Nixon, were willing to respond to the demands of minorities, women, and the poor.

However, the American administrations of the late 1960s were not willing to adopt straightforward, but perhaps politically suicidal, programs to redistribute wealth. Instead they relied on deficit financing to cover the simultaneous expansion of the military and the welfare state. In any other country such a policy would have led to an immediate fiscal crisis and to stern action by the IMF, but the unique position of the dollar as the source of value for all Free World currencies allowed the US to export the funds needed to pay both for the war and for its prior security commitments in Europe and east Asia, while still printing money to pay for expansions of the welfare state (Block 1977: 182–4). When the American policy finally led to crisis, it was a crisis of global governance. In 1971 the Nixon administration argued that the result of this policy, the growing US balance-of-payments deficit, was not solely an American responsibility because much of it could be explained (quite plausibly) by the American forces stationed overseas to protect Europe and Japan, or (less plausibly) by the unusually liberal trade policies of the United States. Therefore, Nixon refused the medicine that the IMF would have prescribed to another economy: devaluing the dollar (which meant increasing the number of dollars it would pledge to give for every ounce of gold). Instead, the US simply decided to break that pledge, no longer backing the dollar with gold and thereby pulling out the keystone that had held up the fixed exchange rate system. Money markets quickly established new, lower values for the dollar against other OECD currencies, but the US dollar remained the world's principal currency, for which there was always a market, even though it was not backed by gold. That left the US with even fewer restraints on its ability to finance budget deficits (Vries 1976: 520; Block 1977: 193–202).

In the meantime the expansion of welfare state entitlements throughout the 1950s and 1960s had strengthened the hand of labor in both the United States and Europe. Some analysts (such as Glyn and Sutcliffe 1972; cf., Offe 1984) began to predict a point when the bargaining power of labor would begin to squeeze out profits. To make matters worse there were some significant signs that demand in the OECD for Fordist goods was becoming saturated (Mensch 1979: 26); every family already had its car and its color TV. Moreover,

244 PROSPERITY AND DISAPPOINTMENT

the cultural revolution of the late 1960s – student demonstrations, environmental awareness, drugs, and drop-outs – all suggested that the material incentives that Fordism could provide were no longer enough to convince everyone in the industrial world to live under the strict authority of the machine demanded by a mass-production/mass-consumption economy. This was certainly not the traditional problem of recurring "underconsumption" that had worried Hobson and influenced Lenin's "orthodox" Marxist view of a capitalist crisis. Instead, it reflected a social-psychological crisis of motivation and a crisis of the national political institutions that provided legitimation for the Free World Order (cf. Habermas 1975: 68–92).

We can summarize the sources of the early stages of the crisis in the Free World, and compare them to the similar forces that affected the Interimperial Order, by considering the four types of conflicts that are inherent to capitalist industrialism and that liberal internationalists tend to ignore (table 7). In each case, the conflict can be thought of as contributing to the overall crisis due to the failure of the political institutions designed to regulate it.

TABLE 7 The crisis of the Interimperial Order and the crisis of the Free World Order compared

INTERIMPERIAL ORDER	FREE WORLD ORDER
Conflicts between Industrial Regions and Less Developed Countries	
Between Austro-Hungary, Denmark, Great Britain, the Ottoman Empire, Russia, Sweden and various nationalists → partial Balkan and Nordic self-determination, strengthening of all nationalist movements	Between the US and militant nationalists of the left → military conflicts Between the industrial capitalist states and OPEC and Group of 77 → oil crises, debate over the NIEO
Conflicts between Alternative Social Orders	
Between the *ancien régime* and the bourgeois order → consolidation of official nationalism, temporary aristocratic support for the nascent welfare state, and fascism as a temporarily successful compromise	Between the US and USSR (and/or China) over support for militant nationalists of the left especially in Indo-China, Lusophone and southern Africa, Afghanistan → protracted military conflicts and crises of defense costs Between the Free World Order and the real world communist alternatives → deterrence, the arms race, and crises of defense costs

Conflicts among Industrial Regions

Between Britain and Germany over trade → calls for imperial preference in Britain and support for the redemption-through-war school in Austria and Germany	Among US, Europe, and Japan over trade and money → breakdown of Bretton Woods system of fixed exchange rates
Among the powers over resources and concessionary investments in the Balkans, the Middle East, China, Africa, and the Pacific → colonial crises	Among the US, Europe, and Japan over accommodation of OPEC and the Group of 77

Conflicts with Workers over Democratic Control

Between capitalists and workers over labor legislation, social security, and extension of the franchise → establishment of nascent welfare states, partial extensions of the franchise, willingness of labor to see victory by nation's adversary as a threat	Between capitalists and workers (and, temporarily, between generations) over the demands of Fordism → expansion of the welfare state, fiscal limits to growth, crises of motivation

Conflicts between the industrialized world and the Third World provided the most persistent problems to the Free World Order, although it is perhaps incidental that the beginning of the long crisis can be tied to the violent clashes in Indo-China. Until much more recently, what the Free World actually promised to those outside the core of industrial prosperity was the populist "development" project: the stronger states and the longer and better lives that came with development in the Third World. What the Free World's western leaders most often resisted (with military force, if necessary) were any Third World attempts to break away from the western order. But only in a few cases did such attempts lead to protracted, violent conflicts – in fact, only when the major communist powers backed local Third World nationalist movements and when the relevant anticolonial forces within the US were overwhelmed by more conservative groups, as was the case in the conflicts in Portuguese and southern Africa and in the more prominent case of Vietnam.

Perhaps it is not surprising that one of these violent clashes would eventually become extremely costly to the US, simply because nationalist movements are inherently so difficult to defeat; yet great military powers often find that difficult to accept.[7] The Soviet Union's similar policy of relying on military force to maintain allied governments along its borders also eventually resulted a protracted and costly war, the one in Afghanistan.

Neither the costs of the Vietnam war nor those of the Afghan intervention would have been enough to trigger a world order crisis if they had not added to the economic burden of the technological arms race. As Partha Chatterjee argues (1975: 216–52), these costs may have been the Achilles' heel of the postwar security system. Nuclear deterrence was, at the very least, widely believed to be what kept the peace between two antagonistic and equally evangelistic social systems, and thus that conclusion became one of those social myths that is indistinguishable from reality; after all, as long as rational people believe they are deterred by an enemy's weapons, they are. Nevertheless, the superpowers had to do something to keep demonstrating the resolve necessary to make their threat of nuclear retaliation plausible. Each side's spending on technologies that might someday give it an advantage over the other was one way to demonstrate that resolve. Of course, that also meant that the other side would have another motivation for engaging in the technological arms race: preventing the other from gaining that advantage. Unfortunately, there was no inherent upper limit to the competitive spending encouraged by the deterrence system. Reductions in hostility – some form of detente – might eventually have allowed the superpowers to find an equilibrium point, but even many cold warriors recognized that if a limit on spending were not imposed by a comprehensive system of arms control – a system of governance that would have transformed both the Free World and the Soviet Orders – the internal stability of one or both of the superpowers' systems might eventually be threatened by the ever-increasing economic burden of defense.

A case can be made that this dynamic was at the core of what happened to the Soviet system. But the same dynamic was only one of many sources of the Free World's crisis. The costs of the arms race merely accelerated the conflict between the US and its allies over the special position the Americans occupied in the international monetary and public finance regimes. The costs of the arms race simply contributed one more factor to the problems of US public finance that became a global issue in 1971.

At Breton Woods Keynes had anticipated the kind of problem that the Nixon administration faced. Keynes had argued for an IMF in which creditor nations would be required to bear a part of the costs of balance-of-payments adjustments, just as the US argued its partners should bear some of the costs of its adjustment in the 1970s (Maier 1977: 620). Unfortunately, back in 1944, when the shoe was on the other foot, the US had embraced the bankers' orthodoxy that creditors should be allowed to determine exactly what costs, if any, they would bear, leaving the IMF without the power it would have needed to weather the later crisis.

Of course, it is unclear if that power by itself would have been enough to avert the Free World's other problems in the 1970s. Keynes's desire to see explicit requirements for creditor nations was part of his program for protecting the full-employment guarantees of the welfare state. But in 1971, in the age of the counterculture and with the beginning of ecological awareness, it was far from clear that the promise of mass consumption that full-employment policies served would be able to dampen the deeper conflict over the democratic control of industry that Keynes, like many liberals before him, had hoped could be diverted by prosperity – a prosperity still appreciated by many of those who remained outside the privileged circles of the Free World Order.

The conflict over democratic control, the deeper contradiction within the liberal internationalist vision, soon disappeared below the surface as the clashes of the early 1970s turned into the economic malaise that would continue into the 1990s. The most widely identified contributor to that malaise, the oil crisis of 1973, partially followed from the US decision to cease to back the dollar with gold. One oil producer, Libya, immediately used the new uncertainty about the dollar's value to justify a sharp increase in the price it charged its traditional purchasers, a successful action that provided the first evidence that Third World raw material producers could influence commodity markets. Two years later, in 1973, Egypt used that evidence to convince all the Arab oil producers, especially the habitually cautious Saudis, that "the oil weapon" could be used effectively as part of the Arab strategy in the October War with Israel. Oil prices rose after the Arab producers stopped sales to the US and the Netherlands (with its key European petroleum port, Rotterdam), and then the previously quite inactive Organization of Petroleum Exporting Countries (OPEC) ratified the increases and began to manage exports to keep prices high (Murphy 1984: 99–101, 112–13).

High oil prices reinforced the "stagflation" that had begun to plague the Free World economy in the early 1970s. High rates of inflation (linked by many economists to US deficit financing) existed alongside low rates of growth (linked by others to the saturation of markers for Fordist goods).

Although analysts in the industrialized core tended to focus only on the effect of high oil prices on the wealthy nations, OPEC's action had an even greater impact on some of the least industrialized countries, especially in Africa where the first oil crisis marked the beginning of two decades of economic decline.

Yet despite this impact, which Third World economists predicted as soon as oil prices jumped, in 1973 African, Asian, and Latin American states rallied behind the oil producers. Once again, the earlier American decision to undermine the Bretton Woods system played a part in this surprising development. The new US economic policy had convinced Third World governments to reestablish the bonds that had linked the anticolonial alliance within the UN. In 1970 that alliance had been in disarray, with the newer, generally poorer, and more numerous African states pushing for development strategies emphasizing poverty alleviation, while the generally older and more industrialized Asian and Latin American states pushed for the kind of greenlining that would promise them rapid entry into the Free World's core (ibid.: 93–6). The American decision opened up an opportunity for a "New International Economic Order" that would satisfy both groups.

The NIEO demands reflected Raul Prebisch's version of Keynesianism and included the whole range of Keynesian proposals that had been left out of global governance under the Free World Order. The NIEO would reestablish the system of fixed exchange rates by focusing on the SDR as the basic reserve asset; this would allow development assistance to become more automatic through a newly established SDR-Link. Moreover, the NIEO would also secure Third World income through commodity agreements attached to a common fund, thus reviving the wartime Allies' idea of how to benefit farmers and those employed in other older sectors throughout the Free World.

While most Third World governments went no further than these self-interested NIEO proposals, both Raul Prebisch (1984) and a number of northern economists, especially those associated with the ILO and with the World Bank's Economic Development Institute, began arguing for a type of global Keynesianism that could also solve some of the North's economic problems – especially the saturated markets for consumer goods reflected in the "stagnation" part of "stagflation." They argued that a more rapid greenlining of the Third World would solve the problem. But to make such greenlining possible, to actually ensure that more of the Third World "took off" in the way South Korea and the east Asian NICs were doing, would require increases in the incomes of the masses in all the countries on the economic launching pad. To achieve that goal, most Third World governments would have to change their "development" priorities.

The populist project of providing relatively low-cost improvements to the lives of the masses would not be enough. Rather than spending the bulk of development funding to serve the politically important interests of the local bourgeoisie and of relatively privileged workers in urban areas, Third World governments would have to focus on increasing the incomes of the vast majority, the rural poor. Policies would have to begin by focusing on basic needs, go on to focus on improving human capital, and finish by abolishing the economic inequities sapping initiative and preventing the kind of agricultural revolution that seems to have preceded the "takeoff" of all societies presently enjoying mass production and mass consumption (Streeten with Burki et al. 1981; Wood 1986: 200; Elsenhans 1991: 146–7).

This global Keynesian vision would not only require northern countries to accept many of the NIEO proposals (albeit with amendments that assured their benefits would go to the Third World's least advantaged), many northern governments would also have to change their views about who their allies were within the Third World. As one German global Keynesian, Hans Elsenhans, puts it, OECD governments would have to look to

> those segments of the [Third World] State-classes which are in a position to enforce social structural change. Often, these reformist segments subscribe to the Marxian critique of capitalism. This is only to be expected as long as the industrial countries of the West use the principles of the market economy as a pretext to reject welfare measures in Third World countries, and the redistribution of income on a global scale. (1991: 160)

Such a change of attitude was a great deal to ask of western governments in the 1970s and 1980s before the fall of Soviet communism and before China's wholesale embrace of the market. Therefore it is not surprising that this version of global Keynesianism did not have that wide a hearing. While it was reflected to some extent in the 1976 Club of Rome report (Tinbergen 1976), the possibilities for cooperation between liberal and Marxist regimes emphasized by Elsenhans and the strict demands that even Prebisch would have placed on Third World governments were not emphasized in the first Brandt Commission report of 1980, a report that came out after the 1979 Soviet invasion of Afghanistan ended the earlier, very brief possibility of East-West detente.

As Susan Strange (1981) points out, although the Brandt Commission's ideas struck a popular cord within Europe, where some governments were becoming skeptical of America's capacity for world leadership (Augelli and Murphy 1988: 169–71), the analysis was ignored in the US and was seriously criticized by European pundits and scholars. The critics rebuked the members of the Commission for their faith in the often quite venal governments found in the Third World, for their simplistic assumptions about the mutuality of interests between those governments and OECD policymakers confronting the continuing problem of stagflation, as well as the results of the second oil crisis brought on by the Iranian revolution of 1979, and for their inability to say anything productive about the "inflation" part of the global economic malaise. Many of the European critics looked across the Atlantic where the new Reagan administration had been able to control inflation by continuing the monetarist policy of exorbitant interest rates begun under Jimmy Carter.

Of course, the Reagan administration did not abandon what many monetarists considered the deepest flaw of decades of Keynesian policy: it did not control US government spending. In fact, the conservative US governments of the 1980s constantly relied on the US's freedom from international macroeconomic discipline granted by Nixon's decision to cease to back the dollar with gold. They eventually amassed much larger debts than those created by Lyndon Johnson when he attempted to expand the welfare state and pursue the Vietnam war without raising taxes. Yet, due to the high US interest rates required by the anti-inflationary, "monetarist" part of Reagan's policy, the dollar tended to retain its value against other currencies.

Through the mechanism of cascading monetarism those high US interest rates plunged the world economy into a major recession at the beginning of the 1980s, a downturn that marked the beginning of a lull in the Free World's crisis similar to the brief European era of good feeling at the end of the 1920s. The recession broke the back of the OPEC cartel; the more populous of the oil producers found they had to sell at low prices both in order to maintain the populist programs that were the source of their legitimacy, and, perhaps even more significantly, in order to service huge development loans taken out when oil prices were high (ibid. 161–4). The end of OPEC's power also meant the end of one source of tension between the US and its allies. Europe stopped considering ways to accommodate the NIEO, and the Reagan administration appeared to reciprocate by reducing the East–West tension raising the specter of a European war; Reagan was helped in that effort by the coincidence of Mikhail Gorbachev's rise to power in the Soviet Union.

The core of the Free World came out of the recession of the early 1980s into a period of sluggish but steady economic growth in the late

1980s, a relief to many when compared to the economic upheavals of the 1970s and early 1980s. Most OECD citizens had become used to the diminished expectations of the end of the twentieth century, while a very few enjoyed the kind of exuberant consumption that had earlier typified the Roaring Twenties. In the US the recession of the early 1980s, in combination with a host of procapitalist and antilabor policies, destroyed the boundary of privilege that had protected many working people. At the beginning of the crisis, sometime between 1969 and 1976, wealth in the US had been distributed more equitably than it had ever been before, one sign of the success of the postwar hegemony. But by 1992 a panel of distinguished economists estimated that this had been completely reversed: the rich controlled almost as much of the country's wealth as in the 1920s, the point in American history when inequality was greatest (Nasar 1992; Harvey 1989: 193). The assault on organized labor, Reagan-era tax policies that gave preference to the rich, and the export of US manufacturing jobs to the low-wage NICs explain the change.

To varying degrees, these factors affected all other OECD economies as well. John Willoughby writes of a growing transnational solidarity of the bourgeoisie throughout the 1980s that has meant the weakening of labor at the core (1989: 94–6). The liberal economy created throughout the Free World had allowed investors to respond to profit squeezes of the 1970s (the increased cost of privileged labor in the welfare states and the saturation of demand) by shifting out of production and into speculative investments in all the new global financial markets encouraged by the revolutions in telematics – especially the global money markets that needed to be so active given the end of the system of fixed exchange rates. The 1980s became an era of frenzied, and successful, "casino capitalism" similar to that in the late 1920s (Strange 1986). But this time around investors could also grab profits by staying in production, but shifting their factories to lower-wage countries (Ross and Trachte 1990: 70–1). Cascading monetarism helped ensure that no OECD government could join labor in a successful defense of the core's boundary of privilege by strengthening the welfare state. When François Mitterrand's French socialists tried to turn back the tide of the Reagan recession in the early 1980s, they proved as ineffectual as the Weimar social democrats who tried to use macroeconomic policy to support the Ruhr strikers of the early 1920s.

Hartmut Elsenhans argues that the weakening foundation of the welfare states means that OECD workers will not be able to prevent the creation of a competing Third World industrial labor force equal to that of the "developed" countries before the end of this century (1991: 15). With that new labor competition will come what Elsenhans somewhat euphemistically calls "the danger of downward equalisation," OECD wages falling toward those in the NICs, and with it, the end of Fordism. Mass consumption would no longer be the basis for mass production. The typical industrial worker in the OECD, like today's average industrial worker in the NICs, would not be able to afford the products that they make, while capitalists would be haunted by the specter of underconsumption, of not having sufficient markets for the goods that can be produced through mass production, the shade that the generalization of Fordism had put to rest.

Underconsumption was not the only ghost of the Great Depression raised in the late 1980s. A new version of the 1930s debt crises appeared as well. Throughout the 1970s private banks had "recycled" OPEC's new wealth by making loans to those eastern European and Latin American states that appeared to be well on their way to becoming industrialized nations. As had been the case with the new states of the 1920s, the big borrowers of the 1970s found they could get better terms from private lenders than those offered under the strict conditionality required by the world organizations. In addition, throughout the 1970s government debts to other governments also increased as poorer states, especially many in Africa, borrowed in order to adjust to the new economic order created by higher oil prices. However, unlike in the 1930s when Germany's reparation debt dwarfed the debt of the new state to private banks, in the 1980s it would be the debt to private banks that would most threaten the international finance system (Fishlow 1985).

The debt crisis of the 1980s might have been addressed by creating more "fictitious capital" to wipe out the debt or, at least, to lower the burden of repayment, perhaps through a vast new issue of SDRs. But the US governments of the 1980s shared the beliefs of their predecessors in the 1920s and early 1930s and this, foreclosed any radical deviation from what was always described as a "market" solution to the crisis. Moreover, in the 1980s many powerful American lenders had the same motives as the French governments of the early 1920s: they hoped to prosper on the basis of debt repayments (Kahler 1985: 373–4).

But by the mid-1980s, after the Reagan recession had reduced western consumption of Third World goods (especially oil), and with interest rates still near all-time records, many of the debts contracted in the 1970s were no longer sustainable. As a consequence, the

North–South compromise at the center of the Free World Order began breaking down even more completely than Fordism had, and the analogy to the interwar years became even more apt. The eminent Mexican economist Victor Urquidi puts it this way: "The essence of the problem, so clearly foreseen by Keynes at the time of the German reparations . . . is that for the debt to be repaid . . . the debtors must develop a sufficiently large export surplus" (1991: 7).

The recession-induced collapse of world markets for Third World goods made that impossible. Therefore, as he continued,

> many countries went into default, which made them ineligible for loans or other forms of financial assistance. Others kept on meeting their interest payments at the expense of growth and development. What came to be termed the "reverse transfer," that is the net out-transfer of financial resources from the developing to the industrialized countries, was the equivalent of reparations payments as if a war had been lost. In fact, the war on poverty, the great struggle for development, had to be given up. (ibid.)

The "reparations payments" of 1980s helped northern economies avoid the deep economic crisis experienced in much of Africa and Latin America. From 1983 onward officially recorded capital outflows from the Third World exceeded investment and aid capital flowing in. If you add reasonable estimates of undocumented capital flight to that amount, the net transfer from the South was of the order of $50 billion dollars per year (Hoogvelt 1991). To give some idea of the magnitude of that figure: all foreign aid would have to be more than doubled for the Third World to break even.

At least in the short run this outcome may have seemed to be a boon to northern investors, just as the antilabor policies of the 1980s must have seemed to be a boon to many OECD employers. But this was only a temporary respite, what Gramsci would call a reassertion of "domination," not the reestablishment of a long-lasting hegemony. In the 1980s, capitalists might be able to dominate workers as they had in the interwar years, and the US might be able to dominate its Free World allies (North and South) the way European members of the Entente dominated Weimar Germany, but in both eras the world order crisis remained.

What Happened to the World Organizations?

It is not easy to assess whether the UN system has done anything to mitigate this world order crisis, or whether the world organizations, despite their growing capacity for self-transformation, have exacerbated it. Certainly they tried to do a great deal that was new in the 15 years between Nixon's new economic policy of 1971 and Gorbachev's first moves to revitalize the Security Council in 1985. It is not surprising that in the face of growing domestic conflicts in the industrialized world and new tensions between developed countries and the LDCs that UN activities in "managing potential social conflicts" outpaced the growth in all other fields except environmental issues, the focus of the UN Environmental Program (UNEP), created in 1972 (figure 7).

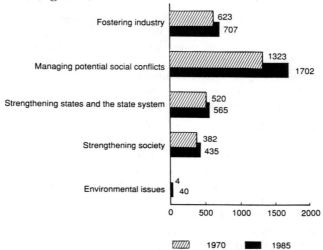

FIGURE 7 Increased activity of world organizations: a comparison of 1970 and 1985 (regular activities, 1966–70 and 1981–5, see appendix on data)

If the world organizations had began to carry out all the activities suggested by their members during these years, the number of new activities would have been even greater.

The UN conducted almost as many global conferences in those 15 years as had taken place in the 75 years before the First World War (table 8). The topics of these conferences correspond to, the purposes of the new activity that did take place: the NIEO debate and the violent conflicts that continued in southern Africa, the Middle East, and Afghanistan predominate. Intercontinental shipping, a prerequisite for the global factory, also remained a constant topic. Finally, and perhaps most significantly, the impact of industrialization on the global environment first became a significant topic of global intergovernmental debate.

TABLE 8   United Nations global conferences, 1974–1985

FOSTERING INDUSTRY

Infrastructure
1974   Liner conferences, Geneva
1974   Law of the sea, Caracas
1975   Law of the sea, Geneva
1976   Law of the sea, New York
1977   Law of the sea, New York
1978   Law of the sea, Geneva
1978   Carriage of goods by sea, Hamburg
1979   Law of the sea, New York
1979   Multimodal transport, Geneva
1980   Multimodal transport, Geneva
1980   Law of the sea, Geneva
1981   Law of the sea, New York
1982   Law of the sea, New York
1982   Uses of outer space, Vienna
1984   Registration of ships, Geneva
1985   Registration of ships, Geneva

Trade
1974   Sale of goods, New York
1979   Business practices, Geneva
1980   Business practices, Geneva
1980   Sale of goods, Vienna
1985   Business practices, Geneva

MANAGING POTENTIAL SOCIAL CONFLICTS

Agriculture
1974   Food, Rome

LDCs
1974   Raw materials, New York
1974   Population, Bucharest
1975   Economic cooperation, New York
1976   Agricultural Development, Rome
1977   Common Fund, Geneva
1978   Common Fund, Geneva
1978   Industrial Development, New York
1978   NIEO General Assembly, New York
1978   Technical cooperation among LDCs, Buenos Aires
1978   Transfer of technology, Geneva
1979   Transfer of technology, Geneva
1979   NIEO General Assembly, New York
1979   Common Fund, Geneva
1979   Industrial Development, Vienna
1979   Science and technology, Vienna
1980   NIEO General Assembly, New York

1980 Transfer of technology, Geneva
1980 Common Fund, Geneva
1980 NIEO, New York
1981 Transfer of technology, Geneva
1981 Least developed LDCs, Paris
1983 Transfer of technology, Geneva
1984 Population, Mexico City
1985 Transfer of technology, Geneva

STRENGTHENING STATES AND THE STATE SYSTEM

Public order and administration
1975 Prevention of crime, London
1980 Prevention of crime, Caracas
1985 Prevention of crime, Milan

Conflict management
1974 Humanity in war, Geneva
1975 Humanity in war, Geneva
1975 Nonproliferation, Geneva
1975 States and international organizations, Vienna
1976 Humanity in war, Geneva
1977 Humanity in war, Geneva
1977 State succession, Vienna
1977 Zimbabwe and Namibia, Maputo
1977 Seabed weapons ban, Geneva
1978 UN forces in Lebanon, New York
1978 Namibia, New York
1978 Disarmament, New York
1978 State succession, Vienna
1979 Indiscriminate weapons, Geneva
1980 Indiscriminate weapons, Geneva
1980 Afghanistan, New York
1980 Biological weapons, Geneva
1980 Palestine, New York
1980 Nonproliferation, Geneva
1981 South Africa, Paris
1981 Kampuchea, New York
1981 Namibia, New York
1982 Occupied Arab territory, New York
1982 Palestine, New York
1982 Disarmament, New York
1983 State succession, Vienna
1983 Namibia, Paris
1983 Palestine, Geneva
1983 Seabed weapons ban, Geneva
1985 Nonproliferation, Geneva

Refugees
1977 Territorial asylum, Geneva
1981 Refugees in Africa, Geneva
1984 Refugees in Africa, Geneva
1985 Emergency in Africa, Geneva

STRENGTHENING SOCIETY

Human rights
1975   Women, Mexico City
1977   Apartheid, Lagos
1978   Racism, Geneva
1980   Women, Copenhagen
1983   Racism, Geneva
1985   Women, Nairobi

Health
1978   Primary health care, Alma Ata
1982   Aging, Vienna

Education and research
1977   Geographical names, Athens
1982   Geographical names, Geneva

ENVIRONMENTAL ISSUES

1976   Habitat, Vancouver
1977   Water, Mar del Plata
1977   Desertification, Nairobi
1981   Renewable energy, Nairobi
1984   Environment and war, Geneva

Source: Willetts (1989).

Unfortunately, the UN did not prove very effective in the first two of these four fields. The Third World used its majority in the General Assembly and other world organizations to create a host of NIEO programs that have little impact simply because the northern powers, led by the United States, refused to fund them. And, until the revival of detente in the late 1980s, UN actions in Afghanistan, the Middle East, and southern Africa were always of secondary importance, primarily because the superpowers and their Third World allies (the US with Israel and South Africa, the Soviet Union with Afghanistan and Vietnam) treated UN actions as illegitimate.

Multilateral attempts to think about modernizing the infrastructure of international trade and responding to international environmental problems proved more successful, if only because they did not highlight the North–South rift opened by OPEC in the early 1970s. But even in these "nonpolitical" fields the UN was often subject to criticism by the OECD's liberal fundamentalist governments of the 1980s. One of the Reagan administration's first actions was to withdraw American support for a long-debated codification of the law of the sea, despite the ways in which it would facilitate both international commerce and an entire new industry of seabed mining. The main problem the Americans had with the new international regime was that it set up a new international public enterprise (in many ways, similar to Intelsat) and an embryonic system of automatic financing of multilateral development assistance. Similarly, in 1982 the US almost withdrew from the ITU, citing the organization's decision to begin a program of technical assistance to the LDCs similar to the programs long established by all the other UN specialized agencies (US Senate 1983: 31).

The United States and its closest allies actually did withdraw from UNESCO, an agency whose constituency of scholars was a good deal less powerful than the many telecommunications companies and their clients who rely on the stable environment provided by ITU regimes. (Of course, going back to Prince Albert's program for exchanging plaster casts of great sculptures, the international institutions involved with education and research have always been the most vulnerable to the cost-cutting measures that typify world order crises.) The Reagan administration also stopped funding a whole series of UN development activities that clashed with its conservative ideology, especially programs aimed at giving Third World women greater control over their own fertility (Crane and Finkle 1987). And the US withdrew much of its funding from the UN as part of an announced strategy of encouraging administrative reform and cost-cutting efficiencies.

Paul Taylor (1991) argues, quite reasonably, that if the US really meant to reform the UN, it chose the wrong strategy. By withdrawing funding the US simply triggered crises within each of the UN agencies. The few that coped and actually instituted administrative reforms found that the Americans would provide little guidance as to what would be necessary in order to regain their support (cf. Coate 1988; Crane and Finkle 1987). In fact, the Reagan and Bush administrations found that they could not promise that support, no matter what the agencies did. Faced with a ballooning federal budget deficit, the US Congress had found that cutting funding for multilateral cooperation was much too attractive.

Nevertheless, if the real goal was to weaken the support given by the UN to the Third World alliance, the strategy made some sense (Augelli and Murphy 1988: 185–9). Attacks on the UN agencies that had done the most to foster the NIEO were consistent with a general Reagan-era opposition to global Keynesianism, especially the policy of preventing the Bretton Woods institutions from creating the resources needed to deal with the debt crisis. Both policies helped the US government retain maximum flexibility in dealing with the short-term problems that its constituents faced as a result of the world order crisis.

The American campaign against the UN system left the world organizations in increasing disrepute and less and less capable of playing a leading role in resolving the world order crisis. After writing *Plenty*, David Hare completed a play that epitomized the problem. He set *A Map of the World* (1982) at a UNESCO conference on poverty that becomes a debate between an embittered Indian novelist of the independence generation (the same generation as the heroine of *Plenty*) and an idealistic British journalist in his twenties. Hare has the younger man defending the Third World movement, the UN, and the welfare-oriented liberal internationalism it represents. The novelist suffers no illusions about these institutions and makes the arguments more often heard from partisans of the Reagan revolution or from the European critics of the Brandt Commission.

Yet, ultimately, Hare lets the younger man win the debate by voicing the opinion that under all the mass of paper, with all of the UN's hypocrisy, the world organizations do get some things done: "crises *are* averted, aid *is* directed," the agencies are at least engaged in trying to make things work better, which is more than can be said of the older man who has given up and retreated "further and further into a right-wing corner of fastidious reaction." The journalist's sentiment echoes the quotation from Oscar Wilde that Hare places at the head of the play:

> A map of the world that does not include Utopia is not worth even glancing at, for it leaves out the one country in which humanity is always landing. And when Humanity lands there, it looks out, and, seeing a better country, sets sail.

By the late 1980s the world organizations could still be seen as such a map, but that was all. A generation earlier they had been part of that country of plenty in which the Free World alliance had landed.

8

TOWARD THE NEXT WORLD ORDER

The utopia to which today's world organizations point remains the one first mapped by Adam Smith and Immanuel Kant and later only partially explored by the nineteenth-century public systems builders and the mid twentieth-century Keynesians. Despite the world order crisis of the last decade we still have reason to believe that the promise of liberal internationalism can again be fulfilled in a new world order more extensive, and with benefits more widespread, than the last.

Some of those who discount the continuing relevance of Smith's project argue that revolutions in the scale of production triggered by wider markets are things of the past. But today's suggestions along this line sound like those of the pundits of 1890 who argued that the movement toward large-scale production had run its course (Thorp 1924: 45), or the economist who claimed in 1948 that "long-term, general, and pervasive increase in plant size throughout most industry has come to an end" (Blair 1948: 151). There was, at the time, some truth in these statements, but in both cases fundamentally new economies of scale and scope would soon fuel decades of growth.

The connection between the scale of markets for industrial goods and new investment certainly still holds in the emerging world of "globalized" production where a "plant" has become a regular set of relationships of purchases among large and small companies, often separated by hundreds of miles, but all contributing to the same value-added chain. In this new world, the typical "plant" remains a connected set of physical processes achieving "scale" results – more output for the same input – and the resources needed to create such systems remain vast. So far, most of the "globalized plants" simply

produce products of older industries at lower costs (usually by seeking lower-wage labor), but, as Adam Smith would have expected, we
can identify a range of new products that would require larger, secure
markets for industrial goods. These range from computers capable of
recognizing voice commands and translating natural languages
(Somerlatte 1982: 29), to a new generation of cost-efficient supersonic transports (Rosen and Williams 1993), to a host of new means
to minimize pollution and restore the environment (M. Porter 1991;
E. Smith 1992). All of these products have such high research and
development costs that they could be recovered only if the resulting
goods could be sold throughout today's major industrial markets: not
only North America, western Europe, and Japan, but also the growing markets of China, India, eastern Europe, and the NICs.

The first wave of transportation and communication infrastructure
that would be needed for such a huge market area has begun to be
put in place. In fact, some of those who study "long waves" of
industrial development (Grübler and Nakićenović 1991) suggest that
the global diffusion of jet aircraft in the late twentieth century so
closely matches that of railways in the European and North American
continents a little over a century ago that we should simply expect
the "third industrial revolution" to arrive in ten or 15 years. This new
industrial revolution would be led by industries producing goods
carried by planes, the way the Second Industrial Revolution was led
by industries producing goods carried by trains.

However, no such inevitable connections exist among the various
long-wave patterns that scholars can find in historical data. In the
future, as in the past, any new period of relative prosperity and peace
will require the creation of new institutions to end stagnation and
conflict. We can look to the past only to help understand the purposes those institutions must serve.

The two long waves of industrial development I have described
here could each be summarized in the verbal formula: *build, thrive,
clash, grab, hoard*.[1] A run of good years followed the building of both
world orders, but faltered as unresolved conflicts came to the surface.
After temporarily resolving these conflicts, capitalists and the most
powerful states succumbed to the temptation of domination and
grabbed for profits through the frenzied speculation of casino capitalism and through liberal fundamentalist public policies that benefited
the rich at the expense of more vulnerable people both at home and
abroad. In the 1930s, at least, the explosion of a few speculative
bubbles led to an era of simple hoarding, when productive, future-
oriented investment continued to be rare.

Ending those unproductive eras of clashing, grabbing, and hoarding required creative acts of intellectual and political leadership designed to extend international civil society in order to secure the wider market areas that new communication and transportation technologies allowed. The new potential markets, thus secured, encouraged the long-term, productive investment needed to begin and sustain the next industrial wave.

This, then, would appear to be the current agenda of global governance. We need to create international institutions that will assure the maximum diffusion of today's most advanced transportation technologies, define rules encouraging trade in the products of the new industries that are next on the horizon, and manage both the current conflicts between those who are more advantaged and less advantaged by the industrial system and the new conflicts that are likely to emerge in the next industrial era.

This agenda could be pursued in many different ways. Some liberal internationalists might endorse the goal of the regulationist Alain Lipietz, of a new industrial wave in which some of the emptiness at the heart of Fordism would begin to be addressed by putting leisure and welfare rather than the mass consumption of new products at the heart of a new pact between labor and capital (1992: 77–110). Similarly, a surprisingly wide range of cosmopolitan institutions – including Japan's Ministry for International Trade and the planning departments of some of the world's largest companies – have concluded that environmental concerns could drive the next generation of rapid economic growth. Some treat this possibility as a tragedy to be averted, but most accept it as an opportunity-laden challenge (Murphy 1992: 62; M. Porter 1991; E. Smith 1992: 73–4).

The argument goes that there are at least three kinds of large investments that could fuel a green wave of industrial growth. First, there is the massive investment needed to replace outmoded, polluting infrastructure (especially power plants, fuel lines, and sewage systems) in the already industrialized world. This is one of the most significant challenges faced by the new governments of eastern Europe, where the environmental inadequacy of the existing infrastructure has been especially marked. Second, there is the significant investment needed to replace older industrial processes with new, more benign substitutes, for example, investing in plants to produce new refrigerants to replace the ozone-destroying refrigerators used by consumers. Investments of this sort are of special interest to the large, newly industrializing nations (Brazil, China, India, Indonesia, and Mexico) because of the damage to the global environment that would result if the populous nations attempt to reach the industrial level of the already rich countries by using the same polluting technologies used by Germany, Japan, and the US when they were in a similar position of economic takeoff. Third, there is the investment needed to build plants producing green consumer products for those in societies with high mass consumption; such products are already demanded by consumers in Germany, Scandinavia and some other parts of the OECD world.

As has always been the case with investments in infrastructure, governments would probably have to make most of the large investments of the first kind. In contrast, industries providing newly industrializing countries with less harmful means of production could become quite profitable, at least in the long run, even if some sort of North–South compromise on development, and some northern financing, were needed in the beginning. Many green consumer products could provide significant returns from the beginning, especially if environmental regulations (requirements to recycle waste and caps on household waste) encouraged rapid adoption of the new products. In any case, laissez-faire would not be enough to intiate a green industrial wave.

Nevertheless, both the nature of the next industrial wave, and both the institutions needed to start it are current matters of dispute. Throughout the "age of diminished expectations" many liberal scholars have looked backward, to the era of the Public International Unions and before, to find models of limited international institutions with none of the perceived failings of the "overtly managerial" UN and the Bretton Woods agencies (Gallaroti 1991: 186; cf. Adelman 1988; Conybeare 1980). Such organizations would not only rely on the market as a political institution, they would also forgo any attempt to overcome powerful market tendencies, for example, by trying to resist the logic of cascading monetarism.

For many years the United States government championed this hyperliberal vision of the institutions needed to end the world order crisis; the policy of the Reagan and Bush administrations to undermine many of the current world organizations served the larger goal of building international institutions for the next world order. President Bush's leadership of the UN-based coalition to reverse Iraq's invasion of Kuwait (and, not incidently, to protect western oil interests) and his willingness to support the explosive expansion of the Security Council's role in managing international conflicts after the breakup of the Soviet Union demonstrated this purpose. This reflected a liberal fundamentalist acceptance of a "nightwatchman" role for the general purpose world organization: the UN would become an instrument both for legitimizing and for sharing the material burden of the use of force within the new world order, a coercive instrument over which the one remaining superpower (along with its four great-power allies who also carry a veto in the Security Council) would retain control (Legault 1992: 21–2).

Despite their tendency toward strict liberal fundamentalism, US policymakers also gave a great deal of thought to the consensus-oriented international institutions needed in President Bush's "New World Order" (cf. Warsh 1992). Throughout the 1980s the US pushed agreements to deregulate international communication and transportation in order to encourage the private production of new infrastructure (Ganley 1987; Golich 1992). American officials demanded that the largest private companies be given even more responsibility for setting industrial standards and that intellectual property rights be strengthened through the expansion of copyright protection to cover software and of patent protection to cover biotechnology. In the most recent round of GATT negotiations the US hoped to replace WIPO's intellectual property regimes, abolishing the requirement to work patents abroad and extending GATT's retaliation procedures to countries whose firms violated trademarks, patents, and copyrights (Vaitsos 1989).

Nevertheless, the Reagan and Bush administrations paid little attention to updating international protections of workers' rights and the US welcomed the check on the expansion of the welfare state provided by the mechanism of cascading monetarism. In GATT's Uruguay Round, which began in the late 1980s, the US pushed hard for agreements to dismantle subsidies for farmers and for some older industries throughout the industrial world, thus offering the Third World an end to the Free World Order hypocrisy of having laissez-faire liberalism apply to southern producers but not their northern competitors.

Finally, the Republican administrations were at their most innovative in sponsoring international institutions to check the casino capitalism of the 1980s short of a financial crash. As a result, a new International Organization of Securities Commissions (Levin 1989; T. Porter 1992) now regulates the new globalized financial markets, and the Basle Accord, worked out within the BIS, has given most of the world's banks the same capital requirements, thus helping prevent the excessive speculation of a few institutions from undermining confidence in the world's vast majority of relatively sound banks (Bhala and Kapstein 1990).

There are good reasons to expect that this attempt at building a hyperliberal world order might be more effective than the one that was tried 60 years earlier. The major incentives today's hyperliberals offer to long-term productive investment – an extended and stricter international regime covering intellectual property – are directed toward those industries that many analysts consider to be among the most likely leaders of the next industrial wave (Mass and Senge 1981). A related US policy of trying to extend the GATT to cover "service" sectors – from advertising and insurance to the various "cultural" industries producing TV programs, music videos, and computer games – also taps into sectors that could continue to grow by leaps and bounds (Alleyne 1992; Alleyne and Sen 1992).

On the other hand, the similar American attempt to use GATT to establish free trade in agriculture and other older sectors has pushed Europe and North America apart, convincing leaders on both continents to emphasize new regional trade liberalization pacts – the North American Free Trade Area (NAFTA) and a newly broadened and deepened European Community – over a global order (Paarlberg 1991). Even so, a hyperliberal world order would not necessarily fail even if its most important trading areas were regional blocs – that is, a somewhat extended NAFTA including the Caribbean, South America, and perhaps even part of east Asia; the European Community with its own near peripheries to the east; and an Asian bloc centered on Japan and China but also including much of southeast Asia and perhaps even Asian Russia. Paul Krugman (1991) argues that, given current costs of transportation and other factors that correlate with geography, a world of three trading blocs might, in theory, provide only marginally fewer welfare benefits than those that could be achieved in the initial phase of any deepening integration across the entire industrial world.

However, by relying on the market to build the transportation infrastructure of global trade, this hyperliberal world would probably never see more efficient links built between the separate trading blocs, such as a new generation of efficient supersonic transports (Rosen and Williams 1993). In the sense, this social order would be less advantageous than an order designed with the lessons of the public system builders in mind. Similarly, relying on the market to establish industrial standards would probably prove to be less efficient than the current system of coordination through industrial committees (Farrell and Saloner 1987) and any move away from WIPO-style requirements to work patents will diminish the incentive to share intellectual property throughout the industrial world

(Penrose 1951: 136, 233). Moreover, the entire range of conflicts related to the growth of industry could increase under a hyperliberal world order.

In fact, new forms of international labor resistance have been growing in many of the more populous newly industrializing countries where liberal fundamentalists hold out the greatest hope for finding relatively inexpensive and relatively skilled labor to staff the new "global" factories: places like Brazil, Mexico, Poland, and South Africa. These movements tend to see workers' interests as opposed both to capitalists and to the state, but not necessarily to the national society. Their international connections have been secured by alliances with global ecological, human rights, peace, and women's movements that have arisen in the political space created by the waning world order. Examples include the consumer boycotts organized by Greenpeace and the Interfaith Center on Corporate Responsibility of the World Council of Churches (Waterman 1988).

Given that the champions of a hyperliberal world do not promise the Fordist era's wide generalization of prosperity or relief from the burden of debt under which many of the low-wage industrialized countries suffer, we should not be surprised that the new labor internationalism already resists this fundamentalist vision. In some of the most populous nations (Brazil, Mexico, India, Indonesia) that resistance could push national governments to put out of the liberal order and become centers of significant antagonistic alternative orders, the way China and the Soviet Union became centers of hostility toward the Free World (Murphy 1990).

Beyond increasing the conflicts that go along with capitalist industrialism, the hyperliberal order would do little to cope with the global environmental issues that have lately absorbed so much of the attention of the UN system and that will undoubtedly continue to be topics of global concern simply due to the rate at which human activity is changing the biosphere.[2] Throughout the 1980s many global Keynesians began highlighting these issues as an argument for their alternative to a hyperliberal world order. Boston University economist Jonathan Harris put it this way: "The future world economic system will have to be based on kind of a global ecological Keynesianism, with significant social direction of capital flows, demand management, and technological choices, to promote ecological sustainability".

There are as many signs of the emergence of this alternative as there are of the world order championed by Reagan and Bush. The "technological choices" made by the US in establishing Intelsat, by

European governments in mapping out a new continent-wide system of high-speed railways (Protzman 1992), and by the many industrial countries now funding designs for a new generation of supersonic civilian jets that would cause minimal environmental damage (Rosen and Williams 1993) all suggest that lessons of the public systems builders have been remembered. In fact, one of the newest communication infrastructures – the "Internet" of global pathways linking public and private computers (usually without cost to individual users) – was built following something very much like the short-distance system for financing railways that John Wright saw as the foundation of global governance over a century ago; institutions may connect to the network simply by agreeing to help others connect to the network through their node.

Moreover, despite the American push to de-emphasize intergovernmental work on industrial standards and to put intellectual property under the GATT, the older regimes encouraging the rapid diffusion of technology are still in place; governments have recently added new commitments, however vague, to encourage rapid sharing of any innovative, environmentally sound technologies that can replace older, polluting practices. These commitments would become increasingly significant if environmental concerns do come to drive the next generation of rapid economic growth.

Whether they do or not depends, as Harris would say, on the "social direction of capital flows" and the particular form of "demand management" adopted by the wealthiest and most powerful states. Alain Lipietz's image of a transformed Fordism directed toward increasing leisure and welfare would be compatible with encouraging the "green wave" of industrial growth to follow the automobile and jet age. Yet, as Lipietz points out, many of the policies needed to begin such an era would, of necessity, involve reinforcing some of the boundaries that separate different nations and different regions: different societies will need to work out different exchanges between increased consumption and increased leisure. As a result, in a "global ecological Keynesian" world order, finance would again have to be made a servant of the welfare state in order to prevent cascading monetarism and guard against capital flight as different states or regions arrive at different social pacts.

Outside the industrialized world this alternative world order would require something more than just the restoration of the populist project of "development" that once strengthened the Third World state. What has been learned from a generation of experience with "development" would need to be used to channel foreign assistance toward the activities that are the most likely to increase mass incomes and, hence, provide the foundation for the kind of economy that the Fordist world has enjoyed (Elsenhans 1991). Paul Streeten, one of the most distinguished economists who has worked on outlining this vision, recommends new international institutions to provide debt relief and guard against further debt crises by opening northern markets to Third World goods and by establishing effective commodity pricing agreements (1991: 126–9). Self-interested justifications that the North could find for these actions include the benefit of having constantly expanding, greenlined mass markets which could help avert future problems of market saturation, as well as, perhaps more significantly, the globally relevant benefit of ensuring that places like Brazil, China, and India do not become mass-production societies by using the same environmentally destructive technologies used by Britain, Germany, and the United States a century ago.

To complete the picture of this alternative to a hyperliberal new world order, perhaps we should imagine the United Nations at the center of a new international security regime that uses coercive force with an eye toward securing accountable governments and the protection of human rights throughout the world. Tatsuro Kunugi (1992, 1993), who was the Assistant Secretary General who dealt with humanitarian and population activities throughout the 1980s, sees a strong connection between the encouragement of the economic policies needed for ecologically sustainable development toward high-wage economies in the industrializing Third World (and in the despoiled former communist states), and the increasing demands on the UN to help establish accountable governments even if that requires multilateral force. The desire of Secretary General Boutros Boutros-Ghali (1992) to see a seamless web among the UN's more coercive "peacemaking" activities and the "peacemaking" that goes on through "development" gives global Keynesians an opportunity to design a multilateral security mechanism that could be central to the next world order, rather than merely a secondary adjunct as it was throughout the Cold War (cf. Mackinlay and Chopra 1993).

However, one of the limitations of the intellectual leadership that can be provided by today's global ecological Keynesians is that few have Kunugi's interest in thinking about positive roles that can be played by military force. Like Jane Addams, Emily Green Balch, John A. Hobson, Leonard Woolf, and the rest of the first wave of critical liberal internationalists between the world wars, most of today's global Keynesians are more apt to be economists than military strategists, and some have Hobson's aversion to professional soldiers, even to those who shared the rest of the critical liberal agenda.

The similarities between the first interwar wave of critical liberals and today's global Keynesians do not end there. Like that older generation, many of today's critical liberals lack the practical experience that gave Keynes the reputation needed to act as an effective intellectual leader. Policy intellectuals can rarely argue that their science *dictates* particular solutions to social problems; they can only claim to provide considered, professional judgments, – as John Ikenberry (1992) shows that the wartime Keynesians did. Their real power, like that of nineteenth-century public system builders, came from the prestige they had gained in the eyes of potential sponsors and benefactors of new international institutions. The Keynesians gained it simply because Keynes's economics helped end the Depression and forge the new compromises between labor and capitalists throughout the industrial world.

While many of today's global Keynesians are men and women of action, unlike many of the League intellectuals, many of the most innovative of todays critical liberals have long worked on practical problems within the UN system. As a result, these analysts were diminished by the crisis of the UN system in the eyes of governments of many of the powerful states that will have to be relied on as sponsors and benefactors of new international institutions.

A few years back Jonathan Harris (1990) argued that it might take a crisis affecting the developed world as sharp as the Great Depression (probably, this time, an ecological crisis) before key policymakers would turn to the solutions offered by Keynes's successors. Since that time more benign paths to becoming effective intellectual leaders have opened up. In 1991, David Warsh, whose business-page columns have closely tracked the jockeying to develop the economic institutions of the next world order, began to see a new political sophistication in the global Keynesian research coming out of the UN, especially in the reports of Mahbub ul Haq's research staff at the UNDP. The arguments being provided for the importance to real development of accountable governments, macroeconomic stability, and a global trading system were more sophisticated than anything being written by liberal fundamentalists. According to Warsh, the UN-based intellectuals had "taken over" some of the most powerful parts of the message of the Reagan-era fundamentalists. Unlike the fundamentalists, the global Keynesians were able to "deliver it everywhere" (Warsh 1991), using new concepts to attach what could be learned from the successes of the Reagan era to issues on which the global Keynesians clearly had something to add to the fundamentalist vision.

One consequence has been a shift in Third World blueprints for a new world order. In the early 1990s the global Keynesians who staffed UNCTAD argued that the Uruguay Round should be capped by the transformation of GATT into a full-fledged world trade organization. In 1992 they helped prepare the texts endorsed by UNCTAD's full membership that included references to a host of principles that earlier had been championed only by the OECD: an unambiguous preference for free markets, disregard of any notion of delinking from the world economy, an equation of democratization and the protection of human rights with development, and all the Reagan-era rhetoric about the need to decrease the corruption and increase the efficiency of governments in the South. Meanwhile, similar signs of convergence came from the "other side" as the IMF's managing director endorsed the idea of "sustainable development" and the argument that Michael Stewart (1984) had made a decade before about the similar logics of cascading monetarism and of mounting problems of transborder pollution in a purely market-based order (Camdessus 1992).

This relatively new idea of "sustainable development," which had first appeared in the early 1970s as part of an antimaterialist critique of Fordism (Murphy 1992: 53–5), has become an important focus of the revised global Keynesian message. Unlike previous attempts to find a global Keynesian alternative to neoliberal fundamentalism, the call for "sustainable development" encouraged support from the kind of business and government interests that had helped create the international social structures of the European Second Industrial Revolution and the postwar Free World Order. These included major firms involved in leading, high-technology industrial sectors and, as was the case a century ago, some of the major industrial states only one tier removed from the leading economic power.

The 1987 report of the World Commission on the Environment and Development, under Norwegian Prime Minister Gro Brundtland (Brundtland Commission 1992), included Stewart's conclusions about the similarity of global environmental problems and the problem of cascading monetarism and added global Keynesian arguments about development in the Third World then being made by critics of the liberal fundamentalist prescriptions championed by the US and the Bretton Woods institutions. The Commission appealed to growth-oriented Keynesians in the North by arguing for agreement on international institutional structures of accumulation that would allow a return to the more egalitarian days of rapid economic growth in the 1960s and 1970s. It appealed to northern environmentalists as well as a growing ecological movement in the South by pointing out both the unsustainability of the North's growth patterns and the planetary responsibilities of Third World governments for maintaining the habitats and the biodiversity of their lands. And it appealed to southern exponents of the failed NIEO, and their northern allies who had supported the earlier Brandt Commission reports, by providing a new, potentially more convincing set of arguments for the North's responsibilities toward the South (Murphy 1992: 56).

Critics of the Brundtland Commission, including S. M. Lélé (1991: 616), admonished it for sneaking in the idea that free trade is almost always desirable. Yet by embracing the globalization of the market economy the advocates of "sustainable development" put themselves squarely in the tradition of liberal internationalism and improved their chances to mobilize powerful business interests to join the other social forces pushing for international responses to contemporary social problems.

The success of this tactic has been reflected in the work of the Business Council on Sustainable Development (BCSD), a new nongovernmental organization that brings together the leaders of a host of the world's largest firms, from the Dow Chemical Company, to Nippon Steel, to India's giant TATA, to Volkswagen. The only thing that all these companies clearly have in common is that all have learned from experience that it can pay to be a first mover on environmental issues. Generalizing from their individual experiences, they have convinced the International Organization for Standardization to establish a Strategic Advisory Group on the Environment to prepare international standards for the "eco-efficiency" of industrial products and services. The aim is to ensure that products have standard "eco-labeling" and that public entities purchasing goods and products look at life-cycle analyses and environmental audits (Schmidheiny 1992: 95).

The self-interest of the BCSD firms is transparent even if it is enlightened. They believe that in a global market of green consumers and of governments increasingly influenced by the environmental concerns of their publics, ISO standards labeling the environmental desirability of every product and service will benefit the BCSD firms, those that already have experience as environmental first movers.

Even though it is at least conceivable that industrial investors could make the North's contribution to sustainable development by themselves, not even the BCSD firms' strategic planners act on that assumption. At Shell, for instance, the strategists want to be sure that "the decisions our businesses make" will work in two different future worlds: "In one . . . regional conflicts plague the world, environmental problems are attacked piecemeal, and low prices shape energy use. In the other, sustainable development takes hold. International cooperation blossoms to combat environmental damage and global warming. Governments discourage fossil fuel use and promote renewable energy" (E. Smith 1992: 74).

Global Keynesians are apt to see the first scenario as what would result from the triumph of the hyperliberal world order and the second as the realization of their own vision. The proximate causes of an inexorable move down the second path may prove to involve nothing more than the policies of the industrial powers that rank just below the United States. For example, if the Japanese Ministry for International Trade maintains its conviction that environmental concerns will drive the next generation of economic growth, and then spends to reposition Japanese industry to take advantage of this development, then it will be in the interest of every firm around the world to invest with that vision in mind.

Japan is also typical of the powers to which global Keynesians will have to appeal to find the sponsors and benefactors of the international institutions needed to help structure such an order. The major political leader of the Free World Order, the United States, is likely to play a less central role. The limited leadership provided by the Republican administrations of the 1980s may have been more than a reflection of their liberal fundamentalism. As Paul Taylor (1991) points out, the limits set in the Reagan and Bush era on contributions to the UN simply continued a trend of decreasing financial support that began in the early 1970s. A Senate report explains the logic of limited US involvement:

> When dealing from a position of technological or economic advantage, it is wise to approach the question of negotiation with caution. If, relative to other parties to the negotiation, a country has the most to give, and already has most of what it is liable to get, striking a satisfactory bargain may require a good deal of careful forethought. (US Senate 1983: 30)

British companies and their government displayed a similar conviction in the last decade of the Long Depression. That conviction cannot be shaken by appeals to the *immediate* interests of American business or to those of the US government. Meanwhile, governments that have not yet had the US's opportunity to form a world community in its own image may be more susceptible to appeals to long-term aspirations for leadership.

However, appeals to the long-term interests of American *businesses* may work. After all, German, Dutch, and Swiss first movers did much better within the economic space created by the Public International Unions than did the British. Analogously, the American business school professors who now worry about the US being the last to jump on to the "sustainable development" bandwagon are actually less worried about the long-term negative impact on the environment of such a policy than they are about the long-term impact on American competitiveness (M. Porter 1991; E. Smith 1992; Rosen and Williams 1993: 29).

In any event, the problem of finding political sponsors and benefactors for the international institutions of the next world order will be at least as complex as it was a century ago. It has been compounded by what the nineteenth-century public system builders might recognize as the "lack of political efficiency" of many of the solutions proposed by intellectuals of the critical tradition to today's North–South conflicts.

Many involve the all-too-visible transfer of new northern resources to the South. This may seem justified given that net financial flows went from South to North throughout the 1980s, and that after 1985 even the World Bank and IMF became net recipients of funds from the countries that, in the Bank's case at least, they are mandated to aid. Nevertheless, most OECD legislatures are unlikely to tax their citizens to reverse such transfers, especially when some governments have to consider unprecedented accumulations of government debt and all face the other consequences of years of slow growth.

There really may be no way around this dilemma, especially as it relates to the funding of multilateral development programs. The costs of the operational development activities far exceed those of any of the other activities of the world organizations, even the maintenance of peacekeeping forces. This means that the traditional pattern of one or few states as the benefactors of new activities will not work very well in these fields. It is one thing to pick up many of the bills for a big global meeting, or even support a secretariat by seconding staff and making voluntary contributions; it is quite another thing to foot the bill for a host of development operations.

There is a lesson in the way the US actually played that benefactor role at the beginning of the Free World Order, but it is not the usual lesson of the Marshall Plan's generosity. Rather, it is the lesson of the Bretton Woods institutions. The initial deposits of gold and hard currencies by the US (and the very few other original members whose money was convertible) created a pool of loan money that could immediately be expanded enormously by the IMF and the World Bank both by fiat and by borrowing. The long-standing Keynesian proposal using increases in IMF reserves to create a pool for development assistance, the SDR-Link, has the same advantage of invisibility, the same political efficiency. Of course, that particular proposal has been unworkable ever since the floating exchange rate system appeared in the early 1970s. Nevertheless, rather than bemoaning either that fact or the inadequacy of today's funding for multilateral activities that comes through the increasing used mechanism of voluntary contributions (Taylor 1991: 380), global Keynesians should recognize that this necessary voluntarism reflects the way that innovation in global governance usually takes place. Calls for new Marshall Plans for the environment, for Africa, or for the former communist countries will be less successful than other proposals that would establish regular (even if initially quite small) sources of development finance linked to a growing part of the world economy.

The work of Ruben P. Mendez (1992) of the UN Sudano-Sahelian Office suggests some possible directions. The most interesting are those that could be connected back to the traditional, proven way in which benefactors have played a role in extending the activities of world organizations by allowing benefits of the new task to be demonstrated in practice before all states are required to bear their part of the burden. Consider recent Norwegian proposals to respond to the demands for less polluting industry from its own environmental groups, not by investing the huge amounts needed to clean the last 5 percent of the pollution from its own advanced factories, but by investing an equivalent amount in reducing the much easier to clean first 95 percent of the pollution from factories in the same industry in China. Perhaps these are the kinds of proposals that will find their way into the final reports of the latest of the global Keynesian projects for designing the institutions of next world order. This is the Commission on Global Governance, following on the work of the Brundtland Commission and aiming "to feed into the discussions on global governance that can be expected to accelerate in the period leading up to the fiftieth anniversary of the United Nations" (Hansen 1993).

Whether or not future historians recognize that anniversary as a turning point in the institutionalization of the next world order, the liberal internationalist project that fostered Keynes's prewer economic Eldorado and the Free World's postwar decades of prosperity is still very much alive. Moreover, the critical version of that project that I have outlined in this last chapter has, today, a surprisingly wide range of supporters, especially in the industrialized world. For example, the conclusions of W. W. Rostow (1985: 222) about the international and regional requirements for a new phase of industrialism that would both restore prosperity and begin to prepare us for a world no longer shaped by heroic materialism are surprisingly similar to Alain Lipietz's view of the international structures of a new industrial wave that would begin to take us beyond the limitations on our humanity imposed by Fordism (1992: 111–26).

To see our way toward that new order, Alain Noël (1993: 23) argues we would do well to adopt the realism underlying the theories of both Marx and Keynes about the fundamental instability of capitalist industrialism, eschewing the search for deterministic laws, but indentifying mechanisms that allow us both to explain social change and to have the foresight to recognize opportunities as they emerge without deluding ourselves into thinking that we can predict what is to come. In doing so we could do much worse than be guided by the principle that Gramsci followed, one that has appeared at the end of so many of the studies of world politics that he has informed: we should take the path toward the next world order full of both the "pessimism of the intellect" that lets us see the extent of the political obstacles to a more humane world, and the "optimism of the will" that lets us begin by assuming that none of them is insurmountable.

APPENDICES

FROM PRINCELY HOBBY-HORSES TO FREE WORLD PROSPERITY: AN ILLUSTRATED JOURNEY

(1) Princely hobby-horses

The Plaster Cast Room of the Victoria and Albert Museum in London showing the fruits of the Prince's pact to exchange copies of works of art.

(2) designed by the new experts in government

Serge Witte profiled in the American edition of W. T. Stead's *Review of Reviews*: "His daring and decisive action in the struggle of tariffs, which led to such a burnishing of bayonets in Berlin, and brought the international centre of gravity to the Russian Ministry of Finance, is, however, only the last of a long series of surprises in the career of this remarkable man, which raised him, in less than twenty years, from a subordinate post in a provincial railway to the most responsible position in the vast Russian Empire, after the Czar's." The hagiography of the designers of a new world had begun.

(3) used information

Clerks at the International Institute of Agriculture work with the most advanced communication and information-processing equipment available in 1910 to compile market data and (in theory) to relay it back to the world's farmers so rapidly that they could counter the market power of the grain trusts.

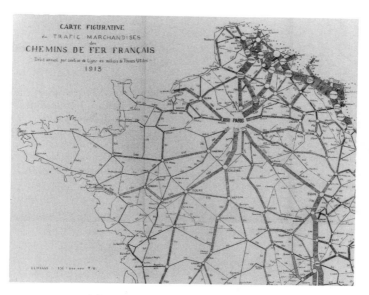

(4) to create a European market

The fat lines crossing the northern and eastern borders on a map of the value of goods shipped by rail across France in 1913 reveal that even this, the most protectionist of Europe's industrial powers, was, on the eve of the First World War, part of a continental economy.

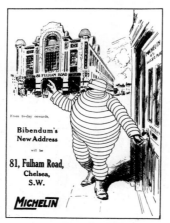

(5) in which the industries of the Second Industrial Revolution could grow.

In the same season that Ford would open the first automobile assembly line, Michelin's trademark character invites London's elite to the firm's palatial new tire showroom and service garage, emphasizing the cosmopolitanism of firms in the new mass production industries.

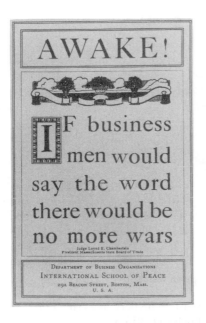

(6) Not liberal fundamentalists, but

The views of Boston publisher Edward Ginn, an important benefactor of interwar experiments in global organization, boldly stated on the cover of an early World Peace Foundation pamphlet.

(7) more direct descendants of the Public System Builders

John Maynard Keynes and Harry Dexter White, architects of the Bretton Woods system.

(8) expanded the agenda of the world organizations,

The image of international development assistance: clearly in the
foreground, but excluded from the conversation, Cape Verdean
peasants watch as an FAO economist, a French entrepreneur, a
planner from the capital, and the leader of the region's cooperative
movement discuss a scheme for labor-intensive farming of
drought-resistance oilseeds to be used in local production of soap
for the French market.

The DC-8 makes history...and <u>remakes</u> geography !

On the wings of the Douglas DC-8, world's most advanced jetliner, will come a new concept of geography almost as startling as the first knowledge that the earth was round.

With its scorn for the boundaries of hours and distance, the DC-8 will make the people of all other nations practically your next-door neighbors.

This new-found opportunity to meet people of other ways and other environments will enrich your life manyfold. It will allow you and your family to broaden your human experiences; to unfold cultures other than your own; to conduct your business affairs easily face-to-face anywhere in the world.

But the DC-8 offers you more than the wider horizons of time and space. It brings you a family history of experience, dependability and comfort unmatched in the annals of flight. It is this *and more* which makes passengers and pilots look up to Douglas. You'll sense it all when you take your first fabulous flight in the ...

DOUGLAS DC-8 JETLINER
Built by the most respected name in aviation

These famous air lines already have purchased the DC-8.

ALITALIA-Linee Aeree Italiane • DELTA AIR LINES • EASTERN AIR LINES • JAPAN AIR LINES • KLM ROYAL DUTCH AIR LINES • NATIONAL AIRLINES • NORTHWEST ORIENT AIRLINES • OLYMPIC AIRWAYS • PANAGRA • PANAIR DO BRASIL • PAN AMERICAN WORLD AIRWAYS • SAS—SCANDINAVIAN AIRLINES SYSTEM • SWISSAIR TRANS-CANADA AIR LINES • TRANS CARIBBEAN AIRWAYS • TRANSPORTS AERIENS INTERCONTINENTAUX • UNION AEROMARITIME DE TRANSPORT • UNITED AIR LINES

(9) ushered in the jet age, and

In 1958 readers of *Life* magazine learn what to expect now that the
first large transcontinental civilian jets have gone into production.

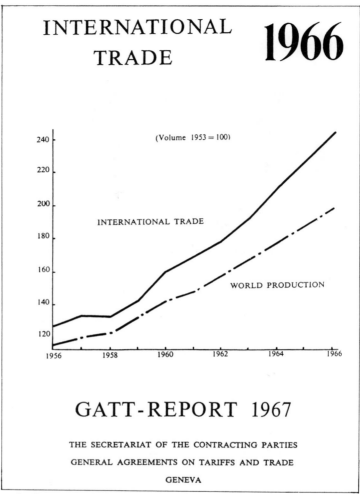

INTERNATIONAL TRADE **1966**

(Volume 1953 = 100)

240

220

200

INTERNATIONAL TRADE

180

160

WORLD PRODUCTION

140

120

1956   1958   1960   1962   1964   1966

GATT-REPORT 1967

THE SECRETARIAT OF THE CONTRACTING PARTIES

GENERAL AGREEMENTS ON TARIFFS AND TRADE

GENEVA

(10) promised to fulfill the liberal internationalist vision.

GATT uses a single image to explain its justification at the height of the Free World Order.

DATA ON THE CIVIL ACTIVITIES OF WORLD ORGANIZATIONS

In the early twentieth century economists and political scientists wrote comprehensive empirical studies of contemporary world organizations. Reinsch's (1911) study of the Public International Unions and Leonard Woolf's (1916) Fabian Society report were typical of the genre. But in the 1930s Salvador de Madariaga – diplomat, historian, and senior officer of the League of Nations – argued that the world order crisis demanded a different kind of analysis. His *The World's Design* (1938) anticipated the new genre that has come to dominate the field. While utopian accounts of ideal world governments continued to be written, comprehensive studies of global governance, of world government "as it is" have become rare. They have been replaced by studies of the global power structure, textbooks that summarize original research, and detailed case studies of specific international institutions (cf. Alger 1970; Dixon 1977; McCormick 1980, 1982).

In recent years the closest approximation to the studies undertaken by Reinsch and Woolf have been compilations of comparable case studies of a number of major world organizations – Cox and Jacobson's (1974) collection on patterns of influence within key agencies at the height of the UN era, a recent set of volumes edited by Groom and Taylor (1990; Taylor and Groom 1988, 1989), and the work carried out over many years by Mark Zacher and his colleagues (Finlayson and Zacher 1981, 1988; Sutton and Zacher 1987; Zacher 1979). My goal was to revive something of that earlier genre by building on the comparable case studies of the 1970s and 1980s.

Herbert Simon (1981) argues that the most fundamental thing we must remember in investigating the origin and impact of institutions is that they are "artificial." They are human creations. To explain any human artifact – from a cathedral to a computer algorithm – we must begin by trying to understand its design.[1]

Unlike architecture students trying to understand a modern building, students of modern social institutions cannot expect there to have been a single set of builders' blueprints. Social institutions are often built following many plans at once, and their occupants almost always "improve" them in diverse ways. Students of social institutions must be more like Henry Adams approaching the cathedral at Chartres. In 1913 Adams looked at the cathedral's mismatched towers and abrupt changes of scale and recognized the work of hundreds of builders following many different plans (Adams 1959). To explain the resulting unity that he, and so many others, also saw, Adams searched for the logic of the building's design, which could be thought of as the reasons it had been preserved by people throughout the centuries. He believed he found it in a "spirit of the age" that moved the church's many designers to build a glorious house for the Virgin, as they would say, "in the way she wanted."

While some liberal apologists may disagree, it would be hard to argue that the design of global governance has ever been as sublime. Nonetheless, the task of explaining it is the same as the one that Adams gave himself at Chartres: we need to look for the unities in the overall design of all the mismatched agencies, with their different mandates, procedures, and histories.

Adams was satisfied that the perspective he had gained through his long struggle to understand modernity gave him a way to see the overall design of Chartres. He offered descriptions of his own insights and a few photographs as sufficient evidence for his conclusions. A generation later art historians would attack the cathedrals with T-squares and compasses, rulers and sextants, arguing that only systematic measurement could verify grand hypotheses such as his (Simson 1962: 13–20).

The method I chose for my study resembled that of this later generation of medievalists. By systematically collecting and categorizing much of the information about the regular, ongoing activities of world organizations to be found in the many studies of particular global agencies, I would be in a position to provide an even stronger case for generalizations about world organizations than they could provide individually.

Others had systematically gathered and categorized information on the military activities of the global agencies (Bloomfield and Leiss 1969; Coplin and Rochester 1972; Butterworth 1978; Alker and Sherman 1980). I concentrated on their nonmilitary, "civil" activities.[2] I began by making a comprehensive list of "potentially universal" intergovernmental agencies – that is, intergovernmental organizations that any state could join – by merging standard lists (Jacobson 1984; Manley 1978; Wallace and Singer 1970) with the Union of International Associations (UIA) list of global and intercontinental intergovernmental organizations. I also included separate references to those world organizations that the UIA considers subsidiary agencies or agencies of a special kind (category E and F agencies) when these agencies were frequently referred to in citations under the universal and intercontinental (A, B, and C) categories. My final list included over 180 agencies.

To locate sources of information covering the entire history of each, I consulted standard bibliographies (Atherton 1976; Baer 1981; Dimitrov 1981; M. Haas 1971; Hüfner and Namann 1971–5; Speeckaert 1965) as well as the subject catalogs of the New York Public Library, which may be unique in having had a policy of collecting works on international institutions since the 1870s. I tried to identify a wide variety of sources for each organization, always including at least one comprehensive source that was as close to an "official history" of the organization as possible, for example, from descriptions of activities written by officials in response to questionnaires.

Following procedures similar to those used by scholars who have created systematic lists of foreign policy events,[3] I read each of the more than 100 sources I had identified. I recorded what each reported as ongoing activities of the over 180 world organizations, excluding only the military actions of the United Nations. Each record was a sentence in which one of the agencies or its subdivisions was the subject and the action was directed outside the agency itself. After completing the coding, I "cleaned" the data set, removing duplicate records, approximately 4,500 records.

I checked the reliability of the data by recoding (making a second record of) a random sample of pages from the source material after the passage of six months and by having a second coder, a student assistant, code the same material. In both cases more than 90 percent of the activities recorded the first time were recorded the second time and no additional activities were recorded.

To check for bias that might be introduced by relying on too few sources I examined the "marginal utility of the last source," the percentage of the total information on the organization added by the source of the smallest number of records on that organization, for the 65 organizations with more than ten records (ten regular activities).

In four cases (the Central Office of International Railway Transport, the International Copyright Union, UNICEF, and UNESCO) the "last source" added more than 10 percent of the records. Thus, if the data set under-represents the activity of any agencies due to inadequate source coverage, these are the organizations whose activities are the most likely to be under-represented.

I then read through the data set to check for what might appear to be logical inconsistencies, cases where one source reports an agency doing one thing and another source reports the same agency engaging in exactly opposite, or at least contradictory, activities and found a small number of contradictions, fewer than 5 percent of the cases, in activities involved with aiding LDCs, but not in other fields.

With these caveats, the resulting data set can be considered a record of all the civil activities of world organizations as reported in recognized published sources, with a bias toward the "official" record. While it would be possible to get a more complete picture of world government as it is by exhaustively consulting archives and by interviewing people who have worked with and within intergovernmental agencies, this data set puts the information that typically can be found in the main collection of a major reference library into a systematic and comparable form.

To be a bit more technical: the cases in the data set are *regular activities* carried out by the same world organization for a period of at least one half-decade (five years). The case records in the data set cover activities from the 1861–5 period to the 1986–90 period. Each record identifies the *agency* (using the letter and number assigned by the UIA yearbooks), the period in which that agency *began* the activity in question, the period in which it *ended* the activity (if it no longer carried it out in 1990), the *verb* the source used to describe the activity (expressed in English in the present tense), and the *object* of the activity, a summary of the rest of the original sentence describing the activity, covering both the receiver of the activity (if one is specified) and the direction of the action. Each record uses a number to identify the *source* and the *page* on which the original information appeared.

Each record includes information on three other clusters of variables: *issues affected* by the activity, the *ways the organization influenced members* relative to that activity, and the *ways members controled the organization* relative to that activity.

Three variables identify the issues affected by the activity. The first, the *political economy issue area* (PEI), uses broad categories, dividing activities according to whether they affected relations between: (1) firms or sectors; (2) workers and employers; (3) LDCs and industrialized countries; (4) states; (5) states and societies; and (6) humanity and the environment.

To supplement and provide alternatives to this scheme my research assistant and I also classified activities by *economic sector* using the four-digit categories of the United Nation's International System of Standard Industrial Categories (UN Statistical Office 1968) and by *governmental sector* using the UN's System of Categories of the Activities of Government (SCFG) (UN Statistical Office 1980). The "areas of responsibility" reported in the text come from aggregations across these schemes. Thus, for example, "public order and administration" includes all cases where PEI = 5 and SCFG = 1.4 (general) and 3.0 (public order and safety).

Eight variables in the original data set identify ways that organizations have influenced members. Following Anthony Giddens (1981: 57), I argued that, at least in the abstract, the most basic characteristics of any social institution include the particular ways it sanctions social actors: providing inducements to act by enabling actors to do things they would not otherwise be able to do, and constraining them to act by imposing coercive sanctions. Ruth Collier and David Collier (1979) provided a model of how to develop a checklist of inducements and constraints relevant to a specific category of institutions (in their case, corporatist states).[4] I followed that model in making a checklist of four inducements and four constraints proposed by scholars as the basic characteristics of different world organizations. (For example, one might say that the ILO can enforce labor standards only because it requires member governments to report violations and allow those reports to be circulated to other governments and to labor and employers' groups throughout the world. Another might say that many members have remained part of the FAO only because of the agricultural information it gathers.) I then used the checklist to answer eight yes or no questions about each activity. Did the activity:

1 support powerful domestic interest groups allied to some member states? (*domestic inducement*);
2 support powerful foreign allies of some member states? (*foreign inducement*);
3 reduce the information costs associated with further international cooperation for member states? (*information cost inducement*);
4 reduce other transactions costs associated with further international cooperation for member states? (*transaction cost inducement*);

5 support powerful domestic interest groups opposing some member states? (*domestic constraint*)
6 support powerful foreign opponents of some member states? (*foreign constraint*);
7 monitor prior commitments made by member states? (*monitoring constraint*);
8 require that coercive sanctions be imposed against member states if they violated prior commitments? (*sanctions constraint*).

Conceivably, the studies I consulted for information about the regular activities of world organizations could have reported that every one displayed all eight of these ways that the organizations could influence member states, but, in fact, only one question, the first one, almost always required a "yes" answer. The data on "influence over members" reported in the text aggregates across these variables:

Supported allies	domestic or foreign inducement = 1, all other inducements and constraints = 0
Reduced cost of cooperation	information cost or transaction cost inducement = 1, all constraints = 0
Supported opponents	domestic or foreign constraint = 1, monitoring and sanctions constraints = 0
Monitored compliance	monitoring constraint = 1, sanctions constraint = 0
Imposed sanctions	sanctions constraint = 1

In the original data set a single categorical variable, *oversight*, identifies how member states control the world organization as it carries out the activity:

1 infrequent oversight under the control of a single member;
2 close oversight under the *unit veto* system;
3 close oversight under *weighted voting* reflecting the issue-specific power of members;
4 close oversight under *majority rule*;
5 infrequent oversight, but officials of the organization do not initiate new programs;
6 infrequent oversight, officials of the organization may initiate programs;
7 little or no oversight.

In the analysis the data categories 1, 5, 6, and 7 are collapsed into "little oversight."

The small differences between the original aggregations and those used in the analysis reflect how some of my own assumptions changed in the course of the study. I also needed to consider different ways to aggregate the data in order to verify it, that is, to check it against other data sets designed to provide a record of all the civil activities of world organizations with a similar bias. No other data set tries to do exactly the same thing. The UIA yearbooks, for example, provide semi-official information on current activities of existing IGOs, but no information on the activities of those that no longer exist.

Nevertheless, one significant part of the data set could be checked against a similar listing. I compared the distribution of activities across issues for the central UN agencies in my data set for the 1986–90 period with the UN's own distribution of "outputs" (separate programs both projected and actually completed) for the 1990–1 budget year (Menon 1992). The UN has recently begun to collect this information in order to compare how well different agencies perform the tasks they take on; thus actual outputs are compared to the projected outputs required by the legislation of members and by the original plans of program managers.

The report of UN outputs considered 27 categories. I disregarded two of these (Legal Activities and Public Information) because activities under these budget categories would be distributed across the functional categories used in my data set. I also included only 10 percent of the activities that the UN report charged to the regional

TABLE A Comparison of study data with UN data on outputs (number and percentage)

	UN:Projected outputs	UN: Actual outputs	Activities in data set
Development and social affairs	947 (*28*)	653 (*28*)	413 (*38*)
Human rights, refugees and relief	660 (*19*)	546 (*23*)	218 (*20*)
UNCTAD and international trade centre	634 (*19*)	332 (*14*)	144 (*13*)
Political affairs and disarmament	486 (*14*)	318 (*14*)	113 (*10*)
Science, technology and transnational corporations	236 (*7*)	163 (*7*)	100 (*9*)
Narcotics	197 (*6*)	115 (*5*)	27 (*2*)
Habitat	135 (*4*)	113 (*5*)	35 (*3*)
Ocean affairs	78 (*2*)	66 (*3*)	21 (*2*)
UNEP	51 (*1*)	43 (*2*)	27 (*2*)
Totals	3424	2349	1097

economic commissions, based on an estimate of the small part of their activities serving all UN members from a more detailed study of the activities of the Economic Commission for Latin America in the 1971–5 period. In order to find comparable categories within my data set I had to further collapse the remaining categories in the UN report to nine.

The largest differences between the data set and the UN's report of actual outputs are in Development and Social Affairs (where the data set includes a relatively larger number of cases) and Political Affairs and Disarmament (where the data set includes relatively fewer cases). The latter is an expected artifact of the decision not to include military operations in the data set. The former may be the result of including too few of the activities of the regional economic commissions in the comparison. Taken as a whole, this comparison provides strong confirmation that the data set accurately represents recent UN activities. The data included above make up only a small part (one-quarter) of all the cases in the data set. Because the same methods have been used to generate the data on the other cases – historical cases as well as the activities of non-UN world organizations – the data set as a whole should provide a similarly accurate calculation of all the activities of the world organizations back to their beginning.

NOTES

Introduction

1 "General introduction," in Galtung (1980: xxi), originally written in 1974. In the 1980 postscript Mendlovitz says that his prediction may have been premature.

2 This social order united the Austro-Hungarian, Belgian, British, Danish, Dutch, French, German, Italian, Portuguese, Russian, Spanish, Swedish empires (and extended beyond them) throughout the generation before the First World War.

3 There is some deliberate irony in identifying the social order formed among the OECD countries and their dependencies as the "Free" World. This is what US policymakers always called it, but officials in other parts of this postwar social order used the designation somewhat less frequently, especially after its origin in Franklin D. Roosevelt's "Four Freedoms" speech had been forgotten. See p. 172 below.

Chapter 1 The Promise of Liberal Internationalism

1 Nelson and Winter (1982: 14–21) provide a concise introduction to evolutionary explanations in the social sciences. Veblen's much older discussion of 1898 is richer but much less precise (Veblen 1969).

2 Keohane calls this a "functional" explanation. Differing uses of this term are bound to be confusing to anyone coming to the literature on international institutions for the first time. Originally, analysts who called themselves "functionalists" were people like Mitrany who used the term to identify themselves with their core hypothesis that international institutions will be more successful, and more likely to contribute to peace and prosperity, if they are designed to serve limited functions necessary for the expansion of world commerce. The alternative view, called "federalist" in the interwar period, was that general authority had to be transferred to a higher level and international law enforced before any of the goals of the liberal internationalists could be

achieved. The functionalist view of that time was based on a critical evaluation of the Public International Unions and the regional IGOs established before the First World War. The "federalists" worked more from an axiomatic legal theory and from a rather narrow reading of the experience of the United States. The predictions of this "functionalism" have tended to be confirmed by later experience, especially when contrasted to the predictions of the world federalists. Jacobson, Reisinger and Mathers (1986) provide the most recent systematic confirmation of a number of functionalist hypotheses. When Keohane writes of "functional *explanations*" of international institutions he does not mean to identify himself with this older tradition. Keohane uses "functional" to denote explanations of social institutions in terms of the purposes they serve for a group of sufficiently powerful actors who are rational and self-interested. While Keohane's functional explanation may account for the existence of international institutions, it does not directly address the questions about the potential sources of lasting global peace and prosperity which are the core concerns of the older functionalist tradition.

3   The Gramscian distinction between intellectual and political leadership, and the two types of political leadership (acting as a sponsor of international discussions and acting as a benefactor of experimental activities) that I argue are needed to create international institutions, parallel the three types of leadership distinguished by Young (1991), whose focus is on the process of international bargaining.

4   The liberals' success has meant, as Cox has argued (1987: 7), that the continuous growth of international civil society has come to represent the kind of "internationalisation of the state" that Gramsci anticipated. Stephen Gill makes the same point by saying that the "internationalisation of civil society" has been part of the "transnationalisation of the state" (1990: 1). Global governance has grown. The state-like institutions that function as political regulators of the world economy have become increasingly international. Some of these institutions exist as cooperative agreements among, or international extensions of, domestic agencies. Others still perform regulatory functions even though they are juridically "private" nongovernmental transnational associations. Other traditions have recognized the same developments in slightly different ways. John Boli, sociologist of the world system, identifies the period since the middle of the nineteenth century as one of "intensification" of "the world polity" that "constitutes" national states (1987; 1990: 17), thus identifying a realm of international social institutions influencing stable patterns of interstate relations. In the early 1970s Samuel P. Huntington (1973: 368) and other neoliberals began writing about transnational organizations (the private voluntary international agencies) as the "revolutionary organizations" in world politics that operate alongside the less revolutionary IGOs. A group of British scholars has long identified the same period as one in which a "world society" of private transnational associations, such as the International Chamber of Commerce, have articulated transnational interests and aspirations and influenced the transformation of the global social order through their impact on states and IGOs (J. Burton et al. 1974).

5 Gramsci would add that these are purely abstract and only a reliable guide to political analysis when a specific political situation has allowed people to see and act on their interests (or, for that matter, their collective aspirations). See Augelli and Murphy (1988: 19–25); cf. Golding (1992: 103).

6 Golding (1992: 68–87) calls the same motivational notion Gramsci's "concept of the will." She perceptively notes its centrality in his political thought, as well as the tendency of scholars to understate its significance.

7 The article which first proposed analyzing social structures of accumulation (Gordon 1980) is a major exception.

8 Inattentive readers of Cox's early articles may miss one important part of Gramsci's political sociology. They might be read as implying that all concrete social orders rest on hegemony and that the task of a social class trying to form a social order is equivalent to the task of securing its hegemony. Actually, Gramsci used a broader concept, *supremacy*, to define the position of the leading class within a historical bloc. Gramsci argued that supremacy could be secured primarily by hegemony (including a type of "unethical" hegemony based on fraud), but it could also be secured primarily through force, by the domination of the leading group over all others. (Writing from a fascist prison in the late 1920s and early 1930s, Gramsci was acutely aware of social orders in which supremacy was secured more by domination than by hegemony.) In any event, in every real social order both hegemony and domination appear. The political task of the group seeking supremacy is to secure hegemony over allied social forces and domination over adversaries. See Augelli and Murphy (1988: 117–37).

Chapter 2   Building the Public International Unions

1 Stead writes only of "four" Unions in Berne because he treats the Patent Union and the Copyright Union as one. Stead traveled constantly and paid special attention to the changes wrought by industry in Europe and America, and to the prospects for world peace through the development of worldwide civic culture as well as through formal international institutions. Recent historians have mined many of Stead's first-person accounts of the economic, political, and social transformations at the end of the last century. See, e.g., William Cronon's (1991: 344–67) use of Stead's reports from America and Robert K. Massie's (1991: 627) reliance on Stead's account of the public reaction to the Boer War.

2 See Mayer's (1981) analysis of the prewar European social order, whose title provided the first part of this sections heading.

3 In the United States, with its rigid two-party system, the process involved conflicts between the "old guard" and "progressives" inside both parties (Skowronek 1982).

4 Traditional diplomatic protocol, which has always reflected the inequalities among aristocrats (let alone between them and the rest of the population) as much as the equality of states, remained. For example, even though

Theodore Roosevelt initiated the call for the Hague Conference of 1907, he yielded the responsibility of summoning the conference to the Tsar, who had called the first Hague Conference in 1899 (Choate 1913: 50–1).

5 The French Count Albert de Mun, a Catholic social reformer, had earlier been another potential sponsor, but, unlike the Kaiser, one without the capacity to assure that all governments would attend a conference (Follows 1951: 70–1, 133).

6 See Edwards (1976: 142–4) and Yates (1989: 19). Yates emphasizes that in large firms committee meetings play both a control function, gaining the uncoerced cooperation of subordinates who are being treated (temporarily) as equals, as well as this function of encouraging innovation. Interestingly, the committee system was one of the very last tools of modern corporate management to be developed. It was an invention of the early twentieth century, appearing long after the conference system, and only then after the stultifying effects of pure hierarchical control had been felt in many firms. The conference system was able to develop earlier simply because national governments had long accepted the contradictory notions of sovereign equality and the hierarchy of states.

7 The story of the penny post is related in many places. One of the most interesting for students of international institutions is an article by John Fairfield Sly (1907), who spells out the intellectual and personal links among leading postal officials in Britain, the United States, Germany, and France in the years leading up to the formation of the Universal Postal Union.

8 Foucault 1979: 218–21. In using Foucault's account we should bear in mind a few of its limitations. His use of Jeremy Bentham's Panopticon prison as the model for all public systems suggests that the development of modern government is the rational working-out of utilitarian ideology. This view had influenced historians of the nineteenth-century revolution in government until MacDonagh's generation demonstrated that many of the original "disciplinary experts" central to that development were not self-conscious utilitarians following "academic" models, but often just problem-solving administrators whose personal paths typically went from using skills as applied natural scientists in government, to becoming professionals involved in "statistics," to thinking up new public systems (MacLeod 1988: 6–12). The Panopticon exemplar also overemphasizes the role of coercion. Ultimately, the Panopticon works due to the constant, but rarely visible or exercised, threat of violence by prison guards. Most of the "systems" under formal international institutions are held together by the promise of rewards more than by the threat of punishment.

9 Similarly, Gramsci wrote, "*laissez faire* too is a form of state 'regulation,' introduced and maintained by legislation and coercive means" (1971: 160).

10 Throughout chapters 2, 3, and 4 the abbreviation of ILO is used for the prewar International Labor Office which was absorbed into the more comprehensive International Labor Organization when it was founded at the end of the war. In subsequent chapters the abbreviation is used for the successor organization.

Chapter 3   The Unions' Work and How It Was Done

1 It was revived briefly under UNESCO's interwar predecessor, the International Institute of Intellectual Cooperation (Greaves 1931: 126), when France was its benefactor.
2 Extrapolated from figures Stead (1899: 30–7) gives for all the Unions in 1898, and from figures Reinsch (1911: 18, 26) gives for two of the Unions in 1910.
3 Strange (1988: 96–101) provides a concise account of the late nineteenth-century financial system's active management. She is especially clear and accurate in recounting Karl Polanyi's reasons in 1944 for focusing on the gold standard (Polanyi 1957) and the limited argument that Charles P. Kindleberger (1973) originally made about the need for American economic leadership after the First World War.
4 In addition, as we will see in chapter 4, the economic logic that Hobson uncovered probably continued to affect the calculations of *British* investors even at the peak of the Second Industrial Revolution.
5 The categories for these examples are taken from Cialdini (1984), a well-documented account of research on the social psychology of influence written for the nonspecialist.

Chapter 4   The Second Industrial Revolution and the Great War

1 Kochan notes, however, that Germany had less experience with mass production of consumer goods (1980: 104–6). Germany's competitive strength lay in specialized machinery and other products purchased by other industrial firms. Unlike the United States, Germany had few giant firms involved in food processing or the other branded products for home consumption. However, if one treats the industrial economies at the center of turn-of-the-century Europe as a single unit, adding Swiss, Dutch, and Belgian firms to those of Germany, the whole unit resembles the United States even more than Chandler suggests.
2 While no consensus can ever be expected about the causes of a single event or a particular war, it should be possible to come to some agreement about both the ultimate and proximate causes of the whole class of great-power wars of which the First World War was just one. This has been the aim of more than 50 years of systematic studies by peace researchers, political scientists, and sociologists – studies that received some of their original impetus from the interwar International Institute of Intellectual Cooperation's program of "scientific" investigations of "the political economy of war and peace" (Pham Thi Tu 1964: 168). The results of this effort may not appear impressive; no scholarly consensus about the causes of great-power war seems to exist. Holsti (1991: 3–5) suggests why by succinctly cataloging the limitations of the majority

of studies: they search only for ultimate causes and they reach contradictory conclusions because most consider only one possible cause at one level of generalization out of the infinite number of possible ultimate causes that could appear at many levels. Yet if we look just at those studies that consider many variables and try, as Holsti does, to pay much more attention to the proximate sources of conflict, the convergence among different explanations appears much greater. Väyrynen's conclusions exemplify that convergence.

3   "Mythical" both in the sense of deriving from a romanticized history and in the sense that Gramsci took the term from Georges Sorel: the Norwegians, Irish, Finns, and other turn-of-the-century nationalists needed only one thing to make the "myth" of their nation real. They needed the collective action of the people identified as one by the myth, collective action that was only possible if all the people believed the myth.

4   It was not, however, primarily the consequence of government policy, which is what Albert O. Hirschman argues in his classic study of Nazi trade policy, *National Power and the Structure of Foreign Trade* (1945, see Hirschman 1980). Written at the height of the Second World War, the book may suffer from the wartime tendency to see only continuity from the Second to the Third Reich. Hirschman disagrees with a fairly sensible statement Hobson made in 1916:

> The widespread employment of German clerks in foreign commercial houses has undoubtedly given German firms a fuller knowledge of their foreign competitors than commercial firms in England possess. But all these arts and practices are nothing else than an intelligent seizure of legitimate business opportunities . . . . The notion that all this expanding trade and finance has been the cat's-paw of the aggressive German state is baseless.

This is not to say that the prewar German trade advance had no strategic consequences. Nor is it to deny that the ideology promulgated in Germany at the turn of the century saw industrial supremacy and trade dominance as admirable signs of a people's mastery. It is simply to note that Nazi policy, the focus of Hirschman's work, differed. Nazi policy was initiated by the state and sponsored by the state with the conscious aim of creating strategically valuable trade dependencies. The state may have supported, but it did not initiate, prewar trade penetration.

Chapter 5   Liberal Learning and the Free World Order

1   Hunt (1987: 46–91) and Adas (1989: 271–342) provide excellent introductions to the American and European attitudes respectively.

2   Coyne to du Pont, March 1, 1921. I am grateful to JoAnne Yates for discovering this letter in the papers of Pierre S. du Pont, and to the Archives of Hagley Museum and Library in Wilmington, Delaware, where they are housed.

3 Gramsci's scholarly work in prison was sustained by indirect correspondence with his friend, the economist Piero Sraffa, Keynes's colleague at Cambridge. Gramsci was also able to order books from a Milan bookstore where Sraffa set up an account (Forgacs 1988: 22–3).

4 The pamphlet has been attributed to Michael Foot, who was to be leader of the Labour Party in the 1980s. It is cataloged under his name in major research libraries and he had used the same pseudonym on an earlier pamphlet attacking fascism. When I interviewed him in 1990 at a Wellesley College symposium honoring C. L. R. James, Foot denied authorship and speculated that the tract was the work of a junior Tory colleague who would have risked the ire of Winston Churchill for expressing such views. Foot noted that, in 1947, in contrast to the Tories, Labour backbenchers were still engaged in a lively public debate about whether it was wise for Britain to become the junior partner in a global condominium with the US, thus, he would have been at no risk if he had signed his name to the pamphlet, with which, by the way, he had agreed at the time.

5 This Darwinian language could also be read as straightforward social science jargon. Veblen, like Gramsci, was greatly influenced by the Italian Darwinian Marxist, Antonio Labriola. Dorothy Ross concludes, "Veblen was the American Gramsci, drawn by the problem of false consciousness and training in idealist philosophy into a revision of Marx's theory of history" (1990: 207). Both Gramsci and Veblen took from Labriola their understanding that material conditions affect human institutions only through habits of thought and action; thus transformation of society requires educative actions to root out "atavistic habits of thought" (Veblen's terms) or "the contradictory consciousness reflected in 'common sense' " (Gramsci's terms).

6 Interpol provides the exception that proves the rule. In the one world organization whose primary purpose it is to increase the coercive powers of its state members, a few legacies of cooperation with fascism were surprisingly long-lived. The organization's first headquarters was in Vienna. It was moved to Berlin and became an adjunct of Hitler's state after the Nazis annexed Austria in 1938. It was only in 1985, under the pressure of a new secretary general who moved to Interpol from Scotland Yard, that the organization began to distribute wanted notices for Nazi war criminals (Riding 1990).

7 By 1925 the academic progeny of the nineteenth-century public system builders even had their own professional organization, the Centre for Research on Collective Economy, with a journal, *The Annals of Collective Economy*, published in three languages and providing a place to debate questions such as whether there were any "natural monopolies" and, if there were, whether they should be regulated or owned by the state.

8 Plischke notes a sharp upturn in US involvement in IGOs directly after the Second World War; the US became newly affiliated with "two dozen multipartite organizations; roughly half were League related and possessed global stature" (1991: 58).

Chapter 6   The Work of the League and the UN System

1   This is using McKeown's "volume" measure of trade openness (1991: 156).
    Using his "value" measure the trading system did not again become as open
    as it had been 1905–14 until the early 1970s.

2   Nau challenges the widely accepted interpretation of White's position
    presented by Block (1977: 46–50), which underlies Ruggie's (1982) and
    Maier's (1977) interpretation of the postwar order. Nau argues that White was
    not a Keynesian and "not a New Dealer" (p. 84). Helleiner's (1992) recent
    reinterpretation of the primary sources demonstrates that this conclusion goes
    much too far. But Nau is correct in arguing that neither White nor Keynes
    anticipated the explosive growth of the welfare state seen in the 1960s, and
    neither would have endorsed continual government deficits. They were trying
    to create an international order in which national countercyclical policies
    could operate; they did not conceive of the IMF as being able to ensure full
    employment, nor did they necessarily agree on the centrality of that goal for
    international economic cooperation. But, as Helleiner demonstrates and Nau
    ignores, the larger social context in which the ideas of Keynes and White
    became significant was the emerging social pact between business and labor
    within which the idea of full employment was central.

3   A slightly different version of some of the arguments in this section appears in
    Murphy and Augelli (1993).

4   Payer's (1982) critique of the World Bank does a good job of documenting this
    role, which has typified its activity since the late 1950s; it is a role that has not
    necessarily changed with the Bank's increased concern with environmentally
    sustainable development in the 1990s.

5   Ghana, India, Kenya, Morocco, Nigeria, Pakistan, Sri Lanka, Sudan, Tanza-
    nia, and Uganda. The other major aid recipients of the 1960s included Greece
    and Turkey (whose aid was coordinated by the OECD) and the US clients,
    Israel, South Korea, and South Vietnam, for whom no IGO played this role.

6   Wood's account of the alternatives to the postwar aid regime considered by
    the United States emphasizes the role of protecting the privileges of American
    farmers and workers (1986: 21–9). He notes that despite American liberal
    rhetoric, the idea of opening all US markets to Third World goods was never
    really considered. But, then, neither were four other "pure" strategies for
    coping with world order problems generated by the Third World's underde-
    velopment: (1) reliance solely on a multilateral aid; (2) reliance solely on
    military containment of the Soviet Union and Third World anti-systemic
    movements; (3) reliance solely on market-induced adjustments in the Third
    World; and (4) acceptance of Third World nationalist revolutions.

7   Cape Verde's president then served as the coordinator of the 22 "most serious-
    ly affected" African nations in their dealings with donors and many of the
    agencies had their regional headquarters in Senegal's capital.

8   In the case of 63, or seven per cent, of the activities of the IGOs in 1939
    the power to initiate sanctions for non-compliance served as a constraint on

state members. None of the Public International Unions had this power in 1914.

9 Of course, what may be considered realistic in one context may appear irrational in others. The International Commission for Aerial Navigation (ICAN) began under a system of qualified majorities or weighted voting reflecting the uneven international distribution of aircraft. But ICAN's system quickly became unworkable because it was perceived as "undemocratic" by members who controlled key airspace and key landing rights. ICAN's regime rested on all states accepting a very strong version of national sovereignty, complete control over airspace, which implied ICAN members were equally powerful. In 1929 ICAN adopted a one state, one vote system in order to solve this problem (Colegrove 1930: 67–8).

Chapter 7   Prosperity and Disappointment

1 British proto-computer scientists concentrated on cracking the codes Germans used in launching rocket attacks. The American program focused on accurately calculating ballistic trajectories when both guns and targets were moving. See Saxby (1990: 94–103) on the early computers.

2 No systematic study has been made of the impact of the massive presence of American military families in the generalization of mass consumption throughout the Free World, but Enloe's description of one single base is typical:

> The expansion of the base in the 1950s had brought subtle but fundamental changes in the townspeople's lives . . . More American soldiers arrived, bringing with them more wives and children. And with the families came American style consumption: "air-transports began to fly into Effingham laden with deep-freezers, washing machines, pressure- and microwave cookers, hi-fi equipment, Hoovers, electric organs and even Persian carpets." Some of the appliances made their way on to the now flourishing local second-hand market . . . ideological overspill from the American model of family life. (1990: 77)

3 Hamilton provides a lively, but thoughtful and specific account of the new Third World industries created by telematics revolution (1990: 25–74). Enloe offers a similar account of Third World clothing production and similar export-oriented industrialization (1990: 151–76).

4 Nau (1990), for example, sees changes in the unity of American "purpose" as one of the major reasons for fluctuations in the prosperity of the Free World Order. His argument combines a somewhat fundamentalist version of liberal internationalism (with its strong preference for laissez faire) with the American exceptionalism that tends to animate advocates of the theory of "hegemonic stability," and with the philosophically idealist "learning" theories of Ernst Haas. The result is a unique, sophisticated, and quite dialectical theory that is a good deal more satisfying than any of its constituent parts, even than Haas's thought-provoking analysis.

5 To those of us schooled in the great-power politics of the industrialized nations, these forms of international support may seem minor and marginal to power politics, but successful nationalist leaders of the postwar era almost all argue that they were critical; decolonization would not have taken place without them. Julius Nyerere's assessment in his introduction to Mason Sears's autobiographical *The Years of High Purpose* (1980) is typical.

6 Kidron (1965) demonstrates that the success of Pandit Nehru's economic nationalism depended on a strong local industrial sector that existed before independence. In 1956, World Bank President Eugene Black made its first real development loans conditional on India giving "private enterprise, both Indian and foreign, every encouragement" (Roy 1967: 96). This helped create an alliance between local industrialists and the government, and at the same time helped avoid an alliance between Indian capitalists and British businesses that would have helped maintain colonial economic relations. Nehru, who was no fan of private enterprise, especially foreign, but who wanted the World Bank's support, proposed policies that would favor local industrialists as a compromise, a compromise the Bank was willing to accept. On the political sociology of decolonization within Britain and France see Kahler (1984), and within the Netherlands, Fennema (1990).

7 Murphy (1988) explores some of the difficulties of defeating identity movements in the context of what UN security activities have done and can do to manage fundamental conflicts.

Chapter 8   Toward the Next World Order

1 Alain Noël (1993) would probably find even this open-ended formula much too mechanical. In his excellent critique of various regulation theories he says that the historical record teaches us that:

> regulation is more akin to the snowforts children build in winter. The participants erect a wall, add a motif – inspired by the neighbor's snowfort – open a loophole, break a side-wall in an unexpected battle, in short, they continuously build and renovate, without ever stopping, until the whole project is finally destroyed by a war, a celebration, or a heavy rainfall. An ongoing project, the snowfort is never finished until it is lost or abandoned. What matters for the participants is less the outcome than the process, less the snowfort itself that the always fragile agreement of all around a common vision, which organizes the games for a period.

I find Noël's image compelling, but more can be said about what happens as the game ends. When the visions that organized the Interimperial Order and the Free World Order stopped being held in common, similar conflicts (*clashes*) came to the fore. In both cases the response of both a significant group of cosmopolitan capitalists and the governments of leading states was to abandon the hegemonic project of liberal internationalism and to seek what Gramsci would call "domination" in the eras of "grabbing" and "hoarding." In both cases these periods (roughly, the 1920s and the 1980s) appeared at times when some of the earlier clashes had ended and a modified version of the older world order was restored. It was as if first some of the largest and most powerful children in the snowfort had worked with close friends to throw out of the game children who wanted to play by different rules (Imperial Germany and the OPEC-led Third World alliance); then the big kids themselves modified the rules in order to lord over the weaker children they had temporarily befriended.

2 Lynton Caldwell makes the point well:

> In sum, until very recently planetary issues were largely confined to those few global phenomena that were of concern to international commerce and to the health of humans and their domesticated animals and plants. Except for health, economic considerations were the prime movers of international and transnational world-wide cooperation. The planetization of economic affairs continues and expands, but it is now being overtaken by an awareness of ecological problems of planetary dimensions, which extend beyond health and economy to considerations of natural resources, quality of life, of ethics, aesthetics, and prospects for the survival of the human species and the biosphere. (1990: 131)

I would add that even "health" began as an issue of "international commerce" and that today's environmental issues, like all the other issues of global governance that have gone before, stem from the triumph of industrialism.

Appendix: Data on the Civil Activities of World Organizations

1 Madariaga called his book *The World's Design* and he is not the only student of international organization to rely on the design metaphor. See Kihl (1971) and see Alker's (1977) development of Simon's ideas.

2 One reason for omitting the UN's military operations from the data set is that these have usually been costly activities involving many personnel, something that is not true of most of the other regular activities of world organizations. In other cases the number of regular activities carried out by a world organization highly correlates with its staff size and with the size of its budget. The only major exceptions have been the two refugee organizations with operational roles, UNRRA during the Second World War and the UN Relief and Works Agency in Palestine.

3 On the strengths and limitations of such data see Azar and Ben Dak (1975), Goldstein and Freeman (1990: 37–41) and King (1989). A great deal of mysticism has surrounded the creation of data useful in studying international relations, much of it a consequence of the hyperbolic claims made for social "science" as against "traditional" prudential, historical ways to understand world politics. My own sense is that the virtues of systematic data-gathering

are no more (or less) than those of taking and keeping good notes: others may later use the information to help answer related questions or to critique the logic of the original inquiry, while, throughout the research, data-gatherers are constantly reminded of their original questions and of the new assumptions that they have made along the way.

4　I am grateful to Hayward R. Alker, Jr. for suggesting the Collier and Collier model.

REFERENCES

Abrahamsson, Bernard J. 1980: *International Ocean Shipping: Current Concepts and Principles*. Boulder, Colo.

Abrams, Irwin 1988: *The Nobel Peace Prize and the Laureates: An Illustrated Biographical History, 1901–1987*. Boston.

Abt, G. 1933: *Vingt-cinq ans d'activité de l'office internationale d'hygiène publique*. Paris.

Adams, Henry 1959: *Mont-Saint-Michel and Chartres* (1913). Garden City, N.Y.

Adas, Michael 1989: *Machines as the Measure of Men: Science, Technology, and Ideologies of Western Dominance*. Ithaca, N.Y.

Addams, Jane, Emily G. Balch and Alice Hamilton 1915: *Women at the Hague*. New York.

Adelman, Carol C.(ed.) 1988: *International Regulation: New Rules in a Changing World Order*. San Francisco.

Adler, Georg 1888: *Die Frage des internationalen Arbeitschnutzen*. Munich.

—— 1891: The Evolution of the Socialist Programme in Germany. *Economic Journal*, 1(4): 688–709.

Agresti, Olivia R. 1941: *David Lubin*, 2nd edn. Berkeley.

Alcock, Anthony 1971: *History of the International Labor Organization*. London.

Alger, Chadwick F. 1970: A Decade of Quantitative and Field Research on International Organization. *International Organization*, 24(3): 414–50.

Alker, Hayward R., Jr 1977: A Methodology for Design Research on Interdependence Alternatives *International Organization*, 31(1): 29–63.

Alker, Hayward R., Jr and Frank L. Sherman 1980: War-Avoidance through Collective Security-Seeking Practices since 1945. Paper presented to the International Political Science Association roundtable on recent scientific contributions to war avoidance, Academy of Romania, Bucharest.

Alleyne, Mark D. 1992: Liberalization in Nonregime Areas: The Twenty-Year Debate over Cultural Industries, from UNESCO's NWICO to the GATT's Uruguay Round. Paper presented at the annual meeting of the International Studies Association, Atlanta, April.

Alleyne, Mark D. and Shinjinee Sen 1992: Fact Sheet on International Trade in Cultural Products. International Communications Program,

Department of Comparative and Regional Studies, American University, Washington, D.C.

Anderson, Benedict 1983: *Imagined Communities: Reflections on the Origin and Spread of Nationalism*. London.

Ashley, Richard K. 1980: *The Political Economy of War and Peace: The Sino-Soviet-American Triangle and the Modern Security Problematique*. London.

Atherton, Axline L. 1976: *International Organization: A Guide to Information Sources*. Detroit.

Augelli, Enrico and Craig N. Murphy 1988: *America's Quest for Supremacy and the Third World: A Gramscian Analysis*. London.

—— 1993: Gramsci and International Relations: A General Perspective with Examples from Recent US Policy toward the Third World. In Stephen Gill (ed.), *Gramsci, Historical Materialism, and International Relations*, Cambridge.

Averitt, Robert 1968: *The Dual Economy: The Dynamics of American Industrial Structure*. New York.

Azar, Edward E. and Joseph Ben Dak (eds) 1975: *Theory and Practice of Events Research*. London.

Baer, George W. 1981: *International Organization, 1918–1945*. Wilmington, Del.

Bailey, Sydney D. 1964: *The General Assembly of the United Nations: A Study of Procedure and Practice*, rev. edn. New York.

Balch, Emily G. 1918: *Approaches to the Great Settlement*. New York.

—— 1972: Toward Human Unity or Beyond Nationalism (1946). In Frederick W, Haberman (ed.), *Nobel Lectures: Peace*, Amsterdam.

Bell, Daniel 1977: The Future World Disorder: The Structural Context of Crises. *Foreign Policy*, 13: 223–8.

Beniger, James R. 1986: *The Control Revolution: Technological and Economic Origins of the Information Society*. Cambridge, Mass.

Bensel, Richard 1990: *Yankee Leviathan: The Origins of Central State Authority in America, 1859–1877*. Cambridge.

Berend, Ivan T. 1974: Investment Strategy in East-Central Europe. In Daems and Wee (1974).

Bernhardi, Friedrich von 1918: A Summary View of Machtpolitik (1914). In Clark, Hamilton and Moulton.

Bhala, Raj and Ethan B. Kapstein 1990: The Basle Accord and Financial Competition. *Harvard Business Review*. (Jan.–Feb.): 158–9.

Bihr, A. 1989: *Entre bourgeoisie et prolétariat. L'encadrement capitaliste*. Paris.

Blair, John M. 1948: Technology and Size. *American Economic Review*, 38(2): 121–71.

Block, Fred L. 1977: *The Origins of International Economic Disorder: A Study of United States International Monetary Policy from World War II to the Present*. Berkeley.

Bloomfield, Lincoln and Amelia Leiss 1969: *Controlling Small Wars: A Strategy for the 1970s*. New York.

Boli, John 1987: World-Polity Sources of Expanding State Authority and Organization, 1870–1970. In George M. Thomas, John W. Meyer, Francisco O. Ramirez and John Boli, *Institutional Structure: Constituting State, Society, and the Individual*, Newbury Park, Ca.

—— 1990: Issues of Sovereignty in the World Polity: An Institutionalist Research Agenda. Department of Sociology, University of Uppsala.

Borkenau, Franz 1942: *Socialism, National or International?* London.

Boutros-Ghali, Boutros 1992: *An Agenda for Peace.* New York.

Bowker, Richard R. 1886: *Copyright, its Law and Literature: Being a Summary of the Principles and Law of Copyright with Especial Reference to Books.* New York.

Boyer, Robert A. 1990: *The Regulation School: A Critical Introduction.* New York.

Brandt Commission 1980: *North–South: A Program for Survival.* Cambridge, Mass.

—— 1983: *Common Crisis North–South: Cooperation for World Recovery.* Cambridge, Mass.

Braudel, Fernand 1981: *The Structures of Everyday Life: The Limits of the Possible* (1979), vol. 1 of *Civilization and Capitalism, 15th–18th Century,* trans. Siân Reynolds. New York.

Brock, Gerald W. 1981: *The Telecommunications Industry: The Dynamics of Market Structure.* Cambridge, Mass.

Brown, Christopher P. 1980: *The Political and Social Economy of Commodity Control.* New York.

Brown, James L. 1936: *Industrial Property Protection throughout the World.* Washington, D.C.

Brown, M. and J. Popkin 1962: A Measure of Technological Change and Returns to Growth. *Review of Economics and Statistics,* 44(3): 402–11.

Brundtland Commission 1987: *Our Common Future.* New York.

Buchanan, R. A. 1988: Engineers and Government in Nineteenth-Century Britain. In MacLeod (1988).

Buisseret, David (ed.) 1990: *From Sea Charts to Satellite Images: Interpreting North American History through Maps.* Chicago.

Burton, John W., A. J. R. Groom, Christopher R. Mitchell and A. V. S. de Reuck 1974: *The Study of World Society: A London Perspective.* Pittsburgh.

Burton, Margaret E. 1941: *The Assembly of the League of Nations.* Chicago.

Butterworth, Herbert L. 1978: *Moderation from Management.* Pittsburgh.

Cafruny, Alan W. 1985: The Political Economy of International Shipping: Europe versus America. *International Organization,* 39(1): 79–119.

Caldwell, Lynton K. 1990: *Between Two Worlds: Science, the Environmental Movement, and Policy Choice.* New York.

Camdessus, Michel 1992: Remarks to the Annual Meeting of the Academic Council on the UN System Held at the International Monetary Fund. Washington, D.C., June.

Cameron, Rondo 1961: *France and the Economic Development of Europe, 1800–1914.* Princeton, N.J.

Campbell, Roy H. and Andrew S. Skinner 1981: General Introduction. To Adam Smith, *An Inquiry into the Nature and Causes of the Wealth of Nations* (1776), Indianapolis.

Canby, Henry S.(ed.) 1943: *Prefaces to Peace.* New York.

Cardoso, Fernando H. 1977: The Originality of a Copy: CEPAL and the Idea of Development. *CEPAL Review,* 1(2): 7–40.

Carnoy, Martin 1972: *Industrialization in a Latin American Common Market.* Washington, D.C.

Caron, François 1974: Investment Strategy in France. In Daems and Wee.

Carr, E. H. 1946: *The Twenty Years' Crisis: 1919–1939*, 2nd edn. London.

Cassen, Robert and Associates 1986: *Does Aid Work? Report to an Intergovernmental Task Force.* Oxford.

Cassius 1947: *The Bretton Woods Plan for World Domination by the USA: Blueprints for a Third World War.* Wellington.

Chalmers, Henry 1953: *World Trade Policies: The Changing Panorama, 1920–1953.* Berkeley.

Chandler, Alfred D., Jr. 1962: *Strategy and Structure: Chapters in the History of American Industrial Enterprise.* Cambridge, Mass.

—— 1976: The Development of Modern Management Structures in the United States and the United Kingdom. In Hannah.

—— 1977: *The Visible Hand: The Managerial Revolution in American Business.* Cambridge, Mass.

—— 1980: Technical and Organizational Underpinnings. In Chandler and Daems (1980).

—— 1984: The Emergence of Managerial Capitalism. *Business History Review*, 58(4): 368–97.

Chandler, Alfred D., Jr and Herman Daems (eds) 1980: *Managerial Hierarchies: Comparative Perspectives on the Rise of Modern Industrial Enterprise.* Cambridge, Mass.

Chandler, Alfred D., Jr with Takashi Hikino 1990: *Scale and Scope: The Dynamics of Industrial Capitalism.* Cambridge, Mass.

Channon, Derek F. 1973: *The Strategy and Structure of British Enterprise.* London.

Chartand, Robert L. and James W. Morentz (eds) 1979: *Information Technology Serving Society.* Oxford.

Chase-Dunn, Christopher 1990: The Limits of Hegemony: Capitalism and Global State Formation. In David P. Rapkin (ed.), *World Leadership and Hegemony.* Boulder, Colo.

Chatterjee, Partha 1975: *Arms, Alliance, and Stability: The Development of the Structure of International Politics.* New York.

—— 1986: *Nationalist Thought and the Colonial World: A Derivative Discourse.* London.

Chenery, Hollis B. 1960: Patterns of Industrial Growth. *American Economic Review*, 50(4): 624–54.

Choate, Joseph A. 1913: *The Two Hague Conferences.* Princeton, N.J.

Choucri, Nazli and Robert C. North 1972: Dynamics of International Conflict: Some Policy Implications of Population, Resources, and Technology. In Raymond Tanter and Richard H. Ullman (eds), *Theory and Policy in International Relations*, Princeton, N.J.

—— 1975: *Nations in Conflict: National Growth and International Violence.* San Francisco.

Cialdini, Robert B. 1984: *Influence: How and Why People Agree to Things.* New York.

Clark, John M., Walton H. Hamilton and Harold K. Moulton (eds) 1918: *Readings in the Economics of War.* Chicago.

Coate, Roger A. 1988: *Unilateralism, Ideology, and US Foreign Policy: The United States in and out of UNESCO*. Boulder, Colo.

Codding, George A., Jr 1952: *The International Telecommunications Union: An Experiment in International Cooperation*. Leyden.

—— 1964: *The Universal Postal Union: Coordinator of International Mails*. New York.

Cole, G. D. H. 1935: Industrialism. *Encyclopedia of the Social Sciences*. New York.

Cole, Jack E. and Richard J. O'Rourke Jr 1983: *Telecommunications Policies in Seventeen Countries: Prospects for Future Competitive Access*. Washington, D.C.

Cole, Jack E. et al. 1977: *A Review of International Telecommunications Industry Issues, Structure, and Regulatory Problems*. Washington, D.C.

Colegrove, Kenneth W. 1930: *International Control of Aviation*. Boston.

Collier, Ruth and David Collier 1979: Inducements versus Constraints: Disaggregating Corporatism. *American Political Science Review*, 73(4): 967–86.

Conrad, Joseph 1971: *Heart of Darkness* (1899). New York.

Conybeare, John 1980: International Organization and the Theory of Property Rights. *International Organization*, 34(3): 307–34.

Cooper, Richard N. 1986: *International Cooperation in Public Health as a Prologue to Macroeconomic Cooperation*. Cambridge, Mass.

Coplin, William and J. Martin Rochester 1972: The Permanent Court of Justice, the International Court of Justice, the League of Nations, and the United Nations: A Comparative Survey. *American Political Science Review*, 66(3): 529–50.

Cox, Robert W. 1977: Labor and Hegemony. *International Organization*, 31(3): 385–424.

—— 1979: Ideologies and the New International Economic Order: Reflections on Some Recent Literature. *International Organization*, 33(2): 257–302.

—— 1980a: The Crisis of World Order and the Problem of International Organization in the 1980s. *International Journal*, 35(2): 370–95.

—— 1980b: 'Labor and Hegemony: A Reply. *International Organization*, 31(1): 159–76.

—— 1987: *Production, Power, and World Order: Social Forces in the Making of History*. New York.

Cox, Robert W. and Harold K. Jacobson (eds) 1974: *The Anatomy of Influence: Decision Making in International Organization*. New Haven.

—— 1977: Decision Making. *International Social Science Journal*, 29(1): 115–35.

Crane, Barbara and Jason Finkle 1987: The Conservative Transformation of Population Policy. *Governance: Harvard Journal of Public Policy* (Winter-Spring): 9–14.

Crane, Rhonda J. 1979: *The Politics of International Standards*. Norwood, N.J.

Cronon, William 1991: *Nature's Metropolis: Chicago and the Great West*. New York.

Culbertson, W. S. 1923: *Commercial Policy in War Time and After: A Study of the Application of Democratic Ideas to International Commercial Relations*. New York.

Curtiss, George B. 1896: *Protection and Prosperity: An Account of Tariff Protection Legislation and its Effect in Europe and America*. New York.

Daems, Herman and Herman van der Wee (eds) 1974: *The Rise of Managerial Capitalism*. The Hague.

Dangerfield, George 1961: *The Strange Death of Liberal England* (1935). New York.

Daniel, Howard 1973: *One Hundred Years of International Cooperation in Meteorology*. Geneva.

Deutsch, Karl W. and Alexander Eckstein 1961: National Industrialization and the Declining Share of the International Economic Sector, 1890–1920. *World Politics*, 13(2): 270–99.

Dickens, Charles 1978: *Nicholas Nickleby* (1839). Harmondsworth.

Dimitrov, Timor D. 1981: *World Bibliography of International Documentation: International Organization*. Pleasantville, N.Y.

Disraeli, Benjamin 1980: *Sybil or the Two Nations* (1845). Harmondsworth.

Dixon, William 1977: Research on Research Revisited: Another Half Decade of Quantitative and Field Research on International Organizations. *International Organization*, 31(1): 65–82.

Doeringer, Peter B. and Michael J. Piore 1971: *Internal Labor Market and Manpower Analysis*. Lexington, Mass.

Doman, Nicholas 1942: *The Coming Age of World Control*. New York.

Donnelly, Jack 1986: International Human Rights: A Regime Analysis. *International Organization*, 40(3): 599–642.

Dubin, Martin D. 1983: Transgovernmental Processes in the League of Nations. *International Organization*, 37(3): 469–93.

DuBoff, Richard B. 1983: The Telegraph and the Structure of Markets in the United States, 1845–1890. *Research in Economic History*, 8: 253–77.

Dulles, Eleanor L. 1932: *The Bank for International Settlements*. New York.

Dyas, Gareth P. and Heinz T. Thanheiser 1976: *The Emerging European Enterprise: Strategy and Structure in French and German Industry*. Boulder, Colo.

Eckhardt, William 1987: Rudolf J. Rummel – Apostle of Peace and Justice through Freedom. *International Interactions*, 13(3): 183–223.

Edwards, Richard 1976: *Contested Terrain: The Transformation of the Workplace in the Twentieth Century*. New York.

Einaudi, Luigi 1910: *The International Institute of Agriculture: Its Labours on Behalf of Economic Betterment*. Rome.

Einzig, Paul 1930: *The Bank for International Settlements*. New York.

Elbialy, Farouk 1963: *La Société financière internationale et la développement capitaliste des pays sous-développés*. Geneva.

Elsenhans, Hartmut 1991: *Development and Underdevelopment: The History, Economics, and Politics of North – South Economic Relations* (1984), trans. Madhulika Reddy. New Delhi.

Engels, Frederick 1962: *The Condition of the Working-Class in England* (1845). In *Marx and Engels on Britain*, 2nd edn. Moscow.

Enloe, Cynthia 1990: *Bananas, Beaches, and Bases: Making Feminist Sense of International Politics*. Berkeley.

Fabian, Larry L. 1985: *Andrew Carnegie's Peace Endowment*. New York.

Factiri, Alexander P. 1932: *The Permanent Court of International Justice*, 2nd edn. New York.

Faith, Nicholas 1990: *The World the Railways Made*. New York.

Farrell, Joseph and Garth Saloner 1987: Coordination through Committees and Markets. Massachusetts Institute of Technology, Alfred P. Sloan School of Management.

Farrenkopf, John 1991: The Challenge of Spenglerian Pessimism to Ranke and Political Realism. *Review of International Studies*, 17(3): 267–84.

Fennema, Meindert 1990: Dutch Policy Networks in the Decolonization of Indonesia. In Raoul Schildmeijer (ed.), *After the Crisis: Political Regulation and the Capitalist Crisis*, Amsterdam.

Ferguson, Tyrone 1988: *The Third World and Decision-Making in the International Monetary Fund: The Quest for Full and Effective Participation*. London.

Fieldhouse, D. K. 1966: *The Colonial Empires: A Comparative Survey from the Eighteenth Century*. New York.

Finlayson, Jock A. and Mark W. Zacher 1981: The General Agreement on Tariffs and Trade and the Regulation of Trade Barriers: Regime Dynamics and Function. *International Organization*, 35(4): 561–602.

—— 1988: *Managing International Markets: Developing Countries and the Commodity Trade Regime*. New York.

Firestone, O. John 1971: *Economic Implications of Patents*. Ottawa.

Fishlow, Albert 1985: Lessons from the Past: Capital Markets during the Nineteenth Century and the Interwar Period. *International Organization*, 39(3): 383–440.

Follett, Mary P. 1918: *The New State: Group Organization the Solution of Popular Government*. New York.

Follows, J. W. 1951: *Antecedents of the International Labor Organization*. Oxford.

Forgacs, David (ed.) 1988: *An Antonio Gramsci Reader: Selected Writings, 1916–1935*. New York.

Foucault, Michel 1979: *Discipline and Punish: The Birth of the Prison* (1975), trans. Alan Sheridan. Harmondsworth.

Freeman, Christopher (ed.) 1984: *Long Waves in the World Economy*. London.

Freundlig, Rainer 1983: Germany. In O'Brien (1983).

Fröbel, Folker 1980: *The New International Division of Labor: Structural Unemployment in Industrialized Countries and Industrialization in Developing Countries*. New York.

Gallaroti, Giulio M. 1991: The Limits of International Organization: Systematic Failure in the Management of International Relations. *International Organization*, 45(2): 181–220.

Galloway, Jonathan F. 1987: Intelsat's Markets and the New Competitors. *International Journal*, 42(2): 256–75.

Galtung, Johan 1980: *The True Worlds*. New York.

Ganley, Oswald H. 1987: Trade as a Key Determinant for the Communications and Information Industry. Working paper of the Harvard University Center for Information Policy Research.

Gartmann, Heinz 1959: *Rings Around the World*. New York.

GATT 1978: *Network of World Trade by Areas and Commodity Classes, 1955–1976*. Geneva.

Gibberd, Kathleen 1937: *The International Labor Organization: The Unregarded Revolution*. London.

Giddens, Anthony 1981: *A Contemporary Critique of Historical Materialism*, vol. 1. Berkeley.

Gill, Stephen 1990: *American Hegemony and the Trilateral Commission*. Cambridge.

Gilpin, Robert 1981: *War and Change in World Politics*. Cambridge.

Gitelson, Susan 1970: *Multinational Aid for National Development and Self-Reliance*. New York.

Glyn, Anthony and Bob Sutcliffe 1972: *British Capitalists, Workers, and the Profit Squeeze*. Harmondsworth.

Gold, Joseph 1969: The Institution. In Horsefield.

Golding, Sue 1992: *Gramsci's Democratic Theory: Contributions to a Post-Liberal Democracy*. Toronto.

Goldman, Nathan C. 1985: *Space Commerce: Free Enterprise on the High Frontier*. Cambridge, Mass.

Goldstein, Joshua S. 1988: *Long Cycles: Prosperity and War in the Modern Age*. New Haven.

Goldstein, Joshua S. and John R. Freeman 1990: *Three-Way Street: Strategic Reciprocity in World Politics*. Chicago.

Golich, Vicki L. 1989: *The Political Economy of International Air Safety: Design for Disaster?* Basingstoke.

—— 1992: Liberalizing International Air Transport Services. Paper presented at the annual meeting of the International Studies Association, Atlanta, April.

Gordenker, Leon 1987: *Refugees in International Politics*. New York.

Gordon, David M. 1980: Stages of Accumulation and Long Economic Cycles. In Terence K. Hopkins and Immanuel Wallerstein (eds), *Processes of the World-System*, Beverly Hills, Ca..

—— 1988: The Global Economy: New Edifice or Crumbling Foundations? *New Left Review*, 169: 24–64.

Gorgé, Camille 1938: *The International Relief Union: Its Origins, Aims, Means, and Future*. Geneva.

Gosovic, Branislav 1972: *UNCTAD: Conflict and Compromise*. Leiden.

Gould, J. M. and Augustus M. Kelley 1949: *Lecture Notes on Types of Economic Theory, as Delivered by Professor Wesley C. Mitchell*. New York.

Gramont, Sanche de 1975: *The Strong Brown God: The Story of the Niger River*. Boston.

Gramsci, Antonio 1971: *Selections from the Prison Notebooks* (1929–35), ed. and trans. Quintin Hoare and Geoffrey Nowell Smith. New York.

—— 1992. *Prison Notebooks, Volume I* (1929–35), trans. Joseph A. Buttigieg and Antonio Callan. New York.

Greaves, Harold R. G. 1931: *The League Committees and World Order*. London.

Greider, William, 1987: *Secrets of the Temple: How the Federal Reserve Runs the Country*. New York.

Groom, A. J. R. and Paul Taylor 1990: *Frameworks for International Cooperation*. London.

Grübler, Arnulf and Nebojsa Nakićenović 1991: Long Waves, Technology Diffusion, and Substitution. *Review*, 14(2): 313–42.

Guillame, Charles-Edouard 1902: *La Convention du Mètre et le Bureau international des poids et mesures*. Paris.

Haas, Ernst B. 1958: *The Uniting of Europe*. Stanford.

—— 1964: *Beyond the Nation State*. Stanford.

—— 1983: Regime Decay, Conflict Management, and International Organizations, 1945–1981. *International Organization*, 37(2): 189–256.

—— 1989: *When Knowledge is Power: Three Models of Change in International Organization*. Berkeley.

Haas, Ernst B., Mary Pat Williams and Don Babai 1977: *Scientists and World Order: The Uses of Technical Knowledge in International Organizations*. Berkeley.

Haas, J. Anton de 1923: *Foreign Trade Organization*. New York.

Haas, Michael 1971: *International Organizations: An Interdisciplinary Bibliography*. Stanford.

Haas, Peter M. 1990: *Saving the Mediterranean: The Politics of International Environmental Cooperation*. New York.

—— (ed.) 1992: Epistemic Communities and International Policy Coordination. *International Organization*, 46(2), special issue.

Habermas, Jürgen 1975: *Legitimation Crisis* (1973), trans. Thomas McCarthy. Boston.

Hall, H. Duncan 1948: *Mandates, Trusteeships, and Dependencies*. Washington, D.C.

Halsey, Frederick A. 1919: *The Metric Fallacy, an Investigation of the Claims Made for the Metric System and Especially of the Claim that its Adoption is Necessary in the Interests of the Export Trade*. New York.

Hambidge, Gove 1955: *The Story of the Food and Agriculture Organization*. New York.

Hamilton, John M. 1990: *Entangling Alliances: How the Third World Shapes our Lives*. Washington, D.C.

Hamlin, Christopher 1988: Politics and Germ Theories in Victorian Britain: The Metropolitan Water Commissions of 1867–9 and 1892–3. In MacLeod (1988).

Hannah, Leslie 1976: *Management Strategy and Business Development: An Historical and Comparative Study*. London.

Hansen, Peter 1993: Outline of the Background and Work of the Commission on Global Governance. Paper presented at the International Cooperation Research Association and Academic Council on the UN System Symposium on Strengthening the United Nations. Tokyo.

Hare, David 1978: *Plenty*. New York.

—— 1982: *A Map of the World*. London.

Hargreaves, Clare 1985: France's Spot Satellite will Vie with Landsat. *Toronto Globe and Mail*, May 17.

Harlow, Alvin F. 1936: *Old Wires and New Waves, the History of the Telegraph, Telephone, and Wireless*. New York.

Harris, Jonathan M. 1990: Global Institutions and the Ecological Crisis. Paper presented at the Boston University World Development Institute seminar series, February.

Harris, Nigel 1986: *The End of the Third World: Newly Industrializing Countries and the Decline of an Ideology*. Harmondsworth.

Harrod, Jeffrey 1987: *Power, Production, and the Unprotected Worker*. New York.

Harrod, Jeffrey and Nico Schrijver (eds) 1988: *The UN under Attack*. Aldershot.

Harvey, David 1989: *The Condition of Postmodernity*. Oxford.

Hatcher, William S. and J. Douglas Martin 1984: *The Bahá'í Faith: The Emergence of a Global Religion*. San Francisco.

Hausen, Marika et al. 1991: *Eliel Saarinen: Projects 1896–1923*. Cambridge, Mass.

Hauser, Henri 1918a: Industrial Penetration (1915). In Clark, Hamilton and Moulton.

—— 1918b: *Germany's Commercial Grip on the World: Her Business Methods Explained* (1916), trans. Manfred Emmanuel. New York.

Headrick, Daniel R. 1991: *The Invisible Weapon: Telecommunications and International Politics 1851–1945*. New York.

Hegel, G. W. F. 1952: *Hegel's Philosophy of Right* (1821), ed. and trans. T. M. Knox. London.

Helleiner, Eric 1992: When Finance Was the Servant: International Capital Movements in the Bretton Woods Order. Paper presented at the annual meeting of the International Studies Association, Atlanta, April.

Henderson, W. O. 1965: *Britain and Industrial Europe, 1770–1870*, 2nd edn. Leicester.

Hill, Martin 1946: *The Economic and Financial Organization of the League of Nations: A Survey of Twenty-Five Years' Experience*. Washington, D.C.

Hill, Norman L. 1929: *The Public International Conference: Its Functions, Organization and Procedure*. Stanford.

Hinsley, F. H. 1963: *Power and the Pursuit of Peace: Theory and Practice in the History of the Relations between States*. Cambridge.

Hirschman, Albert O. 1958: *The Strategy of Economic Development*. Princeton, N.J.

—— 1977: *The Passions and the Interests: Political Arguments for Capitalism before its Triumph*. Princeton, N.J.

—— 1980: *National Power and the Structure of Foreign Trade* (1945), expanded edn. Berkeley.

Hobsbawm, Eric 1987: *The Age of Empire: 1876–1914*. New York.

—— 1990: *Nations and Nationalism since 1780: Programme, Myth, and Reality*. Cambridge.

Hobson, Asher 1931: *The International Institute of Agriculture*. Berkeley.

Hobson, John A. 1904: *International Trade: An Application of Economic Theory*. London.

—— 1912: *The Evolution of Modern Capitalism*. London.

—— 1915: *Towards International Government*. London.

—— 1965: *Imperialism: A Study* (1902). Ann Arbor, Mich.

Hoffman, Ross J. S. 1933: *Great Britain and the German Trade Rivalry, 1875–1914*. Philadelphia.

Hogan, Michael J. 1987: *The Marshall Plan: America, Britain, and the Reconstruction of Europe, 1947–1952*. Cambridge.

Holborn, Louise W. 1975: *Refugees: A Problem of Our Time*, vol. 1. Metuchen, N.J.

Holsti, Kalevi J. 1991: *Peace and War: Armed Conflicts and International Order 1648–1989*. Cambridge.

—— 1992: Governance without Government: Polyarchy in Nineteenth Century European International Politics. In James N. Rosenau and Ernst-Otto Czempiel (eds), *Governance without Government: Order and Change in World Politics,* Cambridge.

Hoogvelt, Ankie 1991: The Debt Crisis and Prospects for Socialism in the Third World. Paper presented at the annual meeting of the International Studies Association, Vancouver, March.

Horie, Shigeo 1964: *The International Monetary Fund: Retrospect and Prospect.* New York.

Horsefield, J. Keith (ed.) 1969: *The International Monetary Fund 1945–1965: Twenty Years of International Monetary Cooperation.* Washington, D.C.

Hounshell, David A. 1984: *From the American System to Mass Production, 1800–1932.* Baltimore.

Howard-Jones, Norman 1975: *The Scientific Background of the International Sanitary Conferences.* Geneva.

Hudson, Manley O. 1944: *International Tribunals: Past and Future.* New York.

Hüfner, Klaus and Jens Namann 1971–5: *The United Nations System International Bibliography.* Munich.

Hughes, Thomas P. 1989: *American Genesis: A Century of Invention and Technological Enthusiasm.* New York.

Hunt, Michael H. 1987: *Ideology and US Foreign Policy.* New Haven.

Huntington, Samuel P. 1973: Transnational Organizations in World Politics. *World Politics,* 35(3): 333–68.

IAEA, 1977: *The International Atomic Energy Agency, 1957–1977.* Vienna.

IIA 1942: *The International Institute of Agriculture: Its Organization, its Works, its Results.* Rome.

IIIC 1946: *The International Institute of Intellectual Cooperation, 1925–1946.* Paris.

Ikenberry, G. John 1992: A World Economy Restored: Expert Consensus and the Anglo-American Postwar Settlement. *International Organization,* 46(1): 289–322.

ISO 1977: *Information Transfer.* Geneva.

ITU 1965: *From Semaphore to Satellite.* Geneva.

—— 1968: *1865–1965: A Hundred Years of International Cooperation.* Geneva.

Jackson, Robert H. 1990: *Quasi-States: Sovereignty, International Relations, and the Third World.* Cambridge.

Jacobson, Harold K. 1974: WHO: Medicine, Regionalism, and Managed Politics. In Cox and Jacobson (1974).

—— 1984: *Networks of Interdependence: International Organizations and the Global Political System,* 2nd edn. New York.

Jacobson, Harold K., William M. Reisinger and Todd Mathers 1986: National Entanglements in International Governmental Organizations. *American Political Science Review,* 80(1): 141–59.

Jacoby, Henry 1973: *The Bureaucratization of the World* (1969), trans. Eveline L. Kanes. Berkeley.

James, C. L. R. 1977: *Nkrumah and the Ghana Revolution.* Westport, Conn.

Jeans, James S. 1887: *Railway Problems: An Inquiry Into the Economic Conditions of Railway Working in Different Countries.* London.

Johnson, Alvin 1914: The War: By an Economist. *Unpopular Review,* 2(2): 411–29.

Johnston, George A. 1970: *The International Labor Organization*. London.

Jones, Charles A. 1987: *International Business in the Nineteenth Century: The Rise and Fall of a Cosmopolitan Bourgeoisie*. New York.

Juda, Lawrence 1981: World Shipping, UNCTAD, and the New International Economic Order. *International Organization*, 35(3): 493–516.

Kahler, Miles 1984: *Decolonization in Britain and France: The Domestic Consequences of International Relations*. Princeton, N.J.

—— 1985: Politics and International Debt: Explaining the Crisis. *International Organization*, 39(3): 357–82.

Kanninen, Tapio 1989: Frameworks for the Monitoring of Emergent or Ongoing Conflicts: Possibility and Feasibility of an Internationally Standardized Framework. Paper presented at the annual meetings of the British International Studies Association and the International Studies Association, London, March.

Kant, Immanuel 1957: *Perpetual Peace* (1795), ed. and trans. Lewis White Beck. Indianapolis.

Katzenstein, Peter 1976: *Disjointed Partners: Austria and Germany since 1815*. Berkeley.

—— 1984: *Corporatism and Change*. Ithaca, N.Y.

—— 1985: *Small States in World Markets*. Ithaca, N.Y.

Keohane, Robert O. 1984: *After Hegemony: Cooperation and Discord in the World Political Economy*. Princeton, N.J.

—— 1989: *International Institutions and State Power: Essays in International Relations Theory*. Boulder, Colo.

Keohane, Robert O. and Craig N. Murphy 1992: International Institutions. In Maurice Kogan and Mary Hawkesworth (eds), *Routledge Encyclopedia of Government and Politics*. London.

Keynes, John Maynard 1932: Economic Possibilities for Our Grandchildren (1930). In *Essays in Persuasion*, New York.

—— 1971: *The Economic Consequences of the Peace* (1920), introd. Robert Lekachman. New York.

Kidron, Michael 1965: *Foreign Investments in India*. Oxford.

Kihl, Young W. 1971: *Conflict Issues and International Civil Aviation*. Denver.

Kindleberger, Charles P. 1973: *The World in Depression, 1929–1939*. Berkeley.

—— 1984: *A Financial History of Western Europe*. London.

King, Gary 1989: Event Count Models for International Relations: Generalizations and Applications. *International Studies Quarterly*, 33(1): 123–48.

Kissin, S. F. 1988: *War and the Marxists: Socialist Theory and Practice in Capitalist Wars*. Boulder, Colo.

Knudsen, Olav 1973: *The Politics of International Shipping: Conflict and Interaction in a Transnational Issue-Area 1946–1968*. Lexington, Mass.

Kochan, Jürgen 1980: The Rise of Modern Industrial Enterprise in Germany. In Chandler and Daems (1980).

Köhler, Dinah A. 1991: Unconditional Surrender, Peace by Default: The German–American Peace Process of World War II. Hons thesis in international relations, Wellesley College.

Kolasa, Jan 1962: *International Intellectual Cooperation*. Warsaw.

Kolko, Gabriel 1965: *Railroads and Reform, 1877–1916*. New York.

Konvitz, Josef 1987: *Cartography in France 1660–1848: Science, Engineering and Statecraft*. Chicago.

Kopp, Karl 1941: The League of Nations and Raw Materials. *Geneva Studies*, 11(3).

Krasner, Stephen D. 1982: Structural Causes and Regime Consequences: Regimes as Intervening Variables. *International Organization*, 36(3): 185–206.

Krugman, Paul R. 1990a: *The Age of Diminished Expectations*. Cambridge, Mass.

—— 1990b: *Rethinking International Trade*. Cambridge, Mass.

—— 1991: The Move to Free Trade Zones. Paper presented at the symposium on policy implications of trade and currency zones, Jackson Hole, Wyo., August.

Kunugi, Tatsuro 1992: The Roles of International Institutions in Promoting Sustainable Development. *Ambio*, 21(1): 112–15.

—— 1993: Promotion of Democratic Governance through the United Nations. Paper presented at the International Cooperation Research Association and Academic Council on the UN System Symposium on Strengthening the United Nations. Tokyo.

Kuznets, Simon 1971: *Economic Growth of Nations: Total Output and Production Structure*. Cambridge, Mass.

Laar, Aart J. M. van der 1980: *The World Bank and the Poor*. Boston.

Ladas, Stephen P. 1930: *The International Protection of Industrial Property*. Cambridge, Mass.

Lancaster, Kathleen L. (ed.) 1982: *International Telecommunication: User Requirements and Supplier Strategies*. Lexington, Mass.

Landy, E. A. 1966: *The Effectiveness of International Supervision*. London.

Laves, Walter H. C. and Charles A. Thompson 1957: *UNESCO: Purpose, Progress, Prospects*. Bloomington, Ind.

League of Nations 1929: *Handbook of International Organizations*. Geneva.

—— 1930: *Ten Years of World Cooperation*. Geneva.

Legault, Albert 1992: United Nations Peacekeeping and Peacemaking. In Legault, Murphy and Ofuatey-Kodjoe.

Legault, Albert, Craig N. Murphy and W. B. Ofuatey-Kodjoe 1992: *The State of the United Nations: 1992*. Providence, R.I.

Leive, David M. 1970: *International Telecommunications and International Law*. Dobbs Ferry, N.J.

Lélé, S. M. 1991: Sustainable Development: A Critical Review. *World Development*, 19(6): 607–22.

Lenin, V. I. 1970: Preface to the French and German Editions (1920). In *Imperialism, the Highest State of Capitalism: A Popular Outline*, New York.

Lens, Sidney 1983: World Government Reconsidered. *The Nation*, Sept. 17: 201 ff.

Lenway, Stefanie A. 1985: *The Politics of US International Trade*. Boston.

Levin, Jayne 1989: Global Greed: The Insider Network of Ellis A.G. *Investment Dealer's Digest*, April 21: 13–19.

Lewis, John P. and Ishan Kapur 1973: *The World Bank Group, Multilateral Aid, and the 1970s*. Lexington, Mass.

Lewis, W. Arthur 1949: *Economic Survey, 1919–1939*. London.

Lih, Lars T. 1990: *Bread and Authority in Russia, 1914–1921*. Berkeley.

Linnemann, Hans 1966: *An Econometric Study of International Trade Flows*. Amsterdam.

Lipietz, Alain 1987: *Mirages and Miracles: The Crises of Global Fordism*. London.

—— 1992: *Towards a New Economic Order: Postfordism, Ecology, and Democracy*. Cambridge.

Lippincott, Issac 1936: *The Development of Modern World Trade*. New York.

Lippmann, Walter 1915: *The Stakes of Diplomacy*. New York.

List, Friedrich 1922: *The National System of Political Economy* (1844), trans. Sampson S. Lloyd. London.

Lister, Frederick K. 1984: *Decision-Making Strategies for International Organizations: The IMF Model*. Denver.

Little, Daniel 1986: *The Scientific Marx*. Minneapolis.

Long, David 1991: J. A. Hobson and Idealism in International Relations. *Review of International Studies*, 17(3): 285–304.

Long, William R. 1935: *Railway and Highway Transportation Abroad: A Study of Existing Relationships, Recent Competitive Measures, and Coordination Policies*. Washington, D.C.

Love, Joseph L. 1980: Raul Prebisch and the Origins of the Doctrine of Unequal Exchange. *Latin American Research Review*, 15(3): 45–73.

Lowe, Boutelle E. 1921: *The International Protection of Labor*. New York.

Luard, Evan 1982: *A History of the United Nations: The Years of Western Domination, 1945–1955*. New York.

—— 1989: *A History of the United Nations: The Age of Decolonization*. New York.

Macaulay, Rose 1983a: *Told by an Idiot* (1923). Garden City, N.Y.

—— 1983b: *The World My Wilderness* (1950). London.

McClure, Wallace M. 1933: *World Prosperity as Sought through the Economic Work of the League of Nations*. New York.

McCormick, James M. 1980: Intergovernmental Organizations and Cooperation among Nations. *International Studies Quarterly*, 24(1): 75–98.

—— 1982: Alternative Approaches to Evaluating International Organizations: Some Research Directions. *Polity*, 14(4): 531–47.

McCormick, Thomas J. 1989: *America's Half-Century: United States Foreign Policy in the Cold War*. Baltimore.

McCraw, Thomas 1984: *Prophets of Regulation*. Cambridge, Mass.

MacDonagh, Oliver 1958: 'The Nineteenth Century Revolution in Government: A Reappraisal.' *Historical Journal*, (1)1: 52–67.

McGowan, Patrick J. with Bohdan Kordan 1981: Imperialism in World-System Perspective: Britain 1870–1914. *International Studies Quarterly*, 25(1): 43–68.

Macht, William H. 1980: *August Bebel: Shadow Emperor of the German Working Class*. New York.

McKeown, Timothy J. 1991: A Liberal Trade Order? The Long Run Pattern of Imports to the Advanced Capitalist States. *International Studies Quarterly*, 35(2): 151–72.

Mackinlay, John and Jarat Chopra 1993: *A Draft Concept of Second Generation Multinational Forces*. Providence, R.I.

McLaughlin, John F. and Anne E. Birings 1984: Mapping the Information Business. In Benjamin M. Compaigne (ed.), *Understanding New Media*, Cambridge, Mass.

MacLeod, Roy (ed.) 1988: *Government and Expertise: Specialists, Administrators and Professionals, 1860–1919*. Cambridge.

McPherson, Logan Grant 1910: *Transportation in Europe*. New York.

Madariaga, Salvador de 1938: *The World's Design*. London.

Mahan, Alfred T. 1898: *The Influence of Sea Power upon History, 1660–1783*, 15th edn. Boston.

Maier, Charles S. 1977: The Politics of Productivity: Foundations of American Economic Policy after World War II. *International Organization*, 32(4): 607–33.

Mair, Lucy 1928: *The Protection of Minorities*. London.

Mance, Harry O. 1944: *International Telecommunications*. New York.

—— 1945: *International Sea Transport*. London.

—— 1947: *International Road Transport, Electrical, and Miscellaneous Questions*. London.

Mander, Linden A. 1941: *Foundations of Modern World Society*. Stanford.

Manley, Robert H. 1978: The World Policy System: An Analytical and Substantive Overview. *International and Comparative Public Policy*, 2(1): 35–138.

Markovitz, Irving L. 1977: *Power and Class in Africa*. Englewood Cliffs, N.J.

—— (ed.) 1987: *Studies in Power and Class in Africa*. New York.

Marx, Karl and Frederick Engels 1932: *Manifesto of the Communist Party* (1848). New York.

Mason, Edward S. and Robert E. Asher 1973: *The World Bank since Bretton Woods*. Washington, D.C.

Mass, Nathaniel J. and Peter M. Senge 1981: Reindustrialization: Aiming for the Right Targets. *Technology Review* (Aug. Sept.): 56–65.

Massie, Robert K. 1991: *Dreadnought: Britain, Germany, and the Coming of the Great War*. New York.

Mayall, James 1975: Functionalism and International Economic Relations. In A.J.R. Groom and Paul Taylor (eds), *Functionalism: Theory and Practice in International Relations*, New York.

—— 1990: *Nationalism and International Society*. Cambridge.

Mayer, Arno J. 1981: *The Persistence of the Old Regime: Europe to the Great War*. New York.

Mendez, Ruben P. 1992: *International Public Finance: A New Perspective on Global Relations*. New York.

Menon, Bhaskar 1992: UN Achieves 77 Percent of Tasks Budgeted for 1990–91. *International Documents Review*, 3(4): 1–2.

Mensch, Gerhard 1979: *Stalemate in Technology: Innovations Overcome the Depression*. Cambridge, Mass.

Meyer, Hugo R. 1905: *Regulation of Railway Rates: A Study of the Experience of the United States, Germany, France, Austria-Hungary, Russia, and Australia*. London.

Milward, Alan S. and S. B. Saul 1977: *The Development of the Economies of Continental Europe, 1850–1914*. London.

Milward, Alan S. and S. B. Saul 1979: *The Economic Development of Continental Europe, 1770–1870*, 2nd edn. London.

Mitrany, David 1933: *The Process of International Government*. New Haven.

—— 1943: *A Working Peace System: An Argument for the Functional Development of International Organization*. London.

—— 1948: The Functional Approach to World Organization. *International Affairs*, 24(July): 350–63.

Morris, James 1963: *The Road to Huddersfield: A Journey to Five Continents*. New York.

Murphy, Craig N. 1984: *The Emergence of the New International Economic Order Ideology*. Boulder, Colo.

—— 1988: Global Institutions and the Pursuit of Human Needs. In Roger A. Coate and Jerel A. Rosati (eds), *The Power of Human Needs in World Society*, Boulder, Colo.

—— 1990: Freezing the North-South Bloc(k) after the East-West Thaw. *Socialist Review*, 90(3): 25–46.

—— 1992: The United Nations Capacity to Promote Sustainable Development: The Lessons of a Year that "Eludes all Facile Judgment." In Legault, Murphy and Ofuatey-Kodjoe.

Murphy, Craig N. and Enrico Augelli 1993: International Institutions, Decolonization, and Development. *International Political Science Review*, 14(1): 71–85.

Nagle, Percival E. D. 1923: *International Communication and the International Telegraph Convention*. Washington, D.C.

Nasar, Sylvia 1992: The Rich Get Richer, But Never in the Same Way Twice. *New York Times*, Aug. 16.

Nau, Henry R. 1990: *The Myth of America's Decline*. New York.

Nelson, Douglas R. 1981: The Political Structure of the New Protectionism. World Bank staff working paper no. 471.

Nelson, Richard R. and Sidney G. Winter 1982: *An Evolutionary Theory of Economic Change*, Cambridge, Mass.

New York University Institute of Finance, n.d.: *The Bank for International Settlements*. New York.

Nier, Kenneth A. and Andrew J. Butrica 1988: Telegraphy Becomes a World System: Paradox and Progress in Technology and Management. In Edwin J. Perkins (ed.), *Essays in Economic and Business History*, vol. 7, Los Angeles.

Noble, Iris 1975: *Interpol: International Crime Fighter*. New York.

Noël, Alain 1993: The Regulation Approach and International Political Economy: A Scientific Realist Assessment. Paper presented at the annual meeting of the International Studies Association, Acapulco, March.

Norris, Frank 1964: *The Octopus: A Story of California*. (1901). New York.

Northedge, F. S. 1986: *The League of Nations: Its Life and Times, 1920–1946*. New York.

O'Brien, Patrick (ed.) 1983: *Railways and the Economic Development of Western Europe 1830–1914*. New York.

OECD 1989: *Geographical Distribution of Financial Flows to the Developing Countries, 1984–1987*. Paris.

Offe, Claus 1984: Crisis of Crisis Management: Elements of a Political Crisis Period. In John Keane (ed.), *Contradictions of the Welfare State*, Cambridge, Mass.

Oliver, Robert W. 1975: *International Economic Cooperation and the World Bank*. London.

Osborne, Thomas R. 1983: *A Grande École for the Grands Corps: The Recruitment and Training of the French Administrative Elite in the Nineteenth Century*. Boulder, Colo.

Overbeek, Henk 1990: *Global Capitalism and National Decline: The Thatcher Decade in Perspective*. London.

Owen, Nicholas 1983: *Economies of Scale, Competitiveness, and Trade Patterns within the European Community*. Oxford.

Paarlberg, Robert L. 1991: Why Agriculture Has Blocked the Uruguay Round. Harvard University Center for International Affairs.

Pagnol, Marcel 1988: *Jean de Florette and Manon of the Springs: Two Novels* (1962), trans. W. E. van Heyningen. San Francisco.

Papi, G. U. 1951: *The First Twenty Years of the Bank for International Settlements*. Rome.

Parker, Margaret T. 1940: *Lowell: A Study of Industrial Development*. New York.

Parker, William N. 1984: *Europe, America, and the Wider World: Essays in the Economic History of Western Capitalism*, vol. 1. Cambridge.

Parkinson, Fred 1977: *The Philosophy of International Relations: A Study in the History of Thought*. Beverly Hills, Ca.

Pavan, Robert J. 1972: Strategy and Structure of Italian Enterprise. Doctoral dissertation in business history, Harvard Business School.

Payer, Cheryl 1982: *The World Bank: A Critical Analysis*. New York.

Peaslee, Amos J. 1956: *International Governmental Organizations: Constitutional Documents*. The Hague.

Pelton, Joseph N. 1981: *Global Talk*. Alphen aan den Rijn.

Penrose, Edith T. 1951: *The Economics of the International Patent System*. Baltimore.

Perec, Georges 1987: *Life: A User's Manual*. Boston.

Perigord, Paul R. 1926: *The International Labor Organization*. New York.

Perlman, Selig 1928: *A Theory of the Labor Movement*. New York.

Peterson, M. J. 1986: *The General Assembly in World Politics*. Boston.

Peterson, Martin 1980: *International Interest Organization and the Transformation of Postwar Society*. Stockholm.

Pham Thi Tu 1964: *La coopération intellectuelle sous la société des nations*. Geneva.

Pijl, Kees van der 1984: *The Making of an Atlantic Ruling Class*. London.

—— 1990: Socialisation and Social Democracy in the State System. In Wibo Koole, Michael Krätke, Henk Overbeek, Raoul Schildmeijer and Kees van der Pijl (eds), *After the Crisis: Political Regulation and the Capitalist Crisis*, Amsterdam.

Pillai, K. G. J. 1969: *The Air Net: The Case Against the World Aviation Cartel*. New York.

Pinder, John 1965: The Case for Economic Integration. *Journal of Common Market Studies*, 3(3): 246–59.

Plischke, Elmer 1991: Evolution of Participation in International Organizations. *Commonwealth*, 5(1): 57–74.

Poats, Rutherford M. 1985: *Twenty-Five Years of Development Cooperation: A Review*. Paris.

Polanyi, Karl 1957: *The Great Transformation: The Political and Economic Origins of Our Time* (1944). Boston.

Porter, Michael 1991: Green Competitiveness. *New York Times*, June 5.

Porter, Theodore M. 1986: *The Rise of Statistical Thinking, 1820–1900*, Princeton, N.J.

Porter, Tony 1992: Regimes for Financial Firms. Paper presented at the annual meeting of the International Studies Association, Atlanta, April.

Prebisch, Raul 1984: Five Stages in My Thinking on Development. In Gerald M. Meier and Dudley Seers (eds), *Pioneers in Development*, New York.

Protzman, Ferdinand 1992: To Track Unity in Europe, Watch its Fast Trains. *New York Times*, Oct. 25.

Pynchon, Thomas 1984: Is it OK to Be a Luddite? *New York Times Book Review*, Oct. 28: 11ff.

Railhac, Pierre 1928: *L'office internationale du vin*. Lyon.

Ranshofen-Wertheimer, Egon-Ferdinand 1945: *The International Secretariat*. New York.

Reinsch, Paul S. 1911: *Public International Unions, their Work and Organization: A Study in International Administrative Law*. Boston.

Ridgeway, George L. 1959: *Merchants of Peace: The History of the International Chamber of Commerce*, 2nd edn. Boston.

Riding, Alan 1990: Interpol Regrets Shady Past, Vows Better Future. *New York Times*, July 15.

Rittberger, Volker 1973: *Evolution and International Organization*. The Hague.

Roberts, Adam and Benedict Kingsbury (eds) 1988: *United Nations, Divided World: The UN's Role in International Relations*. Oxford.

Robertson, A. F. 1984: *People and the State: An Anthropology of Planned Development*. Cambridge.

Robinson, Arthur H. 1982: *Early Thematic Mapping in the History of Cartography*. Chicago.

Robinson, E. A. G. (ed) 1963: *The Economic Consequences of the Size of Nations*. New York.

Robles, Alfredo C. 1994: *French Theories of Regulation and Conception of the International Division of Labor*. New York.

Rosen, Robert and Louis J. Williams 1993: The Rebirth of Supersonic Transport. *Technology Review* (Feb. Mar.): 22–9.

Rosenberg, Nathan 1976: *Perspectives on Technology*. Cambridge.

Ross, Dorothy 1990: *The Origins of American Social Science*. New York.

Ross, Robert J. S. and Kent C. Trachte 1990: *Global Capitalism: The New Leviathan*. Albany.

Rostow, W. W. 1948: *The British Economy of the Nineteenth Century*. Oxford.

—— 1985: *Eisenhower, Kennedy, and Foreign Aid*. Austin, Tex.

Rothschild, Emma 1973: *Paradise Lost: The Decline of the Auto-Industrial Age*. New York.

Rothstein, Robert L. 1979: *Global Bargaining: UNCTAD and the Quest for a New International Economic Order*. Princeton, N.J.

Roy, Ajit 1967: *A Marxist Commentary on Economic Developments in India, 1951–1965*. Calcutta.

Ruggie, John Gerald 1982: International Regimes, Transactions, and Change: Embedded Liberalism in the Postwar Economic Order. *International Organization*, 36: 379–415.

Rupert, Mark Edward 1990: Producing Hegemony: State/Society Relations and the Politics of Productivity in the United States. *International Studies Quarterly*, 34(4): 427–56.

Russell, Robert 1977: Governing the World's Money: Don't Just Do Something, Stand There. *International Organization*, 31(1): 107–27.

Russell, Ruth B. with Jeannette E. Muther 1958: *A History of the United Nations Charter: The Role of the United States 1940–1945*. Washington, D.C.

Salas, Rafael M. 1979: *International Population Assistance*. Oxford.

Salter, James A. 1927: *The Economic Consequences of the League*. London.

Sampson, Anthony 1981: *The Money Lenders: Bankers and a World in Turmoil*. New York.

Sands, Saul S. 1961: Changes in Scale of Production in United States Manufacturing Industry, 1904–1947. *Review of Economics and Statistics*, 43(4): 365–8.

Saxby, Stephen 1990: *The Age of Information*. New York.

Scelle, Georges 1953: The Evolution of International Conferences. *International Social Science Bulletin*, 5(2): 241–57.

Schattschneider, E. E. 1975: *The Semisovereign People*. Hinsdale, Ill.

Schenkman, Jacob 1955: *The International Civil Aviation Organization*. Geneva.

Scherer, F. M. et al. 1975: *The Economics of Multi-Plant Operations: An International Comparisons Study*. Cambridge, Mass.

Schiff, Eric 1971: *Industrialization without National Patents: The Netherlands 1869–1922 and Switzerland 1850–1907*. Princeton, N.J.

Schmidheiny, Stephan 1992: *Changing Course: A Global Business Perspective on Development and the Environment*. Cambridge, Mass.

Schumpeter, Joseph 1934: *The Theory of Economic Development* (1912), trans. Redvers Opie. Cambridge, Mass.

—— 1955: The Sociology of Imperialism (1919). In *Imperialism and Social Classes*, trans. Heinz Norden, New York.

Scott, Andrew M. 1982: *The Dynamics of Interdependence*. Chapel Hill, N.C.

Scott, James B. 1911: The International Court of Prize. *American Journal of International Law*, 5(3): 302–24.

—— (ed.) 1917: *Reports of the Hague Conferences of 1899 and 1907*. Oxford.

Sears, Mason 1980: *Years of High Purpose*. Lanham, Md.

Sewell, James Patrick 1975: *UNESCO and World Politics*. Princeton, N.J.

Shotwell, James T. (ed.) 1934: *The Origin of the International Labor Organization*. New York.

Silverstein, Harvey B. 1975: *Superships and Nationstates*. Boulder, Colo.

Simon, Herbert A. 1981: *The Sciences of the Artificial*, 2nd edn. Cambridge. Mass.

Simson, Otto von 1962: *The Gothic Cathedral* (1956), 2nd edn. New York.

Skowronek, Stephen 1982: *Building the New American State*. New York.

Sly, John Fairfield 1907: The Genesis of the Universal Postal Union. *International Conciliation*, 233: 395–443.

Smith, Adam 1981: *An Inquiry into the Nature and Causes of the Wealth of Nations* (1776). Indianapolis.

Smith, Anthony 1980: *The Geopolitics of Information*. New York.

Smith, Anthony D. 1988: The Myth of the "Modern Nation" and the Myths of Nations. *Ethnic and Racial Studies*, 11(1): 1–26.

Smith, Brian H. 1990: *More than Altruism: The Politics of Private Foreign Aid*. Princeton, N.J.

Smith, Delbert D. 1969: *International Telecommunications Control*. Leiden.

Smith, Emily T. 1992: Growth versus Environment. *Business Week*, no. 3265: 66–75.

Snow, Marcellus S. 1976: *International Commercial Satellite Communication*. New York.

Sommerlatte, Tom W. H. A. 1982: Strategic Approaches to Office Automation. In Kathleen Lancaster (ed.), *International Telecommunication: User Requirements and Supplier Strategies*, Lexington, Mass.

Sorel, Georges 1961: *Reflections on Violence* (1906), trans. T. E. Hulme. London.

Sorokin, Pitrim A. 1937: *Fluctuations of Social Relationships: War, and Revolution*, vol. 3 of *Social and Cultural Dynamics*. New York.

Speeckaert, G. P. 1965: *Selected Bibliography on International Organization 1885–1964*. Brussels.

Spengler, Oswald 1926: *The Decline of the West* (1923), trans. Charles Francis Atkinson. New York.

Stead, W. T. 1899: *The United States of Europe*. New York.

Steenson, Gary P. 1981: *Not One Man: Not One Penny: German Social Democracy 1863–1914*. Pittsburgh.

Stephens, Carlene E. 1985: Before Standard Time: Distributing Time in Nineteenth Century America. *Vistas in Astronomy*, 28(1–2): 113–18.

Stern, Philip van Doren 1975: *The Pocket Book of America*. New York.

Stewart, Michael 1984: *The Age of Interdependence: Economic Policy in a Shrinking World*. Cambridge, Mass.

Stone, Norman 1983: *Europe Transformed, 1878–1916*. Cambridge, Mass.

Strange, Susan 1974: International Monetary Fund: Monetary Managers. In Cox and Jacobson.

—— 1981: Reactions to Brandt: Popular Acclaim and Academic Attack. *International Studies Quarterly*, 25(2): 328–42.

—— 1986: *Casino Capitalism*. Oxford.

—— 1988: *States and Markets: An Introduction to International Political Economy*. London.

Streeten, Paul 1991: Global Prospects in an Interdependent World. *World Development*, 19(1): 123–33.

Streeten, Paul with Shahid Javed Burki et al., 1981: *First Things First: Meeting Basic Human Needs in the Developing Countries*. New York.

Streit, Clarence K. 1940: *Union Now*. New York.

Sutton, Brent A. and Mark W. Zacher 1987: A Theory of International Regulation. Paper presented to the Berkeley-Stanford colloquium on international institutions.

Taylor, Paul 1991: The United Nations System under Stress: Financial Pressures and their Consequences. *Review of International Studies*, 17(4): 365–82.

Taylor, Paul and A. J. R. Groom (eds) 1988: *International Institutions at Work*. London.

—— (eds) 1989: *Global Issues in the United Nations Framework*. Basingstoke.

Tedlow, Richard S. 1990: *New and Improved: The Story of Mass Marketing in America*. New York.

Teitel, Simon 1975: Economies of Scale and Size of Plant. *Journal of Common Market Studies*, 13(2): 92–115.

Thomson, Valentine 1930: *Briand: Man of Peace*. New York.

Thornton, Robert L. 1969: *International Airlines: A Study in Adapting to Change*. Ann Arbor, Mich.

Thorp, W. L. 1924: *The Integration of Industrial Operations*. Washington, D.C.

Thullen, George 1964: *Problems of the Trusteeship System: A Study of Political Behavior in the United Nations*. Geneva.

Tickner, J. Ann 1987: *Self-Reliance versus Power Politics: The American and Indian Experiences in Building Nation States*. New York.

—— 1990: Reaganomics and the Third World: Lessons from the Founding Fathers. *Polity*, 23(1): 53–76.

Tinbergen, Jan (coordinator) 1976: *Reshaping International Order: A Report to the Club of Rome*. New York.

Tomlinson, John D. 1938: *The International Control of Radiocommunication*. Geneva.

Toulmin, Stephen 1990: *Cosmopolis: The Hidden Agenda of Modernity*. New York.

Toussaint, Charmain E. 1957: *The Trusteeship System of the United Nations*. London.

Tracy, Michael 1964: *Agriculture in Western Europe: Crisis and Adaptation since 1880*. London.

UN, 1963: *A study of Industrial Growth*. New York.

—— 1965: *Industrial Standardization in Developing Countries*. New York.

—— 1968: *Everyman's United Nations: A Handbook on the United Nations, its Structure and Activities*, 8th edn. New York.

—— 1979: *Everyone's United Nations: A Handbook on the United Nations, its Structure and Activities*, 9th edn. New York.

—— 1986: *Everyone's United Nations: A Handbook on the United Nations, its Structure and Activities*, 10th edn. New York.

UNDP 1992: *Human Development Report*. New York.

UNIDO 1982: *Changing Patterns of Trade in World Industry: An Empirical Study of Revealed Comparative Advantage*. New York.

Union of International Associations 1982: *Yearbook of International Organization, 1981*. Brussels and Paris.

—— 1985: *Intergovernmental Organizations Directory, 1984/85*. Munich.

UNRRA 1948: *The Story of UNRRA*. New York.

UN Statistical Office 1968: *International Standard Industrial Classification of all Economic Activities*. New York.

—— 1980: *Classification of the Functions of Government*. New York.

Urquidi, Victor L. 1991: Can the United Nations System Meet the Challenges of the World Economy. The John W. Holmes Memorial Lecture to the annual meeting of the Academic Council on the United Nations System. Mexico City, June.

US Interstate Commerce Commission 1940: *Early European Experience with the Railway Passenger Fare Zone System*. Washington, D.C.

US Senate 1879: *The International Monetary Conference of 1878*. Washington, D.C.

—— 1893: *The International Monetary Conference (1892)*. Washington, D.C.

—— 1983: *Long Range Goals in International Telecommunication and Information: An Outline for United States Policy*. Washington, D.C..

Usher, Abott P. 1918: The Theory of the White Man's Burden, (1916). In Clark, Hamilton and Moulton.

Vaitsos, Constantine V. 1989: Radical Technological Changes and the New "Order" in the World-Economy. *Review*, 12(2): 157–89.

Väyrynen, Raimo 1983: Economic Cycles, Transitions, Political Management, and Wars between Major Powers. *International Studies Quarterly*, 27(4): 389–418.

Veblen, Thorstein 1917: *An Inquiry into the Nature of Peace and the Terms of its Perpetuation*. New York.

—— 1966: *Imperial Germany and the Industrial Revolution* (1915), introd. Joseph Dorfman. Ann Arbor, Mich.

—— 1969: Why Economics is not an Evolutionary Science (1898). In *On Marx, Race, Science, and Economics*, New York.

Vernon, Raymond 1966: International Investment and International Trade in the Product Cycle. *Quarterly Journal of Economics*, 80(2): 190–207.

Von Laue, Theodore H. 1987: *The World Revolution of Westernization: The Twentieth Century in Global Perspective*. New York

Vries, Margaret G. de 1976: *The International Monetary Fund 1966–1971: System under Stress*. Washington, D.C.

Wallace, Henry 1943: *The Century of the Common Man*. New York.

Wallace, Michael D. and James David Singer 1970: Intergovernmental Organization in the Global System: A Quantitative Description. *International Organization*, 24(2): 239–87.

Walter, F. P. 1957: *A History of the League of Nations*. London.

Warsh, David 1991: As the World Turns: Yesterday's Polemics to Today's Pieties. *Boston Globe*, July 7.

—— 1992: The Alphabet Agencies of the New World Order. *Boston Globe*, Mar. 8.

Waterman, Peter 1988: The New Internationalisms; A More Real Thing than Big, Big Coke? *Review*, 11(3): 289–328.

Webb, Herbert 1910: *The Development of the Telephone in Europe*. London.

Wedgewood, Ralph L. and J. E. Wheeler 1946: *International Rail Transport*. New York.

Wee, Herman van der 1987: *Prosperity and Upheaval: The World Economy 1945–1980* (1983), trans. Robin Hagg. Berkeley.

Weiss, Thomas J. 1976: Economies of Scale in Nineteenth-Century Economic Growth. *Journal of Economic History*, 36(1): 39–41.

Welles, Sumner 1943: Blueprint for Peace. In Canby.

White, Horace 1893: The Gold Standard: How It Came into the World and Why It Will Stay. Address presented to the Congress of Bankers and Financiers at Chicago, June 20. New York.

Wilford, John N. 1981: *The Mapmakers: The Story of the Great Pioneers in Cartography from Antiquity to the Space Age.* New York.

Wilkenfeld, Jonathan and Michael Brecher 1984: International Crises 1945–1975: The UN Dimension. *International Studies Quarterly,* 28(1): 45–68.

Wilkins, Mira 1974: *The Maturing of Multinational Enterprise: American Business Abroad from 1914 to 1970.* Cambridge, Mass.

Willetts, Peter 1989: The Pattern of Conferences. In Taylor and Groom.

Willkie, Wendell L. 1943: *One World.* New York.

Willoughby, John 1989: Is Global Capitalism in Crisis? A Critique of Postwar Crisis Theories. *Rethinking Marxism,* 2(2): 83–102.

Wilson, F. G. 1934: *Labor in the League System: A Study of the International Labor Organization in Relation to International Administration.* Stanford.

Winham, Gilbert 1977: Negotiation as a Management Process. *World Politics,* 30(1): 87–114.

—— 1986: *International Trade and the Tokyo Round Negotiation.* Princeton, N.J.

Wood, Robert E. 1986: *From Marshall Plan to Debt Crisis: Foreign Aid and Development Choices in the World Economy.* Berkeley.

Woodbridge, George 1950: *UNRRA.* New York.

Woolf, Leonard S. 1916: *International Government.* London.

World Bank 1985: *World Development Report.* Washington, D.C.

World Peace Foundation 1985: *1985, 75th Anniversary Report.* Boston.

Woytinsky, Vladimir S. and Emma Savely Woytinsky 1955: *World Commerce and Governments: Trends and Outlooks.* New York.

Wrege, Charles D., Ronald G. Greenwood and Sakae Hata 1987: The International Management Institute and Political Opposition to its Efforts in Europe, 1925–1934. Paper presented at the Business History Conference, Wilmington, Del., April.

Wright, John 1851: *Christianity and Commerce, the Natural Results of the Geographic Progression of Railways, or A Treatise on the Advantage of Universal Extension of the Railways in our Colonies and other Countries and the Probability of Increased National Intercommunication Leading to the Early Restoration of the Land of Promise to the Jews.* London.

Wright, Quincy 1930: *Mandates under the League of Nations.* Chicago.

—— 1942: *A Study of War.* Chicago.

Yates, JoAnne 1985: Internal Communications Systems in American Business Structures: A Framework to Aid Appraisals. *American Archivist,* 48(2): 141–58.

—— 1986: The Telegraph's Effects on Nineteenth Century Markets and Firms. In Jeremy Atack (ed.), *Business and Economic History,* Second Series 15: 149–63.

—— 1989: *Control through Communication: The Rise of System in American Management.* Baltimore.

Yoshiro, M. Y. 1968: *Japan's Managerial System: Tradition and Innovation.* Cambridge, Mass.

Young, George 1918: Immediate Antecedents in the Near East (1914). In Clark, Hamilton and Moulton.

Young, Oran R. 1991: Political Leadership and Regime Formation: On the Development of Institutions in International Society. *International Organization*, 45(3): 281–308.

Zacher, Mark W. 1979: *International Conflict and Collective Security 1946–1977*. New York.

Zimmerman, Eric 1917: *Foreign Trade and Shipping*. New York.

INDEX